WESTMAR COLLEGE LIBRARY

147545

P9-DMC-005

The Psychoanalytic Study
of the Child

VOLUME X

The Psychoanalytic Study

of the Child

VOLUME X

MANAGING EDITORS

Ruth S. Eissler, M.D. Heinz Hartmann, M.D.
Anna Freud, LL.D. Ernst Kris, Ph.D.

EDITORIAL BOARD

United States

Ruth S. Eissler, M.D. Lawrence S. Kubie, M.D.
Phyllis Greenacre, M.D. Bertram D. Lewin, M.D.
Heinz Hartmann, M.D. Rudolph M. Loewenstein, M.D.
Edith B. Jackson, M.D. Marian C. Putnam, M.D.
Ernst Kris, Ph.D. René A. Spitz, M.D.

Great Britain

Anna Freud, LL.D. Willie Hoffer, M.D., Ph.D., L.R.C.P. Edward Glover, M.D.

EDITORIAL ASSISTANT

Lottie M. Maury

INTERNATIONAL UNIVERSITIES PRESS, INC.
New York   New York

BF
721
.P8

+55.4
P974
v.10

Copyright, 1955, International Universities Press, Inc.

Library of Congress Catalog Card Number: 45-11304

Second Printing, 1965

Manufactured in the United States of America

70943

CONTENTS

Problems of Ego Development

Genetic Problems

Problems of Psychosexual Development

Clinical Presentations

PROBLEMS OF EGO DEVELOPMENT

NOTES ON THE THEORY OF SUBLIMATION[1]

HEINZ HARTMANN, M.D. (New York)

It has frequently happened, in psychoanalysis as in other fields, that concepts first devised to account for some more or less occasional observations were later used to refer to phenomena of a far more general nature than had been anticipated. In such cases, these concepts often preserve for a time the imprint of the specific situation they were originally meant to cover, but gradually detach themselves from the particular discoveries which had given rise to their formation. They get more or less integrated into the total field of experience and thought, which process often requires redefinition. To demonstrate this in detail would certainly be a worth-while subject for the historian of psychoanalysis. Suffice it here to remind you of Freud's concept of defense of the nineties, as compared to a later phase in which defense had acquired a structural definition and was recognized as one aspect of general psychology equally relevant for the development of the normal as of the later pathological individual. Or think how the conceptualization of aggression has changed, until finally aggression was realized to be, and defined as, one of the basic instinctual drives. As a third example, I may mention narcissism. Here, too, you will notice several reformulations; the fact that Freud has not quite consistently synchronized the concept of "narcissism" with the level of his later insights and theories has, in this case, led to quite some uncertainties and contradictions in psychoanalytic thinking and literature.

The subject of my contribution to this panel, the concept of sublimation, shows a somewhat similar development. When first used by Freud, "sublimation" referred to certain cultural or otherwise highly valued achievements and to their derivation from instinctual, which meant at the time sexual, sources. These phenomena were also studied as ways to avoid conflict while still achieving discharge, to escape the necessity of repression; their relations to the reaction formations of the latency period, their role in artistic creation was recognized. Partly realized was

[1] Introduction to the Panel on Sublimation, held at the Midwinter Meeting of the American Psychoanalytic Association in New York on December 4, 1954.

also their relation to symptom formation on the one hand and symbolization on the other hand. All this was described by Freud and other analysts
before ego psychology had come to be acknowledged as a chapter of
psychoanalysis in its own rights. Later studies on sublimation tend to
emphasize its relations to the build-up of the ego in general and to
specific ego functions. As in the case of narcissism, we find in Freud's
later work new ideas on the subject which, however, he has not quite
explicitly developed or used for a redefinition of "sublimation" in terms
of his more recent work.

Despite the broad and general use made by analysts of the concept of
sublimation and despite many attempts to free it from ambiguities, there
is no doubt that a certain amount of discontent with some of its facets is
rather common among us. Different aspects of sublimation, as usually
defined, have been criticized by Sterba (1930), Bernfeld (1931), Glover
(1931), Levey (1939), among others. Brierley (1947) speaks of sublimation
as an "omnibus term" which comprises a great number of actually different activities. Jones (1941), limiting his indictment to earlier usage only,
refers to "the days when analysts were prone to cite the blessed word
'sublimation' as the deus ex machina in all social and idealistic impulses."
At any rate, it is, I suppose, these uncertainties surrounding what is one
of our basic concepts, that have led to this topic being chosen for a
thorough discussion at this Midwinter Meeting.

The most common definition refers to sublimation as a deflection of
the sexual drives from instinctual aims to aims which are socially or
culturally more acceptable or valued. There may also be a change of
objects. In this definition, sublimation is actually a special case of displacement, special in the sense that it includes only those displacements
that lead to the substitution of worthy aims. The advantage of this approach was that it clearly stated that the highest achievements of man—
art, science, religion—may have and often have their origin in libidinal
tendencies. But some authors, e.g., Bernfeld (1931) and Sterba (1930),
have objected to this definition, pointing out that it is always questionable to include value judgments in the definition of a mental process—
which, of course, does not mean that the function of valuation cannot
be made the object of empirical studies. At any rate, on the basis of such
a definition every inquiry into the relations between sublimation and
the creation of values rests more or less on a *petitio principii*.

It was, therefore, a reasonable suggestion to eliminate the element of
value judgment and to speak of ego-syntonic aims (Bernfeld). This important emendation still left many questions unanswered. We are used
to saying that in sublimation ego aims are substituted for instinctual aims,

which may be accompanied by a change of objects. But is it really true that it depends only on the aims (and objects) whether or not we can speak of sublimated activities? Here we meet the problem of the relations between sublimation and sexualization. Some definitions of sublimation leave open the question what the differences between the two processes are; or rather, they forget to make this distinction. Clinically, we know that sexualization of ego functions, beyond a certain limit, interferes with proper functioning, while in a large field of human activities successful functioning depends on sublimation.

In the case of sexualization, we often say that an ego function has, mostly unconsciously, been invested with a "sexual meaning." I remind you, e.g., of certain forms of inhibition, described by Freud in *Problem of Anxiety* (1926). However, this concept of "meaning" is in need of clarification. Obviously, in the case of sublimation, too, we may find unconscious genetic determinants of a sexual character. One could try to relate the differences between sublimation and sexualization to the preponderance of the secondary or the primary process; to the degree to which the functions in question are, or are not, reality-syntonic; to whether suppression of the function can lead to anxiety; to how likely it is that the ego activity changes into direct instinctual gratification, and so on. All these are no doubt relevant aspects of that distinction and some of them I will take up later. At any rate, it seems that a clear presentation of this problem calls for the introduction of metapsychological concepts. And for the purpose of our discussion we will retain the fact that basing the concept of sublimation on the aims of behavior only, will of necessity fall short of a satisfactory definition. We will also realize that one short-coming of such a definition that makes no distinction between sublimation and sexualization is caused by its neglect of the considerable differences we find in the stability of ego functions, even of those whose instinctual core is very much alike; differences in resistivity against regression and sexualization—that is its neglect of what I am used to calling degrees of secondary autonomy of the ego. Postponing the discussion of the energic aspects, the aspects of the modes of energy involved, we may say that the stability of sexualized ego functions and their integration are usually less secure and that they more easily follow the pull of regressive tendencies.

Developmentally speaking, one main trend can be characterized as away from instinctualization of ego functions toward greater (secondary) autonomy, that is, better protection against instinctualization and regression. The degrees of autonomy vary, of course, from individual to individual, according to the developmental stage, and to different functions of the ego.[2] If we take an over-all picture of an individual ego, the degree of autonomy is correlated with what we call ego strength, though it is not its only source.[3]

The dependence of ego function on needs is marked in the infant. During the whole of childhood, newly acquired ego activities show a considerable lack of stability, or a tendency to get temporarily reinvolved in the conflicts and instinctual demands that contributed to their development. The child develops special methods to counteract such regressive tendencies (Anna Freud, 1951; Kris, 1951).

We probably all agree on the developmental relevance of early libidinal cathexis of ego activities. But I should, in this case, not yet speak of sublimation—which has been done, though, by some analysts—because of the reasons just mentioned and because of others not mentioned so far. However, I should think that there is a variety of ways in which these early libidinal cathexes of ego activities may influence later sublimations. Melanie Klein (1923a) equates the capacity to cathect ego activities with libido with the capacity to sublimate. She also thinks that libidinal fixations on speech and pleasure in movement constitute the preconditions for the capacity for sublimation.

The spreading of cathexis on objects, functions, and aims somehow or other related to the original ones is in fact part of the primary process. Thus the ego, and already the precursors of the fully developed ego, become invested with drive energy. This is a significant factor which partly accounts for the relative emphasis on certain ego functions in the growing child and also for the timing of their development.[4] But such characters of the primary process, as, e.g., displacement, come soon to be partly integrated by the ego and to be used for its own purposes, e.g., defense (Anna Freud, 1936). Displacement is, in a way, also a form of primordial learning, inasmuch as it widens the child's grasp of his outer and inner world (Hartmann, 1952). As to symbolization, its importance for the development of the ego and particularly of sublimation has been

[2] For an interesting discussion of the stability of ego functions in the psychoanalytic process, see Jokl (1950).

[3] In discussions of this kind, the early value-tinged concept of sublimation proves to be still very much alive in the minds of many of us. The place in a theory of sublimation of the problems at which it originally aimed I shall briefly outline toward the end of this paper, in terms of Freud's later ideas. At this point, however, it may be good to remind ourselves that the concept of secondary autonomy refers to the stability of ego functions only, in the sense just outlined, and not in any way to the "value" of the activities in question or of their results.

[4] I do not propose to discuss here the factor of primary autonomy of the ego. Later I shall say a few words about the not unlikely hypothesis that the ego draws, in its development, also on other than instinctual sources of energy.

repeatedly stressed by Melanie Klein (e.g., 1930). Hand in hand with the full integration of the precursors into the gradually developing ego go certain changes in the mode of cathexis we shall have to describe. From that stage on, while one aspect of these functions can still be described as "vicissitudes of an instinct"—you remember that Freud (1915) describes sublimation in this way, among others—it becomes necessary to add a description of their role in the setup of the ego.

I think it should greatly facilitate our understanding of these developments if we here introduce some distinctions. Speaking of sublimation: quite apart from the specific process of sublimation,[5] which we will discuss later, there is a difference between the (sublimated) cathexis of an ego function, on the one hand, and the (sublimated) cathexis of the aims toward which this function is directed, and of the objects through which the aims are achieved, on the other hand. The cathexis of objects of thought or action is not identical with the cathexis of the functions of thought or action. Clinically, we know that aims which presuppose a high degree of sublimation may be retained, though the functions are regressively instinctualized (as in sexualization). This difference holds good also in another respect: we have to distinguish the pleasurable character of an activity from the pleasurable character of its aims. It also seems advisable, which I may note here parenthetically, to differentiate between ego function and the representation of the self, the neglect of which has considerably handicapped our understanding of a variety of phenomena that are frequently lumped together under the heading of "narcissism" (Hartmann, 1950, 1953). There is, of course, interaction between the two aspects I mentioned. What I want to note here is that some concepts of sublimation referring to the aims only and not to the functions, which are equally important for our understanding of the ego, are less suitable for the advancement of ego psychology.

Even today, we know much more about the origin of specific contents of sublimations, of specific goals, or of interests in a given material, or subject, etc., than of the role of sublimation in the build-up of ego functions (though here, too, important work has been done[6]), and the genesis of the process of sublimation is far from being clearly understood. To trace the specific contents of sublimation to their sources was actually the central issue of research on sublimation for a long time. We can establish

[5] The word "process" has, in analysis, been used to cover different meanings. One, I think, fruitful attempt to give it a definite place in our field has been made by Brierley (1944).

[6] See Anna Freud (1936) on intellectualization, and more recently, for instance, Rosen (1953).

genetic connections of this kind in much of our clinical material. That the child's conflicts, his instinctual behavior and fantasies, and his anxiety reactions, at least codetermine the contents of later sublimation, was, of course, an important discovery. If one would say—and it has been said—that sublimation is the repetition of an infantile situation, this is certainly in a way true as far as the contents are concerned; though it does not fully clarify what the particular features of sublimation are. The knowledge of an artist's conflicts and unconscious fantasies often does not sufficiently explain why their working out takes the form of art (see also Kris, 1952). The thesis which considers sublimation a victory of the id (over the superego; Róheim, 1943) is certainly due to a failure to distinguish between the function of sublimation and its genetic aspect. This hypothesis neglects the fact that forces originating in the id may be used by the ego and even turned against the id. It is again an instance—we touched at the problem before, in speaking of secondary autonomy—of a kind of genetic fallacy: the actual function is equated with its history, or rather reduced to its genetic precursors, as if genetic continuity were inconsistent with change of function.[7]

Fortunately, detailed genetic studies usually do more than emphasize the persistence of past conflicts and fantasies in the contents of present sublimations. They often show us the functions that sublimation had in *statu nascendi* and how it is used in the development of the ego, in its relations to id, superego, and reality. They can give us answers to the question which are the actual situations that either promote sublimation or interfere with it. In this respect, child observation which has given us certain clues, might become even more helpful in tracing the impact of objects, object relations, identifications, etc., on concrete sublimatory achievements as well as on the different question of the individual capacity for sublimation.[8] It is probably true that, as Freud states, this capacity is partly inborn—which will appear to us even more plausible today, since we have come to realize that ego functions no less than

[7] I think that the distinction between function and genesis, and the recognition of the principle of change of function, are inherent in what, in analysis, we call the structural point of view. Of nonanalytical psychologists, Buehler (1929) and Allport (1937) have clearly stated the problem, and the latter has systematically developed this aspect of psychology. Both, though, failed to realize its actual role in the framework of psychoanalytic theory, and they consider it contrary to basic tenets of analysis. Most analysts, however, would, I suppose, agree that it is one of the significant features of psychoanalytic psychology that Freud has succeeded in integrating the genetic approach with a structural viewpoint. See also Hartmann (1939, 1950).

[8] After having written this paper, I read the one by Ernst Kris on "Neutralization and Sublimation: Observations on Young Children" (this Volume, pp. 30-46). His child observations actually fulfill, in a highly suggestive way, what I had in mind here.

instinctual tendencies may have a hereditary core; but Freud never doubted that external influences, too, have a part in it. Also we would be glad to hear more, in this discussion, from the child analysts and analytic child psychologists, about the typical or individual timing of sublimations. The "beginnings of sublimation" are variously described to coincide with the latency period, with the beginning of the oedipal phase, but also with much earlier stages of development. Of course, the answer to this question will be different according to whether the original, narrower concept of sublimation is used, or a much broader one, to which we now turn.

In *The Ego and the Id* (1923) Freud equates desexualization and sublimation; and thought processes are quite generally subsumed under sublimation. Somewhat later (1926) he stated—again quite generally—that the ego works with desexualized energy. As I said in the beginning, Freud has not systematically synchronized the concept of sublimation with the new level of his psychological thinking; but there are implicit in the statements just quoted fundamental changes which ought to be spelled out and challenge further development. Here the stage is reached at which sublimation, as other psychoanalytic concepts before, refers to a psychological process, this process being a change in the mode of energy, away from an instinctual and toward a noninstinctual mode. This formulation eliminates the doubts concerning earlier concepts of sublimation that did not account for the clinically essential differences between sublimation and sexualization. Moreover, we see the relations between displacement and sublimation in a new light; not only the aims are (usually) changed in sublimation, but also the mode of the cathexis is. It is even likely that the same aim of the ego may be pursued at times with less, at times with more, sublimated energy; this can be studied in the play of children and in other developmentally relevant ego activities:

The process of sublimation can be linked with several mechanisms, of which displacement is only one. I just mention identification, whose importance in this respect has often been emphasized by Freud and many others. Even more important, the correlation between change of mode of energies, on the one hand, and change of aims or objects, on the other hand, has again become a topic of empirical research, being no longer prejudged, as it was, by too narrow a definition. On this basis, the role of sublimation in the formation of objects, particularly constant objects, can be hypothesized (Hartmann, 1952). Freud approached this subject in speaking of the "tender," or "aim-deflected" strivings toward an object and thought that "if we want," we could consider them as a "beginning" of sublimatory processes. I suppose we could assign them their place as one of the many shades of neutralization in the continuum from fully instinctual to fully neutralized energy, a subject we shall have to deal with later.

That all ego functions are fed by desexualized or sublimated energy (later we will say: by neutralized energy), is indeed only the last touch Freud gave his gradually evolving ideas on the ego, which step by step emphasized its importance in mental economy. It is with this turn in his theory formation that the problems sublimation poses become essential for our metapsychological understanding of the ego. If we agree with Freud's later proposition, we will tend to see in sublimation not a more or less occasional happening but rather a continuous process, which, of course, does not exclude temporary increases or decreases in sublimatory activities. This hypothesis will, of course, also be one more reason for us, and a decisive one, not to limit any longer the study of sublimation to culturally or socially valuable achievements only. The earlier definition poses an essential difference between some striking sublimatory achievements and other, less obvious ones, though the fundamental psychological process, we want to define, is probably the same in both cases; and, continuing this trend of thought, we cannot attribute, as was done in the past, the "capacity for sublimation" to "the few" only. Obviously, while Freud's later definition emphasizes an essential relation between creativity and the ego, this does not do away with the many psychological problems creativity poses. The striking expression of sublimation we call "creativity" may be quantitatively, but is certainly also in a subtler way, different from other ego achievements.

Taking as his point of departure the same passages in Freud's later work I just mentioned, Glover (1931), in a penetrating study of the subject, comes to the conclusion that "some qualitative change in energy may prove to be the only metapsychologically valid criterion of sublimation." The advantages of the concept are manifold, particularly in the study of specific ego functions, and some of these advantages have been mentioned. Glover suggests a definition which includes displacement together with the change in the mode of cathexis. About the role of displacement, I said a few words before. But the question of what the relations between various mechanisms, as displacement, identification and others, and the energy transformation actually are, is in many respects in need of further study. At any rate, it seems essential that the nature and relevance of this basic process of energy transformation be clearly conceptualized and that we comprehend its role in the build-up and the functions of the ego.

Something similar to this, i.e., a conceptualization aiming at the basic processes, has been attempted in regard to other concepts of psychoanalysis and has considerably helped to clarify our thinking on developmental psychology, on clinical problems, and so on. Thus we are used today to defining "defense" in general terms, topographically, dynamically, economically, and structurally. In speaking of a particular defense mechanism, we will add a statement on its specific characteristics and functions. We would rather not include into its definition anything beyond this, as, for instance, the possible long-range consequences of defense as regards neurosis, health, perversion. Many of us would agree today that in speaking of "successful defense," we refer to the fact that the function of the defense mechanism has been performed, its aim has been reached—and not to the possible long-range outcome of health or disease.[9] The latter type of definition would threaten every study of the relations of defense to health and disease with the danger of begging the question.

If we want to achieve the same level of psychological definition in the case of sublimation, we will here, too, have to eliminate all references to "normalcy" or "abnormality," which are frequently included. Thus we cannot accept the frequently used distinction between "true" and "not true" sublimation, if it is drawn with this implication in mind. This certainly does not mean that no correlation of capacity for sublimation, or degree of sublimation of specific ego functions, with states of health or disease exists, or that it is irrelevant. The opposite is true (which, of course, does not imply that in the concatenation of factors that lead to disease, no functions enter which are fed by sublimated [neutralized] energy; see later). At any rate, it is preferable not to prejudge the question. Thinking again of the analogous situation of defense, you will remember how many misunderstandings were created when on the basis of the correct insight into the role of defense in neurosis, it was deduced, which is not correct, that every defense leads necessarily to pathology.

The next question, though essential for our orientation in this field, I will treat rather briefly. I have discussed this aspect of our subject in a series of papers published partly together with Kris and Loewenstein, in the last few years. We have accepted Freud's idea that sublimation of libido is a process by which the ego is provided with energy appropriate to its special needs, that is the energies the ego uses for its specific functions are as a rule not instinctual, they are desexualized. But is there a parallel to this with aggressive energy? I assume, in agreement with Melanie Klein, Kris, Loewenstein, Menninger, Lampl-de Groot, Hart,

9 I know that Fenichel (1945) defines this differently.

and others, that the mode of the aggressive energies too can be changed, in a way comparable to desexualization. It also appears that this desaggressivized energy is no less important for the formation and the function of the ego than is desexualized libido. This, then, implies that self-destruction is not the only alternative to aggression being turned outward; neutralization is another alternative (Menninger, 1942;[10] Hartmann, 1948; Hartmann, Kris, and Loewenstein, 1949). If desexualization is really correlated with defusion of instincts (Freud, 1923), the possible dangers inherent in such defusion could still be counteracted, as long as the capacity to neutralize aggression is unimpaired. If we further assume that self-preservation is, in man, to a considerable degree a function of the ego (Freud, 1939), we will come to the conclusion that it is actually dependent on neutralization.

We call neutralization the change of both libidinal and aggressive energy away from the instinctual and toward a noninstinctual mode.[11] The process of neutralization is essential in what we usually call sublimation, and it is mostly this aspect I am dealing with in this paper. But what is the relation of the two terms? There are several terminological possibilities. We may continue to speak of sublimation only in the case where neutralization of libido is involved, because this is the way it was meant by Freud and is still dominant in analytic literature. One may also use the word sublimation for the desinstinctualization of both aggression and libido, making it a synonym of neutralization (Menninger, 1942). An alternative suggestion (Kris, 1952) would reserve the term for the change of aims, often associated with neutralization. Again, the term is sometimes used for the nondefensive, in contradistinction to the defensive ego functions, and for their aims and cathexis. This question of nomenclature cannot be too important in itself and, for the purpose of my presentation, a decision between these alternatives does not seem necessary. What I want to remind you of here is just that much of what I said before about "sublimation," refers to the process now defined as "neutralization." In what follows, you will see from the context where I speak of this process and where I refer to other aspects often associated with the concept of sublimation.

Beyond emphasizing the central position of the process of neutralization in general in the build-up of the ego, and in its differentiation from

[10] Menninger (1942) even considers aggression more important in "sublimation" than libido. See also Brierley (1932).

[11] This term has occasionally been interpreted as referring to instinctual energy somewhere in between libido and aggression. But this is at variance with the term as we use it here. Also, "neutralization" does not mean instinct fusion—though the two processes may be interrelated (Hartmann, Kris, Loewenstein, 1949).

the id, a certain number of more specific hypotheses are necessary to organize and clarify our thinking on the great variety of phenomena we have in mind in speaking of ego functions. In what follows, I shall, then, attempt to develop some such propositions based upon Freud's statements quoted above, on the desinstinctualized character of the mode of energy used by the ego. It is, of course, in elaborating the implications of these propositions, and their applications with respect to specific problems, that their usefulness will have to be tested.

The question is often discussed in analytic literature whether moral masochism, or play, or any number of phenomena "are" or "are not" sublimations. But this is not just an either-or question. I think, it comes closer to observable facts, to speak, as I suggested, not just of two modes of energy of each drive: instinctual or neutralized. Both clinical experience and theory point to the probability that there exists a continuum of gradations of energy, from the fully instinctual to the fully neutralized mode (Hartmann, 1950; Kris, 1950; Rapaport, 1950).

If we accept this proposition, the next problem would then be what degrees of neutralization are commonly used for certain ego activities. Individual differences, differences as to situation and developmental level have of course to be considered. But some generalizations may be hypothesized. To draw my example from aggression: there is the unmitigated form of free aggression; the aggression the superego uses in its relations to the ego is already partly modified; even further removed from instinctual energy is the one the ego, according to a hypothesis I developed elsewhere (1950), employs in countercathexis—but it is still aggression and also retains that element of aggression, "fight"; the highest degree of neutralization of aggression, we find in nondefensive ego activities. It is not unlikely that differences between instinctual and neutralized energy go mostly parallel with the differences between primary and secondary processes. This would mean that in this respect, too, transitory phases have to be considered.

That changes in the degrees of neutralization do not without exception coincide with a change of the aims, I have mentioned before in discussing sexualization (see also Hartmann, 1952). To trace systematically the ontogenesis of ego functions from the angle of change of aims and change in the mode of energy is obviously a subject too broad to be broached here. May I repeat what I said before: that, aside from primary autonomous ego functions, and before the ego has been established as an organization, primordial aims and functions come under the influence of libidinal and aggressive displacements and symbolizations. In the course of development, their cathexes will be neutralized, and they will gain a certain degree of autonomy vis-à-vis the instinctual drives, which happens in constant interdependence with processes of maturation. Secondary autonomy is certainly dependent on neutralization. But it would be erroneous to assume that every—maybe transitory—cathexis of a function with neutralized energy constitutes autonomy in the sense we use the term (that is, stability of an ego function, or, more precisely, its resistivity against regression and instinctualization).

Once the ego has accumulated a reservoir of neutralized energy of its own, it will—in interaction with the outer and the inner world—develop aims[12] and functions whose cathexis can be derived from this reservoir, which means that they have not always to depend on ad hoc neutralizations.[13] This gives the ego a comparative independence from immediate outside or inside pressure, a fact that one is used to considering (though usually not in this terminology) as a general trend in human development. Thus we may say that while displacements partly determine the directions neutralization takes, it is also true that neutralization can lead to displacements, because, as a rule, different degrees of neutralization are not equally well suited for all aims and functions of the ego (I remind you of what I said about degrees of neutralization of aggression, in their relation to different functions; see also Kris, 1952).

There are considerable variations in this respect also from one individual to the other. And in the same individual the level of neutralization, as to one specific function, is not constant.[14] It seems, furthermore, that neutralization of libidinal and of aggressive energy varies independently—or rather partly independently. Berta Bornstein's discussion will refer to this point.[15]

[12] That the ego sets itself aims was emphasized by R. Waelder long ago (1936).

[13] Stating this more completely and with reference to the relationships of the ego and the id (here I do not want to broaden this statement to include the interactions with the superego), we may say: the ego accepts some instinctual tendencies and helps them toward gratification, without change of aims or of the mode of energy involved. In other cases, it will substitute ego aims for aims of the id. This can be done in a variety of ways. The ego aims may lie in the direction of id tendencies; they may be opposed to them (countercathexis); the third group are those nondefensive aims the ego, as I just said, sets itself in the course of development. Ego aims will normally be fed by neutralized energy and achieve a certain amount of secondary autonomy. But ego aims may, under certain conditions, also be cathected with instinctual energy—the case we call sexualization and aggressivization. In the first case, that is the one in which these aims use neutralized energy, the energy is either drawn from ad hoc acts of neutralization, or provided by the reservoir of neutralized energy at the ego's disposal.

[14] Kris (1952) introduced the concept of "energy flux," defined as "the transitory changes in energy distribution and redistribution such as the temporary and shifting reinforcement, of sexual, aggressive or neutral energy as it may occur in the course of any type of activity."

[15] Her material has not yet been published.

Sublimation (which here means neutralization) of instinctual energy is mediated by the ego (Freud, 1923).[16] Freud has particularly emphasized the role identification plays in this process (it is a well-known fact that disturbance of identification often leads to disturbance of sublimation), but it is unlikely that neutralization can be achieved in this way only. Whether, generally, in neutralization object libido has first to be transformed into narcissistic libido—a problem related to the one I just mentioned—is a question not easy to decide. Because of certain variations in terminology, I could not even say positively that this was always Freud's opinion. You know that Freud, and others, have often equated "narcissism" with the libidinal cathexis of the ego. In this sense, the statement that neutralization proceeds through a narcissistic phase could be tantamount to the one mentioned before: that neutralization is mediated by the ego. But narcissism was also meant to refer to the libidinal cathexis of the self (not the ego), as opposed to object cathexis, and this definition of narcissism seems to me in many respects preferable to the one mentioned before. If we accept it, we may then speak of self-representation (in the case of libidinal cathexis: narcissism) in opposition to object representation; but self-representation in this sense is not identical with the cathexis of ego functions. It becomes clinically and theoretically important to make a difference between the cathexis of the self-image, on the one hand, and of ego functions, as thought or action, which may be object-directed as well as self-directed, on the other hand (Hartmann, 1950, 1953). This, applied to our subject, leaves the hypothesis unchanged that neutralization proceeds through the ego (or its precursors). But, if we make that distinction, we will be inclined to say that while a change to narcissistic cathexis will certainly often be one step in neutralization, as, for instance, in identification, this step is not a necessary prerequisite of neutralization in general.

It is well known that in sublimation (neutralization) the ego allows a certain amount of discharge of the original tendencies, provided that their mode (and, often, their aims) have been modified. Pleasure gain by sublimation has been often emphasized by Freud and others. The amount of energy that can be discharged this way varies in the estimate of different analysts. The fact itself that sublimation provides us with an outlet, in a different mode, of instinctual impulses has been made the basis for its distinction from reaction formation (Sterba, 1930; Glover, 1931; Fenichel, 1945). Reaction formations originate in defensive measures of the ego. They will also later be used in their countercathectic aspects, but we

[16] And, in view of what we shall discuss later, we may add, already by the precursors of the ego, before the ego as a definite system has been established.

should not forget that, e.g., reactive character traits will, in the course of development, be invested also with other, nondefensive functions in the framework of the ego (quite apart from the fact, noticed by Freud long ago, that they may also feed on instinctual tendencies opposed to the ones they were built to ward off). This confronts us with a rather complex issue. Glover subsumes reaction formation under displacement, defining it as a displacement into the opposite. The next step would try to account for it in energic terms. It sometimes appears from analytic writings that sublimation is used as a word for the nondefensive achievements of the ego (see, however, later), which points to the dynamically speaking correct opposition of defensive and nondefensive ego functions. With respect to the modes of energy used, according to Freud's later formulations which I take as a point of departure here, reaction formations too (and for that matter, all countercathexes) work not with instinctual but with some shade of neutralized energy. Still it may be that countercathexes can be characterized as also energically differing from other ego functions, which may, at least partly, explain why, according to Freud, they are "set apart" in the ego. As I mentioned before, it seems likely that defense against the drives (countercathexis) retains an element (fight) that allows of their description as being mostly fed by one mode of aggressive energy, and that this mode is not full neutralization. In this sense, countercathexis in repression appears to be a good example to be contrasted, also as to the energy it uses, with the nondefensive ego functions. Reaction formation (e.g., in character traits) is a less good example, because, as I said, here the countercathectic function is often overlaid with other functions of the ego. It is not unlikely, though it may appear paradoxical from a certain point of view (see below), that the nondefensive ego activities have a higher discharge value than the countercathexes. The typical reactive character formations would have an intermediary place—representing on the one hand a defense, on the other hand nondefensive functions.[17] Furthermore, the shift of energy from one ego function to another one seems easier achieved among the nondefensive functions. But this is not to say that defenses cannot also to some extent draw on the reservoir of various shades of neutralized energy that the system ego has at its disposal. The comparative rigidity of the cathexis of some ego functions, as against the comparative ease with which the cathexis of others is changed, is a scarcely explored chapter of psychoanalysis.[18] We have learned from Freud the differences in mobility between primary and secondary processes, and also that, as a rule, secondary

[17] Freud occasionally describes reaction formation as a case of sublimation.
[18] See, however, Hartmann (1950, 1953), Kris (1951, 1952), Rapaport (1951).

processes are characteristic of the ego functions.[19] However, we see that there are differences in mobility also between various ego functions. We could try to correlate these differences with degrees of neutralization, and this might actually be part of the truth; but maybe not the whole truth. Some of the most challenging problems of psychoanalysis might become approachable if one were to resume Breuer's and Freud's work on bound and mobile cathexis extending it to the varieties of ego cathexes. Here it must suffice to remind you that the system ego, besides the more localized investments of specific ego functions, disposes of reserves of neutralized energy that can be shifted to points where it is needed. It is probable that in certain psychoses these operations are interfered with, maybe concomitantly with impairment of neutralization (Hartmann, 1953).

We spoke of various degrees of discharge being correlated with various ego functions. But there is also another case relevant for our understanding of the discharge aspect of neutralization. In many situations that call for action, it is probable that the ego appeals to the id for energic support (this is, of course, an anthropomorphic description; but you understand what I mean). It is further likely that the appeal is mostly made to those forces in the id which, genetically speaking, represent the precursors of the ego activity in question (Hartmann, 1952). Ego and id activities, though often antagonistic, would here be synergic, as they frequently are (Freud, 1926). In these cases there will be an increase in the amount of instinctual energy of the id discharged through the ego, in a more or less neutralized mode. It would be an example of one of those "switching" operations of the ego, of which there are many.

This way of admitting the forces of the id will not interfere with autonomy, as long as the ego's capacities for control and neutralization are unimpaired. The ego's faculty to accept this help without functional disturbance varies from one individual to the other, and also as to specific functions. The process, though in itself normal, has one aspect that can be described as regressive, and I want at this point to remind you again of Kris's work on "controlled regression" (since 1934).

So far, in opposing defensive and nondefensive ego functions, we have only scantily referred to the fact that there is a defensive aspect to neutralization (or sublimation) too. Sublimation has often been described as a defense mechanism also, and it is true that it represents one of the most efficient means to deal with "danger" threatening from the drives. Thus it can be used as defense, though it is not always and often not only defense,

---

[19] For the cases in which ego functions depend on the use of the primary process, see Kris (1934).

as it takes care, economically speaking, of the nondefensive functions of the ego too. We may add that even where it serves defense, sublimation is hardly a "mechanism" in the usual sense (Fenichel, 1945; Hartmann, 1952). There is also this difference, if we compare it with other defensive measures, that the change of instinctual to neutralized energy forms at least one element of its definition, thus setting sublimation apart from other defense methods, the concept of none of which refers to a change in the mode of energy. We may say that the process of neutralization in itself, and in general, can serve defensive purposes, far beyond the more special case in which certain shades of neutralized aggression are used in countercathexis.

As I mentioned before, it can also be closely linked with some real defense "mechanisms," as identification or displacement. More complex is its relation to repression. It has often been said that early repressions may interfere with neutralization (Freud; Melanie Klein, 1932, and others); but also that successful repression may be a prerequisite for neutralization (Nunberg, 1931). Jones (1941) states that there is "an optimum point, where there is neither too much nor too little repression, in relation to which the maximum amount of sublimation occurs." That repressions can handicap neutralization is an uncontested clinical fact. Still, this is certainly not the necessary outcome of every repression. Also, while Freud originally thought that repression makes the energy of the repressed drives definitely unavailable for other purposes, he later (1924; 1926) considered an alternative to this outcome, namely that it may be taken over by the ego and used in, e.g., identifications. Just in passing I may mention that if we use the broader definition of neutralization, there is actually a double correlation with repression; while repression often interferes with neutralization, impairment of the latter can, on the other hand, prevent the formation of stable repression, as, I think, is the case in schizophrenia (Hartmann, 1952, 1953).

From what I said, it already clearly appears that neutralization (the change of the purely instinctual strivings into a mode of energy more appropriate to the functions of the ego, together with the delay of immediate instinctual discharge, the control by the ego) plays a decisive part in the mastery of reality. The formation of constant and independent objects, the institution of the reality principle, with all its aspects, thinking, action, intentionality all depend on neutralization. According to Hart (1948), it is a compromise between instinct and reality (see also Hendrick, 1943). As I said before, if we accept Freud's statement that self-preservation, in man, is mostly taken care of by the ego, we come to understand neutralization also as a powerful help to this central biological aspect of man, not as its opponent as it has occasionally been described. Besides reality testing and the mechanisms of adaptation, the integrating (or synthetic, or organizing) functions share in the maintenance of self-preservation and they too are not purely instinctual in character but mostly belong to those that work with neutralized energy, though they may be in part genetically traceable to the instincts (Freud, 1923; Nunberg, 1931), as are other neutralizations.

We have discussed the neutralization of libidinal and aggressive drives, pointing to what these two forms of neutralization have in common, but also to some of their differences, e.g., in relation to specific functions of the ego; I also mentioned that neutralization of libido and aggression do not of necessity run parallel to one another. Here I want to add a few words to what was also hinted at before: the possibility that there exist other, noninstinctual sources of neutralized energy. Most of the energy active in the psychic apparatus originates, according to Freud, in the drives. But a later hypothesis of his which may be relevant for this question assumes that there exists a hereditary core not only of instinctual, but also of ego functions. This idea I have developed, as to some of its implications, in my work on the primary autonomy of the ego (Hartmann, 1939, 1950, 1952), which prepares the ground for the possibility just presented: namely that part of the mental energy—how much or how little we can hardly estimate—is not primarily drive energy but belongs from the very first to the ego, or to the inborn precursors of what will later be specific ego functions, and maybe also to those apparatus that come gradually under the influence of the ego and in turn influence its development. It is true that such a hypothesis, though appealing on many grounds, cannot today be proved. But this is equally true of the hypothesis that really all mental energy stems from the primary drives. Both assumptions lead ultimately back to physiology (Hartmann, 1950).

Not only the longest known, but also still the best studied sources of neutralized energy are the sexual drives. May I insert here some remarks on a problem, widely discussed in analytic literature: the question of what kinds of sexual energy lend themselves best to sublimation. The question has been answered in various ways. In one passage, Freud (1917) states about sublimation that "it consists in the abandonment, on the part of the sexual impulse, of an aim previously found either in the gratification of a component impulse or in the gratification incidental to reproduction, and the adoption of a new aim, etc." Freud (1908) also considers the occurrence of sublimation as a consequence of sexual abstinence (for the case of the scientist). Here he implies the sublimation of genital libido, and, in the first quotation, he states that both pregenital and genital libido may be sublimated. In another passage (1908) he assumes that the greatest part of sublimation has its origin in pregenital strivings. Fenichel (1945) and even more definitely Deri (1939) think it unlikely that genital libido can be neutralized, and Flescher (1951) seems to share this opinion; while others, like Sterba (1942), allow at least of the occurrence of some degree of genital sublimation. Both Fenichel's and Deri's thesis is deduced from theoretical premises which I cannot go into at this point. Personally, I cannot fully agree with those premises nor, therefore, with their arguments for discarding genital sublimation. That normally a considerable part of pregenital impulses is sublimated, is very likely true. But I do not see any definite reason to deny the occurrence also of neutralization of genital libido. Alpert (1949) emphasizes the apparent contradiction that even when the genital level has been reached, only pregenital strivings should be sublimated. There is some uncertainty also as to the question whether only object libido can be sublimated. Glover (1931) points to the fact that at least part of the pregenital tendencies, from which so much of the sublimation is derived, are not object-directed. These and related questions do not necessarily enter the definition of sublimation. But these and other differential considerations may become relevant if we study the developmental aspects of neutralization, or the relations between certain of its forms (as to gradation, as to origin, and so on) on the one hand, and specific contents, or functions that it serves, on the other hand. I first realized the relevance of this latter category of problems in studying the energic aspect of countercathexis, about which I said a few words earlier in this paper.

As mentioned before, it is difficult to ascertain when neutralization starts in the child. It has often been traced to early frustrations and renunciations. Hart (1948) has particularly emphasized that renunciation which comes from love is more likely to promote neutralization than the one which comes from fear. The child's siding with reality demands (Anna Freud, 1954) and the early identifications are no doubt an important step in the use and spreading of neutralization.[20] At any rate, we have to assume that neutralization starts very early, if we follow the lead of Freud's later definition which seems to me the most logical one. It must start even before the ego as a definite system is established and before constant objects are constituted—because it is likely that

20 For the formation of early countercathectic energy distribution in their relation to neutralization see Rapaport (1950, 1951) and Hartmann (1952, 1953).

these achievements already presuppose some degree of neutralization.[21] This also implies that neutralization cannot be assumed to be initiated by the superego, though its secondary relations to the superego are clinically and developmentally of paramount importance. That certain types of superego formation may interfere with neutralization is amply documented clinically. Alexander (1923) stressed the point that every tendency to self-injury may handicap it. On the other hand, the aspect of the superego that Freud calls the ego ideal is most influential in determining the direction of neutralization on certain aims or functions —which does not mean, as Freud reminds us, that the capacity for sublimation is in any way proportional to the sublimity of the demands.

This is obviously one of the problems that stood at the beginning of psychoanalytic research on sublimation: the question of the meaning and the origin of those sublimations which are syntonic with the demands of the ego ideal. Today we would say that this is not "the problem" of sublimation or neutralization, but it is certainly one aspect of it. It was necessary to broaden the concept—maybe so much that some of you feel uneasy with it—in order to make it maximally fruitful for our understanding of ego functioning (some of the pertinent problems I have presented to you today) and for a comprehensive view on ego-id relations. On the basis of these insights, the old sublimation problem, sublimation in art, religion, etc., has, then, to be attacked anew. If our reasoning is correct, we should expect to find that the later formulations prove more elucidating, even in regard to those "cultural achievements" than the original concept was meant to cover. So far differential research along these lines has not been done in all the fields relevant to that subject. But it has been done for one of them: art and the artist. I think that a work like that of Kris, *Psychoanalytic Explorations in Art* (1952), which uses the later and more complete conceptual framework, does bear out this expectation.

To summarize: we found that while conceptualization of "sublimation" has changed, the most important single factor among several that at one time or another entered its definition, is the process of desinstinctualization (neutralization). In adopting a broad concept of neutralization I follow Freud's later formulations on desexualization. It opens the way to many problems essential for the metapsychology of the ego and of ego-id relationships. Because of obvious reasons, the earlier concepts have not become, and could not become, equally meaningful in this respect.

21 Aspects of sublimation as, e.g., the elaborate stratification described by Bergler (1945) belong obviously to a much later age.

In studies about "sublimation," situations that give rise to neutralization, or the genetic determinants of its contents, or the mechanisms that are often connected with it, etc., are sometimes not clearly set apart from the process itself, a neglect which has often led to ambiguities. I have suggested in this paper to consider, besides the general character of the process, the twofold (or probably trifold) origin of neutralized energy in the two drives (probably also in the ego);[22] the capacity to neutralize which varies individually, according to the developmental level, to the situation, etc.; the incentives to neutralization, under the pressure of the id, under the direction of the ego (and later of the superego); the ontogenesis of neutralization; the neutralized cathexis of aims of the ego, as opposed to that of ego functions; the role of neutralization in defensive as well as nondefensive ego functions and the difference of cathexis of these two sets of functions; the gradations or shades of neutralization, in particular with respect to the various functions they serve; the partly different use of neutralized libido and neutralized aggression; the correlation of neutralization with secondary ego autonomy.

I know that this introduction to our discussion falls considerably short of a systematic presentation, and I am fully aware of the tentative character of some of the hypotheses I introduced. The accent was on the importance of Freud's later concept of desinstinctualization for the psychology of the ego, and, on the other hand, on how our understanding of some aspects of sublimation (neutralization) can benefit by the introduction of ego-psychological propositions. I also tried to give you some indications where potential ambiguities lie, and where, on the other hand, fruitful possibilities of future investigation may be found.

BIBLIOGRAPHY

Alexander, F. (1923), The Castration Complex in the Formation of Character. *Int. J. Psa.*, VI.
Allport, G. (1937), *Personality*. New York: Henry Holt.
Alpert, A. (1949), Sublimation and Sexualization. *This Annual*, III/IV.
Bergler, E. (1945), On a Five-Layer Structure in Sublimation. *Psa. Quart.*, XIV.
Bernfeld, S. (1931), Zur Sublimierungslehre. *Imago*, XVII.
Brierley, M. (1932), Some Problems of Integration in Women. *Int. J. Psa.*, XIII.
—— (1944), Notes on Metapsychology as Process Theory. *Int. J. Psa.*, XXV.
—— (1947), Psycho-Analysis and Integrative Living. *Int. J. Psa.*, XXVIII.
Buehler, K. (1929), *Die Krise der Psychologie*. Jena: Fischer.
Deri, F. (1939), On Sublimation. *Psa. Quart.*, 1939.
Fenichel, O. (1945), *The Psychoanalytic Theory of Neurosis*. New York: Norton.

[22] A terminological note is to the point here. Strictly speaking, energy that from the start belongs to the ego can, of course, not be termed "desinstinctualized" or "neutralized." It could be called "noninstinctual" and is probably best called "primary ego energy."

Flescher, J. (1951), *Mental Health and the Prevention of Neurosis*. New York: Liveright.

Freud, A. (1936), *The Ego and the Mechanisms of Defense*. New York: International Universities Press, 1946.

—— in collaboration with Dunn (1951), An Experiment in Group Upbringing. *This Annual*, VI.

—— (1954), Psychoanalysis and Education. *This Annual*, IX.

Freud, S. (1908), 'Civilized' Sexual Morality and Modern Nervousness. *Collected Papers*, II. London: Hogarth Press, 1933.

—— (1915), Instincts and Their Vicissitudes. *Ibid.*, IV.

—— (1917), *Introductory Lectures to Psychoanalysis*. New York: Boni and Liveright, 1920.

—— (1923), *The Ego and the Id*. London: Hogarth Press, 1927.

—— (1924), The Passing of the Oedipus Complex. *Collected Papers*, II.

—— (1926), *The Problem of Anxiety*. New York: Norton, 1936.

—— (1939), *An Outline of Psychoanalysis*. New York: Norton, 1950.

Glover, E. (1931), Sublimation, Substitution and Social Anxiety. *Int. J. Psa.*, XII.

Hart, H. (1948), Sublimation and Aggression. *Psychiat. Quart.*, XXII.

Hartmann, H. (1939), Ichpsychologie und Anpassungsproblem. *Int. Ztschr. Psa.*, XXIV. Translated in part in: *Organization and Pathology of Thought*, ed. D. Rapaport. New York: Columbia University Press, 1951.

—— (1948), Comments on the Psychoanalytic Theory of Instinctual Drives. *Psa. Quart.*, XVII.

—— (1950), Comments on the Psychoanalytic Theory of the Ego. *This Annual*, V.

—— (1952), The Mutual Influences in the Development of Ego and Id. *This Annual*, VII.

—— (1953), Contribution to the Metapsychology of Schizophrenia. *This Annual*, VIII.

—— Kris, E.; Loewenstein, R. M. (1949), Notes on the Theory of Aggression. *This Annual*, III/IV.

Hendrick, I. (1943), Work and the Pleasure Principle. *Psa. Quart.*, XI.

Jones, E. (1941), Evolution and Revolution. *Int. J. Psa.*, XXII.

Jokl, R. (1950), Preservation of Sublimation in Classical Psychoanalytic Procedure. *Bull. Menninger Clin.*, XIV.

Klein, M. (1923a), The Role of the School in the Libidinal Development of the Child. In: *Contributions to Psycho-Analysis*. London: Hogarth Press, 1948.

—— (1923b), Infant Analysis. *Int. J. Psa.*, VII.

—— (1930), The Importance of Symbol-Formation in the Development of the Ego. *Int. J. Psa.*, XI.

Kris, E. (1934), The Psychology of Caricature. *Int. J. Psa.*, XVII, 1936.

—— (1950), On Preconscious Mental Processes. *Psa. Quart.*, XIX.

—— (1951), Opening Remarks on Psychoanalytic Child Psychology. *This Annual*, VI.

—— (1952), *Psychoanalytic Explorations in Art*. New York: International Universities Press.

Levey, H. (1939), A Critique of the Theory of Sublimation. *Psychiatry*, II.

Menninger, K. (1942), *Love against Hate*. New York: Harcourt, Brace.

Nunberg, H. (1931), *Allgemeine Neurosenlehre*. Bern: Huber.

Rapaport, D. (1950), On the Psychoanalytic Theory of Thinking. *Int. J. Psa.*, XXX.

—— (1951), *Organization and Pathology of Thought*. New York: Columbia University Press.

Róheim, G. (1943), Sublimation. *Psa. Quart.*, XII.

Rosen, V. (1953), On Mathematical "Illumination" and the Mathematical Thought Process. *This Annual*, VIII.

Sterba, R. (1930), Zur Problematik der Sublimierungslehre. *Int. Ztschr. Psa.*, XVI.

—— (1942), *Introduction to the Psychoanalytic Theory of the Libido*. New York: Nervous and Mental Disease Publ. Co.

Waelder, R. (1936), The Principle of Multiple Function. *Psa. Quart.*, V.

NEUTRALIZATION AND SUBLIMATION

Observations on Young Children[1]

ERNST KRIS, PH.D.

The problems with which Hartmann[2] found himself confronted when surveying the concept of sublimation, its history and its vicissitudes, are familiar to me from a similar but much more restricted attempt which I undertook some years ago (Kris, 1952).

In this publication my attention was focused on art and creative activity. I was at the time faced with the fact that sublimation was being used to designate both transformations of energy and displacements of goal; that is, activities in which this transformed energy was being discharged. In my discussion I suggested that the term *neutralization could be conveniently used to designate the relevant energy transformations,* and that the term *sublimation* might be reserved for *the displacements of goal.* This terminological division, I thought, would help to avoid misunderstandings which tend to arise because of the fact that displacements of goal can take place without the energy used in the activity having been neutralized, or because these activities can be continued when the formerly neutralized energy has become deneutralized (i.e., "instinctualized," "sexualized" or "aggressivized"). The use of the terms neutralization and sublimation as two relatively independent variables seems useful for the following reasons: The division preserves the term sublimation and attaches it to its original meaning. However, my attention was centered on the study of a specific activity, i.e., "art," and I believe that the study of specific activities represents an important subject for future psychoanalytic investigations. "It seems possible not only to organize the structural characteristics of various types of activity according to the opportunities they offer for more or less direct discharge

[1] From the Child Study Center, Yale University School of Medicine. Presented as a contribution to the Symposium on Sublimation at the Midwinter Meeting of the American Psychoanalytic Association, in New York City on December 4, 1954.
[2] See "Notes on the Theory of Sublimation," *this Volume,* pp. 9-29.

of instinctual energy, but also to organize them according to the degree
of neutralization of libidinal and aggressive energies which they require"
(Kris, 1952, p. 27). A further reason which led me to suggest the distinction of terms leads thus to a specific problem. I feel that many problems
of neutralization, and particularly some ontogenetic aspects of it, can
best be investigated if viewed in conjunction with the influence that
certain activities exert on the process itself. In the course of this presentation this point will be illustrated by examples.

The relationship between goal displacement and energy transformation is naturally that of a circular interdependence. However, as the child
grows, so does complexity, so that the choice of activity is increasingly
determined by the interaction of many factors. Some concern the influence of endowment; others are more specifically related to the problem
of discharge of id impulses, the aspect which is best known from our
clinical experience.

> Expectations are significantly limited when we hear that a certain pa-
> tient is an actor, a dancer, a cartoonist, or a dress designer. They are less
> limited but still significant when we hear that he is a writer, painter, archi-
> tect, or poet. In all these cases—in the first instances more definitely—we
> expect that certain typical conflict constellations will more likely occur than
> others: The problem of rapidly changing identification may be crucial in
> the actor, that of coping with exhibition in the dancer, the wish to distort
> others in the cartoonist, and to adorn them in the dress designer; but each
> of these dominant wishes—which we here have mentioned only in order to
> characterize one direction of our expectations—is clearly merged with in-
> numerable other tendencies in the individual, and each of them is rooted
> in his history. According to clinical experience, success or failure in these
> professions depends, among other factors, on the extent to which the activity
> itself has for any particular individual become autonomous, *i.e., detached
> from the original conflict* which may have turned interest and proclivity
> into the specific direction [Kris, 1952, p. 29].

To the psychoanalytic study of what is commonly called creative
activity the relation of ego and id is of particular importance. It is a
powerful factor not only in the experience of the creator but also in the
reaction of his audience. The specific functions of ego autonomy in this
connection have certainly not been sufficiently explored. Our guidepost
is still Freud's suggestive hint, when he speaks of a peculiar "flexibility
of repression" as distinctive feature. As implementation of this thought,
I proposed many years ago that the control of the primary process and
generally the control of regression by the ego may have a specific signifi-

cance for the creative process (Kris, 1934, 1935). Only recently two observations suggested to me an additional approach. The first of these observations started out from analytic experience with professional "creators." In the analysis of one such individual, a particularly successful man, it became evident that a sharp cleavage existed between routine work and work in which he was fully, one might say, personally engaged. The first type followed a formula; the second was deeply and, as it were, inextricably interwoven with his present and hence also with his past conflicts: the process was a painful one and accompanied (preceded or followed) by a more or less intensive acting out of the same conflicts in the transference or in his life situations. It later appeared that the cleavage between the two types of creative activity was one of degree only; that in routine or formula work the experiences of the "true" or "great" creative process appear reduced to signals and that it is justified to say that "in every process of creation the gradual emergence from conflict plays a part" (Kris, 1953). This then led to the following assumption: It may be useful to distinguish between "the permanent or relatively permanent investment of the ego with neutralized aggressive or libidinous energies" on which secondary autonomy in ego functions mainly depends, and "the energy flux, i.e., transitory changes in energy distribution and redistribution such as the temporary and shifting reinforcement of sexual, aggressive and neutral energy as may occur in the course of any type of activity" (Kris, 1952, p. 27). The first, the permanent investment of the ego, represents what Hartmann (1955) describes as the reservoir; the second, the transitory changes in energy distribution and redistribution, the flux, represents instinctual energy which may or may not be added. The capacity to neutralize can then be viewed as determined by both the reservoir and the flux. Creative individuals may be characterized by a particular span between both.[3] However, the usefulness of similar distinctions seems somewhat limited, their relation to observable phenomena tenuous, unless other factors are taken into account, factors related to the individual's endowment. While one part of them, those connected with the strength of instinctual forces, remains in the area of those necessary assumptions which at the present time cannot be specified, another factor has become somewhat more tangible through one of Hartmann's suggestions (1955). He points to the possibility that the permanent investment of the ego may in part consist of energy of noninstinctual origin.[4] When Freud hinted at the existence of such energy sources, it seemed

[3] A more detailed typology of creativeness would obviously have to take a larger number of variables into account.

[4] For a similar suggestion see Jacobson (1954).

difficult to find a place for them in psychoanalytic thinking. Now this assumption seems to have become eminently useful. The energy might be thought to stem from the apparatus of the ego, and we might add that, by its quantitative variations it may influence the investment of the ego with neutralized energy. To put the vista which this opens into a highly condensed example: the endowment of the gifted facilitates the development of his capacity for successful activity.

The suggestion that a sharper distinction between energy reservoir and energy flux might throw some light on the vicissitudes of creative processes was, as I said before, brought to my attention by two kinds of observations. While I mentioned that the first was gained in analytic work, I did not refer to the second: they are of a different nature and connected with the study of nursery school children.[5]

I shall briefly report on three types of observations. The first will deal with the relationship of neutralization of drive energy to a specific type of activity; the second is meant to illustrate in even more aphoristic form two contrasting ways in which identification may influence the process of neutralization. The third tries to illustrate the possible influence of earliest object relations on the development of the capacity for neutralization.

II. The Easel in the Nursery School

There is an easel in every well-run nursery school; on the ledge there are pots neatly set apart, in each one color and one brush. Why is the easel there? How do the two to fours or fives who use it behave? What can we learn from watching them?

The literature has no systematic answer to these questions. The few who have studied the problem have been attracted by the product:[6] The masses of more or less well-organized colors distributed over white sheets of paper, out of which in the later years configurations and even representations emerge. In recent years the easel paintings of nursery children

5 The impressions I am going to report have been obtained in the course of my participation in various research projects in the Child Study Center at Yale University, School of Medicine. They owe their focus to the fact that I have had the privilege to organize some psychoanalytically oriented investigations in creative activity under a grant from the Arthur Davison Ficke Foundation of this City. Some of this work, to be published under the editorship of Dr. K. M. Wolf with the assistance of Mrs. Robert Bury, deals with creative sublimation in early childhood. For data from other studies I feel particularly indebted to Dr. Rose W. Coleman, Miss Eveline Omwake, Drs. Sally A. Provence, Samuel Ritvo and Albert J. Solnit.

6 I found the comprehensive material presented by Alschuler and Hattwick (1947) very useful; see also Friess (1952).

have been largely viewed as projective material and used for diagnostic purposes. This particular viewpoint will be neglected here. We turn, at least initially, not to the product but to the process of production.

The two- to three-year-old child in front of the easel finds itself in a situation which as a rule does not satisfy one of his most urgent demands: the situation does not allow for imitative role play. Hence there are many who use the easel only as a starting point for other activities; their interest focuses on the apron which has to be put on before painting, on washing of brushes, the cleaning of pots, or more generally on cleaning of what has been soiled for this purpose.

But let us leave this longlasting and time and again repeated cycle of playful housewifery and turn to the child that stays at least for some time before the easel. There are significant and typical moments: There is the first stroke and its result. The transposition of the kinesthetic experience of the arm movement with the big brush onto the trace on the sheet is to some two-and-a halves a significant experience. It is not a totally new experience; the principle is familiar from the handling of pencil or crayon. But the broader scope of the movement, the larger and brighter result on the sheet is bound to attract interest. There something has been done; dare we say "created"?

Some children are, as it were, soon captured by the expansiveness of the movement; the hesitancy of others is gradually overcome—and in some instances the motor pattern alone can serve as the child's signature.

These and similar individual differences offer a promising field for study. I shall neglect many alluring sideroads and concentrate on the problem with which almost all those who stay with the easel for their nursery years meet at one point: the battle against the impulse to smear which the medium itself stimulates. (I do not here enter into the problem how easel and finger painting compare in the opportunities for discharge which they offer.) That battle apparently sets in without a clear temporal relation to the stage of bowel training, i.e., irrespective of the fact whether bowel training has been completed or not and, if completed, whether it was a light or a bitter, a short or a protracted experience.

The battle against smearing starts not at once and its intensity is subject to great variations. There are children who start to mix colors in the pot, others who change the brushes and by putting the green brush in the blue pot achieve their first result. There are children who for some time produce monochromes, then add a second and third color kept strictly apart; then a slight shading starts until the mixing becomes wilder and wilder. At one point the sheet will look like a cauldron. In any one painting the whole process of defense and eruption may be repeated. The smearing may start after ten or more minutes of work, and then an explosive process may take over, sometimes supplemented by excited stamping, clutching of the genitals and rhythmical rubbing of the brush against the sheet—briefly by a passionate outburst.

There is the four-year-old who has sensed the danger. When in the nursery school much interest had been focused on easel painting, he, a highly verbal gentleman with a great capacity for a dry but gentle kind of what might be called "pre-humor," was suddenly heard to say: "I wish I would like to paint." And when he finally yielded to the (slight) pressure of the group and the temptation itself, his apprehension seemed justified. He was one of those whose temper carried him finally into a violent outbreak of excitement.

Let me turn to another example: this time we will start from the product. A brown mass irregularly shaped but placed approximately in the center of the sheet; not dirty but somewhat repulsive. The painting of the three-and-a-half-year-old is almost unambiguously representative: he has painted fecal matter, and calls it "a big one."

A study of the *process* of painting reveals that the result at first was not easily or painlessly achieved, that the first sheets in brown were not covered in a wild discharge. He went to great length to mix on the sheet out of pure yellow, pure blue and shining red the right shade of brown. The effort involved in achieving this mixture could be studied "experimentally." The teacher added green to the colors previously available. Now the mixing became more arduous. For some weeks it seemed as if green would prevail, but then Tommy learned the trick and once more he was able to produce the desired brown masses.

Tommy's interest in "brown" was highly overdetermined. He was under psychiatric treatment for a stool retention of unusual severity and long duration. The symptom itself, closely linked to his struggle with his mother, who actually—not figuratively—provoked it, represented at the same time an identification with her. Tommy had been aware of his mother's pregnancy, and of the birth of a baby that died a few days after birth when Tommy was sixteen months old, and of a second pregnancy which had started when he was twenty-six months old.

Tommy's painting in the nursery school had in the past not shown unusual features. He turned to the series of brown themes after he had been witness to a dramatic spontaneous abortion of the mother.[7]

Under the influence of this experience and his rising anxiety, the goal of displacement was lowered, and after this lowered goal had first

---

[7] He simultaneously developed stuttering.

been achieved by a well-co-ordinated production process, deneutralization became noticeable in his painting behavior; he learned to mix the
brown in the painting pots and filled the sheets with it while stamping,
and masturbating in trembling excitement.

Let us now turn to the question how other children try to cope with
impulses which, activated by the medium, become threatening. Some
retreat after more or less bold attempts at color mixing into monochrom-
atic drawing, others interrupt their work when temptation approaches:
they ask the teacher to remove the sheet, start on a new one and interrupt
once more when the point comes at which the tension rises. (This naturally is not the only reason for their wish to complete their work at a given
point. The sheet may satisfy some of their intentions and they may feel
that to continue might mean to destroy it. Only in careful analysis of
individual cases is it sometimes possible to determine what "completion"
signifies to the child at any given moment in his development.)

Defenses against the danger may appear in strange combination: a
particularly illustrative one was displayed by a four-and-a-half-year-old
boy who has obsessional-compulsive mechanisms of various sorts at his
disposal. He is intellectually far advanced, and intellectualization has
become his preferred tool in coping with conflicts. His colors tend at first
to be simply isolated, in band-like configurations. But then he turns
from bands to shapes, squares and rectangles, outlined in one, filled in
another color; seen over the course of a nursery year, his work conveys
the impression of a sequence of solutions of the problem of balance in
shape and color—so consistently that observers are able to establish the
chronological sequence of the paintings, as they might do it in viewing
the work of say Cezanne. And yet there is little thrill in looking at this
boy's achievements; only when he borders the danger zone, the attraction
to the observer seems to increase. During two phases of the year's work
his paintings are flooded with red: shortly after a suddenly performed
tonsillectomy, and six months later when in an organized play situation
the operation was re-enacted.

With those children who stay at easel painting and do not abandon
it at one point of the conflictual period, other less dramatic but no less
significant methods of conquest of the danger can be studied. Already
at an early stage the pleasure in mixing and smearing may appear combined with pleasure in interesting color contrasts, rare shading, balanced
shapes and fantastic configurations. During the fourth and fifth year
these configurations tend to be named, and gradually (typically during
the fifth year) the representational elements take charge. Fantasies become
attached to shapes. An early stage shows similarity to adult doodling: the

brush produces and the child names the configurations. It plays both at rendering and combining recognizable or not so recognizable shapes and at developing and combining fantasies. The primary process is at work, but while it emerges, first attempts at control—or at pretense of control—can be noticed. On later stages the fantasy content becomes elaborate, stories may be expanded, and some of those faithful to the easel achieve what seemed to attract them when the first stroke of the broad brush created that bright trace on paper: but now their product is "organized," they "make" a world of things. This progress requires renunciation of direct discharge. The neutralization of energy can, as it were, be watched. There always is initially a defensive move to ward off the temptation. There comes in every child's painting development the moment when the dripping paint is being resented, when the disorder it produces disturbs the child, when mixing of colors is done with particular care, and when out of the cauldron some signs of a tasteful arrangement emerge—all this with individual differences for which we can account only rarely.

The easel painting of nursery school children is here being used to illustrate the interdependence of drive discharge and goal displacement, of neutralization and sublimation. The point I should like to make is that as maturation proceeds, as the inner world grows, as new pleasures in fantasy and mastery become accessible, the structure of the activity itself influences the process of neutralization.

The easel then stands in the nursery, because it is thought that instead of the sudden and "total" suppression by reaction formation of a component drive of anal satisfaction, the child should be offered an activity, which, as catalyst, stimulates further neutralization. In the course of this process the easel painting of the nursery years comes into being. It is difficult to account for the attraction many of these paintings exercise on adult observers. The most plausible explanation may well be that some of the conflicts which the child experienced, some of the intensity of the struggle between id and ego, some pleasure at compromise, some triumph is shared by their adult admirers. The transparence of the id, the charm of the infantile, may have led educators and artistically inclined people to lift the color scribbles in loose designation into the category of the sublime: they do so when we speak of children's art.

III. THE ROLE OF IDENTIFICATION AND OBJECT RELATION

The experience of the children who perform as easel painters has here been viewed in the light of one problem: we tried aphoristically to illustrate how during a given phase of development one component drive, stimulated by the medium, breaks through neutralization, how deneutralization and reneutralization follow each other. The processes described can be viewed as exemplary: most activities of two's and three's (and sometimes those of older children,) are constantly threatened by a regressive trend; the break-through of immediate instinctual gratification is almost at any time a possibility, depending on the amount of stress and direct stimulation to which the child is exposed (Kris, 1950). The structure of the activity, pure or constructive play as the case may be, supplies an incentive for increased neutralization, and on the other hand the capacity to neutralize codetermines the preference for any one activity. But the general aspect of what is here being viewed as childhood behavior is, I believe, of less interest than the place of these vicissitudes in the development of the individual. Macroscopic observation itself suggests the problem, since individual differences seem to be most significant where attitudes of children to organized activity are concerned. Preference for any one activity, the range of such preferences, the degree to which the child can endure difficulties, solve problems, elaborate fantasies, and at the same time discharge instinctual tension, have to be taken into account.

A whole range of problems for the study of initial steps in ego functioning opens itself before our eyes. But only where a large set of data on any individual child is available, where influences of the various figures in his home and environment are accessible and the child's history is known in some detail can such questions gain full meaning. The two cases about whom I report in the following are part of a longitudinal study, which supplies the required data.[8] It is a single episode in the life of a charmingly smiling girl of two and a half which I should like to choose as starting point: One day in November, four weeks after she had first learned to handle the brush on the easel, Evelyne sets to work. As usual the young lady, at the time a painter in monochrome blue, selects her brush and color. She carefully drives it over the paper and a circle emerges. She looks at it for a while, then sets in it eyes, nose and mouth and clearly says, "Halloween."

The achievement is an extraordinarily advanced one. The elaborateness of the performance leaves no doubt about the intention, and circumstances before the painting throw light on the motivation. Evelyne is a fearless child; her courage and independence are outstanding, but a few days before the painting she had an attack of prolonged terror and fright. She reacted to children with Halloween masks.

8 The study is supported by the Commonwealth Foundation.

The painting reproduces this impression. The active repetition of the passively experienced terror is here not entrusted to play. Evelyne can represent what she wants, and she wants to represent what frightened her. Active repetition is entrusted to a higher level of imagination and action: Evelyne herself, unaided as always, produces the mask in a painting.[9] We may describe the step she has taken from three aspects: The drawing requires an unusual degree of skill, which cannot be achieved without neutralization; the goal, a re-productive painting, is very highly set for her age, at least a year or a year and a half ahead of others; and this capacity is mobilized by a painful experience and serves to cope with it. The model of similar behavior, familiar from latency age, and there described by Anna Freud (1936), is extremely rare at Evelyn's age. Can we determine some of the factors which enabled Evelyne to act on a level, which is not only out of the range of her peers, but which even much older children will reach only rarely?

Evelyne is highly advanced in all her intellectual achievements. She is not very sociable, but determined and resolute even if alone. When she came to nursery school she impressed the teacher as the most mature and best predictable of the children, as the one who sought least help, was least dependent, and least forlorn when the mother left. In fact, her independence is demonstrative and energetic. Nothing in her behavior indicates disturbance; all seems smooth and even. However, there are differences in her skill. She has less ability in motor achievements than in others; and during a whole year at the nursery she sets to work on this area, purposefully determined, and yet full of high spirit, she learns to ride a bike. And in her very independence and courage she is a striking simile of her mother.

During the very period in which she drew the Halloween mask she was engaged in a bitter fight with her mother, in the battle for toilet training. In this battle, induced and fostered by the mother, the child tortured the mother by a highly complex sequence of behavior, best described as aggressive sweetness. The singularly interesting fact is that trait by trait the child's handling of her mother could be transposed a generation backwards: Evelyne's mother had used similar techniques when she struggled against her own mother's impositions. A long and detailed story of the interaction between mother and child starting from

[9] Evelyne was at the time a master in role and fantasy play, an ability which, like that of representational painting, has stayed with her. We find her at three and a half enacting Alice's adventures in Disney's version. The problem of why the active repetition of what seemed to have been her first fearful experience was entrusted to painting rather than to role playing raises many intriguing questions, which are reserved for a more detailed report on Evelyne's personality development.

birth and largely based on observations by Dr. Provence will present answers to the question on how such a closeness of identification came about. Here it suffices to say that Evelyne's mother is a gifted, highly introspective, and according to all clinical criteria, normal woman who devoted to her child a maximum of attention. It was less in the area of intimate physical contact that this intensity became manifest; there is some reason to believe that the lack of motor skill in Evelyne may have to do with this. But no opportunity for mental stimulation was missed. Imagination seemed to mold every contact with the child. The very history of feeding is one in which mental stimulation was communicated jointly with an almost puritanical scale of values by a skillful combination of indulgence and deprivation. The control of impulses, e.g., the distraction from a period of masturbation by thigh pressure at seven months were entrusted to stimulation by play and later by fantasy. At fourteen months the child was able to recognize in a cookie into which she had twice bitten the shape of a dog; at nineteen months her play with imaginary companions started; she is one of the children whose infantile fetishes, the transitional objects of Winnicott (1953), soon became fantasy beings in their own rights.

The creation of an inner world and the ability to produce the Halloween mask are connected in various ways. Visual stimulation played a decisive part in the contact of mother and child—and then there is the crucial fact that the mother herself was a drawing teacher and drew for her child. The child was never "taught" to draw. There was never explicitly a premium set on her achievements, and yet every one of Evelyne's achievements meant much to the mother. The skill which Evelyne displayed is only one in a broad picture of a relationship in which learning by imitation becomes part of the molding of personality.

This is one example out of several which I might have chosen to illustrate the point that the activity to which neutralized energy can be directed, is likely to be the most significant to the child, the choice of sublimation most successful when this activity at the same time represents a bond with the love object.

This is only a special instance of a more general principle; the richness of needs simultaneously satisfied by any sublimation, the overdetermination of the activity or the multiple functions which it fulfills have always been considered to be of decisive importance. When the activity satisfies the most important need of the child, the wish for closeness to the parent, we may expect it to be of great significance indeed.

Evelyne was thirty months old when she painted the Halloween mask.

It is not her skill or what it means prospectively which is likely to interest us most but rather the factor behind it: the extraordinary capacity to neutralize, the extent of her secondary ego autonomy.

I now turn to an example meant to illustrate a different and, in some sense, opposite aspect of the problem:

The relationship of Anne to her mother had gone through dramatic vicissitudes.[10] The normally born and originally active little girl soon showed signs of decline in her development under the care of a mother whose unconscious set-up revolted against the double narcissistic mortification of having to give up her career and of having to devote her attention to a girl. The developmental picture of the child between six months and twelve months resembled that of children in institutions. Under the influence of a variety of circumstances the picture changed around one year, when particularly a developmental spurt of the child enabled the mother to find an outlet for a fantasy: She became the child's devoted teacher, as her father had been her own teacher. The ambivalence in the relationship did not subside, but a complex interaction, in which aggressive elements played a part comparable to that which more frequently libidinal elements play between the small child and his mother, opened the way for a workable and even satisfactory relationship. Anne developed into an anxious but active and gradually sociable two-and-a-half-year-old whose behavior was compounded out of friendliness tempered by a "be-a-nice-girl" comportment and a genuine "touch-me-not" attitude. She had some outstanding achievements to her credit: her vocabulary and language development were extraordinary, her pronounciation immaculate, and her ability to name and recognize pictures was above that of her age group. These were the areas in which the mother's ambitions were most marked.[11]

Initially the interest in picture books facilitated the separation from the mother in nursery school, and was the bridge on which Anne moved to closer attachment to one of the teachers. During a brief period, when the relationship of mother and child was once more obscured, both Anne's achievements were subjected to a slight regressive trend. The mother was pregnant and could not decide to let her child know about her pregnancy. During this period Anne's speech became excited and somewhat more infantile, its use defensive. At the same time her handling of books changed in character: she would anxiously go from one picture

10 See for a history of Anne's development, Coleman, Kris, Provence (1952).
11 See a report by Dr. Marianne Kris at the extraordinary meeting of the New York Psychoanalytic Society and Institute in honor of Miss Anna Freud at Arden House, N. Y., on May 7, 1954.

to the other in restless search for what she needed.[12] No other symptoms of regression were noted: in the rigorous atmosphere in which she was brought up a regression in cleanliness or sleep might have been too dangerous. But the area which she chose for regressive behavior was the one in which she had established the relationship with her mother. She had acquired mother's attention by performance, and performance deteriorated first: the energy was clearly deneutralized. No similar regression affected Evelyne's development. Her reaction to the birth of a sibling at two was reinforced resistance to bowel training, whereas her ego functions, "her character" remained unaffected. The areas in which neutralization had been achieved remained autonomous. Anne's choice of sublimation, the mastery of language, never reached the freedom and scope of Evelyne's achievements, but the fundamental difference between both children seems best characterized if we make a very general assumption: In Evelyne the capacity to neutralize was early developed, in Anne this general capacity did not reach a comparable stage: Most areas of her behavior were free from instinctual outbreaks, but in none was neutralization carried as far as with Evelyne. While Evelyne soiled at two and a half, in those activities in which neutralization had been achieved the degree of neutralization seemed extraordinary. It is a difference which, I believe, can be well expressed in terms of the "reservoir" and the "flux."

We may assume that in Evelyne the permanent investment of the ego is far advanced, but the flux is left relatively free. In Anne the flux is well controlled, but the degree of neutralization is not comparable; there is something reactive and defensive about her achievements. Though these differences must have many roots, some, we may assume, are likely to be connected with the quality of the early relationship of the two mothers to their two children.[13]

[12] Anne's behavior with the picture book supplies a further example for the relationship of neutralization to sublimation: On the first level, the picture-book activity serves to alleviate the anxiety. When connected with the separation from the mother, it has a defensive quality. We therefore assume that neutralization has been carried to a given point. In the mother's absence the shared activity is simply repeated with a substitute. This defensive performance breaks down when difficulties between mother and child arise. Though the activity with the picture book, i.e., the sublimation continues, the energy neutralization seems lowered.

On a third level the activity is used in a new context. Instead of mere repetition, initiative and problem solving can be noticed. After the mother had been able to tell Anne about her pregnancy, their relationship improved. When Anne sees a sad child, she now comes over to him with a picture book, sits down, and suggests that she would "read to him a story." (These and similar instances in Anne's behavior were noted by Lottie M. Maury.)

[13] They are naturally also related to the personalities of the mothers themselves.

IV. OBJECT RELATION AND INITIAL STEPS IN NEUTRALIZATION

Since the early 1930's the influence of early object relations on ego development has been a much-discussed topic of psychoanalytic work in various areas. In viewing this work from the vantage point of neutralization and sublimation, it seems obvious that emotional deficit in child care affects specifically the capacity to neutralize—so obvious, in fact, that it is scarcely necessary to review the evidence in detail.

A word first need be said about one group of clinical pictures in which the corroborating impressions are highly suggestive but ambiguous— the psychotic children. There the interaction between the defect in the child and in the mother, the reaction of the mother to an unsatisfactory "receiver," and the reactions of the child to an initially or reactively unsatisfactory "sender" of stimuli leads to a large number of puzzling phenomena repeatedly discussed and clarified particularly in Mahler's contributions (1952). The deficient neutralization of libidinal drives has been repeatedly implied in the literature. However, it is my impression that the deficient neutralization of aggression is equally pathognomonic (and this may sharpen our eye for the lack of synchronization in the neutralization of aggressive and libidinal drive energy in other children, thus pointing to an area in which even variations of normal behavior could be fruitfully studied from a new vantage point.) But the complexity of the clinical pictures in this area excludes them from more detailed discussion on this occasion.

I now turn to another group of data. They concern the developmental deficit in institutionalized children. The findings reported are derived from a detailed longitudinal study of individual children by Drs. R. W. Coleman and S. Provence, some results of which will be published in the near future. The study confirms in a general way previously established knowledge (Spitz, 1945) but presents more detailed and in many instances unexpected findings. However, I bear sole responsibility for the selection of data here mentioned and the conclusions drawn.

The decline in the general response and developmental picture of these children, some of whom were institutionalized shortly after birth, starts even with apparently well-endowed individuals at five months. It does not affect all areas measured by tests with equal intensity. Motor functions are on the whole at first (up to six months) less affected than others, and fine motor activity less than gross motor activity. (One might say the body needs a mother to stimulate it; the self-stimulation of the hands is more effective.) That language development or response to human contact should be more severely affected, needs hardly an explanation. In our context, however, it is particularly interesting that no activity that involves higher organization of discharge, problem solving, and thinking as related to action, develops as it does in normals. Individual variations as to the degree of maturity at birth play a decisive part, and the investigators gained the impression that the resistance to deprivational experience constitutes some sort of measure for intactness or for some other total factor of endowment. Moreover, the maturational processes themselves change the picture. Maturation, as it were, proceeds in spite of impediment. During the second half of the first year rocking dominates the picture. But, though mostly delayed, the institutionalized children here studied "learn" to walk. These and similar steps in maturation initiate around one year a shift in the total picture. It seems that some substitutions and restitutions are being attempted; yet the total achievement level (as measured by developmental tests) does not rise. Much more impressive than the quantitative data are the clinical impressions. The investigators feel the absence of "driving power." What lacks is the initiative. Imitation comes easier than self-initiation of action; and though equipment facilities brought about by growth are at the child's disposal, they are not being used. It should be added that none of the children studied showed the depressive reaction to the separation from the mother described by Spitz and Wolf (1946), since the separation had taken place at a very early stage. In certain areas, the impression arises that one can actually differentiate purely maturational forces from those which show influences of the environment. The area where this differentiation is clearest is that of earliest language development.

Seen in conjunction with the assumption concerning the existence of two kinds of energy at the disposal of the ego, the following hypothesis becomes feasible: one might assume that maturational processes are more closely connected with noninstinctual energies and that the organization of action and problem solving is more dependent on the neutralization of instinctual energy. If this neutralization does not occur to a sufficient extent and/or degree, even the flow of noninstinctual energy tends to tarry. Only the combination of both energies in the investment of the ego leads to the normally expected developmental steps during the later part of the first and the second year of life.[14] Such an assumption encroaches, as Hartmann (1955) said, on the competence of the physiologist. We therefore continue on lines more familiar in psychoanalytic theory.

[14] A separate set of assumptions might naturally envisage the possibility that the conditions of institutional care affect the quantity of available instinctual energy itself.

The neutralization of instinctual energy does presumably not occur or does not become effective in institutionalized children because a central love object is absent. We have learned from Freud (1931) that the child's development is largely determined by the general tendency to repeat actively what has been and is being passively experienced in infant and child care; Freud speaks of the child's identification with the active mother. We assume that through this identification the child develops certain action units, which seem to include some more complex motor performances and adaptive movements as they occur in the contact between mother and infant. These action units, we assume, require and stimulate neutralization.

The study of two interacting processes, of maturation and adaptive patterning in response to the mother's ministrations, might enable us to approach the question of how specific types and modalities of maternal care can be related to the development of the capacity for neutralization of instinctive energy in the child.

In my own mind (1950), I had viewed the opportunity for simultaneous discharge of libidinal and aggressive energies, their earliest fusion in discharge, as a favorable factor. But it can be no more but one among many.

A more comprehensive approach can be suggested if we generalize some of the assumptions recently made by Winnicott (1953) in the study of transitional objects. To put his thought in briefest outline: Grossly defective maternal care fails to stimulate the child's earliest mental processes. These earliest mental processes tend to supplement whatever satisfaction the child obtains by the illusion of complete satisfaction. The "ordinarily devoted mother" gratifies the child's needs at any given time only to some extent; there is always some slight deficit, some discontent. This discontent, Winnicott argues, is filled by the child's capacity to imagine full satisfaction. Not only extreme deprivation but also extreme indulgence eliminates the incentive for mental activity.[15] In this set-up, mental activity, which is related by Winnicott to an equipment factor (he chooses, I believe erroneously, the I.Q.), stands as it were at the beginning of what might be called initiative for independence. The assumption of a hallucinatory stage (Ferenczi) can thus be related to specific experience of the infant; it can be integrated with other assumptions, for instance, those concerning the relation to the mother and the growth of the apparatus itself. The capacity for appropriate illusion seems to constitute one of the earliest stages in neutralization. It would

15 See in this connection Hartmann, Kris, Loewenstein (1946).

be the one which predominantly and typically depends on the interaction
between mother and child, and prepares the way for identification.

BIBLIOGRAPHY

Alshuler, R. and Hattwick, B. W. (1947), *Painting and Personality: A Study of Young
    Children*. Chicago: University of Chicago Press.
Coleman, R. W.; Kris, E.; Provence, S. (1953), The Study of Variations of Early
    Parental Attitudes. *This Annual*, VIII.
Freud, A. (1936), *The Ego and the Mechanisms of Defense*. New York: International
    Universities Press, 1946.
Freud, S. (1931), On Female Sexuality. *Collected Papers*, V. London: Hogarth Press,
    1950.
Friess, A. (1952), The Study of a Child: Her Paintings and Personality. *Sarah Lawrence
    Studies*, VI.
Hartmann, H.; Kris, E.; Loewenstein, R. M. (1946), Comments on the Formation of
    Psychic Structure. *This Annual*, II.
Jacobson, E. (1954), The Self and the Object World: Vicissitudes of Their Infantile
    Cathexes and Their Influence on Ideational and Affective Development. *This
    Annual*, IX.
Kris, E. (1934), The Psychology of Caricature. See Kris (1952).
—— (1935), Comments on Spontaneous Artistic Creations by Psychotics. See Kris (1952).
—— (1950), Notes on the Development and on Some Current Problems of Psycho-
    analytic Child Psychology. *This Annual*, V.
—— (1951), Some Comments and Observations of Early Autoerotic Activities. *This
    Annual*, VI.
—— (1952), *Psychoanalytic Explorations in Art*. New York: International Universities
    Press.
—— (1953), Psychoanalysis and the Study of Creative Imagination. *Bull. N. Y. Acad.
    Med.*, XXIX.
Mahler, M. S. (1952), On Child Psychosis and Schizophrenia: Autistic and Symbiotic
    Psychoses. *This Annual*, VII.
Spitz, R. A. (1945), Hospitalism: An Inquiry into the Genesis of Psychiatric Conditions
    in Early Infancy. *This Annual*, I.
—— and Wolf, K. M. (1946), Anaclitic Depression. *This Annual*, II.
Winnicott, D. W. (1953), Transitional Objects and Transitional Phenomena. *Int. J.
    Psa.*, XXXIV.

ON DISCOVERING ONE'S IDENTITY

A Case Report

PAUL KRAMER, M.D. (Chicago)[1]

The prolonged analysis of a very ill patient provided an opportunity to reconstruct in some detail early experiences pertaining to the discovery of one's own ego, or rather of those segments of the ego that embody the sense of one's identity. The term identity is used to denote the awareness of one's self as an entity separate and distinct from one's environment, specifically, earliest environment. The intention of this presentation is the demonstration of factors that stimulated an accelerated and precocious development of the sense of identity, and to trace how the forced discovery, having proved an experience of traumatic significance, led to a faulty ego development of an unusual nature, and to certain pathological consequences for the total personality of the patient.

Whether or not this contribution to ego pathography adds in some measure to our understanding of normal ego development is not to be determined on the basis of the study of only one case, though some related questions appear to merit further inquiry. The material may be considered in the light of the old problem of the relationship between ego development controlled by inherited factors, and that stimulated by the variable aspects of necessity, but generalizations should be deferred until additional information has been collected, including particularly that to be gained from the analytic study of children.

Since the observations contained little fundamentally new or unexpected findings, no review of the pertinent literature was attempted. The study is presented because of the relative scarcity of published clinical material of this nature, though theoretical considerations are numerous. The material was obtained in the course of an analysis of several years' duration, though it is mainly concerned with problems and phenomena which dominated a stage of the treatment lasting somewhat longer than

[1] I am indebted to Dr. Samuel Lipton for his assistance in the preparation of this manuscript.

47

two years. I have not attempted to organize the analytic material in a logically consistent sequence, but have chosen a collection of examples from the patient's material germane to the main topic of the report. They will be presented in the approximate order of their appearance in the course of the analysis. This order did not always correspond chronologically to the actuality of the patient's childhood.

The familiar tendency of analytic material to emerge in fragments, sometimes separated by months, should be borne in mind. The paper was written largely from memory, with the help of auxiliary mnemonic devices, such as short key notes made at irregular intervals in the course of the treatment.

The patient, a middle-aged man, had been suffering for many years from a variety of diffuse anxiety symptoms. Predominant and most disturbing were his agoraphobia and claustrophobia. He could neither leave familiar surroundings, such as his home and his office, nor could he stay without severe anxiety in a room other than one familiar to him. He was forever concerned with the question whether and how he would be able to leave the room. When in his car, he could extend his travels to the limit of a few miles from his home, but then he was constantly worried about the condition of the engine, the tires, and about other mechanical possibilities of damage to the car which might leave him stranded. He was for years unable to describe his anxiety or to give an account of what he feared. All he could say was that he was plagued by a terrifying feeling expressed in the words, "I can't make it." He was able to add nothing further for a very long time.

After some years of work the patient finally began to reproduce in detail, in acting, in dreaming and in fantasy, those early infantile experiences which were underlying his symptoms. Memories reaching back into the first three years of life began to emerge, at first in the form of his reliving strange sensations and bewildering experiences, in everyday life and in the transference. Eventually those were transformed into memories, though the patient had much difficulty in verbalizing them. This was true particularly of those early experiences, to be described, which seem to have occurred while he was still inarticulate—in fact, while he was just learning to speak. He was at the time between one and three years of age. During the part of the treatment period with which this paper is concerned, the patient was wont to enter the analyst's room with a seemingly unrelated word or a sentence on his lips. This then became a central point around which an important infantile experience could be reconstructed. I shall give a few examples. Once the patient came into my room repeating the words "Upside down, upside down!" He did not know where the expression came from, nor why he used it, but mentioned that all morning this expression had compulsively pushed itself into his awareness. He also felt dizzy, and objects moved strangely, scintillating in a snake-like fashion, in front of his eyes. He was frightened, and expected one of his severe anxiety attacks to develop. He barely managed to come to the analytic session. After describing all this with great tension, and after he had for some time remained anxiously sitting on the edge of the couch, he stretched out and relaxed. Then he suddenly recognized an image of a tree in a pool of water, upside down, and his own image, also upside down in the water. He then recalled the origin of the scene he described. There was indeed a little creek passing behind the house in which he lived when he was less than two years old, and he recalled the feeling of wonderment and some anxiety on seeing his image so reversed in the water. He recalled reaching for it and causing the water to ripple. The image became distorted, and this puzzled and frightened him. The changes in the image because of the rippling water were reexperienced by him in the form of the scintillating distortion of objects this morning. He remembered further that at the same time in life he observed his own shadow, tried to grasp it with his hands, and was frightened by its change of shape and disappearance as he bent down to touch it.

On another occasion the patient came with the statement, forcefully and repeatedly expressed, "I saw myself!" Again the words impressed themselves on his mind with great force. He had a feeling of conviction, which he could not explain, that this expression was connected in an important manner with his anxieties. Some days later he added some words to the sentence, and it now was: "I saw myself and I got frightened." By way of involved association chains, and experiences of great weakness, smallness and helplessness, vividly felt by him in every life situation and in the analytic hours during those days, he arrived finally at a distinct and emotionally highly charged series of memories, here to be recounted in the approximate order of their emergence, though, as already mentioned, it may not be the order of their occurrence in the actuality of his early childhood.

He saw himself looking up toward his mother and becoming aware of her large abdomen. She was at the time pregnant with his brother, who was born when he was twenty months old. He reached for her, called and cried, apparently wishing to be lifted and carried. Instead, the mother stepped back out of his reach and addressed him in a firm fashion. A feeling of great helplessness and an awareness of his smallness and weakness overcame the child at that moment. It was instructive to observe how all this was re-enacted in the present. A characteristic example follows: On the day on which this memory emerged I had as usual greeted him at the door of the waiting room. He was sitting there with a deep frown on his face, looking perplexed and unhappy. His arms were spread away from his body in an awkward manner. On seeing me his face lit up, he rose rapidly to his feet and came toward me. He later reported, along with the already mentioned reference to the sentence, "I saw myself and I was frightened," that he had been feeling weak and faint all day. He had a headache, his eyes were burning, his throat was dry and he had felt an odd tension around his mouth. He was also aware of a momentary feeling of great relief when he saw me coming toward him. When on the couch, all symptoms disappeared, to his amazement. He explained later that he could no longer reproduce them because "mother" was here and he did not have to cry and feel weak, unhappy and anxious. He then said, after a few moments, that he had a sudden feeling which he expressed as "You are not there." He felt himself on the verge of an attack of anxiety but prevented its emergence by looking at me and convincing himself that I was there. It became evident that this experience was one of many through which the child recognized to his painful disappointment that he and mother were separate entities and that he had no control over her. Thus the experience of discovering his self proved a painful, in fact, as I shall endeavor to show later in this study, a traumatic experience. It seems that in consequence of the discovery that he had no control over his mother, he made other disturbing and thwarting discoveries, which further accentuated his feeling described later as "I saw myself and I got frightened." We succeeded in reconstructing many episodes relating to such experiences. He recalled that he awakened more than once because of hunger and because of being wet. He called his mother by crying loudly. She did not come. The child became enraged because of her failure to appear and finally screamed in a fit of rage and frustration until nearly exhausted. At this stage he found himself unable to stop his screaming and sobbing. He suddenly perceived the rage itself as separate from himself, and as something he could not control. This experience caused a feeling of panic to rise in him. His feeling of weakness in controlling his environment was augmented by his helplessness in mastering happenings within himself.

On a later occasion the patient reported a sensation, rather than a sentence, intruding itself on his consciousness. He felt himself, to use his own words, "stepping out of the analyst's body," more precisely, from his legs. It was as if he were a child barely reaching above the analyst's knees, emerging to walk a few steps on his own, only to get frightened and anxious to return and merge with the analyst again, but finding himself unable to do so and then becoming terror-stricken. As this illusion was analytically investigated, the person of the analyst was replaced by that of his father, and finally, by that of his mother. During this time many sensations and fragments of fantasies appeared, indicative of the child's early concept of seeing himself and his mother as an inseparable entity.

The beginnings of discovery of the self seemed stimulated by occurrences which were, on the one hand, passively endured painful sensations, and on the other, active attempts to increase the range of his functions. Our evidence indicated that this period of ego-finding occurred at the time when he was learning to walk, that is, when he was a little over a year old. During our work on this material, the patient experienced sensations which could readily be interpreted as those of a child learning to walk, exuberant at his success, and frightened by failure. The patient forced himself to take longer and longer walks away from his home, set himself goals, one, two or three streets away and insisted on going by himself, rather than with his wife, as was his previous custom. He found himself glancing back anxiously as if to see whether she watched him. He looked for support toward the walls of the buildings, toward lampposts; he felt dizzy; his knees were faltering; he had sensations of falling forward, and found himself impelled to spread his arms ahead of him to break the fall. On reaching his goal he was bathed in perspiration, anxious, but also secretly elated. The comparison with the child learning to walk was his own and was not suggested to him by me. During the same time he described thoughts of being unable to get up from the chair in the waiting room by himself, and said that he felt his hands lifting in a helpless manner toward me and his face turning up as if to appeal to the mother (analyst) to help him or raise him. I had on many occasions observed what he described quite clearly.

At times the patient spoke of a strange and disturbing feeling of deadness involving all of his body except the organ or limb that was active at the moment. For instance, he was aware of feeling only his eyes when he was looking at something, or his hands when he touched something with them, or his mouth when he tasted food. These sensations led to memories that as a young child he had known similar feelings. He recalled a time when he could feel only his face when he cried, only his penis when he urinated, only his eyes when he looked at his mother, while the rest of his body felt numb or absent. This was a very bewildering and frightening sensation. Still later he explained that during the same period of childhood he felt only those parts of his body as alive that were in direct touch with his mother. He once said: "Only that part of me lived through which mother's love flowed into me."

An important and unsuspected aspect of his castration anxiety found its explanation in connection with these experiences. He reported that at one time in childhood he felt his penis alive only when he masturbated. The mother's prohibition of the masturbation removed the feeling (of life) from the penis. It felt dead, absent. On that basis he developed vaguely formulated, but intensely felt fears that his mother could render him dead, altogether, at her will. Once again the feeling of helplessness contributed to the awareness of his separate and feeble identity as contrasted with that of his mother.

During the same period of treatment he reported that for months he had been relying on seeing a woman working in his office building at a certain desk whenever he passed through the hall on the way to or from his own place of work. When on occasions she was not at the accustomed place, he found himself looking for her frantically, and asked desperately, "Is she there, is she there?" On such occasions his mouth became dry, his throat sore, his voice hoarse, his eyes burned, and he had diffuse pains in his chest and in the muscles of his arms. Shortly before this symptom subsided, and following his discovery of its infantile predecessor, he added that at times he had a taste of sour milk in his mouth or, as he eventually described it, a taste of "burped-up milk." This whole set of reactions proved to be almost an exact repetition of his sensations and feelings in very early childhood when he found himself alone, with his mother gone, and not responding to his frantic calls. His eyes burned with tears, he was hoarse, his throat was sore, his mouth was dry from crying, and his muscles ached from the exertion.

The patient throughout life had been extremely preoccupied with a morbid concern over food. He was forever finding its taste peculiar and was convinced of it being spoiled. He discarded huge quantities of food which he thought unfit for consumption, to the great annoyance of his wife. He insisted that the members of the family refrain from eating food which he declared spoiled. One day he reported a short dream: "Mother is away. I am in the kitchen and out of my mouth some brown stuff flows into the basin." In the course of his associations he launched into the description of an experience which he told with absolute conviction of its reality, although it must have occurred, in keeping with his memory of the locale of the occurrence, when he was less than two years old. He saw himself on the floor, and as he said, not only playing with his feces (something which he had reported on previous occasions), but also eating them. He described his mother's coming upon him and angrily reprimanding him. Moreover, she forced him to swallow a huge quantity of what he believes must have been castor oil. Then he recalled the resulting explosive bowel movements and the feelings of great weakness, emptiness and near collapse that followed them. He had the sensation that the stool and urine would never stop flowing and "that he would turn inside out." He retained from this, and from other experiences of that time, the feeling that the mother did not wish him to keep anything for himself, that all he had belonged to her, and that whatever he kept he had stolen from her. This ideation played a large role at a somewhat later stage of his development when it gave a distinctive color to his castration anxiety. The castration threat was experienced as coming from the mother before it was related to the father, and was felt with no less intensity than that later ascribed by him to the father. After the memory emerged he reported that a few days earlier he and his family had gone to his favorite restaurant. He ordered oysters—a dish for which the restaurant is particularly well known. But this time he could not eat them. They had a distinctly fecal odor. He refused the oysters and tried a salad with his favorite dressing. It tasted like castor oil. Though intellectually convinced that the food was perfect and in spite of his observing that it was enjoyed greatly by the other family members, he found himself unable to eat it. The following day another of the sentences, which we had come to recognize as heralding the emergence of early infantile material, appeared in his mind. This time the words were, "How weak I am." They proved to refer to the state of weakness and emptiness following the castor oil treatment. He described vividly the state of despair connected with the recognition of how little he was able to control the actions of his own body, how weak he was in comparison with his mother, who had such absolute control over him and could force him, magically, as he thought, to experience most unpleasant and frightening sensations.

Perhaps a year after the castor oil treatment there occurred an episode of illness referred to in the family tradition as his "appendicitis." He recalls intense abdominal pain and a feeling of great thirst. This culminated in nausea and vomiting, after which he felt well. Analysis brought forth the information that he was at that time preoccupied with the idea that if only he could manage to hold back his stool and to abstain from eating and drinking,[2] he then would be strong like the mother, and like all grownups, since weakness was already identified with inability to control his bowels. He did indeed refuse food and drink and became severely constipated. It was the resulting condition that was suspected to have been an appendicitis. It appears probable that the threat of a possible operation induced him to give up this particular behavior pattern.

I should like to interpolate an explanatory statement which may be germane. The condensed description may have created the impression that the patient experienced his childhood reactions, feelings and sensations in the manner of an adult observer and reported them in an articulate, precise manner. Nothing could be further from the truth. Many days, weeks, or months of patient work often passed between the first appearance of one of the sentences mentioned or some other symptom and its final explanation. Though his native intelligence was of a very high order, the patient was an unsophisticated and non-intellectual man, completely unfamiliar with psychoanalytic literature, whose rough background and limited education had in no way prepared him for intellectual and theoretical analytic constructions. His memories and reconstructions appeared slowly and often in fragmentary fashion, but nearly always as spontaneous productions of his own. When complete, they emerged with much emotion and an inner conviction of their truth. Many of the states of feeling he reported were quite foreign to my experience and could not have been constructed by me. In fact, I had learned that attempts on my part to introduce interpretations in accordance with my thinking sometimes delayed the clarification of the material. When the patient felt my skepticism he was restless and resentful, and his confidence appeared shaken until the mistake was cleared and he eventually supplied the memory material underlying a particular symptom. As a rule, the symptom then disappeared.

One day the patient spoke with great feeling of the intense empathy he felt with a child lost in a crowd or in a store. He experienced the feelings of the

[2] This material was introduced by another of his "headline" sentences. This time the phrase was "stooling and sucking."

child in this situation with the most painful vividness and realism. The bewilderment, anxiety, the longing for the mother were felt by him as if his own. While speaking of this he recalled distinctly that as a child he often had the feeling, "I am so small I will get lost because mother won't see me." Therefore not only to see the mother but to be seen by her was important to the child, and later to the adult, when a mother figure substituted for the original.

A few weeks later, the patient once again presented us with a phrase that emerged into his consciousness with insistent force. The phrase was "Up and down, up and down." Its meaning was completely puzzling to him. The emergence of this phrase was accompanied by the sensation that objects in his field of vision moved up and down, and also by uncomfortable, though vague, sensations in his body. The patient spoke about certain preferences in food, such as his wish that his oatmeal contain small lumps rather than be completely fluid. Then came a feeling of dislike for liquids in general and for water in particular, and memories emerged of protesting and crying because he was given water rather than milk or semisolid foods when he was a very small child. Finally he added the construction, supported by fragments of memory, of being held on his father's shoulder and "burped," and rocked up and down to stop his crying. He described the feeling of seeing objects bouncing in front of his eyes without knowing what the objects were. He had not yet learned to name them or to recognize their function. Again though much of this was construction, it was accompanied by a feeling of conviction of its correctness.

In another few weeks the patient reported that "something about noise" kept coming into his mind. All he could say at first was that he had the feeling that the noise had something to do with the feeling which he described as "How weak I am." Two days later while taking an afternoon nap he was startled out of his sleep by a tremendous crash. He jumped up in terror and asked his son what crashed, only to be told that nothing had. However, it seems that the son had sneezed. That same day the vision of turning railroad wheels with sparks flying from them came to him, and then there appeared the memory of a time when he suffered from a childhood disease, probably measles, and was lying in a darkened room. Toward evening the shades were raised and the windows opened. They lived at the time in an apartment above his father's shop. The windows in his room were level with an elevated railway structure. He was periodically startled and badly frightened by the noise of the passing trains, and fascinated by the sight of the turning wheels throwing sparks when the brakes were applied. He called for his mother, but she did not come to him. They lived in that apartment when he was twenty-two months old. He remembered further the feeling of having played happily with a young aunt a few days before his illness. Then he found himself sick, very uncomfortable and unhappy, unable to see the favorite aunt. The patient said: "Talking of being weak, that's when I really saw myself. I could not get mother to come to me, and I could not throw the sickness off." He emphasized the last

part of the statement. Again, the experience of remaining alone when frightened, and the simultaneous occurrence in his physical being of events beyond
his power to control, the discomfort of the illness, contributed to the painful
awakening of his self-awareness. An earlier, and more significant incident of
similar character is to be described shortly.

Among the patient's many and frequently changing symptoms were several
sets of complaints outstanding in terms of their persistence and the intense
emotional and intellectual preoccupation which the patient devoted to them.
One of these symptom complexes involved his eyes. He suffered frequently
from a suddenly occurring disturbance of vision which he described as "streaks
of lightning" appearing before his eyes and interfering with his vision. This
was originally accompanied by a sensation of shock, of dizziness, a feeling of
sudden weakness and of inner emptiness, and a fear of utter collapse. The
patient further reported the sensation that things were forever flying into his
eyes, but when he examined the eye, or had his physician examine it, nothing
was ever to be found. For the longest time the derivation of these symptoms
remained hypothetical. It was easy to observe that they occurred when the
patient was troubled by someone leaving his vicinity. He himself associated it
with the reaction of rage at the departing person. This explanation was
undoubtedly partially correct, but it left many questions unanswered.

One day the patient came to the hour in a state of acute panic. His secretary
was leaving for her vacation the next day. He felt paralyzed by fear, anticipated
a "break-down," and felt helpless with rage and frustration. He also had the
eye symptoms described above, and was convinced that some foreign body had
flown into his eye. In his associations he suddenly saw a picture of a breast
being pushed at him. No, he corrected himself, it pulls away, and he cannot
stop it. He then spoke of a feeling of hunger and weakness, and of his having
a "weaker magic" than the breast. On the following days the patient continued
to express sensations of hunger and of confused helplessness. He spoke of a
fear of dying, and of his concern over the painfulness of the slow passage of
time. "How will I stand it till the evening. I feel hollow and cold inside. I have
to go five days[3] without food. I shall die of hunger." Resentment and rage
were also prominent in his feelings. Further work made it appear very probable
that the patient was indeed re-experiencing, in his eye symptoms and in the
accompanying anxious sensations of weakness, hunger, frustration, and rage,
reactions to which as an infant he had become subject when he had been
weaned or, at any rate, when his mother suddenly had taken him off the
breast. We had learned that this did happen fairly often during his infancy
because of her having to attend to the store while she was nursing him. She had
interrupted the nursing many times under such circumstances. It appears likely
that on pathways whose nature must of necessity remain speculative, the sudden
increase of tension and of the level of discomfort upon the abrupt withdrawal

[3] The duration of the secretary's absence.

of the breast expressed itself in a sensation of shock with certain visual manifestations, later appearing as the "streaks of lightning" before his eyes. Perhaps
it is more correct to say that the shock may not as much have caused the visual
impressions repeated in the symptoms, but that these impressions, having been
in some unknown way connected with the catastrophic events producing the
shock, became invested with the affective qualities related originally to the
distressing experiences.[4] The time factor involved seems important in these
considerations: I mean, the suddenness of the traumatic occurrences, the necessity for an adjustment to a frustration more rapid than it was possible for the
infant to accomplish. Nor was it possible for him to absorb and neutralize the
stimuli causing his discomfort as rapidly as they invaded the imperfect, indeed
the still embryonic, ego organization. During the working-through period of
this material the patient voiced complaints of too much being expected from
him, of his being pushed too fast, and of things being expected before he was
ready for them.

It seems that the early experiences of abrupt removal from the breast were
telescoped together with another set of very early traumata that have now to be
described. Together with the weaning they are perhaps the earliest in the series
of experiences leading to the discovery of the patient's identity.

In the course of his treatment the patient often complained of a number of
uncomfortable symptoms which tended to make their appearance simultaneously.
He felt feverish (the patient was forever taking his temperature), and his
muscles ached. He felt distress in his chest, a burning in his throat, and was
subject to an unpleasant cough. As usual, numerous medical examinations
failed to reveal a sufficient organic cause for the patient's complaints. The
symptoms made their appearance when a separation from a significant person
had occurred in the patient's life, or when he was threatened by such a
separation in a way which he feared he could not control. It was also conspicuous that on several occasions a separation accompanied by these symptoms
was followed by an estrangement from the object. It was henceforth viewed
with a lack of trust, and, in fact, with deep suspicion. We shall return later to
this particular circumstance.

In the course of once again relating the complaints just mentioned, the
patient added that he had an unfamiliar bitter taste in his mouth and had to
"burp" repeatedly. He corrected himself to "I mean belch." He said, "I wonder
whether that's the medicine they gave me when I had the double pneumonia."
He had sporadically alluded to this illness without ascribing it much significance. Family tradition had it that at the age of certainly less than eighteen
months, perhaps as early as nine months, he had suffered seriously from what
was termed "double pneumonia." He was repeatedly told that he had nearly

---

4 It is hardly necessary to emphasize the fact that the eye symptoms of the patient
were highly overdetermined, deriving genetically and dynamically from several
sources. Here only the factors germane to the topic of this study are considered.

died at the time. A connection between his symptoms and the early illness was suspected. We were at first inclined to regard such an assumption with skepticism until, when reporting the recurrence of the same set of symptoms on a later occasion, the patient mentioned that he was disturbed lately by sudden variations in his state of consciousness, a vagueness and absent-mindedness not characteristic of him, and by contradictory rapidly alternating feelings of attraction and repulsion toward his wife. He could find no cause for these vacillations and not even a rationalization offered itself to his puzzled mind.

The analytic study of these symptoms convinced us that they were indeed related to the early illness, the "double pneumonia," and that his uncomfortable sensations and the strange changes in his ego feeling and in his relations to the people around him represented a repetition of his experiences at the time of the early illness. The material pointed to the fact that the baby may have reacted to the discomfort of the illness with the expectation that the agency which he did not yet at this time perceive as distinct from himself, and which in the past had promptly removed unpleasant stimuli will do so again. But this time the expectation was not fulfilled and the infant discovered painfully that this agency, the mother, was not a part of, but separated from him, and not subject to his wishes; moreover, that she must have had hostile intentions toward him, or else why should she have withdrawn from him, and ceased to alleviate his discomfort; and further, that he had no capacity to influence this discomfort, in terms of removal of the pain within him, or in removing himself from the sources of his pain. The responsibility for his discomfort he now ascribed to the "newly separated" hostile mother. "Mother did not help me out. She did not want me," was a frequent lament of the patient at this time. It was brought forth with great intensity of feeling. I am unable to convey the expression of despair and anguish contained in the patient's behavior and words. During the same period the thought appeared in his mind: "I don't own the house, the house owns me." The thought proved to reflect the recognition of the infant that it was not he who controlled the all-powerful mother, but she who controlled him.

It is self-evident that the occurrence of logical thought sequences and constructions is not assumed to have taken place in the infant in the form we have descriptively used here. The description intends no more than to convey in words preverbal affective reactions, which appear to represent early stages of the formation of an ego. The matrix from which this process of ego formation took its course, the "nucleus" of the ego, we assume to have existed in some as yet undefined form before its onset.

I am inclined to see in the patient's grave early illness, along with the other early experiences described, an important predisposing factor for the development of his particularly intractable neurosis. The forcible and sudden, rather than gradual, interruption of his unity with his mother, and the infant's "interpretation" of this event as a consequence of the mother's hostile intent, led to a burst of precocious development, an accelerated and premature formation of an ego extremely narrow in scope and limited in its capacity for further growth. On the basis of an ego so impaired, the development of a malignant neurotic pattern took place. Some details of this process are to be described in the following part of this study.

II

At one time, well along in his treatment, the patient began to refer to a part of himself as "the little man." He also resorted to expressions like "the little king," and "the little lord," to describe the same aspect of his personality, but the "little man" remained the one most frequently used. Distinct from the rest of his personality, the "little man" first came into evidence in the analysis when the patient became aware of the resistance which this part of him offered to the treatment and to the analyst. He, the "little man," mocked and ridiculed the interpretations and suggestions made by the analyst. He seemed most obstinately determined to prevent improvement in the patient's condition. The "little man" was suspicious and distrusted the analyst and engaged in "snickering behind his back." One day the patient exclaimed in anger: "There is a Goddamn little man in me that keeps laughing at you while you talk." From then on the patient habitually used this expression to describe a part of himself which he perceived as sharply distinct from the rest of his personality.

We learned that a correct interpretation often resulted in the "little man's" secretly laughing at our expense—"The little man now laughs," the patient was wont to say, in a low voice, with an expression of listening to something within himself.

It gradually became quite clear that the "little man's" activity was by no means limited to the analytical situation. He objected sharply to the patient's attempts to transgress the limits of his self-imposed restrictions on walking and traveling. He did not want the patient to become friendly with anyone and insisted that the patient trust no one. The enjoyment of pleasure and gratification, of rest and peace, was categorically prohibited by the "little man." "He won't let me live," became a frequent phrase with which the patient described the relationship of this part of himself to the rest of his personality. The obstructive and interfering influence of this "little man" was most evident when the patient was about to obtain pleasure or experience an improvement of his condition, or when he attempted to make use of a freedom of movement otherwise restricted.

Superficially this appears like the description of a primitive, archaic, and harsh superego. Further study revealed that indeed primitive superego features and the "little man" were overlapping. But fundamentally this phenomenon appeared to be an isolated part of the ego, an area of condensed narcissistic reaction to the early perception of the patient's own weakness and helplessness. It seems that a mobilization of narcissistic ego resources occurred under the impact of the painful discoveries of the child's helplessness, and that these resources became condensed into an ego area which from then on acted as the "little man." This ego segment did not at first contain identifications in terms of those that enter into the superego formation, though such identifications later became added to it. It remained an isolated ego element, continuing to lead a sort of autonomous existence. At times it utilized the superego content that adhered to it, or overlapped with it, for its purposes. For instance, guilt feelings were used to enforce behavior conforming to the "little man's" demands.

One day the patient sat up with a disturbed expression on his face and declared "we are missing something, we are missing the guilt. What makes me knock myself down like that? It must be because I am guilty." Further study made obvious that he had no reason for guilt, nor did he really feel it, but that he felt compelled by his "little man" to find some means to prevent the rest of his person from enjoying a particular situation, a situation implying greater mobility and some pleasure. In this connection the patient once expressed the idea that it could not be true that the hold which the "little man" had on him was a result of a deep guilt, as he, the patient, had often thought. When he discussed fantasies about his having stolen the mother's breast, so that she could not feed the other children, it occurred to him that if he could prove that he did not steal the breast, he would free himself of the "little man." But then he recognized that this was not so. He realized that such a proof of his innocence would indeed deprive the "little man" of a particular weapon, by means of which he exercised his control over the patient, but by no means free the patient from his pervading influence.

To return to the situation offering pleasure and mobility, it became clear in the analysis, that such situations reawakened ancient fears of venturing too far away from the mother (mother substitute), with the corresponding idea that he will not find his way back. When that happened the "little man" became active and began to interfere with the patient's activities. The "little man" took over, in a distorted fashion, the function which the mother fulfilled before the patient discovered himself as being separate from her. Nevertheless, it is dubious whether this occurred on the basis of a true identification that takes place following an object loss, since, at that stage, the mother had not yet been perceived as an object but as a part of himself. What he lost was to him a protecting and supporting part of himself, whereupon he proceeded to mobilize the remaining resources into the "little man" figure, from now on entrusted with the protective functions which until then were an integral component of the mother not yet separated. The establishment of the "little man" in the ego in effect denied the earliest experience of separation from the mother. When discussing the early disturbances of his relationship to his mother, the patient used to say: "The little man took over mother's job when my brother was born," and "The little man kept on where mother left off, that's why I won't give him up." Once the patient remarked with great emphasis, "When mother was with me I didn't know that I existed, when she was not there I realized that I existed, I felt myself as myself, and that was a frightening thought. . . That is how I felt this morning when N. was not in the office."

As the different stages of libido development passed and the child was subjected to traumata peculiar to each, they lent specific features to the "little man." Moreover, it seems that this ego segment also actively attracted libidinal energy to itself as if deliberately hoarding such libidinal cathexes to increase its power. Most impressive was the contribution of the anal-sadistic phase to the libido reservoir of the "little man" and hence to the character and demeanor of the ego part so named. The patient spent many weeks re-experiencing it in the transference, remembering details of and elaborating on his early childhood relationship to the bowel function and his fantasies regarding his stools at that period. He became vividly cognizant of the magic and omnipotent powers which he ascribed to the stool in childhood. At one time while speaking about the relationship between the "little man" and the fantasies of the omnipotent stool, he said: "The magic stool and the little man merged and became one. They took each other as partners." This spontaneous description graphically bore witness to the manner in which the ego segment of the "little man" drew to itself anal-sadistic libidinal energy.

Of interest for the genesis of the patient's dominant symptom, his agoraphobia, was his identification of the process of awakening, which was often accompanied by much anxiety, with being eliminated as feces from the mother's body. On the basis of slowly emerging memories the patient suggested that this particular fantasy may have originated in infancy when he awakened and found himself covered with feces which had become cold and irritating. The waking anxiety itself was described by him as very much like the anxiety of his agoraphobic attacks. In this context it should be added that he also equated falling asleep with merging with the mothers' breast. He reported fantasies and hypnagogic hallucinations in which he saw himself "falling into mother's breast." Waking up was undoubtedly an anal birth for the unconscious of the patient, and falling asleep a reunion with the mother. Both processes were consequently often associated with anxiety, the first with fear of separation, the second with the dread of total merging with the mother. They were therefore opposed by the "little man," who, in a certain sense, offered himself to the rest of the ego as a mother equivalent from whom separation was never to occur, and the union with whom was not to result in the cessation of individual existence. This ego element consequently sought to draw all libidinal energies unto itself, instead of allowing them to flow over to other objects. We shall return later to these features of the "little man" phenomenon, and shall also refer to the manner in which the separation from him was perceived and elaborated on the phallic level, as castration anxiety, and in which the "little man" became invested with phallic-narcissistic libido and significance.

As a consequence of the fact that the "little man" so voraciously appropriated libidinal energy during all stages of libidinal development, there occurred a sharp increase of secondary narcissistic cathexis, with resulting diminution of the available libido for true object relationships. This was poignantly expressed by the patient in his frequent complaint: "The little man won't let me love," paralleling the already mentioned reproach that "The little man won't let me *live*."

Two childhood experiences, one reconstructed on the basis of analytic material and the other clearly remembered on the basis of reconstruction, had greatly contributed to the process of development and final crystalization of the phenomenon of the "little man."

At an advanced stage of the analysis, on an occasion when the patient for the first time in many years permitted his wife to leave town for a few days, he experienced the following sequence of events. For some days before his wife's trip, he complained about a painful swelling of his legs. During her absence he called me a number of times to report his concern because of a violent bout of diarrhea and cramps. In fact, he believed he had observed a bit of blood and mucus in the stool. For some reason he felt impelled to check his weight. He discovered with surprise and concern that he had lost some six pounds within a few days, or so he believed. He was worried lest a pathological growth might have caused some obstruction in his bowels. He was nauseated and was troubled by a strong urge to vomit, though he did not do so. He felt bloated and could tolerate only soft-boiled eggs as food. The analysis of these events and sensations led to the patient's recognition that he had re-enacted in these few days his experiences at an age of twenty months when the brother next to him in age was born. In fact, he reproduced his observations of his mother's pregnancy and delivery in great detail. Their living conditions at the time made it very probable that he could have made such observations in detail. He also recalled that in the period immediately following he felt what he today described as a constant rage against the mother and the newborn child. His memories, though uncertain, indicated that he had reacted to his brother's birth, and to the corresponding change in his mother's attitude, with a giving up of the already acquired capacity to control his bowel function. He soiled himself occasionally to the great discontent of his mother, who insisted on early training and on scrupulous cleanliness.

A phase of negativistic behavior toward the mother seems to have followed immediately afterwards. The patient described a feeling of estrangement from the mother in this period and stated definitely, "That is when the little man got quite a boost, right then at that time."

The second experience, eventually clearly remembered, was as follows. Once again he introduced the subject by a phrase that appeared suddenly in his mind, without immediately evident relationship to the current material. The phrase was—"Pleasure and death," and later, "Pleasure is death."

He recalled pictures of a tall vase with some evergreens in it, then a procession which he recognized as a funeral, and finally the picture of a dead man in a casket. It then emerged that when he was about three, his mother had surprised him masturbating and had sharply reprimanded him for it. "She gave me hell," he said. On the afternoon of the same day she took him to a funeral, where he saw a dead man for the first time in his life. He recalled being bewildered by everything he observed and asking his mother repeatedly why people wanted to die. He could not remember his mother's answer, but it became clear to him that he had assumed that death was an action of will, and that since one wanted to do only things that were pleasurable, dying people must have wished to die. Although he did not recall what his mother said to him, he knew that his belief was shattered by her reply, and that he came away with the feeling that death was the ultimate punishment for forbidden pleasure, and not a pleasure in itself. He suspected that he took his mother's explanation to be a threat of death to him, if he were to continue the forbidden masturbatory activity. Since he believed his mother had the power of life and death over him he took her threat seriously. Our material indicated that he did not give up masturbation, but that with the help of the by-now formed ego segment, the "little man," he obstinately continued, at least for a time, masturbatory practices. However, he carefully concealed them from his mother, and developed the philosophy that a crime is one only when one fails to get away with it.

It is of interest to pursue further the effect which the different stages of libido development had on the character of the "little man" phenomenon. The review shows, not unexpectedly, that characteristics of each stage were grafted upon this ego segment, and when fully developed, the "little man," like the patient's manifest character, possessed such features as oral greed, anal obstinancy, and phallic narcissism. These features did not appear fused together, nor were they consistently displayed by the "little man." On the contrary, they were readily forsaken and appeared to slide off, as it were, whenever the justification for the "little man's" existence was challenged. The patient might, for instance, be involved in a stubborn argument, insisting on some minor habit or custom in his office or his home, or he might be engaged in the boastful exposition of his success in business, and carry on this account with great abandon. But if it happened that in the course of such episodes a reference to a trip, or to someone's leaving the patient's vicinity occurred, then there followed immediately a sudden and complete change of mood and attitude on the part of the patient. He gave up his vehement argument, or stopped his self-confident boasting and became preoccupied with the thought, "I cannot make it." At the time when he began to perceive the functioning of the "little man" in him, this thought was accompanied by the feeling that it was the "little man" calling him to order, and warning him to observe his self-imposed limitations. Such observations were very frequent, though it is difficult to convey in description the impressive ease with which the derivatives of the various stages of libido development were drawn to and again shed by the "little man." They had clearly not been integrated in a permanent manner into the total ego organization.

Of great interest is the relationship of the "little man" to anxiety. It appears that when the function of developing anxiety was used to produce a signal for the danger of loss of love, or loss of object relationships, it was experienced by the ego components other than the "little man." On the other hand, situations where anxiety signaled a danger from an unduly powerful, or rapidly increasing instinctual tension, or when the threat was one directly affecting the body of the patient, the anxiety was experienced by the ego part which he called his "little man." The ego development as reconstructed from the patient's history makes this division understandable. The "little man" formed no object relationships,[5] and was in fact established in an effort to make such relationships unnecessary. It will be remembered that the separation of the "little man" from the rest of the ego occurred as part of the discovery of the patient's separateness from his mother, at a stage when the

[5] In the sense of an investment of genital, or aim-inhibited libidinal energy in the object.

mother was not yet felt as an external object, but was perceived as one with the child. These experiences were accompanied by painful sensations within the infant, such as hunger, the discomfort and pain of childhood diseases, uncontrollable outbursts of temper and various unpleasant bodily reactions to which I have referred previously. The observation was therefore not unexpected that anxiety from similar sources, i.e., from threats to the bodily self, or from increased instinctual tension, continued to be called forth and acted upon by the "little man," whereas the anxiety signaling the threat of object loss or loss of love was actuated and perceived by the rest of the ego capable of object relationships. Though there was a distinct difference in the patient's manifest experience of the two kinds of anxiety, this difference does not lend itself to easy description. The overlapping of the two, and the fact that the anxiety in the "little man" part of the ego was frequently provoked by an initial anxious reaction in the ego proper offer obstacles to a clear differentiation.

The "little man's" anxiety seemed indeed to have a more consuming character, and often deserved the term panic. It contained the fear of personal dissolution, of total collapse, and the patient was utterly helpless when under its spell. In late stages of the analysis he described these particular emotions correctly as a fear of his own feelings. He referred to the primitive untamed emotions of his early childhood and their successors in his unconscious. He said: "My feelings must appear goofy, crazy, to the adult."

This anxiety was called forth, as mentioned, by threats to the patient's bodily integrity, and by the dangers of instinctual tension. In addition, the same reaction resulted, whenever the "little man" was confronted with evidence of omnipotence other than his own, or "more powerful" than his own. For example, upon hearing of someone else's illness or death, the patient experienced the anxiety described above. This was in keeping with the observation that the "little man" had become established in an almost automatic, reflex-like manner, in response to the perception of his own weak and helpless self, i.e., as a compensatory narcissistic reaction to the impairment of the feeling of infantile omnipotence.

In contrast, the anxiety felt by the patient's ego proper seemed pale and not dramatic. Since the ego's mature object relationships were in themselves inconspicuous, their loss, while damaging, caused no effects such as called forth by the threats to the security of the "little man." Were it not for certain observations, now to be reported, we might not have become cognizant of the fact that two kinds of anxiety were experienced by the patient in two psychic localities within the ego. A number of the patient's self-observations indicated clearly that often while the patient was in the throes of great anxiety, the "little man" in him experienced no anxiety, but felt triumphant. This reaction occurred when the anxiety attack was occasioned by the threat of object loss, for instance, when a friend was leaving town, or the analyst announced a forthcoming interruption of the treatment. At times, while experiencing a spell of acute anxiety during the analytic hour, the patient was wont to say: "The little man smiles"; or "The little man now laughs." Yet, the patient was undeniably very troubled by anxiety. It was obviously the rest of his ego, distinct from the "little man," that experienced the anxious affect. It is significant that the anxiety in these instances lacked the deeply disruptive character of the near-panic states experienced by the patient when the "little man's" position and security were threatened. The "objects" whose loss threatened the ego in these instances were contemporary objects of the ego proper, not of the "little man." The latter's object, of course, was but one, himself, or the mother as a part of himself. Only the danger of separation from *that* object and from its symbolic representatives, the patient's home, office, or car, and his wife, evoked a stormy, incapacitating anxiety reaction in the "little man," a reaction which in turn badly frightened the ego proper. The ego, one felt, then found itself in the position of a bewildered, shocked, and completely helpless onlooker.

The triumphant reaction of the "little man" when not he but the ego proper felt anxiety, became intelligible in terms of the self-preservative function of this ego segment. It felt triumphant when it had succeeded in asserting its domination over the ego, and in preventing it from risking a repetition of early traumatic experiences occasioned by the removal of objects conceived as part of himself. The patient directly stated that it was as if the "little man" were saying to him, "I warned you to beware of becoming attached to that person, now that you come to depend on him, he is leaving you ... You must love no one but me ..."

The acute phobic state reactivated the "memory" of the sensations and feelings at the very moment of the traumatic separation, and by means of the development of the anxiety affect warned against the threatening repetition of that experience. It was the successful avoidance of a repetition of the trauma that provided the basis for the triumphant feeling of the "little man," whose very creation was the first act of mastery of the trauma by at least a part of the ego. This was accomplished by a rift in the infantile ego which remained present throughout life. When the so-achieved mastery was in danger of failing, the "little man" experienced anxiety of catastrophic intensity. The patient eventually learned to distinguish between the "little man" and his ego proper. The acquisition of the capacity to make that distinction was therapeutically of considerable importance for the patient.

The consequences of the division in the patient's ego were, of course, not limited to the experiences of anxiety but extended to other ego functions and ego attitudes. For instance, the patient's relationships to the same object regularly contained sets of characteristics, at times contradictory, attributable to the "little man" in him, and to the ego proper. The patient's manifest attitudes to others depededed on the proportion in which the "little man" and the rest of his ego determined the quality and quantity of libido attached to the object. The acquisitiveness of the "little man" in regard to libidinous energies in general restricted the ego in relating genital and aim-inhibited libido to objects. On the other hand, the "little man," dominated by the time and circumstances of his coming into being, and the aims of his continuing existence, directed only pregenital libidinous energies to the same object. Thus the picture of the patient's object relationships was characterized by an obtrusive component, the "little man's" pregenital attitudes, and a much less conspicuous contribution from the ego proper.

I must elaborate on a significant feature of the patient's object relationships, to which I have repeatedly, if briefly alluded. I mean the "little man's" fateful attitude of obstinate enmity toward objects in general. We saw in this trait a manifestation of the fundamental narcissistic position of the "little man," of the wish to maintain the illusion of his omnipotence, and of the striving to protect the patient from the risk of abandonment by his objects.

I referred in the first part of this study to the mistrust and suspicion engendered in the patient when in his infancy the mother failed to alleviate his suffering during a grave illness. We suggested then that he had interpreted this failure as a consequence of the mother's hostile intent. The eminently characteristic tendency of the "little man" to mock and ridicule everybody, so conspicuous in the transference, may well have been rooted in the experiences during that early and dangerous illness.

We further recognized in the "little man's" animosity toward objects evidence that this ego part was invested mainly with pregenital narcissistic, and especially, anal-sadistic libido quantities. The analysis revealed an additional significant motivation for the refusal of the "little man" to permit to the ego the establishment and cultivation of object relationships.

During one period of the analysis the patient was troubled by strange sensations that occurred while he engaged in free associations concerning the analyst. Whenever he was affectionately inclined toward the analyst, he felt as if his whole person was "flowing together" with that of the analyst and becoming one with him, and as if he himself was about to disappear in part, or even completely. This feeling was very vividly perceived by the patient. His description of it was clearly expressive of a profound reaction and certainly not just an allegorical allusion to a libidinous impulse. He was deeply frightened by the bewildering experiences, and made visible efforts to shake himself free from them. It was during that period of the analysis that he spoke also of the sensations of "walking out" of the analyst's body, mentioned previously in a different connection. In the course of dealing with this material, the patient gave much biographical information, illustrating the continuance in his unconscious of childhood fantasies of his belonging to his mother, who, he felt, owned not only his body and its contents, his stools, but also his thoughts, and his feelings. He was but a temporarily separated part of her, existing by her grace, and at any time subject to be reunited with her. The notion of mutual cannibalistic incorporation and the projection of his own wishes to incorporate and dominate the mother contributed to the determinants of this fantasy.

The patient's life was replete with examples of his continuous struggle to retain an identity of his own, and of his endless protest against being owned and dominated by his mother. He was compelled to engage in never ceasing clashes with her in actual life. He enacted similar conflicts with a series of mother substitutes, and in fact, with all objects, including those of only passing significance for him. The main feature of his argument was regularly the accusation that the person failed to show him due consideration, kindness, or love, and instead endeavored to dominate, exploit and "take over" the patient completely. The transference situation offered many opportunities to examine this conflict of the patient. The immediately obvious, perhaps self-evident meanings of the patient's complaint—the projection of his own wishes to dominate the mother substitutes on the very figures he wanted to control, and the identification with his in fact possessive and dominating mother— were important, but not the only determinants of his reactions. It was also the transference situation, of which an illuminating example was quoted above, that eventually provided us with a further narcissistic derivation of the patient's compulsive behavior pattern. It stemmed in the main from his unconscious conviction, supported by the corresponding unconscious wish, that a "complete" object relationship was identical with the re-establishment of the ego state that existed before the separation from the mother, i.e., before the birth of the "little man."

Consequently, it was the narcissism of this ego segment, intent on self-preservation, that rebelled against the development of object relationships. In the last sense, the formation of such a relationship meant fusion with the object, and the forsaking of personal existence as an identity of his own. This was clearly an unacceptable fate, both for the narcissism of the ego, most richly centered in the "little man," and for the latter's illusion of omnipotence.

We must return briefly to one of the "little man's" primary aims, and his perhaps most important function, i.e., his efforts at restoration of the lost early infantile omnipotence and the continuous protection and preservation of it. This aim was in direct conflict with the tendency to preserve the patient's personal identity. Re-establishment of the omnipotence was most completely accomplished by total reunion with the mother. The sense of omnipotence was essentially the ego feeling that existed before the awareness of his separateness from the mother arose in the patient. A characteristic statement of the patient was: "For a moment I felt real omnipotent today—with you sitting there, and no one else around, I felt I had you all to myself! The little man was king! But then I got anxious again . . ." Since that total reunion was unacceptable to the ego, compromise solutions had to be found.

It was illuminating to observe how the patient had succeeded in establishing himself as unquestioned and absolute master of household and business, though he was unaware of his efforts in that regard until late in the course of his analysis. His behavior bore the mark of a person who tolerated no opposition and who surrounded himself with people too weak to oppose him effectively, thus creating the illusion of his omnipotence. But simultaneously, the means the patient used to support his omnipotent position were those of the naively peremptory, yet feeble child rather than those of a masterful man. He alternately wooed the allegiance and good will of his friends and employees with gifts and favors, and strove to make them as totally dependent on him as he felt dependent on them, and at other times ordered them about, expecting complete and immediate obedience. He tolerated opposition with poor grace, and punished it sooner or later. The development of anxiety, and his general discomfort when someone in his vicinity departed, though consciously painful, gave him a welcome excuse to demand their constant presence and subservience to his wishes. It was a typical and frequent occurrence that he asked me, "Shall I let him go?" referring to a prospective departure of an employee, or a relative. His tone of voice implied categorically that he took his right to prohibit the departure for granted, and made no distinction between his power to enforce obedience to such prohibitions and the right to exercise his power. Needless to say that he was forever feeling exploited, misused and inadequately appreciated by the people around him. He justified his insistence on their loyalty and devotion by constantly pointing to the generous treatment which they received from him. These protestations concealed poorly his possessive and autocratically dominating attitude, an attitude which reflected the persistence in him, unchanged, of the purely narcissistic object relationships of the pregenital child, particularly that at the height of the anal-sadistic phase of development, when the belief in one's omnipotence seems to enjoy a last powerful upsurge before being gradually eroded by the combined pressure of reality and of the growing intellect.

The very formation of the isolated ego part of the "little man" was to some degree a successful effort at restoration, and the continued existence of this ego element a successful preservation, by way of structuralization, of the sense of omnipotence lost in childhood. The price paid for this success by the personality of the patient was clearly a heavy one, as so often it is, when, to borrow a description from Freud, a prehistoric ego structure remains preserved as a fossil in the body of the ego, alien to its more advanced and differentiated elements.

At the danger of appearing redundant I should like to refer once more in broad outline to the development of the "little man" ego element.

The process of the separation of the "little man" from the rest of the ego appears to have taken place gradually in earliest childhood, and was concluded around the patient's third year of life. It seems to have completed the development of an ego identity within him. A succession of narcisisstic injuries on every level of early development resulted in the loss of the feeling of infantile omnipotence, and marked dramatically the child's helplessness toward external influences (the mother's behavior toward his needs) and internal events (hunger, affective reactions, control of body functions and of disease). Thus was brought home to the child his separateness from the powerful mother, and the recognition of his own identity as feeble and vulnerable was forced upon him. Compensatorily, a separate structure in the patient's ego was erected, and this proved of fateful significance in the development of his personality and for the whole pattern of his life henceforth.

But have we not spent altogether too much effort to contrive the existence of an ego structure which is in reality nothing but the familiar result of an identification with the denying, controlling and directing mother? I believe that the answer to this question is definitely negative.

Our observations have shown conclusively that the "little man" became established primarily before the mother existed as a separate entity, and identification with her occurred only later, after she had become an object distinct from himself. Undoubtedly many features of the mother were then added to the image of the "little man."

In later years identifications with a few beloved objects, who had offered him affection but had later disappeared from his life, were also added to the image of the "little man," so that the patient on occasion could say, "The little man is all the people that loved me and went away and died." It goes without saying, that with the advent of the phallic stage, the "little man" also acquired a superimposed phallic narcissistic significance.

An illuminating example will illustrate this, and supplement the discussion of the large contribution which this particular process made to the structure of the patient's phobic fears of dissolution, when separated from mother surrogates.

In the course of the treatment there appeared memories of his observing his mother undressed and noting her genitalia. This at first seems to have made little impression on the child, though he was puzzled by the appearance of a "dark spot" where he expected to see the penis. It seems that he waited for the reappearance of the penis, thinking that it had "gone" but would return. There was also evidence of other explanatory attempts which he made to himself at the time, such as that the penis was hidden inside or that it would grow. Then, perhaps a year or more after the initial observation, there seemed to have taken place a shocking realization that the penis would never return to the mother. The circumstances of this discovery remained obscure, but there was evidence that it may have been connected with the observation of a primal scene. The patient said, "My fear of going outside started right there." He came to the conclusion that he must have decided that he in his entirety could disappear and remain "gone," as he had convinced himself that his mother's penis had vanished, never to return.

It became clear that he had identified with the missing penis of his mother, and eventually incorporated this identification into the structure of the "little man," not unlike the fetishist who rebuilds the woman's lost phallus in his fetish. It appeared evident from the previously reported material that this identification with the penis was grafted on an already preformed ego structure, which at this point drew to itself additional, now phallic narcissistic, libidinal energies.

This personification of the primitive narcissistic ego seemed a depository of what in terms of early psychoanalytic theory was described as the ego instincts of self-preservation. The "little man" was indeed almost omnipotent in his practical invincibility. He defended this position by avoiding all instinctual dangers, which in effect perpetuated the illness, and by enslaving a mother substitute, the patient's wife, whom he had succeeded in making so utterly dependent upon himself, that he could be certain of her being available at his command at all times. The isolated existence of this ego segment interfered with the development of a properly integrated ego, and impaired its function of synthesis. In this fashion there came to exist a house divided within the ego itself, and the total effect was that of a weak, helpless, impoverished and limited ego, even though actually a part of it, the "little man," gave every evidence of possessing great power. Here it was not only the superego that opposed the ego as harsh taskmaster, but an isolated part of the ego itself that was not the result of an identification with the parents, but a segment split off in consequence of the necessity to sustain life with a support suddenly lost. It evolved not out of lost object relationships, as in superego formation proper, but in response to the discovery of one's own weakness. The "little man" represented no moral standards and no ego ideal to be followed. "The little man has no conscience," the patient said on several occasions. He had no regard for, and no relationships to, objects other than those devoted to self-preservation. It cannot be truly said that the "little man" followed the pleasure principle, the *gaining* of pleasure not being one of his objectives. On the contrary, the "little man" objected sharply whenever the patient sought pleasure, or was tempted by the prospect of pleasure. A beautiful spring day invited a walk or ride in the country, very much loved by the patient. Promptly anxiety, tension, and varying physical symptoms developed, as if to warn the patient to resist the temptation. In fact, no price was too high to keep the patient under the "little man's" domination. "The little man," the patient said, "will rather let me die than enjoy myself, or get well." This statement appeared at first at variance with our realization that the "little man's" function was to preserve the patient's life. The discrepancy was resolved when we understood that indeed, from the point of view of the pleasure-seeking id, the "little man" wanted it to "die," i.e., to forsake all striving for pleasure, while at the same time, from the point of view of the ego, the "little man" strove to keep the patient alive, since to him pleasure had the ultimate meaning of death. He once said: "The little man won't let me *live* [i.e., pleasurably], but keeps me *alive,* in a jail."

On the other hand, it was not entirely correct to assume that the "little man" was unable to or did not experience pleasure. Though not engaged in seeking the experience of pleasure as such, for its own sake, he was capable of a sense of pleasurable gratification when his aims were realized. At times, when he succeeded in asserting his will, against the wishes of others, i.e., when he exercised his omnipotence, the intensity of this pleasure rose to that of a feeling of triumph. Only too often the "others" included the patient's own personality as distinct from the "little man" himself. A sadistic tinge was unmistakably and almost invariably present in the "little man's" experience of pleasure. This is not an astonishing finding. As we have seen, the ego part termed his "little man" by the patient, became definitely isolated, and thus prevented from further development, at the height of the anal-sadistic stage of libidinal development, a circumstance which readily accounted for many of the "little man's," and consquently of the patient's, conspicuous characteristics.

In so far as the "little man's" concern was self-preservation one could describe his functioning as a perversion of obedience to the reality principle, since normal functioning implies modification of the pleasure principle to correspond with realistic conditions, and not the complete forsaking of all pleasure. The patient once reported the memory that at one time early in childhood, he became absolutely determined that "he will never let it happen to him again." He said he "made an oath" to that extent. Months later the meaning of this oath became clear. It received its clarification when we had reviewed in detail the beginnings of the "little man." It represented the determination to protect himself from the feeling of weakness, helplessness and rage which accompanied the discovery of his identity, the labor pains, as it were, at the birth of his self-awareness as a person separate from his mother, and the reaction to the loss of the feeling of infantile omnipotence.

It is self-evident that I have in this discussion limited myself to an emphasis on the development of ego identity and its role in the pattern of the patient's character and symptomatology. Many other factors not referred to entered into the structure of his highly overdetermined symptoms. To mention but a few important matters, pregenital fantasies of cannibalistic incorporation, and of the reverse, i.e., fantasies of being devoured by the mother, played a conspicuous role in his case. The patient's analysis also taught me that the familiar interpretation of walking as symbolic of sexual intercourse with the mother, and the role of the originally strong pleasure in movement (Abraham), had to be qualified in his case. It was not a genital sexual intercourse, but an anal-sadistic destructive sexual attack, that was symbolized by his walking. It was particularly prohibited, and consequently productive of anxiety because of its archaic destructive character. Pregnancy and birth fantasies as well as destructive wishes against the pregnant mother and the children in her (the patient was the second oldest of eight) were also prominent. However, I believe that equally significant factors in regard to the impairment of his total functioning were undoubtedly those described in terms of his earliest ego development.

III

I have attempted to demonstrate the beginnings of the development of a sense of personal identity in early childhood, as it could be reconstructed in the analysis of a middle-aged man. This development was, in the case of my patient, a painful process initiated by events of a traumatic nature, and was not successful in its results. The cause for the failure can, as always, be found only in a combination of components, with their relative proportion to each other remaining indefinite. It is impossible to exclude constitutional factors. One of these may be seen in an inherent disproportion between the intensity of instinctual drives and the capacity for their mastery. Early frustrations, the mother's impatient attitude, the discrepancies between her demands for the child's maturation and the infant's innate ability for growth, were other factors involved. A factor of perhaps paramount significance is to be seen in the consequences of the patient's debilitating organic disease in early infancy. This traumatic event undoubtedly initiated, indeed enforced a process of partial ego maturation at an age earlier, and a rate of speed greater than was natural to the infant.[6] We believe to recognize in this latter circumstance, i.e., the necessity for adaptation at a speed exceeding the infant's capacity, an important factor among those causing development deviating from the normal. Thus, necessity instead of providing a stimulating factor became a traumatic influence on the ego development.

In all of the patient's later life, his character, his behavior patterns, and the symptomatology of his neurosis showed the influence of two mutually contradictory tendencies. The desire to unite again with the mother, to prevent forever her separating from him, and to insure the persistence of the feeling of infantile omnipotence based on a not yet interrupted unity with the mother—all these represented one set of paramount motivations in his life. The other was an equally intense

6 A stubborn ego resistance in the treatment stemmed from the patient's anxious opposition to the timing and the speed of changes which, he thought, were expected of him.

effort to forestall such a complete reunion with the mother, to prevent the loss of identity, and the personal death involved in total reunion with her. In consequences of the traumatic circumstances of the discovery of the child's painful separateness from the mother, an ego segment, the "little man," was isolated from the rest of the personality. One of the main functions of this separate structure remained through life the task to prevent either one or the other of the above-mentioned tendencies from gaining the upper hand, and from threatening the individual's existence, either through final separation from the mother, or through merging with her.

Stated differently, the task of the separated ego segment was to realize the motivations mentioned above as fully as possible, yet without permitting the life-threatening total reunion with the mother. The establishment of the separate ego entity, and, with it, the development of the severe neurosis, thus may be said to have secured the patient's life, at the cost of a crippling inhibition of the ego's freedom of movement, a far-reaching renunciation of instinctual gratifications, and the occurrence, through life, of attacks of paralyzing anxiety.

AN UNUSUAL FUNCTION OF AN AMNESIA

K. R. EISSLER, M.D. (New York)

A middle-aged patient reported in her analysis that she had barely any recollection of her mother prior to the age of five or six. Whereas she recalled other adults who spent time with her, such as an aunt, a maid, and her siblings, she could not remember that her mother spent any time with her as a child. This was blatantly contrary to the objective evidence she received from others that her mother had devoted most of her time to her upbringing and went to work only after the patient had reached an age when longer-lasting daytime separations are usually tolerated by the child.

Her recollections of her mother during the period after her mother started to work away from home flowed with greater richness and consistency. She recalled distinctly that her mother phoned home one day and told the maid that she had found employment. The maid seemed happy about it, but the patient "did not know why she was so happy." At other times the event was described in greater detail: "I was home during lunchtime. X [the patient's next older brother] was there. The maid was excited. I remember clearly I felt as if something had been put over on me. I felt different from X. I had a feeling I was apart from the two other people there. It came as a shock. I must have been aware that mother was looking for a job. I did not want her to have a job. I experienced it as meaning that she would be in a different world, as if she were going on a long trip, as if it had nothing to do with me and that I would be isolated. It is the only memory that has emotions. I felt confused and did not know what was going on. I am sure I felt hurt." The patient had spoken previously about this event as if she had not responded emotionally to it, but she explained that at her first report she recalled only the way she reacted but not the way she felt on hearing of her mother's employment. Thus we can say that this moment divided her life into two parts: prior to it almost no recollection of her mother, and subsequently the usual variability of periods of more and less numerous memories.

This patient showed here a peculiarity which one often encounters in a different context. There are many patients who recall the moment of first sight of a newborn infant but are completely amnestic of the time of their mother's pregnancies. In these instances too one observes the peculiar line of demarcation regarding recollections of the mother, centered in a well-defined and well-remembered event. As with the aforementioned patient, one then receives the impression that these patients suffer from a retrograde amnesia. We may learn that traumatic effects which we customarily attribute to a mother's pregnancy and her enforced biological withdrawal from the child can at times be easily provoked by other, and less dramatic, events. This patient, being the youngest of several siblings, was spared the crises in which the older siblings regularly get entangled on the appearance of competitors, and nevertheless she formed psychopathology strongly reminiscent of that which a child may evolve in conjunction with the appearance of a new baby.

Thus the patient's amnesia does not seem to show anything remarkable. She appeared to suffer from a simple amnesia covering the period when she received her mother's affection profusely. From then on she had to shift with less pleasure from this source, because her mother through force of circumstances had to cut down the time spent with her youngest child. Consequently, the patient repressed recollections of a pleasure which was no longer obtainable.

One can well imagine that the child's adjustment was greatly facilitated by her saving herself from longings for gratifications which the world stubbornly denied her. The drawbacks entailed by such a radical therapy will not be discussed here but can easily be imagined by the clinician, who will not be surprised that one of the patient's symptoms was separation anxiety.

Yet this patient's amnesia may appear in a different light when we learn that it was not only the result of repression but served also other functions, one of which was the gratification of an aggressive impulse. By striking out any recollection of her mother's participation in her upbringing, she formed the image of a mother not interested in her, negligent and devoid of affection. The repression was an outright attack, amounting to a reproach against her mother: "It is not only that you spent no time with me since you went to work; you never spent any time with me."

From Hartmann's inquiries into the metapsychology of the ego, we know that the energy used up in some defense mechanisms stems genetically from aggression (Hartmann, 1952, pp. 24f.). The absorption of aggression in the form of neutralized energy by the work of certain defense mechanisms is part of the general internalization of aggression. Yet in the clinical instance under consideration the effect of the amnesia went much further. The amnesia per se, the absence of those contents which it had stricken from consciousness, gratified the resentment which the patient had felt against her mother for the withdrawal of a gratification formerly accorded to her so profusely. A factor relating to an object relationship was directly expressed in the activation of a specific mechanism which had the function of eliminating from consciousness specific biographical contents. We expect such an effect rather from a neurotic symptom which autoplastically achieves what under favorable conditions leads to an alloplastic action (Freud, 1924b, p. 280), but it is striking that a single defense mechanism should achieve so much.[1]

Even more surprising was the observation of still another function which was delegated to this amnesia. If one considers for a moment what effect it would have had upon the patient if her early life had actually been such as in her amnesia she claimed, it will be noticed that her mother's acceptance of employment would not have affected her at all, since the withdrawal of never-enjoyed pleasures cannot have any effect. The amnesia served here the function of protecting the psychic apparatus on a more archaic level than that on which the avoidance of displeasure and the gain of pleasure are the principal goals. One is reminded—by contrast—of Freud's comment upon the repetition of the traumatic situation in the dreams of patients suffering from traumatic neuroses. There the patient is compelled to return over and over again to the traumatic situation as soon as contact with reality and the activation of most ego functions has been stopped, as happens in sleep (Freud, 1920, pp. 37-38).

The patient's amnesia had the function not only of denying that she had suffered a trauma, but also of experiencing the world as one in which no trauma can occur. To have recollected the trauma would have meant the admission of vulnerability, because of the possibility of repetition. Such a possibility, however, would have created a condition of permanent anxiety. The clinical picture which the patient presented left no doubt that her disturbances were not manifestations of hysteria. In this neurosis, I believe, the amnesia serves the purpose of avoiding displeasure. Yet we know that the hysterical patient is prone to be traumatized over and over again. In my patient this tendency was absent. She lived a calm, serene life with a minimum of emotional expression. She maintained the highest standards in her profession, but she did not participate in what she was doing. Her achievements were, she claimed, accidents of good luck, and her various activities were experienced as reactions enforced by the variety

1 As early as 1910 Freud described such a factor, though the opposite one, in the repressions of homosexuals: "Through the repression of love for the mother he [the homosexual] conserves this love in his unconscious and from then on remains faithful to the mother." Freud (1910, p. 413), my own translation

of situations to which she was exposed. Evidently her amnesia must have achieved results beyond those encountered in hysteria. The price the ego had to pay for these results was also concomitantly larger. Yet one hesitates to make one single mechanism responsible for so much. Clinical evaluation makes it far more probable that it was a cluster of mechanisms—such as we customarily encounter in symptom formation—that participated in the formation of the amnesia.

Indeed, if we scrutinize the amnesia more sharply, we discover that the patient's original description was: "My mother did not spend any time with me when I was a child," which is really the description of a screen memory. Only later, when she found out from other members of her family that her mother had actually spent considerable time with her, did she substitute a description sounding like that of an amnesia, namely: "I cannot recall that . . . ." I wonder, however, how often it may happen that what appears on the clinical level like a childhood amnesia is in reality a screen memory with a negative content.[2] Or, to use an analogy of Freud's when discussing repression in contrast to other defense mechanisms, I ask whether most childhood amnesias are not comparable to corruptions of an original text rather than to omissions of words (Freud, 1937, p. 339).

The problem is reminiscent of a casual remark made by Freud (1916) when he said that "any attempt to explain hallucination would have to be made from the starting point of a *negative* hallucination rather than of a positive one" (p. 118).[3]

If this clinical example should be accepted as sufficient proof that in the formation of a childhood amnesia other mechanisms than repression may participate, one wonders whether the resistance against the lifting of a childhood amnesia may depend on other than only quantitative factors. It is quite possible that those patients whose childhood amnesia has left a more or less devastating effect upon their ego development and whose amnesia was formed by an array of mechanisms will put up a quantitatively much stronger resistance than customarily encountered in hysteria, in which form of neurosis the childhood amnesia was effected by repression alone, according to present theory. Be this as it may, the problem necessitates a few remarks about repression in general.

As is well known, in 1926 Freud took up again the concept of defense which had initially held a central place in theory (Freud, 1894, 1896)

---

[2] Freud (1899) wrote of negative screen memories "whose subject matter stands in a contrary relation to the suppressed material" (p. 67). To a certain extent this amnesia would fall into that category.

[3] Italics by Freud.

but was replaced later by the concept of repression (cf. Anna Freud, 1936, pp. 45f.), suggesting a new program of research, namely the detailed study of the various defense mechanisms, only one of which is repression. In 1926 Freud seemed to have temporarily attributed to repression a minor role (or at least a less important one than previously) in so far as he considered the possibility that "repression is a process which has a special relation to the genital organization of the libido and that the ego resorts to other methods of defence when it has to secure itself against the libido on other levels of organization" (pp. 84, 85), and further that "it may well be that before its sharp cleavage into an ego and an id, and before the formation of a super-ego, the mental apparatus makes use of different methods of defense from those which it employs after it has attained these levels of organization" (pp. 157, 158). Both these new viewpoints, if confirmed by clinical observation, would require an evaluation different from the current one regarding the bearing of the repression mechanism upon the development of the psychic apparatus. Yet in 1937 Freud wrote: "Repression is something quite peculiar, more sharply differentiated from the other mechanisms than those are from one another" (p. 338). This statement makes me feel that Freud attributed to repression a greater significance later than he did around the time of writing *Inhibitions, Symptoms and Anxiety* (1926). This historical suggestion, however, is not decisive for what follows. I have only wanted to show that there seems to be inherent in the problem of repression a factor which makes the proper evaluation of the mechanism rather difficult. The reason for this state of affairs is, I believe, a certain ambiguity in the use of the term "repression" as applied in two different situations: in the one case it signifies the mechanism by means of which a psychic element (or combinations of elements) is removed from consciousness (or the ego); in the other, it refers to the state such elements are in after their removal from consciousness or ego, namely, the condition of being repressed. It goes without saying that a successful act of repression leads to a content's becoming repressed, but it does not follow that all contents found in the repressed part of the personality got there through the previous activation of the repression mechanism. Yet the way in which the term "repression" is customarily used today implies this very conclusion in most instances.

Turning toward another difficulty, I should like to point out that no defense mechanism is known which would not result in something psychic being repressed, isolated and denied.[4] This can be easily proved if *all* the

---

4 Although various authors have tried to bridge this difficulty by suggesting specific definitions, I think our clinical work and the reliable presentation of clinical findings is still greatly hampered by basic lack of clarity.

consequences which occur when one of the known defense mechanisms is activated are checked. Thus, the following remarks can be found regarding isolation in *Inhibitions, Symptoms and Anxiety*. Freud (1926) called it a "surrogate" and a "variation" of repression (p. 73) and described its effect as "the same as the effect of repression with amnesia" (p. 76). I should suggest that for the time being a difference be made between mechanism and the effect it has on the psychic elements subjected to it; in other words that we temporarily assume that a content may be in a state of repression without necessarily having been subjected to the repression mechanism, but that other mechanisms may possibly achieve the same result.

Freud (1926) showed that the main motor of repression leading to childhood neurosis was—in the clinical examples he demonstrated— anxiety over an external danger, and since then we have been accustomed to look for the external dangers which originally set the process of defense into motion.

However, I raise the question whether this is really true of all forms of pathology. Is it perhaps possible to divide our patients into two groups, according to which of the two groups of motives prevailed among the instigators of the defensive process, namely whether the motive was anxiety over an external or over an internal danger. In the process of maturation the motives for defense become quite generally dangers from within the personality, and—as Freud has shown— the principal danger in the adult becomes the fear of the punishing superego (Freud, 1926, p. 111; and Anna Freud, 1936, p.59), representing an internal danger. Yet this occurs at a time when the psychic apparatus has become fully differentiated into its several provinces. If, however, the main motives for the initial activation of the defensive process prior to the differentiation of the personality are internal dangers, then we may expect particularly serious forms of psychopathology.

Aggravating as the effect of fears of external dangers such as castration fears are upon the development of the child's personality, I believe the effect of fears of internal dangers is still more disastrous.[5] Anna Freud (1936, pp. 63f.) has described one such fear of internal danger in the child prior to the establishment of the superego as dread of the strength of the instincts, and Waelder (1930) says that "the ego experiences each excessive *crescendo* of the instinctual forces as danger for itself and independently

---

[5] I assume that both groups of motives play their role in the development of the child, but clinical effects will be different depending on which kind of anxiety prevails and in the service of which anxiety the defensive work is principally done.

of any consequences menacing from the outside, a danger to be destroyed and its organization overwhelmed" (pp. 47, 48).

I believe that the patient whose amnesia I have described shows still another fear of an internal danger, namely the danger of stimulation per se.

The child would thus have to cope with three groups of dangers:

(A) The danger of not meeting the requirements of the reality principle. The corresponding fear is mainly represented by castration anxiety and the fear of loss of love.

(B) The danger of not meeting the requirements of the pleasure principle. The corresponding fear is the dread of the strength of the instincts.

(C) The danger of not meeting the requirements of the nirvana (constancy) principle (Freud, 1920, p. 71; 1924a, p. 256). The corresponding fear is the fear of stimulation.

Although clinical experience abundantly confirms Anna Freud's observation (1936, p. 64) that the child uses the same defense mechanisms no matter where the source of danger lies, I still think that possibly the clinical outcome is not identical. Tentatively, I suggest that the more the motives of defense stem from the fear of internal danger, the greater will be the prospect that later a psychosis or some other malignant disorder will develop. The more the fear of reality prevails among the primary instigators of defense, the less will the later disorder infringe upon the patient's contact with reality. If this suggestion should be confirmed by further clinical observation, it would fall within Waelder's law of isomorphism (1951, pp. 173, 176), which says that the form in which the warded-off material returns as a symptom depends on the defense mechanism by means of which it was originally warded off. My own observation, if proved correct, may, however, require a slightly different formulation, namely that the *motive* for the original defense may be reflected later in the symptom.

The reader may easily, and rightly, criticize the drawing of so many theoretical conclusions from such a paucity of clinical material. Perhaps I may, if belatedly, justify this disproportion by calling attention to one clinical point which may prove the unusualness of this amnesia: Is it not strange that the memory of the traumatic event (the mother's withdrawal of affection) was so well preserved in the patient, and that the large number of antecedent experiences which, by their very pleasurableness, made the withdrawal traumatic, were repressed?

Do we not rather expect the memories of traumatic events to become the victims of repression? And does not this reversal of selection of the material to be subjected to repression require extensive theoretical speculation?

BIBLIOGRÀPHY

Freud, A. (1936), *The Ego and the Mechanisms of Defense.* New York: International Universities Press, 1946.
Freud, S. (1899), Screen Memories. *Collected Papers,* V. London: Hogarth Press, 1950.
—— (1910), Eine Kindheitserinnerung des Leonardo da Vinci. *Gesammelte Schriften,* 9:371-454. Leipzig, Wien, Zurich: Internationaler Psychoanalytischer Verlag.
—— (1916), Metapsychological Supplement to the Theory of Dreams. *Collected Papers,* IV.
—— (1920), *Beyond the Pleasure Principle.* London: Hogarth Press, 1948.
—— (1924a), The Economic Problem in Masochism. *Collected Papers,* II.
—— (1924b), The Loss of Reality in Neurosis and Psychosis. *Collected Papers,* II.
—— (1937), Analysis Terminable and Interminable. *Collected Papers,* V.
Hartmann, H. (1952), Mutual Influences in Development of Ego and Id. *This Annual,* VII.
Waelder, R. (1930), The Principle of Multiple Function. *Psa. Quart.,* V, 1936.
—— (1951), The Structure of Paranoid Ideas. *Int. J. Psa.,* XXXII.

STREPHOSYMBOLIA: AN INTRASYSTEMIC DISTURBANCE OF THE SYNTHETIC FUNCTION OF THE EGO[1]

VICTOR H. ROSEN, M.D. (New York)

It is probable that symptomatic disturbances of reading and spelling are of multiple etiology.[2] The present paper, however, is concerned with a fairly discrete, well-recognized disability in the recognition of printed words and the reproduction of words in writing. This disability is usually characterized by normal intelligence and normal learning capacity in other areas. It is found about four times as frequently among males (Blanchard, 1947). Reversal of letters as individual symbols and in their sequence within the word is the most frequent source of error in both reading and writing, but it is not the only error encountered. This gives rise to an impression of a right-left disorientation in these patients which, however, has no counterpart in their orientation in general (see Cole, 1951; Bender and Schilder, 1951; and Schilder, 1944; Orton, 1939; to the contrary).

These cases were first systematically described by Hinshelwood (1917) under the title of "Congenital Word Blindness." Orton (1937, 1939) continued this structural concept in more definitive form, introducing the term "strephosymbolia" to denote a failure to achieve complete right-left orientation through what he conceived to be a conflict between the memory images of the two cerebral hemispheres, one of which had failed to establish complete dominance in organizing visuomotor patterns. Dearborn (1933, 1938) proposes a similar concept based upon learned rather than congenitally determined patterns of sensorimotor function. Many

---

[1] Presented at the New York Psychoanalytic Society Meeting of January 11th, 1955.

[2] Blanchard (1928, 1935, 1947), Cole (1951), Crisp (1949), Dearborn (1933, 1938), Durrell (1940), Fernald (1921), Freud (1904), Gates (1933, 1941), Hincks (1926), Hinshelwood (1917), Hildreth (1934), Kirk (1934), Ketcham (1951), Knight (1952), Launay (1952), Orton (1937, 1939), Pearson (1952), Phillips (1934), Selzer (1933), Sterba (1943), Strachey (1930), Sylvester and Kunst (1943), Tulchin (1935), Witty (1936a, 1936b), Woody (1934), Young (1938), and others.

investigators have since thrown considerable doubt upon both of these hypotheses from clinical and experimental considerations. Young (1938), Tulchin (1935), and Hincks (1926), first stressed emotional difficulty and personality problems as general determinants of reading disabilities. Blanchard (1947) is the first to investigate the problem psychoanalytically. She stresses the use of a phonetic "speech writing" in one case as a form of revenge against the female teacher who stood for the mother who had abandoned the patient. She also discusses the disability in relation to the symbolic meaning of the alphabet where letters are often conceived as threatening, orally aggressive wild animals. Bender and Schilder (1951), and Schilder (1944) who studied graphic art in children with reading disabilities, utilized a Gestalt approach and attempt a synthesis of structural and dynamic concepts. They see the defect as an isolated disorder in gnostic intellectual functioning in which written words and letters cannot be integrated and differentiated in terms of the spoken word due to disturbances of brain development. (Psychoanalytic problems connected with spelling are also discussed by Freud, 1904; Sterba, 1943; and Knight, 1952.)

The present paper will attempt to demonstrate that the so-called strephosymbolic disturbance consists of a failure to synthesize the ordinal aspect of the word, which is a function of its phonetic qualities, with the visual elements of the word. This is especially evident where one finds different visual elements standing for identical phonemes. An attempt will also be made to demonstrate that this disturbance resembles a phylogenetic phase in orthographic evolution, namely, the transitional stage between idiographic scripts and the syllabary alphabet. In the present case, the failure of synthesis of the higher discriminatory functions of the auditory and visual spheres has its analogue in the patient's primal scene fantasies and in the pattern of his object relationships. It is contended, although the evidence for this is by its nature somewhat inconclusive, that precocity of the "reading readiness stage" of ego apparatus development plays a decisive role in its genesis.

CASE REPORT

This patient has already been reported in some detail in a previous paper on mathematical illumination (Rosen, 1953). The present summary, therefore, will be merely a brief recapitulation of this history with some additions which are pertinent here and were not directly pertinent to the material then under consideration.

The patient was a twenty-one-year-old graduate student of mathematics when he first came for analysis. He was about to enter graduate school to become a candidate for a doctoral degree. He sought analysis for two seemingly separate problems. The first was his inability to form any lasting relationships with women, and the second was a disability in reading and spelling of the so-called strephosymbolic type which threatened to interfere with the fulfillment of his academic ambitions. His arithmetical and mathematical ability was of the highest order. There were no speech problems as far as verbalization was concerned. The patient had managed to compensate for a good deal of his reading deficit by an excellent auditory retentive memory which enabled him to pass courses at the college level in all subjects. He was the youngest of three children. Both parents held scholarly achievements in high esteem. The father held a high academic position in a leading university. From earliest infancy the patient is said to have been a very sensitive child. At an early age he had shown an extreme intolerance of loud noises. At the age of three he was subjected to a flash-bulb exposure during the taking of an indoor family photograph. It is said that his eyes teared and appeared reddened for several days thereafter. One of his present complaints is still a marked photophobia, especially on awakening in the morning. At the age of fourteen, he complained of being able to see floating specks in his peripheral areas of vision and a diagnosis of "drusen" due to floating vitreous opacities was made by an ophthalmologist. Glasses are worn for myopia. The curious game of playing with his visual accommodation was also recounted during his analysis. The patient suffered from a severe pavor nocturnus at about the age of four to five years, whose disappearance is covered by a screen memory of finding that his mother had left a pillow in bed next to him to simulate a body after one of his visits to her bed following a nightmare. He still talks of this event as a "shameful hoax to play on a small child." The patient began his schooling with kindergarten in his fifth year. It took several months before his mother was able to leave him alone in school. The first and second grade of school seemed to have gone fairly well. He has a relative amnesia for the third and fourth grade. These were the years in which subsequent reading and spelling tests revealed that he had the greatest learning difficulty. They are perhaps also the years of greatest emphasis on these subjects. Attempts to tutor him in reading and spelling began in the fifth grade and continued in college where the patient spent two summers at a reading clinic. In his fifth grade a diagnosis of "strephosymbolia" was made. His mother was told that it was due to a congenital failure of one side of his brain to achieve dominance.[3] The test curve in reading and spelling performance reveal an initial average level with a sharp drop at the third and fourth year levels and a gradual improvement in the spelling of eighth and ninth grade words. First attempts to teach him to read were by the tachisto-

[3] The patient has been consistently right-handed throughout his development. Numerous tests of lateral dominance at various times are said to have confirmed this fact. However, the family pattern reveals that his father and oldest sister are both left-handed, while his mother and younger sister are right-handed.

scopic word and picture recognition method. Later it was found that he could
do somewhat better when the "old-fashioned" phonetic method was substituted.
The patient's arithmetical ability was well in advance of his years. At the age of
nine he could use a slide rule accurately for complex arithmetical computations.
He had very little recollection of being taught arithmetic. His talent in this
field was unnoticed at first and more or less overshadowed by the reading deficit.
His mathematical ability was not discovered until the eighth grade when the
patient was allowed to go ahead of the class in plain geometry and later algebra,
both of which he mastered in an unusually short time. During this period of his
schooling a striking character change was noted. Previously a shy and timid
child who was usually found on the periphery of the group, he became more
assertive in class relationships and was sometimes thought of as arrogant toward
the less advanced students with a tendency to use his learning in an overbearing
manner. His progress in mathematics in college was rapid and he was recognized
as having a superior talent in this area. In graduate school he has done some
original work in mathematics. He is mainly interested in rather esoteric fields of
pure mathematics. He is also interested in symbolic logic. His work has shown
a high degree of a capacity for "illumination" in regard to difficult problems,
which is the mark of the creative mathematician. The strephosymbolia was not
discussed in the previous communication (Rosen, 1953) in order to keep the
problem from being unduly complicated. However, it was present as a symptom
requiring dynamic understanding from the very beinning and at all stages during
the analysis. It was stated in the previous communication that the patient had
had a series of mirror dreams in which the unconscious meaning of the reversal
of letters in words began to emerge. The full meaning of one of these dreams in
connection with his strephosymbolic symptom did not become clear until very
late in his analysis. This dream was reported as follows:

> I am in the garden at home with B. A woman's voice is directing me. She is
> short and blond. She was walking on a stone path away from me. I find
> myself looking through a glass window which is also a mirror. She appears
> to have a disease and the glass indicates that it is "verboten" to get closer.
> I write to her on the window backwards and to the left so that she can read
> it without having to reverse the words. I recall the letters E, R, and W. It is
> like writing with soap on a looking glass. On the other side, there is a garden
> party. The garden is filled with elegant people. Someone is commenting
> about my parents in French and Russian.

The letters in the dream reminded him of his reading and spelling defects.
The looking glass reminded him of Lewis Carroll who is also a mathematician.
When Alice looked through the glass, one room was warm and homey. The other
side of the glass is cold and strange. At the age of two or three the patient's care
was given over largely to a "Fräulein," the short blond woman of the dream.
(Later it was found that this lady was really from one of the Slavic countries

which is probably another determinant of the reference to Russian.) The arrangement was partly due to the illness of an older sister, which necessitated a good deal of the mother's attention. This was experienced by the patient as a severe rejection by his mother, and his clinging to her was intensified thereafter. The soap in the dream referred to masturbatory practices. Coldness is one of his complaints against his mother and represents his feelings concerning the relationship between his parents who sleep in different rooms. It also represents his feelings about both parents' inability to have sexual desires or to create children. He conceived of his father, particularly, as an asexual being. In his own words, "My father must have conceived us by artificial insemination." The written word is for communication with people who are at a distance. Writing also refers to his love letters which are elegant but devoid of any real warmth. This complaint of the distance between his parents and their artificiality with each other is reproduced in his own complaint, i.e., "the inability to meet women on an ordinary human level." The meaning of the foreign languages in the dream did not become clear for some time. Later it became apparent that French is a language that he must learn in order to complete his Ph.D. requirements. He is fearful of the difficulty that he will encounter in learning to read and spell in French. Russian stands for the cold war and the distance between the Eastern and Western hemispheres. They are both meaningless to him by ear. Russian is meaningless both auditorally and visually since it utilizes an unfamiliar alphabet.

Other aspects of the patient's history revealed his concern about the creative process, his denial of the pregnancy of a young woman in her eighth month, and his interest in artistic production. It was pointed out in the previous communication that for some time in the analysis the patient brought small samples of his creative production, mostly poems in free verse, small drawings and abstract sculpture. The bringing of written productions continued for some time, and fortunately for the present study it was not interpreted until a fairly large number of samples of his writings had been collected. It seemed on one occasion that these written productions represented not only the presentation of his creative work to the analyst but also a request for more direct help in the problem of his spelling. The patient confirmed this transference wish on a subsequent occasion.

The following list of misspelled words were encountered at random in a series of uncorrected hand-written poems and essays which the patient handed to me. For a considerable period of time there did not appear to be any principle involved. The first impression of his spelling errors had a random quality. Later it was found that the misspelled words could be placed in two groups, the significance of which will be discussed in more detail below. For the present it will be sufficient to note that one type of error arises from an attempt to revisualize the word without recourse to its phonetic attributes while in the other group, the phonetic qualities are retained but one would expect the writer to be disturbed by the visual inaccuracies:

Attempts at Visual Reproduction (idiographic)	*Attempts at Phonetic Reproduction* (phonographic)
Piviot (pivot)	Inmoast (inmost)
Truning (turning)	Growning (groaning)
Retalion (relation)	Cloke (cloak)
Thoery (theory)	Theery (theory)
Turnes (turns)	Gross (grows)
Metadates (meditates)	Stachure (stature)
Bouyant (buoyant)	Brest (breast)
Eygipt (Egypt)	Wherels (whirls)

It is more difficult to elicit the comparable data from reading, since direct observation of the patient's reading habits were not readily available. However, one experience recounted in the analysis serves as a clue. The patient was in the habit of taking a bus for his appointment from a certain corner. There was a grocery store on this corner whose name was unknown to the patient. On several occasions he caught himself trying to remember the sequence of the letters in the name. The letters were "G-R-I-S-T-E-D-E-S." On comparison, the following day he found that he had made various errors in the order of the letters but that he recalled the individual letters correctly. He confessed in recounting the following experience that he would have been ashamed to ask the pronunciation of the name, although he frequently bought groceries there. One Lincoln's Birthday while waiting for his bus, a lady tried the door of the store and he overheard her say to a companion, "I didn't know that Gristedes was closed on Lincoln's Birthday." The patient suddenly realized how the name was pronounced and said it to himself several times on his trip to his session. (He had introduced the session by saying that several passengers on the bus had looked at him oddly since he seemed to be talking to himself.) At this time I asked him if he could now spell the word that he had just discovered how to read. He suddenly realized that he no longer could picture the correct letters and had only a hazy notion of the appearance of the word. In his first attempt he now spelled it "GRISTEADY'S," a better phonetic equivalent of the word he had learned than an idiographic one.

During the course of the analysis there was a very striking improvement in the patient's reading. As far as one can tell at the present time he reads at an average speed. No such comparable improvement has occurred in his spelling, although he notes that he can frequently tell when a word "looks" wrong and in contrast to his former state he is able to proof read and correct his own written productions to a large extent.

DISCUSSION

Hinshelwood's (1917) theory of congenital alexia and dysgraphia has been unable to withstand the neuroanatomical and neuropathological objections of subsequent findings in acquired and congenital aphasic defects. The lesions postulated by Hinshelwood to explain so-called congenital alexia would have to be not only miraculously selective but bilaterally symmetrical as well, to fulfill the criteria of clinical experience.

Orton's (1939) hypothesis still finds wide acceptance in many circles today (Gates and Bond, 1936; Hildreth, 1934; Kirk, 1934; Phillips, 1934; Selzer, 1933; Woody and Phillips, 1934), although much work among experimental and educational psychologists is opposed to it (see McFee, 1952; Ketcham, 1951; Witty and Kopel, 1936a, 1936b). Orton bases his theory of conflicting memory images in equipotential cerebral hemispheres upon several observations with strephosymbolics, namely, the tendency to sinestrad reversals which he calls "static reversals" (see also Davidson, 1935) when they occur in letters alone, and "kinetic reversals" when they occur in the order of letters within the word, and the relatively greater speed of learning of mirror writing and mirror reading that is found in these patients. Orton also evokes evidence of at least latent ambidexterity[4] in regard to other functions that tend ordinarily to be lateralized such as the use of a dominant eye or a dominant leg, etc. Orton (1937) makes interesting and astute observations in regard to these patients but formulates the problem in what would appear to be hypotheses from which psychological considerations are largely excluded.

A consideration of the evolution of writing has yielded some interesting data which appear to be relevant to the present problem. These data are largely derived from Diringer (1948) and Ogg (1948). Recorded communication probably takes its origin from the cave painting of the paleolithic period, although it is probable that this early cave painting had a magical-religious rather than an aesthetic or communicative function. The earliest written records with a clearly communicative motivation are the pictographic scripts found among many primitive peoples. These used direct representation of objects themselves in a story sequence. With the progress of civilization, pictographs gradually gave way to idiographic writing where the representation of the object comes to stand for an idea rather than for the object itself. Idiographic writing is still a prominent element in ancient alphabets such as the Chinese. Idiograms are an important part of early Egyptian hieroglyphics. The decisive stage in the transition from idiographic writing to the phonetic alphabet comes by

4 The hypothesis presented here does not imply that functional lateralization is an irrelevant aspect of the problem, but would rather consider that such failures of lateralization, where they appear in cases of strephosymbolia, can also be explained as concomitant disturbances of intrasystemic synthesis rather than as a cause of the disability.

way of phonograms where the visual representation of an object is no longer utilized to convey an idea but denotes the sound of a verbal syllable. Alphabets making use of such phonograms are known as syllabary alphabets. Of these Japanese, Kana and ancient Sumerian cuneiform are usually cited as examples. The phonetic alphabet in which a single symbol or combination of discrete symbols (the diphthongs) comes to stand for a speech sound is the last stage in the evolution of the modern alphabet. This is an obvious "economy of energy expenditure" compared to the syllabary alphabet in that it reduces the number of visual symbols that have to be remembered in order to reproduce the same range and variety of speech sounds. Early Egyptian hieroglyphics contain all elements of the various stages of the evolution of the writing process. Idiographic and phonographic symbols appear in succession and combinations.

The direction of writing has been an important corollary of the evolution from pictography to phonetic script. In *hieroglyphics,* Diringer says, "the direction of writing was normally from right to left, the signs facing the beginning of the line. Sometimes, however, inscriptions were written from left to right, and sometimes for purposes of symmetry, in both directions. In the latter case, each of the two parts usually faces toward the center reading from there outward." Early *hieratic* writing which followed *hieroglyphics* was usually vertical. The direction of writing was probably a further synthesis with kinesthetic phenomena. Actually, sinestrality and dextrality of script is a later development than even the phonetic alphabet. Early Greek writing which is clearly alphabetical still utilizes the principle of "boustrophaedon" or "ox turning" (i.e., like an ox plowing a field). If one line reads from left to right then the next would read from right to left with complete reversal of all alphabetical symbols. Other directional peculiarities recorded by Diringer are the following: An ancient script discovered in 1929 in Syria known as *Ugarit* consists of a cuneiform alphabet which is apparently unrelated to the ancient Summarian or Assyrian languages. One tablet has been found in this script where the letters appear to be a kind of mirror writing or analogous to what today would be called printer's "offset type." The *Bataks,* a primitive group in Sumatra, use a syllabary script. They begin at the bottom of the page on the left hand side and place letter above letter in a vertical column until they reach the top. They then return to the bottom again in the next column to the right. *Pictish Oghamic,* an ancient Druid script discovered in Ireland, is read vertically from bottom upward. The *Phaistos* disc, an undeciphered script from Crete and Asia Minor, utilizes a spiral sequence of symbols reading from right to left and from the interior of the disc toward its periphery. Paleographers are of the opinion that the kinesthetic peculiarities of writing were most often determined by the properties of writing instruments and the media used in a particular culture. These they believe gradually became assimilated into the symbolic characters. Whatever the truth of the matter, it is easily observed that the closer one comes to a phonetic alphabet, the more consistent are the conventions concerning a strict directional character to writing. The more primitive the script, the greater the latitude in this regard. It is quite obvious that less confusion would be introduced by varying the direction of pictograms as long as a sequence was maintained than a similar flexibility in regard to phonetic symbols.

Pedagogy (Durrell, 1940; Harris, 1948) is well aware of the analogous stages in the learning process of the child in regard to reading and writing from pictography to phonetic concepts. The tachistoscopic teaching method is an implicit recognition of the transitional stages of development in this regard. What would appear to be relevant here is the similarity between the transitional character of the patient's reading and writing pattern and similar transitional phases in the evolution of the written word.[5] The early Egyptians, who read or wrote in hieroglyphic characters had to be prepared to oscillate between an idiographic visual system and a phonographic auditory set of symbols as the conventions of their writing demanded. One has a hunch that the first step in Champollion's historic deciphering of the Rosetta Stone must have been a triumph of the capacity for a kind of "controlled regression" (Kris, 1950) in reading and writing patterns. The sudden realization that some symbols were to be read as phonograms and others, the so-called "determinatives," were to be read as idiograms led to the unraveling of the hitherto undecipherable secrets of ancient hieroglyphics. The patient seems to perform in the same manner. His spelling errors and similar, but not as clearly demonstrated, slips of reading can be understood as alternating attempts to reproduce or understand the word either purely as a visual configuration of symbols or as a phonetic sequence of syllables. Orton gives an interesting example of a similar process in a fourteen-year-old girl who read the word "phenomena" as "fmonia." When she was asked what was meant by "fmonia," she parried the question with the query: "Do you mean the liquid or the disease?" Obviously, her interchange of "phenomena" and "pneumonia," according to Orton, was the result of the visual similarity

5 It is not intended here to suggest that the patient's disability has anything to do with the somewhat dubious concept of "phylogenetic regression" by comparing his defect with an incomplete stage in the development of the written word. Rather the similarity is meant to call attention to the analogy between the synthetic processes in the cultural evolution of a sublimation and its formation as an individual ego structure.

of the words, while that of "pneumonia" and "ammonia" rested on their auditory likeness. In normals, a similar disturbance may occur occasionally. It is to be noted how frequently when the spelling of a word seems to be forgotten it will be spelled "by ear" and then written to discover if it looks right.

In his discussion of the synthetic functions of the ego, Nunberg (1931) states, "The ego's capacity for synthesis manifests itself during the formation of the superego, not only in its mediation between the inner and outer world and its assimilation of the two, but also in the manner in which it unites, modifies, and fuses the separate psychic elements within itself." Nunberg goes on to suggest that the synthetic function derives its energy from the erotic components of the id and is the ego process which represents the creative process, which in its most elemental form is seen as the fusion of male and female elements to form a new human being. Also relevant in this connection is a statement of Hartmann (1951): "So far we have come to see ego development as a result of three sets of factors: inherited ego characteristics, influences of the instinctual drives and influences of external reality; to these we have to add as a fourth factor the influences different functions of the ego exert on each other."[6]

In this case we seem to be dealing with an individual whose development of idiographic ego functions is seen to be intact as evidenced by his extraordinary capacity to utilize mathematical symbols and concepts.[7] Functions that are elaborated upon the auditory sphere and have a purely phonographic pattern are likewise intact and highly developed. This patient speaks well. He has a large vocabulary. His diction is excellent. He is addicted to classical music and, as was noted in the previous history, has a hobby which consists of building high fidelity recording sets of unusual sensitivity. He has also in the past had a fair aptitude at playing a woodwind musical instrument (but was unable to play from written musical notation). Why then should his defect show itself in that one area of ego functioning where a high degree of integration between idiographic and phonographic symbolization is required? The present thesis suggests that these functions, as long as they can be utilized separately, fall within the sphere of ego functions utilizing neutralized energies, or what Hart-

[6] An example of this in almost pure culture would be the mutism or distortion of speech development secondary to varying degrees of early acquired or congenital deafness.

[7] In this connection and also in relation to the formulations that follow, it is of some interest to note Kris's (1950) concept of decathexis of external objects in extraordinary feats of preconscious mentation, and Hermann's (1926) suggestion that in mathematics and logic there is a decathexis of objects and a hypercathexis of the relationship between objects.

mann (1939, 1950a, 1950b, 1951) has also called "secondary autonomies" (see also Hartmann, Kris, Loewenstein, 1946) but that in combination they become invaded by the primary process and fall victim to the patient's basic conflict.

It is to be recalled to what extent the parental figures in this patient represented for him auditory and visual functions (Rosen, 1953). Mother was a poetess. She had been an English major at college. She was a great lover of music. One of the patient's complaints about his mother is that as a small boy she used to talk to him too much about her troubles—"things that should have been reserved for adults." In this respect he was utilized as a listening post to compensate his mother for his father's inadequacy as a companion. There were times when his mother's talking went to such lengths that he found himself listening to her tones and inflections, removing his attention from the content of what she was saying. In identification with his mother, the patient still writes poetry, listens for long periods of time to music and builds high fidelity record players. The patient's father was a man "closeted in his study." His complaint against his father is: "We never had anything to say to each other." His father's profession was connected with a microscope. The familiar image of his father is a man sitting in his study peering into a microscope. Father is also a camera "fan." He has a large film library. He annoys the rest of the family with his propensity to break in on all occasions with his flashbulb or movie camera. At the age of three it was his father's flash bulb, while taking a family picture, that allegedly produced the patient's photophobic response. When the patient was eight, his father suffered from a detached retina of one eye. At the age of fourteen, the patient suffered from visual disturbance diagnosed by an ophthalmologist as "drusen." The patient's scoptophilic impulses were detailed in the previous report in connection with his pavor nocturnus at the age of five. At this time it was necessary to keep a light burning in his room at night. It is also noted that the patient's first dream in analysis (Rosen, 1953) represented a scoptophilic wish to see father's erection. In brief, then, father is associated with the idiographic processes. Mother is represented in the area of auditory integrations. The two fail to be synthesized in the same manner that it is difficult for the patient to conceive of father and mother in terms of any kind of togetherness or in a mutual creative function. This had also shown itself in the transference when for some time the patient had withheld from me the name of the woman analyst who was treating his "girl friend," for fear that we would "get together behind his back."

In this connection, it is interesting to refer back to some Rorschach material that was reported also in the previous paper and which appeared quite inexplicable at that time. It was reported that the tester noted three extremely unusual features in the patient's actual perceptual experience.[8] The first she described as so rare that it had been noted by the tester in only two cases examined by the Stress Tolerance Test among battle casualties. This she described as a synesthesia involving visual stimuli and sound. She stated that the patient heard the sound given by the impression of "fighting cats" in one of the cards. The other dysesthetic responses described are not relevant in the present context. The failure of synthesis between visual and auditory functions in the written word appears as a primitive synesthesia to the unstructured visual percepts of the Rorschach patterns, i.e., in the form in which it probably exists at an early stage in object conceptualization (Piaget, 1954).

The question can now be asked why, in spite of the identification of these two ego-apparatus functions with parental figures, should failure of the synthetic process take place? One feels that it is necessary here to invoke a highly theoretical speculation which, however, was already implicit in the previous report on this case. Here it was pointed out that there was an extraordinary precocity in the mathematical talent of the patient which was also a rather consistent feature in the history of mathematical geniuses and lightning calculators who had been previously studied. Some speculation on this problem was offered, based upon the investigations of Bergman and Escalona (1949), concerning the probability of precocious ego development, in certain cases of infantile psychosis and also cases of unusual talents, which derives its initial impetus from processes set in motion by the congenitally low threshold of the stimulus barrier in certain infants.[9] Reference should also be made to Hartmann's formulation (1939, 1951, 1952) (also see Hartmann and Kris, 1945) concerning the possibility of having to consider uneven advances in the maturation not only of the ego as a total structure but also in regard to various sectors within the ego in relation to each other. To explain the involvement of the idiographic and phonographic functions of the ego in the area of conflict in this patient one might suppose that as with his mathematical ability these apparatuses had matured to a greater degree than would ordinarily be found in a child of similar age. There is some evidence that the patient's Slavic governess, who was herself studying English when he was three years of age, had also managed to teach the patient to read and write a few simple words. At least such a legend exists in the family. It would then be possible that a maturational phase

8 The psychological testing was done by Dr. Molly Harrower.

9 In this connection also see Fries and Woolf (1953) in regard to the role of "congenital activity types" in ego development, particularly in its sensory functioning.

for synthetic auditory and visual functions—the so-called "reading readiness" stage (Harrison, 1939) which ordinarily does not occur until the
latency period in most children—would in this patient have been ready
to function at the height of the oedipus complex during the period of
the pavor nocturnus. One of the standard genetic hypotheses of psychoanalysis has been that the taming of the instinctual drives of the pre-
oedipal and oedipal phases, ushers in the latency period which makes
possible the education of the child. It would seem that some revision of
this formulation is necessary. The maturation of certain ego apparatuses
is better described as the *sine qua non* for the child's acquiring of specific
intellectual functions. These maturational phases usually coincide with
certain stages of libidinal development under average conditions, but one
is not necessarily dependent upon the other. Thus the optimal period for
the education of the child in regard to language appears to be the period
from about fifteen months to roughly five years (Gesell and Ilg, 1946).
Thereafter language is continually acquired but at a greatly reduced rate
of learning. In the case of reading, the maximum learning ability appears
to begin at about the age of six years and to increase rapidly during the
next two or three years, gradually leveling off in later childhood. Marked
variations on either side of the norm are encountered according to the
general principle of the "normal distribution curve." The vicissitudes of
an ego function may well depend upon the id phase in which it appears.
One would also expect mutual influences and modifications (A. Freud,
1952), but the appearance of the ego function must be considered relatively independent of the id phase. The "reading readiness stage" is,
according to this hypothesis, a variable maturational phase of the synthesis of verbal-auditory and visual-ideographic ego functions.[10] It is
characterized by the appearance of the child's capacity to grasp the concept of phonograms. By precocious development it may become involved
in the oedipal conflict and thus fail to become part of the "conflict-free
sphere" (Hartmann, 1939) as would be expected under average conditions.

Finally an attempt should be made to bring this formulation into a
coherent relationship with the hypothesis developed in the study of the

[10] Schilder (1944) expresses a neurological point of view with certain similarities,
although he does not view the ego disturbances in quite the same light nor relate
it to id phases. "These variations are probably due to a different development of
those parts of the brain which are indispensable for the process of reading. In the
serious cases we probably deal with a dysfunction of a cortical apparatus. This
dysfunction expresses itself in the integrating and differentiating difficulty, in optic
mistakes concerning letters and in increased mirror tendencies. The inherent mirror
tendencies as well as mirror tendencies originating from other sources, and intellectual
difficulties, may alter and increase the primary trouble which is an isolated trouble of
gnostic intellectual function."

patient's successful mathematical sublimation (Rosen, 1953). At that time the importance of the capacity for decathexis of the image of the object (Kris, 1950), in enhancing the speed and mobility of the preconscious problem-solving function, was emphasized. Evidence was adduced to indicate that the child calculating prodigies who lose their special capacities as they mature, do so, in so far as they begin to "treat numbers as written symbols and become conscious paper computers rather than preconscious lightning calculators." Many lightning calculators, it was indicated, could not distinguish one written arabic numeral from another. Those who became educated and retained this ability did so by retaining the capacity to decathect the image of the written symbol. In other words, the capacity is possible in a child who has not developed a certain stage of "object concept" (the written symbol) or in the adult who has the capacity for a "controlled regression" (Kris, 1950) to this more primitive ego level. Piaget (1954), in studying the stages of the development of the concept of "object permanence" in the infant, stresses the importance of early intersensory co-ordinations: "In the case of sight and hearing, there exists at the outset no objective identity of the visual image with the auditory image [the development of these is then discussed]. . . . In short, intersensory co-ordinations contribute to the solidifying of the universe" (i.e., helping to give objects their external substantial character). The final stage of this process is, according to Piaget, the "concept" (image) of the object as a complex intersensory synthesis after the object itself has vanished. The written word is an advanced stage of such complex intersensory synthesis. In the case at hand a primitive level of this aspect of the process of "objectivation" has been demonstrated. It interferes demonstrably with the development and retention of visuophonetic word images. In the case of mathematical operations, however, it serves as a distinct advantage. The mathematician operating with abstractions or attenuated images has a shorter distance to traverse for his "controlled regression," if the intersensory syntheses of his object world are less "solid."

SUMMARY

A case is presented involving the analysis of a young mathematician who suffers from a developmental dysgraphic and dyslexic defect or so-called "strephosymbolia." Evidence is presented to indicate that his writing errors arise from oscillations between attempts to reproduce words in phonetic fashion without regard to their visual appearance or alternatively in idiographic fashion without regard to the ordering of phonemes necessitated by the sound of the word. It is suggested that phylogenetically his disturbance is similar to a transitional stage in the development of writing between idiographic forms and a syllabary alphabet with incomplete development of the concept of phonetic writing. It is suggested that the basic conflict in this case arises from the primal scene fantasy which associates father with visual activities, mother with auditory functions and which conceives of them as two separate unloving human beings who are incapable of producing a child except by artificial insemination. It is further suggested that secondary autonomy has been achieved in the visual and auditory perceptual functions of the ego when utilized separately, and that conflict invades these areas only in their synthetic function related to recognizing and evoking phonetic words and images. At this point their synthetic product becomes invested with primal scene significance. The genetic origin of the disability may be due to precocious maturation of certain ego sectors involved in visual and auditory perceptual processes so that they become involved in the oedipal conflict at a crucial stage in their development. Thus they are prevented in their synthetic relationship from forming a new, completely autonomous structure as they might have, had their maturation been somewhat delayed. An attempt is made to indicate the relationship between this disturbance of interperceptual synthesis and the enhancement of preconscious problem-solving operations in mathematics which utilize attenuated "unsolidified" images.

BIBLIOGRAPHY

Bender, L. and Schilder, P. (1951), Graphic Art as a Special Ability in Children with a Reading Disability. *Med. Wom. J.*, LVIII, 11-18.

Bergman, P. and Escalona, S. (1949), Unusual Sensitivities in Very Young Children. *This Annual*, III/IV, 333-352.

Blanchard, P. (1928), Reading Disabilities in Relation to Maladjustment. *Ment. Hyg.*, XII, 772-788.

—— (1935), Psychogenic Factors in Some Cases of Reading Disability. *Am. J. Orthopsychiat.*, V, 361-374.

—— (1947), Psychoanalytic Contributions to the Problems of Reading Disabilities. *This Annual*, II, 163-188.

Cole, E. M. (1951), Specific Reading Disability. A Problem in Integration and Adaptation. *Am. J. Ophthal.*, XXXIV., 226-232.

Crisp, W. H. (1949), The Psychology of the Poor Reader. *Rocky Mount. Med. J.*, XLVI, 833-836.

Davidson, H. P. (1935), A Study of the Confusing Letters B, D, P and Q. *J. Genet. Psychol.*, XL, 458-468.

Dearborn, W. F. (1933), Structural Factors Which Condition Special Disability in Reading. *Proc. Am. Assn. for Mental Deficiency*. XXXVIII, 266-283.

—— (1938), Aniseikonia as Related to Disability in Reading. *J. Exper. Psychol.*, XXIII, 559-577.

Diringer, D. (1948), *The Alphabet: A Key to the History of Mankind*. New York: Philosophical Library.

Durrell, D. (1940), *Improvement of Basic Reading Abilities.* Yonkers, N. Y.: World Book Co.

Fernald, G. M. and Keller, H. B. (1921), The Effect of Kinesthetic Factors in the Development of Word Recognition in the Case of the Non-reader. *J. Educ. Research,* IV, 355-377.

Freud, A. (1952), Mutual Influences in the Development of the Ego and the Id. *This Annual,* VII, 42-50.

Freud, S. (1904), The Psychopathology of Everyday Life (VI. Mistakes in Reading and Writing, pp. 87-94). *The Basic Writings of Sigmund Freud.* New York: Random House, 1938.

Fries, M. E. and Woolf, P. J. (1953), Some Hypotheses on the Role of the Congenital Activity Type in Personality Development. *This Annual,* VIII, 48-62.

Gates, A. I. (1941), The Role of Personality Maladjustment in Reading Disability. *J. Genet. Psychol.,* LIX, 77-83.

—— and Bennett, C. C. (1933), *Reversal Tendencies in Reading: Causes, Diagnosis, Prevention and Correction.* New York: Bureau of Publications, Teacher's College, Columbia University.

—— and Bond, G. L. (1936), Relation of Handedness, Eyesightedness and Acuity Dominance to Reading. *J. Educ. Psychol.,* XXVII, 450-456.

Gesell, A. and Ilg, F. L. (1946), *The Child from Five to Ten.* New York: Harper.

Harris, A. J. (1948), *How to Increase Reading Ability.* New York: Longmans, Green.

Harrison, M. (1939), *Reading Readiness.* Boston: Houghton Mifflin.

Hartmann, H. (1939), Ich-Psychologie und Anpassungsproblem. *Int. Ztschr. f. Psa. u. Imago,* XXIV, 62-135.

—— (1950a), Psychoanalysis and Developmental Psychology. *This Annual,* V, 7-17.

—— (1950b), Comments on the Psychoanalytic Theory of the Ego. *This Annual,* V, 74-96.

—— (1951), Technical Implications of Ego Psychology. *Psa. Quart.,* XX, 3-43.

——, Kris, E. (1945), The Genetic Approach in Psychoanalysis. *This Annual,* I, 11-29.

—— —— , Loewenstein, R. M. (1946), Comments on the Formation of Psychic Structure. *This Annual,* II, 11-38.

Hermann, I. (1926), Das System Bw. *Imago,* XII, 203-210.

Hildreth, G. (1934), Reversals in Reading and Writing. *J. Educ. Psychol.,* XXV, 1-20.

Hincks, E. (1926), *Disability in Reading and Its Relation to Personality.* Cambridge, Mass.: Harvard University Press.

Hinshelwood, J. (1917), *Congenital Word Blindness.* London: Lewis.

Ketcham, W. A. (1951), Experimental Tests of Principles of Developmental Anatomy and Neuroanatomy as Applied to Pedagogy of Reading. *Child Development,* XXII, 185-192.

Kirk, S. A. (1934), A Study of the Relation of Ocular-Manual Preferences to Mirror Writing. *J. Genet. Psychol.,* XLIV, 192-205.

Knight, E. H. (1952), Spelling Disability as a Symptom of Emotional Disorder. *Bull. Menninger Clin.,* XVI, 84-91.

Kris, E. (1950), On Preconscious Mental Processes. *Psa. Quart.,* XIX, 540-550.

Launay, C. and Borel-Maisonny (1952), Un cas de dyslexie specifique. *Sem. Hosp. Paris,* XXVIII, 1455-1459.

McFie, J. (1952), Cerebral Dominance in Cases of Reading Disability. *J. Neurol., Neurosurg., & Psychiat.,* XV, 194-199.

Nunberg, H. (1931), The Synthetic Function of the Ego. In: *Practice and Theory of Psychoanalysis.* New York: International Universities Press, 1955.

Ogg, S. T. (1948), *The 26 Letters.* New York: Thomas Y. Crowell.

Orton, S. T. (1937), *Reading, Writing and Speech Problems in Children.* New York: Norton.

—— (1939), A Neurological Explanation of Reading Disability. *Educ. Record,* XX, 58-68.

Pearson, G. H. J. (1952), A Survey of Learning Difficulties in Children. *This Annual*, VII, 322-386.

Phillips, A. J. (1934), Relation of Left Handedness to Reversals in Reading. *Elem. English Rev.*, XI, 97-98.

Piaget, J. (1954), *The Construction of Reality in the Child*. New York: Basic Books.

Rosen, V. H. (1953), On Mathematical "Illumination" and the Mathematical Thought Process. *This Annual*, VIII, 127-154.

Schilder, P. (1944), Congenital Alexia and Its Relation to Optic Perception. *J. Genet. Psychol.*, LXV, 67-88.

Selzer, C. A. (1933), *Lateral Dominance and Visual Fusion*. Cambridge, Mass.: Harvard University Press.

Sterba, E. (1943), On Spelling. *Psa. Rev.*, XXX, 273-276.

Strachey, J. (1930), Some Unconscious Factors in Reading. *Int. J. Psa.*, XI, 322-331.

Sylvester, E. and Kunst, M. S. (1943), Psychodynamic Aspects of the Reading Problem. *Am. J. Orthopsychiat.*, XIII, 69-76.

Tulchin, S. (1935), Emotional Factors in Reading Disabilities in School Children. *J. Educ. Psychol.*, XXVI, 443-454.

Witty, P. A. (1936), Sinistral and Mixed Manual-Ocular Behavior in Reading Disability. *J. Educ. Psychol.*, XXVII, 119-134.

—— and Kopel, D. (1936), Factors Associated with the Etiology of Reading Disability. *J. Educ. Research*, XXIX, 449-459.

Woody, C. and Phillips, A. J. (1934), The Effects of Handedness on Reversals in Reading. *J. Educ. Research*, XXVII, 651-662.

Young, R. A. (1938), Case Studies in Reading Disability. *Am. J. Orthopsychiat.*, VIII, 230-254.

70943

MOTIVATIONS IN LEARNING

EDWARD LISS, M.D. (New York)

INTRODUCTION

Definition of Learning

Learning is the psychosomatic process by which an idea or action originates and is then applied. Learning is as basic to human nature as are the automatic physiological processes in which the organism must engage in order to survive. Inasmuch as the production of energy, particularly in the young, goes far beyond the demands which physical growth utilizes, there is a substantial residuum of energy which can be applied for many purposes besides the routine needs of repair and growth. This surplus energy, when used for exploration and experiment, carries with it the sense of gratification which comes with accomplishment. Unless it is so directed it turns against the organism to its detriment.

The dynamic school of psychology can bear witness to what evils follow frustrated energies, what neurotic tensions and patterns result when sublimation or the direction of energy from its primitive aim to one that is culturally higher does not take place.

The psychoanalytic field is potentially the investigating instrument par excellence of both the conscious and unconscious forces which pervade human action and direct its destiny. Each psychoanalytic patient is an exhibit of the interplay of the forces which enter into the process of action or counteraction, affording the psychoanalyst an excellent opportunity to inquire into the dynamics and goals which condition the common experience of learning. In the past academic research has been of a mechanistic, almost stereotyped nature. Undoubtedly some of it has been extremely helpful for pedagogic purposes. On the whole, however, it has hardened into ritual and made rigid the process of learning, which should be dynamic and constantly in action, and if it is to be broadening, must be fluid and flexible as well. It is essential, of course, that there be a certain amount of basic formal technical equipment for the pedagogue, but when carried too far, this leads to pedantry and sterility. In every field the truly great investigators have had a flair for the imaginative and the artistic, a free play of thought which has often enabled them to bridge gaps of the unknown and to arrive at end thoughts which, though intuitive, proved valid. Some few academic investigators of the educational process have pointed out goals and have discussed motivation, but they

100

have done it as though motivation were a cold and pulseless drive. When motivation, or the incitement to learning is regarded in the round, as it were, with due consideration for the individual history, background, and life experience of the two participants in the learning process—the teacher and the student—we see that learning is a warm and throbbing and very much alive part of every human being.

Cultural Influences

For an understanding of the forces that motivate learning we turn, before Freud's time, to the philosophers rather than to the pedagogues. Francis Bacon sounds off the keynote which we should bear in mind constantly, for he predicted and previsioned these forces. Bacon mentions three categories: "fantastical learning, contentious learning, and delicate learning which is vain and affectatious." He admonishes us: "I would give one general admonition to all, that they consider the true ends of knowledge and not to seek it either for the gratification of the mind or for contention or that they may despise others or for emolument or fame or power or such low things but for the benefit and use of life and that they perfect and govern it in charity." For contemporary broadening of this concept we look to John Dewey, who views learning as a total experience for the individual.

As we have all noticed in the growth of human knowledge from time to time, coincidental discoveries or evaluations take place in different parts of the world. This has been most dramatic, for example, in the fields of psychology and education, where Dewey's philosophy with regard to education has been particularly striking as a correlation of Freud's work. Their conclusions dovetail into each other so beautifully that it is hard to believe that in some uncanny fashion they have not been in communication with each other. It is an experience indeed to see how much one rounds out the work of the other.

If we translate the concepts of these great thinkers into everyday practice, then the motivations behind learning should be the spirit of Christianity, in which learning is an instrument given to an individual for social purposes rather than for egotistical gain and self-aggrandizement. This brings up the question of the psychology of the individual and to what purposes and ends he forwards his acquired knowledge. Implicit herein is the study of man. Whatever conclusions are reached are conditioned too by the psychology of the investigator. His own total personality, the sum of his prejudices, his bias, and his wisdom enter into the formulation of his concepts and his conclusions. Hence induction and deduction are conditioned by the gestalt and the associative experiences of the individual investigated and of the investigator.

We cannot claim complete knowledge of a matter as complex as motivation; conclusions are inevitably subject to some questioning, and as the exposure of some motivations may lead to implications that may appear quite unattractive to the investigator, they may act as a deterrent to open inquiry. But to the scientific investigator the factors which enter into the performance of an act, whether they be egocentric or social, should not lead to blocking; they should rather evoke helpful elucidation and constructive recommendation. Basically, of course, there must be ego satisfaction, and the choice of any professional activity and investigation in the learning field has unquestionably arisen out of his own needs for satisfaction. There may be contradictory factors, as well, but if the end result is good and an artistic performance, the negative motivations should be of secondary significance.

It has long been a contention that the learning process is a composite of physiological and emotional factors and that the ultimate intellectual acquisition is a sedimentation of these processes. This may strike the reader as a rather bizarre concept when he has heretofore been taught to look upon intellectualization as purely cerebral. To appreciate fully what learning can be, regardless of what we often see it is, one should go back to one's childhood and revive those fleeting moments of ecstasy with which one was suffused when new knowledge was suddenly glimpsed and new experiences encountered. That early freshness and pleasure are emotions which we rarely experience in later life. By the artist and other creative personality this original pleasure is more frequently recaptured, sometimes wtih pain. One must ask oneself why something which came so ecstatically in the beginning had subsequently become so distressing. If we consider intellectuality as the brain child, then we must review what brought about this end result and try to understand the insemination, gestation and birth of an idea.

THE PROCESS OF LEARNING

Learning in Infancy

Parent-Child Relationship.—Learning in early infancy is a constant physiologic interchange between the adult and the infant. Into this experience are woven the reactions of the environment to the infant's early physiological interests, which in the beginning are commendable but which with time have to be repressed and sublimated. This is the basis for the necessary psychic sublimation of early physiological practices, such as food intake and body disposition of incorporated material. The first learning problem is centered around the body or self, which is instinctively demanding and unyielding, for its actual existence is dependent upon the satisfaction, directly or through substitutes, of these survival urges. The compromise of self in relation to others comes only with time, when the psyche is able to differentiate between extrinsic and intrinsic phenomena, and when the infant is able to grasp the difference between the self and all that is not self.

Learning in infancy is then the weaving of a pattern in which the adult and the child are like the warp and woof in the slow evolution of a design. In this warp and woof we have the interpersonal relationship between adult and child and the formation of character. Basic egocentrism and what we refer to as narcissism are centered around the by-products of physiology, which are the creative objects of the infant and the core of his sensual self. They must either be gratified, or compromised with in order to bring about social acceptance. Only through the love and affection which comes from our relationship to others and in which we find basic security is it possible to transmute the body products into the highest aspects of man's creativity. To learn means the social acceptance of all body values and the conversion of some of these values, through the alchemy of sublimation, into creative activity.

To the infant and the well-adjusted parent, biology is not a matter of disgust. On the contrary, pride and accomplishment are associated with these by-products. Morality represented by shame and disgust, and the need for the repression of this pride, create the first great trauma to which learning exposes the organism. What the child eats and what he does with it are matters of the highest interest to him, and this interest involves every sense of the human organism. However, with time some of these fundamental interests become taboo socially, but never privately, and to the invalid and the scientist only are permitted the privilege of this pristine interest. For the individual these are acceptable indulgences when illness enters the picture, and what has been forbidden is again permissible. At such times the solicitude of the environment sanctions the forbidden and repressed early emotional focusing on body functions.

There are special areas and orifices of the body which are unusually endowed with emotional significance and erotic sensitivity—they are the skin, muscle actions, the mouth, anus and the genitals. Inasmuch as the parents' attitude toward body functions and products varies from culture to culture, the erotism inherent in habit training, such as in eating, defecation and urination, is particular to each culture, since through each parent are transmitted traditional practices as permissive or restrictive. This is not a new idea to the pediatrician, even one who is not

oriented along psychoanalytic lines. He knows the intensity of body interests and can sense quickly the background of the nurse or governess
in the family picture by the attitudes which the child has picked up
toward body functions. In severe illness and marked degrees of emotional
disturbance this becomes quite patent again.

The better part of the first three years are centered around eating
habits, bowel control, and bladder regimes and locomotion. For the
gratifications and inhibitions which are inherent in these functions the
parents instinctively, as they themselves have been guided, substitute
other interests and activities. With the advent of the child into the formal
school at the age of six, substantial substitutions have taken place.
Approximately at this period the instinctive personal relationships, primitive and sensuous, between parent and child, should have quieted down
and a broader socialization, apart and separate from body interests, will
have received added impetus. To the psychoanalyst, this implies the
resolution of the oedipus complex (age of physical erotism).

Sibling Relationships.—Concurrently with this oedipal phase, in
families where there are siblings, social relationships and the varied
interests of childhood are experienced through and with these siblings.
This brings about, as all experiences do, certain effects upon those
participating: it conditions learning or the acquisition of knowledge
through mutual experiences, in terms of relationships with contempo-
raries. For many years we have used the terms "vertical" and "horizontal"
influences on learning, referring thereby essentially to learning through
parent images and through contemporary contacts. The child who has
had the fortunate experience of a good and full home is infinitely better
prepared for learning and for life, not alone because of the security
engendered by sound human relationships, but because there has been
the give-and-take of experiences with children who are somewhat older
and those who are somewhat younger. Then, too, there are additional
opportunities to review universal physiological values and experiences
on a contemporary level.

In our discussion of the motivational dynamics of learning we have
put so much emphasis on this early period because many learning disabilities are centered around rejection or acceptance of the contribution
of those individuals who have the role of educator, guide, friend or peer.
Rejection of the educator frequently is a carry-over of previous unfortunate experiences with adults in the family and sometimes siblings.
This personal component in learning may account for the fact that some
individuals are better able to learn from persons than from books, and
vice versa.

Physiological Basis of Learning

Inherent in all survival is the application of the five senses. The five senses are organic components, physiological interconnecting units. There is no such thing as an exclusive sense experience—that is, we cannot conceive of seeing things without the whole body structure being involved, nor can we think of hearing or tasting or smelling as a meaningful experience unless the total organism participates. For instance, the investigations made by the Research Division of the Dartmouth Eye Institute bring home to us how much of the body is involved in the visual experience and how complex is the interrelationship of many sense organs when an individual goes through the technique of reading. The reports from Sarah Lawrence College entitled "Teaching the Individual" and "Psychology for Individual Education," and Daniel Alfred Prescott's "Emotion and the Educative Process" are significant contributions which explore the social dynamics of the acquisition of knowledge.

Inasmuch as the total organism is involved and participates in any sensory experience, there is no such thing as a sharply localized reflex without intermediate participation of other body segments. Once this is understood, the physical constitution as a factor in determining skills and accomplishments receives its just emphasis. To the psychoanalytic school the realization of the amount of energy and emotion centered around body physiology is an old story. The concept of depots of pure libidinal endowment such as the orifices of the body—mouth, anus, genital regions and skin surfaces, and their function in the relationship between the child and its environment—receive the consideration which we feel they are entitled to. The stress is on infancy and early childhood as an experiment in living in an environment which permits some biological indulgences and taboos others. This determines how deeply, how sensitively, and how in some instances ineradicably, patterns of learning are laid down with physiological cores.

Does this shed any light on the philosophical definition of what is mind? I think it does. It is not only the brain and the central nervous system but the sum total of the human psychophysical entity.

Student-Teacher Relationship

Teaching and learning are closely allied and one actually grows out of the other, for the teacher of tomorrow is the student of today, and the teacher of today was the child of yesterday.

Learning is conditioned by the parent-child relationship. The earlier relationship conditions the subsequent teacher-student pattern for good or evil when the problem is no longer body action but derivations or substitutes for physiological satisfaction which we call sublimation.

In a very interesting schematization of our current setup there is a certain underlying awareness of learning by the educator's concept of mental growth, which is confirmed by the psychodynamic findings in the study of emotional maturation.

NEONATAL—	Oral		⎰Nursery
POSTNATAL—	Anal	Oedipus	⎱
	Urethral	Complex	
	Phallic		Kindergarten
LATENCY—			⎰Elementary School
PREPUBERTY—		Adolescence	Junior High School
PUBESCENCE—			Senior High School
ADOLESCENCE—			Collegeᶜ

The pre-elementary school is the arena, the place for the acting out of further experiences in relationships. Here occurs the transmutation of interests in body and body products into interests which are socially more acceptable. Eventually these interests form part of the treasury of the creative activities of man—the sciences and the humanities. The graduation, as it were, from parents and parent surrogates at home to the educators who function in nursery and kindergarten provides an elaboration of the social structure with which the growing child experiments. Through this widened social structure he explores human relationships, permissiveness and inhibitions. This is a period and an area not alone of the expansion of the human variations to which he has to become adjusted, but a profound, almost revolutionary change from physiological interests to purposeful activity. It represents a basic, if still inept and clumsy, orientation in human creative activity. For out of the biological comes the beauty which brings comfort and satisfaction to all the senses.

The Role of the Teacher

The educator in these areas of nursery and kindergarten must be more physiologically oriented than cerebral, to make this transmutation as easy or smooth for the child as possible. The educator, however, carries with him (or her) a sedimentation of his own childhood experiences in this area, the prejudices which go with it, or the feeling of comfort and well-being which comes with the handling of materials that do not disgust, do not create overt tension and incompatibility within the growing child.

Each teacher unconsciously assumes a parental role with the group. This carries with it a sense of power, and the important question is how will that sense of power be used? Will it be utilized for his own essential satisfaction or for the creativity and sublimation which gives power to others? The choice has been conditioned by the concept of parental role as laid down in his own life experience. Where he himself has been the victim of abuses of that responsibility in his own childhood, he could very well carry over the same tyranny in his relationship with sensitive, impressionable and all-too-fluid young personalities. If, however, his has been the good fortune to have had benevolent parents, then we find a happy family in the classroom. It can also be true that having learned the evils at home of the corruption of power, such a person might swing pendulum-like from easy practices to ritualization and discipline. There is the opportunity also to work out his own early childhood practices with siblings. He may then play the dual role of parent and intuitive sibling who understands and appreciates the situation at that specific time and phase of growth. It is an ideal, of course, and one not too often met with, for how few of us retain consciously the ability to place ourselves into the child's world?

To summarize, the teacher can function as a good parent because he had a good parent; as a poor, insecure parent with power which is used aggressively; or as a good parent in reaction to the poor parents he has had the misfortune to be exposed to. Of these three categories the first is the most desirable, the second should not teach at all, and the third may function well with good end results as far as the students are concerned, but undoubtedly at a great expense of energy and tension on the part of the educator. One might here use the yardstick of fatigue, for the type of fatigue from which one recovers quickly is most evident in the first category, whereas teaching done by the third category drains inordinately the energies of the teacher. After all, to the educator his classes are his phantom children who gratify a fundamental biological urge inherent in all of us. There is a source of constant rejuvenation which can come from good teaching, for here is a renewal of youth through living with the young. Unfortunately, too few older persons ever recapture it.

The Role of the Student

The classroom becomes the stage for the acting out of the pasts of teacher and student. The residual patterns, good and evil, many of them unconscious, take over and affect the learning process. The educator must understand this, for like the psychoanalyst or therapist, he plays a role which is often thrust upon him, irrespective of his own wishes. The image which he represents to the conditioned child frequently is at complete variance with his actual personality. Under these circumstances, it is necessary to interpret this bewilderment to the educator, for only if he is aware that the child's conception of him may be something quite irrelevant to his real personality, can he evaluate the seemingly bizarre and apparently mismotivated conduct of his student.

To the child fortunate enough to have a good parental imago and a good teacher, the introduction to school is a happy event. To the child whose reaction to the new situation is conditioned by a bad parent, it will take some time to undo the pattern of anxiety and fear and aggression, overt and latent, which was incorporated by his previous unfortunate experience. These children start off on the wrong foot and require complete reorientation. They have to learn that in this world there are also good parents. Naturally, the projection upon the teacher of good or bad parent is easier if the sex of the educator is identical with the parent in question.

Thus the attitude of the child toward the teacher grows out of the child's past. The attitude of the child to his schoolmates has likewise been influenced by his past experience, with siblings in this case who have proved that blood is thicker than water, or who have created a civil war. It is interesting to observe to what extent a good sibling relationship at home is conducive to an easy approach and facility with the child's fellows at school. The child whose home is a battle for supremacy will usually conduct himself accordingly in the classroom, and the ramifications of this belligerency must be understood in the light of what has gone before. The child who is an only child has missed out on the experimental theater at home and comes to the classroom as a novice, requiring slower initiation and much patience before he becomes a part of the inner circle. He may be a timid and bewildered spectator on the periphery, or to cover up his timidity, he may become a bellicose maverick. In the child's adjustment to this new environment and in his struggle for status, he will be motivated by the inherent need of every individual to receive respect for his individuality. It is important for the child's whole future whether this respect is to come through love or through aggression, through an acceptance of power which is based on dominance or through conduct which brings affection to him.

Sex and Learning—Masculine and Feminine Identification

We find that each culture has its own concepts of masculinity and femininity, and that these mores influence learning. These concepts become compartmentalized and often rigid, almost ritualistic in their practice. Like all rituals, many of them are based on defenses against fear rather than on actual facts. It takes a great deal of time to break through such formulations, as may be witnessed by some of out current concepts of education for both sexes, in which we speak of such vague entities as the masculine and feminine mind or basic endowment founded on color or lack of color in individuals. Nonetheless, each culture has its own mores as to what is a masculine attribute and what is a feminine activity. Worldwide investigation indicates to the anthropologist how much such attributes are conditioned by the historical background of the people and how the interpretation of what is masculine and what is feminine varies from culture to culture. In many cultures, as in our own, the emphasis for the male is on activity, essentially physical activity and physical prowess. This concept is engendered in the young male and is something which remains the core of his self-evaluation. Any deviation in fundamental skills requiring physical strength and aggression is regarded as lack of potency in males.

The emphasis on physical activity rather than cerebral function is an important aspect of the younger years. It conditions the attitude of the growing organism throughout its later years and affects its attitude toward learning. In some individuals it goes underground and creates a core of insecurity with regard to book learning, which in turn leads to an attitude of disparagement toward intellectuality and intellectuals. This was forcibly brought out in recent history when the battle between the so-called "practical" man and the "professor" was fought not on an objective basis, but colored by these emotional remnants from childhood.

Sex-oriented identification and its influence on learning is not confined to the male, for the female trying to break through the traditional concepts of maleness and femaleness (*Kinder, Küche, und Kirche*) not only has to contend with the social hostility which for generations has defined the woman's status, but within herself she hears a small voice that doubts the wisdom of an alteration of her ways.

In the family drama, where acculturation is taking place most actively, cerebral function and manual labor may become sex-linked, with the result that the former appears to be the female role and the latter the male one. Often in homes where the self-made successful father has manifested his creativity in trade rather than in academic pursuits and activities, the mother, with more opportunities for leisure available to her as a benefit from generations of pioneer toil, has become the so-called cultured member of the family. This presents an easier identification for the female than for the male siblings. In such cases intellectualism becomes enmeshed in feminine identification and creates difficulties for the boy in the resolution of the oedipus complex and the adoption of a truly masculine role.

Alternative of Intellectuality or Sex

Here is a certain danger that there may be some reinforcement of the young male's concept that cultural acquisition is effete. This may condition the learner to an acceptance of an exaggeratedly biological role for him or her in society. With the acknowledgment, however, that intellectuality is not a special adornment of either male or female, but a part of a composite which makes for a well-balanced individual, culture and sex can then be accepted as fully compatible with the biological destiny of whatever individual is involved. In too many instances we find the "either-or" concept: on the one hand, the intellectual who will not accept sex, on the other, the sexually active individual who will not accept intellectuality. The end results are varying degrees and combinations of this fusion or diffusion. The greater the acceptance of the symbiosis of these two components, the more sound will be the individual and his functioning as a problem-solving and creative personality, and the less will this process of fusion be conditioned by anxiety which interferes with the learning process.

We can say that the *learning process* has gradations which vary from the mature, which we term wisdom, to and through the neurotic, and in its ultimate disorganization ends in a psychotic type of creativity. To the psychoanalyst who regards maturity as a fusion of the infantile sexuality phenomena and the resolution of the oedipus complex, the acceptance of sex and intellectuality as one and inseparable is indispensable for growth. In some of those in whom infantile sexuality has taken the place of mature sexuality, a transposition in emphasis is manifested from mature genital functioning to cerebral activity. Biologically, one gets the impression that the emphasis has been displaced from the "lower" genital, erotic area to the "upper" head zone, what analysts regard as a transposition from below upward. That process which leads to the creation of an object can be likened to the insemination, gestation and birth of a brain child, which has for its substance the transmutation of flesh and spirit into a creative unit.

Mature Creativity—Intellectuality and Sex

Mature creativity is creativity with a minimum of disturbance of sexual potency. This means that the early biological experiences have been accepted by the individual with reasonable equanimity, and that

shame and disgust at body functions and body products are at a minimum. Although there is present reasonable repression of body interests
in accordance with the demands of social morality, prudishness is dis-
dained and wholesome curiosity is permitted. This attitude pervades all
phases of man's interests and promotes exploration and experiment in
the varied areas of his activities and practices.

A personal psychoanalysis, if successfully consummated, is in actuality
a learning process which permits a rectification resulting from tangential
infantile sexual experiences and an exploration of the ramifications of
the oedipus complex. Such examination leads to changed attitudes and
a more economic disposition of man's energies for biological and emotional usage. The ambivalence which is so much a part of each and
everyone of us is brought to a minimum. Conflicts between right and
wrong are no longer in terms of black and white, there is more synthesis
and less antithesis, more give-and-take, which can be applied to the
whole process of growth and adjustment. Inherent in this is the ability,
which the individual acquires, to utilize the best for today's maturation
of man's contributions from the past, and with this new-won security to
meet with less fear the uncertainties of the future.

Utilization of Learning—Sadistic and Masochistic

Whether the child's activities are in the physical area which we think
of as play, or in the cultural field in which we include not alone the three
R's but also the timorous beginnings of the arts, our concept of learning
centers around whether we are dealing with a social utilization of knowledge and action (sublimation) or whether we are confronted, in a very
subtle way, with an egotistical and sadistic use of learning. The precon-
ditioning of the individual and the basic security or insecurity which his
human relationships have built up affect the purposes behind the acquisition of learning. His inner security makes it possible to utilize these
broadening activities with pleasure to the self and with pleasure to others.
Such noncompetitive learning does indeed build up a sense of power,
but it is power which does not corrupt the user or the sharer. However,
since maturation in all human beings by no means keeps pace with
growth, at certain times this power may be used aggressively. Under such
circumstances, there may be pleasure for the acquirer but not often for
society. In the secure person, however, sooner or later learning for learning itself brings satisfaction.

To those individuals whose sense of power is unbalanced by insecurity, learning, like other acquisitions, becomes a tool for the aggrandize-
ment of the individual at the expense of others. Knowledge, which is

commonly quoted as power, now follows along the lines which Lord Acton has forcibly brought to our attention in his famous expression "Power corrupts and absolute power corrupts absolutely." In such instances where intellectuality is used aggressively, it becomes a weapon with sadistic connotations. The antithesis of sadism, of course, is masochism. In circumstances of this type, the learner becomes a victim of the poisons which he has himself generated and which he utilizes against the illusory threats and retaliation of his rivals. In consequence, the pleasure goal of this, as of all accomplishments, becomes pain-laden.

In many cultures, as in ours, the mere acquisition of intellectuality is often regarded with reverence. We are prone to forget that the laws of accomplishment are the same, whether the accomplishment be a crass materialistic end or a social contribution. All too frequently we have overlooked the great potentialities for corruption (sadism) which can and often do go with perverse utilization of intellectuality. We think in this connection of propaganda and many types of publicity practices. The masochistic by-products of such practices and the rebound that they have upon the character of the individual have hitherto lain in the field of psychiatry rather than in education. Again and again we have seen what an important part the element of fear, which is behind the sadistic and masochistic utilization of learning, plays in bringing individuals to the institutions for the mentally ill. How often has the mere acquisition of grades, honors and degrees in school, college and university brought all too little happiness in later life. What a sorry end comes to many a so-called "genius" and uniquely endowed child! High intellectual potentiality with a low index of maturation and emotional stability carry inherent threats of ultimate futility and frustration.

Creative or Social

Ego growth implies knowledge used creatively. The mature individual utilizes learning for the benefit of others as well as for himself. The growth of knowledge carries with it responsibility for its usage for social ends. In such use there are impressive values for the enlightenment of others. It can mean fair exchange and richness and beauty for all.

Knowledge used egotistically may be regarded as intellectual royalism. It is a power instrument which corrupts all who come into contact with it, and particularly those who utilize it. Intellectuality is but a step to action, and the action may be good or evil, depending upon the motivation which prompts the use of the intellectuality. Whether the pen is used for demagogy and harmful propaganda or for the Word is more determined by man than by the elements around him.

Symbols

Man created symbols for a purposeful end. Through them he is able to face reality in its protean forms. He has created out of the animate and the inanimate, instruments which should be hedonistic and pleasurable, and likewise through them he has been able to meet the fears and displeasure of past experiences with less distress. Each of us is a participant in a world of symbols which reaches back in time to the beginning of man. Some of these symbols are universal; some are culturally determined and vary with race, creed and color; still others are unique to each individual. Through his own life history the meaning of a symbol has a specific personal value built up for him through the associations which have been part of his particular past experience. These symbols close the triangle which we are dealing with when we evaluate the *learning process,* comprising teacher, student and the material that is the medium of their activity and exchange. The past as a psychosomatic entity determines the success or failure of this process. The successful consummation of learning is wisdom, which enables the individual to utilize symbols with a minimum of demoniacal anxiety and a maximum of pleasure.

In using the term "demoniacal" we refer to the bizarre evaluation of a symbol because of the unfortunate associations which accompany its past evolution. In dream interpretation this is made particularly overt, for there symbols and their implications are disinterred through free association. Thus for some "beach" may mean the utmost in pleasurable experiences—a summer of rest, social contacts, glorious play of clouds in the setting sun or early sunrise; for others, perhaps a near-drowning or an unfortunate love affair. Likewise for some the alphabet and numerals may be associated with early pleasurable acquisition of knowledge, and for others with the first painful and inept stumbling steps to learning.

Learning Disabilities
>   I. Organic
>   1. Congenital Defects
>   2. Acquired Defects
>   II. Psychosomatic
> III. Affect or Functional Psychic Disabilities
>   1. Neuroses
>   2. Psychoses

When one attempts to analyze the difficulties of learning one must bear in mind that constitutional defects play a significant role. Nature's response to a defect is threefold: (1) an acceptance of that defect with a hypertrophy of other sense activities; (2) a flight from defect, so that the loss of function is greater than the actual defect present; (3) an over-compensating functioning of the defective sense organ. The first makes the best of the defect and functions with satisfaction, although within restricted limits. In the second instance, such as a person with a visual defect, he will utilize the eye very little because of a sense of anxiety at the partial impairment of that organ. Under these circumstances other sensory organs, such as the ear, may take over increased activity, and the defect in one organ may be compensated for by another one. In the third category the individual regards the handicap as an incentive to extra activity. A rather bizarre end result occurs when that visual activity becomes more pronounced than one would expect as possible from the amount of defect present.

Learning disabilities may be divided into three types: (1) Those which can be helped through simple pedagogic techniques. (2) Those which will not respond to the classical pedagogic methods, but which, because the disability is a single manifestation of a complex maladjustment, require psychiatric therapy. (3) There is a third category in which, when the psychiatric aspects of the problem have been alleviated, the patient is ready for pedagogy. This actually is the essence of a rehabilitation program, and in order for it to be successful, the timing for the utilization of these various fields is to be carefully considered and directed.

Many of the learning blocks fall into (1) psychosomatic disturbances, and (2) affect disturbances which lead to and are part of a functional psychic disability. Under the heading of organic learning defects we have the obvious congenital or acquired organic dysfunctions due to somatic pathology. This may involve any of the five senses and locomotion, and it is in this area, when diagnosed, that the current remedial techniques are most applicable. Contrary to the general impression, the percentage of this type of student is comparatively small. The abnormal birth category—moron, idiot and imbecile—requires special educational emphasis upon manual activities such as are available in the crafts and certain crude art forms.

There is a predominating group, however, which is best diagnosed by the projective testing. This group falls into the field of psychiatry, because it is interrelated with the traumata which have interfered with emotional development and have drained off energies from the growth process into all forms of disturbances of a neurotic and at times psychotic nature. For their detection and evaluation some form of the Rorschach test is essential and helpful.

Each organic defect, if it is of a minor nature, creates for the organism a challenge to sublimation. Should the organism be suffused with anxiety, it can and often does negate the function of that sense so that we have a defect which simulates organic disturbance and yet actually is psychic in its origin. This psychic component may center around past experiences with adults or with siblings which now have their counterpart in the classroom. In this category we sometimes see good results not based on any special pedagogic technique but because of the transference or interpersonal relationships which exists between the tutor and the retarded student. As yet it is primarily a matter of experimentation as to whether a male or female tutor will be able to function best in this role, unless we go intensively into the life history of the student and his parental relationships. For some, the isolated "only child" role which is played in the tutor-to-student relationship is effective because it eliminates the competitive sibling images with which such children have to cope. In our educational system there are countless cases where there is an apparent obstruction to learning in a specific subject and where the family background is such that there is a healthy and happy relationship, with no particular difficulty in the resolution of the oedipus complex. Cases of this sort often respond to the technical skill of an understanding educator. Yet one is impressed with a specificity in subject skill which is quite individual. Why are certain individuals utterly inept in the sciences and others uninterested in the arts? Why are these incompatible in many normal (sic) individuals? Some are language inhibited and there are others to whom linguistics come easily. These are challenging areas for research.

THERAPY

Therapy seems a formidable term to use for a subject which primarily has been considered in the realm of pedagogy. However, when we come to those individuals who have developed psychiatric problems as we see them in the neuroses and the psychoses in all of their variations, the learning situation is beyond the scope of the usual pedagogic techniques and becomes a matter of psychiatric and pedagogic teamwork. We must bear in mind, too, that very frequently, learning which is implemented by neurotic and psychotic patterns may be deceptively successful in the classroom and at times lead to brilliant scholarship. But there are other manifestations of libidinal distortions which lead to ultimate dissolution of the learning process.

The role of the analyst through the transference neurosis not only recapitulates the oedipal shortcomings but indirectly, and at times directly, touches upon the whole learning trend. With the release of pathological libidinal fixations, energy is released, and again becomes free flowing, and searches out new activities. We then observe pedagogically significant and at times dramatic interests in new fields, and by the alleviation of repressive activities based upon anxiety, a revival of old interests in a much more functional and creative fashion. There are very few of our patients who do not, during the course of successful psychoanalytic therapy, widen their interest in the arts, or further their intellectual curiosity and exploration.

The paramount consideration in evaluating any learning situation is the allotment of suitable roles to the physician, the pedagogue and the psychiatrist. No investigation should be undertaken unless a complete physical examination has been performed, for the vagaries of infections are such that at times only with difficulty can central nervous system pathology be determined. With the assurance that the organic aspect of our problem has been properly evaluated, we are faced with a major decision as to the timing of the contributions of psychiatrist and educator. Where there is evidence that adequate pedagogic approach has been unsuccessful, it becomes the function of the psychiatrist to take over. When certain aspects of repression have been lifted, and the patient becomes more amenable to learning through a release of tensions and anxiety, the inherent desire of the organism to grow can be utilized. This, of course, is dependent upon the insight of the patient and his awereness of the elements which have unfortunately blocked his intellectual efforts. Tutoring then becomes advisable to aid reviving interests which have been encapsulated. The personality of the educator is here of great significance and the psychiatrist can give wholesome and helpful recommendations in the choice of the educator. This implies educators who are psychologically oriented, and sensitized not only to techniques but to interpersonal dynamics.

The experience which has been gained with individuals in psychotherapy carries over into the whole field of rehabilitation. Convalescence requires specialized education in which not alone individuals but groups should be exposed to a program that co-ordinates the contributions of medicine and education. The therapy of the sick and convalescent, whether the illness is organic or functional, physical or psychic, will draw upon the contributions of all disciplines. It will be an educational program, no longer limited to academic halls, and it will call upon the best in medicine, education and the knowledge gained through the techniques applied in psychodynamic therapy.

GENETIC PROBLEMS

COMMENTS ON THE METAPSYCHOLOGY
OF SOMATIZATION[1]

MAX SCHUR, M.D. (New York)[2]

A Sample Case

In 1946, while I was engaged in a pilot study which attempted to investigate various dermatological entities by analysis of representative cases, a twenty-two-year-old female in her fifth month of pregnancy was admitted to the skin ward of Bellevue Hospital with the diagnosis of a generalized atopic eczema. Her extremities and her face were affected most, but hardly any part of her body was free of lesions. There was extensive lichenification and secondary infection. Her skin was so thick that it was difficult to find a vein for a blood test. She suffered from intolerable itch, culminating in attacks which mostly occurred at 8 or 11 P.M. and were accompanied by extreme anxiety. Only very high doses of chloral hydrate brought some relief. She was not aware of cases of dermatoses or of any manifestation of the allergic state in her family. She did not know exactly when her skin lesions started but remembered being treated for them at the age of six. During her analysis it became apparent that she had had the first skin eruption at the age of one and had started with typical lesions in the cubita and poplitea at the age of three. At nine the lesions appeared on her face. The first generalized outbreak occurred when she was fourteen and a half years old. Since then she had spent a good part of her life in various hospitals.

During the initial trial period it seemed rather doubtful whether this case could be approached analytically. It was extremely difficult to get this patient to talk. She spoke in very primitive short sentences, with a peculiarly harsh voice. It sounded a little bit like barking. She was extremely distrustful. Her intelligence seemed limited, her educational level was quite low. It soon became evident that she was putting up the strongest possible defense against any positive transference. She was unable to follow the basic rule.

The present severe exacerbation of her disease had coincided with her marriage. She had been working in a war plant where she met her husband. After prolonged dating with sporadic sex play—which she abhorred—she gave in and had intercourse. She experienced no satisfaction; on the contrary, she

[1] As exemplified by analyses of skin disorders.
[2] From the Psychoanalytic Institute of the New York State University.

soon developed attacks of itching each time she saw him. Yet she married him hoping that in the course of married life her condition might improve. Instead she got worse. Her husband worked late hours. Toward the evening she would become restless, get eruptions and/or attacks of itching. Frequently she would refuse intercourse. She developed obsessive thoughts that she might kill her husband by stabbing him. This made her feel guilty, "because he was so decent to me." Soon she had to be hospitalized for several weeks because her skin was so bad. After she came home, she thought that she might improve by having a baby. She became pregnant. It was then that her attacks rose to the present intensity.

Why was she so afraid of her husband? Dreams and slips of the tongue pointed toward her father. After many weeks of analysis the following story began to emerge: she was the third of five siblings, the only girl. The younger brothers were born when she was three and five and a half years old respectively. Her father was an alcoholic, frequently unemployed, the family often on relief. When he received his pay—or relief check—he brought home liquor, got drunk, and raped the girl. She placed the first of his attempts to the age of six. During her analysis she realized that it started earlier, when she was five—most probably he began to masturbate her when she was three. These practices started during the pregnancies of his wife. Although he threatened that he would kill her and her mother if she would tell, the child asked her mother for help. Her mother refused, because "it might bring disgrace upon the family and could spoil the future of all the boys." It soon became apparent that she hated her mother even more intensely than her father. When the mother went out to see friends in the evening, the little girl implored her to stay home but to no avail. Then she knew it would happen again. She would lie in her bed trembling while the father started to drink. When she was about eleven he started to penetrate her. Only after she started menstruating at thirteen her father discontinued his attempts.

The possibility of hysterical fantasies had to be considered. However, during her analysis the patient discussed the matter with her mother, who repeated her previous excuses, thereby confirming the truth of the story.

The father also used to beat her and the boys. He would, for instance, accuse one of the boys of stealing and would beat him mercilessly until the boy confessed. The girl he accused of sex play with her oldest brother, and tried to make her confess. He was furious that she never would confess to anything she had not done. In her analysis she reacted for years to the basic rule and interpretation of unconscious material with the same resentment and anxiety she had experienced then. It was the father all over again demanding her confession. After her mother refused help, she never confided in anybody. Being a Catholic, she went to confession at intervals, but had never come out with this story. Yet she was afraid "that people might know." Her face would often break out before she went to church, where she fainted repeatedly. She was constantly preoccupied with the wish to kill her father, specifically by stabbing him with a dagger. In her analysis she brought frequent dreams with such content. When she was fourteen, her father had a stroke with a right hemiplegia and died after a short illness. She could not attend the funeral because she became acutely ill. She had fever, severe headache, and suffered from a prolonged weakness of her right hand. Later while walking on the street she frequently had the sudden feeling that her father was still alive, and she would expect him to turn up around the corner, or wait for her at home. She deeply resented that he had died a natural death, before she had grown big and strong enough to kill him.

In the years after her father's death her skin grew steadily worse, and in addition she also developed the following symptoms: she would suddenly fall asleep wherever she went, at school, even on the street. Most probably she was suffering from narcolepsy, a symptom which disappeared when she was about seventeen. She also had prolonged periods of amenorrhea during which she would gain considerable weight.

She described herself as a tomboy during her childhood, playing mostly with her brothers and their gang. She was aware of her resentment that she was not a boy, a resentment which had the usual unconscious background. In school she was below average, partly due to the frequent hospitalizations. In her adolescence she withdrew from the plays with boys. She became increasingly shy. She masturbated only once with a fantasy of the practices of her father and her wish to kill him—an obvious wish to assume the role of the male aggressor—and was so horrified of her orgasm that she never dared to try it again. At sixteen she once had intercourse with a farm boy in a haystack—she called it being raped. There was hardly any dating. When she was seventeen her mother remarried. She was deeply unhappy. On her nineteenth birthday, nobody gave her a present. In the evening her mother went out with her stepfather and left her and the younger brothers without any dinner and hardly any food in the icebox. She went out, swallowed a bottle of tincture of iodine and was brought to Bellevue. Some time after this episode she started to work in a factory and felt for the first time somewhat sheltered and accepted. There she met her present husband. To have intercourse and to attempt a more positive object relationship proved too much of a strain and precipitated the crisis.

The analysis of this patient lasted about four years. One of the two main difficulties was the handling of her transference neurosis. Any upsurge of positive transference feeling with sexual connotation created overwhelming anxiety and violent hostility—manifestly often directed against her husband or her son. Any negative transference created fear of punishment, specifically abandonment. The reactions to these conflicts merged with the second difficulty: the role of her skin during her analysis, especially in her acting out. In my discussion of this focal point I shall also include material obtained from other cases.

We have here to consider the following skin phenomena: (1) itching; (2) scratching (and other manipulations occurring in other dermatoses); (3) eruptions of new lesions; (4) secondary elaboration of the skin lesions.[3]

Itching may be experienced as a *concomitant* or an *equivalent* of a variety of affects. The distinction between the terms "concomitant" and "equivalent" demands a rather lengthy detour.

RESOMATIZATION OF ANXIETY RESPONSES

The affect first to consider is anxiety. The best and simplest over-all definition of anxiety is still that given by Freud in *Inhibitions, Symptoms and Anxiety* (1926): "Anxiety is reaction to danger." Let us add here: to danger, *present or anticipated*. In Freud's definition danger implies the anticipation of a potentially "traumatic situation," a situation in which the reacting individual experiences utter helplessness. Freud, with certain reservations, attributed this response to danger to the ego, and we have learned to consider this reaction as an essential ego function. In my study on the "Ego in Anxiety" (1953) I tried to correlate complementary series of anxiety responses to the state of the ego.

As any other ego function, reaction to danger is both the result of a complex development and *subject to regressive phenomena*. The application of the genetic principle to anxiety as an ego response implies the recognition of its phylogenetic origin in a biological response, of its genetic link with the reflexes of animals, and of its innate character in the newborn. That is to say that this specific function, as well as other functions of the ego, has its autonomous roots (Hartmann, 1939, 1950).

In the infant, precursors of the anxiety reactions show among others the following characteristics: a tendency to diffuse discharge phenomena and a lack of co-ordination in motor response. While the reactions of the infant occur mainly in response to a disturbance of homeostasis, the reaction to this disturbance may in turn create an even more profound disturbance of this very equilibrium (Stern, 1951).

From this undifferentiated state maturation proceeds in several directions. One, for example, is the development of co-ordinated muscle function. Another is the maturation of the mental apparatus. There is a parallel of development, and mutual interdependence, between the maturation of the central nervous system and of the motor apparatus, the stabilization of homeostatic processes, and the emergence of secondary thought processes as an essential part of ego formation. All this results

---

[3] There is, of course, a considerable overlapping of the material discussed under these subheadings.

in an increasing desomatization of reactions to certain excitations. The development tends toward maximal use of integrated automatization of muscle action, toward replacement of action by thought and reduction of vegetative discharge phenomena. In the adult the ego's reaction to danger actually consists of several components which occur more or less simultaneously, and can be separated only by subjecting them to analysis.

One of the ego functions crucial to reaction to danger is reality testing. The perception and the evaluation of the situation enables the ego to differentiate between potential or present danger. Simultaneously, the ego experiences a reaction to this evaluation. In situations of only potential danger the ego experience of the normal adult is restricted to a certain awareness of danger. This experience is genetically linked with the affect anxiety, but has assumed the characteristics of a thought process and therefore stimulates "problem solving" (Kris, 1949). It shares with the anxiety reaction its relation to danger, with a thought process the potentiality to remain in the unconscious and the absence of obvious discharge phenomena.[4]

We may add here the following hypothesis which follows closely Kris's (1949) reasoning expounded by him in a different context. Discussing Freud's introduction to Varendonck's work (1921), specifically Freud's suggested distinction between freely wandering fantastic thinking[5] in contrast to intentionally directed reflection, Kris states (p. 311): "The ego we[6] assume, has two kinds of bound energy at its disposal, neutralized energy, and libido and aggression in their not neutralized form. Fantastic, free wandering thought-processes tend to discharge more libido and aggression and less neutralized energy, . . . reflective thinking in the sense of Freud, problem solving as we would prefer to say, serves to a higher degree the autonomous ego interest. Discharge of libido and aggression is therefore likely to be minimized and that of neutralized ego-energy to be of greater relevance." In his comment to this passage Rapaport (1951b, p. 487) states that "corresponding to the degree of neutralization of cathexes are the degrees to which thought is organized according to the primary or secondary process; the transition between these forms of thought-organization is fluid." We may add here that the degrees of neutralization are equally fluid. The ability of the

4 "Awareness of danger" as a form of ego experience corresponds, as will be seen, to Freud's "signal anxiety" (1926) and also to Fenichel's "tamed anxiety" (1945a) and Rapaport's "structuralized anxiety" (1953).

5 Rapaport's (1951b) translation of Varendonck's paper uses the term "fantasy-thinking" which reflects the meaning more adequately.

6 Hartmann, Kris, and Loewenstein (1949).

ego to neutralize energy and to use such neutralized energy in its responses constitutes another achievement of maturation.

My hypothesis assumes the interdependence of the ego's faculty to use secondary processes and to neutralize energy, and the desomatization of responses. It assumes, on the other hand, that resomatization of responses is tied up with prevalence of primary process thinking and the use of deneutralized energy.

In the anxiety reaction the ego operates with energies it has at its disposal, which may be libido and/or aggression in various degrees of fusion, or neutralized energy in various phases of neutralization. In the example of the ego's response to anticipated danger this whole response has become thoughtlike. *My hypothesis would assume that throughout this response the ego operates with secondary processes, uses thoroughly neutralized energy, and that these facts explain that somatic discharge phenomena are practically absent.* This ego response applies best to the response of a "normal" ego or of the "conflict-free" part of the ego (Hartmann, 1939) to the anticipation of external danger.

As the next step let us investigate the ego's response to instinctual demand. The demand may reach the systems Pcs. and Cs. more or less unaltered. The ego again applies reality testing—including the testing of superego reactions—and either allows or refuses access to the motor apparatus and/or to discharge. Based on the evaluation of the situation the ego may treat this demand as potential danger, and, to use an anthropomorphic image, behave throughout as it normally does toward potential *external* danger: i.e., operate with neutralized energy.

The constellation changes with the upsurge of an *unconscious* incestual demand or its derivatives. Again the ego has to evaluate the situation. We know that the ego automatically treats such demands as dangerous (we speak here of people whose conflicts in such areas have not been resolved by analysis). Yet when we scrutinize the ego's functions in this situation, we meet with a basic difference: in the evaluation of *this* instinctual danger the ego loses its ability of reality testing. The demand may have represented danger decades ago. But differentiation between past and present has disappeared. This part of the ego now operates on the level of primary processes. We here recognize the phenomenon we are used to call regression which can be expressed and studied in structural, topical and, as will be seen, also in psysiological terms. The ego responds to this—regressive—evaluation of inner danger with certain measures to avoid or eliminate the danger, e.g., it establishes or reinforces defenses.

On closer analysis, however, we distinguish a twofold aim of the ego:

the obvious one is the elimination of danger. The second aim is the following: it is useful for the ego's economy if the whole response is kept on the level of thinking which, according to Freud's formulations in this context, is "an experimental dealing with small quantities of energy" (Freud, 1932). It tries even in the sphere of defenses to utilize secondary thought processes, e.g., by treating the instinctual demands as external danger and by using such mechanisms as rationalization or intellectualization (A. Freud, 1936). If successful, the ego experience may, even throughout *this* situation, be limited to an awareness of danger; it may still operate with prevalently neutralized energy. Accordingly, discharge phenomena and resomatization of responses may be absent. To summarize, the ego succeeds in avoiding a regressive reaction to a regressive evaluation of danger. This constellation corresponds to what Freud has described as signal anxiety.

Let us now proceed with the discussion of other anxiety situations and start again with what may be called "normal reaction" in a situation not of potential but of present danger. The ego responds first with a quick appraisal of the situation and an optimal mustering of all its resources (Freud's "protective action," 1917). In such a situation the ego experiences a different shade of anxiety which can be designated as fright, and we may assume that it utilizes nonneutralized energy—probably predominantly aggressive energy.[7] We can accordingly register somatic discharge phenomena. If the situation becomes traumatic, the experience of the ego can reach the state of panic with an abundance of somatic phenomena up to shock. The ego will then operate exclusively with nonneutralized energy. It may be of interest to note that in the state of panic the ego may also operate with nonneutralized libido, and we may encounter such discharge phenomena as orgasm.

The ego function may deviate from the normal in the direction of the neurotic response by regressive evaluation of danger and by regressive reaction. Instinctual demands may become danger, and a potential danger situation may be evaluated as present danger or even as a traumatic situation. The reaction in such situations may also undergo far-reaching regression. If we take as a model the example of the hungry infant missing the breast (Freud, 1926; Rapaport, 1951a), we may say that in the hierarchy of situations absence of the mother threatens hunger, and thus represents danger of danger, i.e., potential danger, while actual

[7] The ego may use and utilize aggressive energy in anxiety, as in any other response. This does not imply that anxiety or any other ego response utilizing aggressive energy is "aggression prevented from discharge," a theory proposed by Flescher (1955) who especially emphasizes the economic factors in anxiety.

hunger represents threat of a traumatic situation. Yet the infant may react to the potential danger of absence of the mother as if it represented actual danger or even a traumatic situation. The same takes place in the neurotic evaluation of danger. In these situations we can also see the re-emergence of infantile types of diffuse discharge phenomena. The long and painful path of maturation may be reversed in an instant. The ego loses the capacity of secondary process thinking. It uses unneutralized energy and desomatization fails. This type of regression we may call physiological regression (Margolin, 1953; Schur, 1953).[8]

My hypothesis links resomatization to the prevalence of primary processes and the simultaneous failure of neutralization. Within this framework the faculty for neutralization can be seen as an important factor in the avoidance of responses which would not only endanger the autonomous functions of the ego but could be injurious to the whole self. We may also assume that, in analogy to other ego functions, the function of neutralization must have its precursors in the undifferentiated "psychosomatic" phase of development.

It is tempting to conjecture that the re-establishment of homeostasis through automatic regulations and/or external need satisfaction may constitute the model for what later is to develop into the ego function: neutralization (see also Menninger, 1954). Neutralization would then represent one of the first barriers against physiological stress (Selye, 1950).

The importance of these considerations for the entire area of psychosomatic manifestations is obvious. If neutralization follows the model of homeostatic regulations, we may expect in children with innate or early acquired abnormalities of homeostatic mechanisms inhibitions of the development of the ego function of neutralization. This assumption seems to be confirmed by the observations of Bender (1950) and Greenacre (1952), who found that such children are predisposed for severe pathology.

While physiological regression is always linked to prevalence of primary process thinking and failure of neutralization, the loss of these ego functions will not always result in physiological regression. Physiological regression and its phenomena depend on innate and environmental factors which together determine the constellation of id and ego development, the predisposition to anxiety or rather to regressive types of anxiety (Greenacre, 1952; Bergman and Escalona, 1949), and the choice

8 In Jacobson's (1954b) terminology this regression results in a return to "centripetal" discharge processes.

of the reacting organ system. All these factors can be summarized as the total condition of an individual (Schur, 1950a).[9]

The individual reaction will be determined also by the following factor: While the ego can tolerate a selected, controlled regression (Kris, 1949) or even seek and enjoy it—as, e.g., in orgasm—the regressive reaction in anxiety is treated by the rest of the ego as danger per se. Close analysis will show that in most constellations of anxiety the ego, respectively its not yet submerged part, desperately tries to re-establish the equilibrium, to restore secondary thought processes, and to resume operating with neutralized energy. This results in what may be called *controlled anxiety* in contrast to a situation of complete regression in which the attempt at restoration has been abandoned or was unsuccessful—a situation of *uncontrolled anxiety*. Between these extremes we are dealing with a complementary series of responses. In controlled versus uncontrolled anxiety we may expect reactions differing not only in quantity but also in quality, with the differences extending to the somatic discharge phenomena.[10]

Finally in the following, a special constellation of regression is described: in all previous examples the subject consciously experiences various shades of anxiety, although the actual content of danger might be hidden or utterly disguised, especially in neurotic anxiety. Occasionally, however, we encounter somatic discharge phenomena which we have seen in the same subject as concomitants of various shades of anxiety reactions, but without his conscious awareness of danger or his experiencing of anxiety. Careful analysis may show that in such situations the regression carried to a preverbal, pre-ego stage of development where reaction to stimuli is in the closest sense psychosomatic (see also Jacobson, 1954b), and where the conscious experience is limited to the awareness of the discharge phenomena which genetically have been present before the emergence of the affect "anxiety." Here we may speak of anxiety equivalents.

After this lengthy detour into the theory of anxiety we may return to our patient. I mentioned that itching occurred very frequently as a concomitant of anxiety.[11] Invariably, however, it turned out to be an

[9] Grinker (1953) seeks a clarification of this multiplicity of contributing factors in the usage of the "field" concept.

[10] For clinical examples see "The Ego in Anxiety" (Schur, 1953, p. 30).

[11] If I discuss separately itching as concomitant or equivalent of anxiety, of hostile affects (anger, rage), of libidinous impulses, etc., I am of course fully aware of the overlapping. The separate discussion is nevertheless necessitated by expediency of presentation.

anxiety situation the analysis of which disclosed various degrees of ego regression. Itching did not occur in situations of actual danger unless analysis could reveal links of such situations with unconscious sources of danger. On the other hand, it was characteristic of this, as it is of many other dermatoses patients, that many facets of their daily lives constitute danger. Some of them have outright phobias, most of them show phobic mechanisms. Frequently, as is to be expected, analysis reveals multiple determination of the anxiety.

A few concrete examples: our patient—as many other patients with itching dermatoses—would itch most after going to bed. One explanation given by patients and dermatologists is the change of temperature. However, our patient —again like many others—would start itching when she no more than considered that it was time to go to sleep. The conscious content was: she would again have a sleepless night, she would scratch and make her skin get worse. After having developed a positive transference toward her analyst, she would think of me and of the sessions—for magic protection. This soon changed into a compulsion to repeat my first name which in turn was tied up with unconscious sexual fantasies and with her incestuous relationship to her father. That is, evening was the time when her father used to rape her, or when he used to come home. Falling asleep then also meant losing control, and on the deepest level it also signified fear of oral incorporation.

, Another situation which precipitated itching was an impending visit to her mother. The upsurge of her hostile impulses brought deep anxiety.[12] The anxiety attacks with violent itching before intercourse which brought her to the hospital have already been described. In all these situations the patient was aware of a certain degree of anxiety. Yet on many occasions, and this occurred much more frequently during her first years of analysis, she also started to itch without any conscious affect. Only after progress in the analysis was it possible to assume here an ego regression to a preverbal level as described in the theoretical discussion. Then, when the patient would wake up itching, it became possible first to guess and then to confirm that such itching was linked with a forgotten dream. In such a constellation the itching was an *anxiety equivalent*.

All these reactions had one factor in common: physiological regression. The ego regression was not limited to a regressive evaluation of danger. In its response the ego operated with deneutralized energy and this corresponded to the re-emergence of somatic discharge phenomena. In the specific constellation of an itching skin disorder this meant the discharge of some unknown substance causing itching. In this case itching occurred in situations of all shades of affects between controlled and

12 An example of overlapping of anxiety and aggressive affects.

uncontrolled anxiety, while in other cases itching occurred in phobic situations where control was at least attempted. The latter cases showed different discharge phenomena in situations of uncontrolled anxiety (Schur, 1953).

Since such patients live surrounded by danger, they develop an attitude of vigilance (Liddell, 1949). They live in constant readiness for anxiety (Freud's [1918] *Angstbereitschaft*; Kubie's [1941] "free-floating anxiety"). This defensive ego attitude is probably the basis of what is commonly called tension and may *also* have its somatic manifestations. Here too the ego may use aggressive energy. In cases of dermatoses, the somatic discharge phenomena of this state may also result in itching.

Somatization and Aggression

Itching also appears with hostile affects. What has been said about anxiety is to a great extent true of hostile affects as well. Hartmann, Kris, and Loewenstein (1949) discussed the aspect of neutralization mainly in connection with aggressive energy. Whenever anger and rage emerge, we assume a certain change in ego control. *This explains the use of less neutralized or nonneutralized energy in these reactions and, in accordance with my hypothesis, also the fact that anger and rage have somatic discharge phenomena.*

The concept of controlled and uncontrolled anxiety has its parallel in the concept of controlled and uncontrolled aggression (Menninger, 1954). In analogy to anxiety, the endless variety of responses in aggression can be understood only in terms of a complementary series. There is a certain parallel between the degree of control, the state of neutralization, and the emergence of somatic discharge phenomena. Here the ego plays the pivotal role. The more the ego operates with secondary processes, the more "adequate" will its response be, which in the main implies that it will be restricted to the present precipitating cause. The more the ego is under the sway of primary processes, the more will its response be influenced by a whole gamut of associative links between the precipitating factor and a multitude of events of the individual's history.

The somatic manifestations of aggression must—in analogy to the anxiety response—depend on the total condition of the individual, comprising at any given moment the sum total of all innate and environmental factors in their intricate interdependency.[13] We may also assume

[13] This may be expressed—to no apparent advantage—in terms of the "total field" (Grinker, 1953).

(again in analogy to anxiety) that the somatic manifestations of these manifold shades of aggression will differ not only in quantity but also in quality.

To complicate matters further: any change in the level of aggression, whether in its quantity or in the state of neutralization or in both, may be, and most frequently is, interpreted by the ego as danger. The content of this danger may be punishment from the outside and/or disapproval of the superego. While the ego reacts to this danger with some shade of anxiety, anxiety may on the other hand bring an upsurge of aggressive impulses.

Even under the spotlight of the analytic situation it is frequently very difficult to determine which affect dominates a specific situation. It is still more difficult to decide whether a specific discharge phenomenon should be attributed mainly to one of the two affects.

Once increased and/or deneutralized aggression has been recognized by the ego as danger, the defensive attitude described above as vigilance may be applied, specifically against an upsurge of aggression. This may result in a special type of tension.

CRITICAL EVALUATION OF THE CONCEPT "REPRESSED HOSTILITY"

Only when we consider all these factors, can we arrive at a physio-pathology of affects and defenses, and can we also understand the degree of oversimplification with which results of animal physiology—particularly Cannon's work—were applied to the formulation of hypotheses in "psychosomatic" research. Cannon (1920) himself mainly established the manner in which the "great" emotions—meaning emotions of a considerable intensity—resulted in a stimulation of the autonomic nervous system. He not only recognized that members of different species, e.g., dogs, show quite different reactions than cats, which he most frequently used for his experiments, but he found considerable variations within the same species. Yet the hypothesis of the role of aggression in human physiology was mainly based on the responses of Cannon's cats, or more specifically on the reactions of his belligerent and ferocious and not of his milder and more domesticated specimens. Thus it has been assumed that if aggression results in a stimulation of the sympathetic division of the autonomic system, "repressed hostility" must result in a "damming up" of aggression and thereby in a "chronic stimulation" of the sympathetic nervous system. "Repressed hostility" then became a catchword to explain a host of somatic manifestations (Alexander, 1950; Binger et al., 1945; Saul, 1939, 1941; and others).

Historically these concepts have their roots in the decisive importance ascribed to the "damming up" of libido as one of the main causes of psychoneuroses, a concept which had dominated Freud's early writings and which had gradually been reduced to its proper place in the whole framework of causative factors.

Alexander and his coworkers elaborated on Cannon's concepts in the following way: They divided the emotional disturbances of vegetative functions into two main categories, corresponding to two *basic emotional attitudes*:[14] preparation for fight or flight, and withdrawal from outwardly directed activity. Inhibition or repression of self-assertive, hostile impulses result, according to Alexander, in a constant state of preparedness with a sustained sympathetic excitation, persisting in the absence of what he calls the consummation of the fight or flight reaction. While the patient suffering from essential hypertension is supposed to exemplify this state of affairs, similar mechanisms were claimed for such diverse entities as rheumatoid arthritis, migraine, urticaria, etc. On the other hand, retreat from a situation to an increased dependency with an increased but repressed need for gratification of help-seeking tendencies is supposed to result in a chronic excitation of the parasympathetic nervous system—with peptic ulcer as a possible outcome.

This is not the place to discuss the many pitfalls of these concepts, from a physiological point of view.[15] It should only be pointed out that any attempt to apply results obtained from animal experimentation in the field of emotions to human physiopathology is doomed to failure, unless it considers all the intricacies of ego function. It is the ego which distinguishes men from animals, and which accounts for the endless variety of our mental processes. While even animal experimentation can distinguish between shades of affects, varied not only in quantity but also in quality (see, e.g., Mahl, 1950), human experiments dealing with anxiety and aggression must apply the concepts of controlled and uncontrolled anxiety and controlled and uncontrolled aggression.

While analytic concepts may thus doubtlessly guide the proper experimental approach, let us examine whether analytic considerations also can contribute *directly* toward the understanding of the somatic manifestations of aggression.

The proponents of the concept of the importance of "repressed hostility"—with Alexander as the main representative—stress in the first place the inhibition and repression of self-assertive tendencies. There-

14 Italics mine.
15 Especially as far as such concepts have been applied to essential hypertension.

fore, to quote Alexander (1950), "frequently the mean blood pressure of the patient becomes substantially reduced after psychoanalytic therapy has succeeded in making him more self-assertive, and such a patient may even become a problem to his environment" (p. 153).

Without discussing here the scientific validity of such therapeutic claims, let us ask: What are the sources of this aggression, as expressed in topical and structural terms? Is it rooted in pregenital or oedipal conflicts? What is the role of the ego? Does it imply a failure of ego control, and what ego functions are involved? Or do we deal here with different *quantities* of aggression?

Let us return to our sample patient to look for possible answers. As mentioned before, itching appeared also as a concomitant of hostile affects and our patient was full of hatred directed consciously against most members of her immediate environment. Neither did she fail to express it. She nagged her husband whom she had completely under her thumb, she quarreled with her mother-in-law, shouted at her little boy and spanked him. If *expression* of hostility and "self-assertiveness" had a cathartic effect and could have released the tension of the "dammed-up" aggression, the patient would not have had somatic manifestations of aggression. Yet during the first years of analysis she reacted with severe itching and/or new eruptions to any upsurge of aggression and in addition was quite a problem to her environment. On the other hand, toward the end of her analysis, she was still occasionally quite angry, no less assertive, but less vocal, more controlled, was *no* problem to her environment, and did not react to her aggression with itching and/or eruptions.

What had changed in the sphere of her aggression? Let us examine her hostility, as directed against her husband, her son, her mother-in-law, and her analyst. We have mentioned her obsessive thoughts of killing her husband which used to increase especially during and after intercourse. In this situation her husband represented her violent, raping father. She also tried to interfere with her husband's relationship with his mother and his siblings. Here he represented her older brothers. She had little patience with her little boy and she could not control her outbursts of anger. Her son represented to her at the same time the incestuous fantasy-child sired by her father, and her younger brothers who had been the objects of violent sibling envy. Her mother-in-law represented her own mother the hatred of whom had dominated every phase of her development. The analyst represented in the transference situation mainly her father, but as long as her skin was unimproved—and this lasted well over three years—he also represented her mother. He failed to cure and protect her—as had her mother. While only aggression against her boy and her analyst were accompanied by guilt feelings, *any* upsurge of aggression increased her skin symptoms.

All these situations have one thing in common: In their evaluation the patient's ego operated on the level of the primary process, thus establishing associative links with infantile material. The patient could therefore not restrict her response to the present precipitating factor but responded to *all* the factors connected by an associative pathway. The reaction could not be adequate, it had to be exaggerated in quantity and sustained for a longer time span.

Hence we may conclude that the emergence of somatic phenomena is linked to ego function. Ego regression, specifically prevalence of primary processes, may result in the failure of another essential function of the ego: the faculty to neutralize aggression. There seems to be a parallel between the prevalence of primary process thinking, the failure of neutralization, and the resomatization of reactions.

The link from the present precipitating cause to the infantile sources of aggression makes the proper "discharge" of this aggression as futile as would be the immediate discharge of any pregenital, e.g., anal-libidinous drive. As long as our patient's aggression was actually directed against the objects of her infancy, she could not discharge her aggression by behaving aggressively. She could not devour her mother-in-law, stab her husband, or castrate her little boy. Thus an element of frustration entered the economic situation. The economic equilibrium in the sphere of aggression is put to additional strain due to the narcissistic regression which follows the somatic symptoms. The narcissistic equilibrium of these patients is extremely unstable. They are as vulnerable as is their skin. Anything which upsets this equilibrium also produces an immediate upsurge of aggression which in turn cannot be neutralized. For *all* these reasons her aggression was accompanied by somatic symptoms. When analysis helped her to solve her unconscious conflicts and restored her essential ego functions, she could respond to the precipitating situation on the level of the secondary process. Her husband was her husband, her son was her son. She was able to shout and scold—and did not have to itch.[16]

The impact of aggression on somatic phenomena can thus be studied analytically on the basis of what Hartmann (1953) calls the "broadened economic approach."

The recognition of the role of neutralization and other ego functions in the economics of aggression raises the question whether the conceptual model of dammed-up tension, borrowed from hydrodynamics, should not

[16] What has been said about our sample case also applies to the other patients with dermatoses on which this study is based. But while this paper is concerned with dermatoses, these concepts apply to all "psychosomatic" disorders.

be replaced. Menninger (1954) suggested the concept of the homeostatic function of the ego. We may use a more specific physiological model and speak of the role of the ego as an organ of adaptation in the sense of Selye, or we may borrow a more up-to-date model from physics, and compare the explosive release of energy after failure of certain ego functions to the results of nuclear fission.

The idea that freely expressed aggression may be desired from a therapeutic point of view is reminiscent of the misinterpretation of analytic principles in certain phases of so-called modern education, when parents used to get the good news from teachers how wonderfully aggressive their offspring was.[17] Actually successful analysis should gradually restore the ego's defective capacity to deal with aggression.

Somatization and Sexuality

Can itching also be the concomitant or equivalent of libidinous impulses? Let us go back to our patient: were the itching attacks she experienced when she considered intercourse with her husband, or when she compulsively repeated the analyst's name, a discharge phenomenon of anxiety or of libido? Unfortunately, we know very little about the true nature of sexual impulses. It might be useful here to quote Fenichel (1945a):

> Chemical changes in the body initiate sensory stimuli in the erogenous zones, bringing forth impulses of a particularly urgent character, demanding actions that lead to changes at the place of stimulation. The physiological basis of sexual impulses is comparable to the physiological occurrences that arouse sensations such as itching or tickling. Insect bites or internal physiological conditions produce chemical changes causing sensory stimuli in the skin, which in turn, create feelings of an especially urgent kind; the impulse to scratch is aroused and scratching finally leads to a change at the source. However, although scratching may be effective through changing the blood supply to the itching area, one gets the impression that scratching represents a remainder of a much deeper biological reflex which is also of basic importance for sexual discharges: the reflex to get rid of organs that create disturbing sensations... An evaluation of the concept of autotomy

---

[17] I am presently treating a patient suffering from, besides his "character neurosis," essential hypertension, spondylarthritis *and* peptic ulcer (with utter disregard of the rules of "specificity"!). He had previously been encouraged to "release his repressed hostility." Fortunately for the patient, he still tried to "suppress" his hostility in his professional life, but let it flow freely in his home. When I tried to analyze the reasons for this behavior, especially toward his wife, he was utterly surprised: was it not bad for his blood pressure to "suppress" hostility?

shows the relativity of the contrast between satisfaction of an instinct and defense against an instinct; the autotomic reflex may be a common root for both the instinctive act and the defense against the instinctive act (p. 56). [See also Ferenczi, 1921.]

In "Repression" Freud (1915a) states:

When an external stimulus becomes internal through harassing and destroying an organ, so that the results are a fresh source of continuous excitement and an increase of tension, it acquires a far-reaching similarity to an instinctual drive. We know that this condition is experienced in pain. [See also Bonaparte, 1952.]

Such considerations may also be applied to itching. As will be discussed later, the sexuality of these cases is predominantly "pregenital," hence a source of extensive conflicts, giving rise to anxiety and to upsurge of aggression. It is therefore difficult to separate somatic manifestations of libido, aggression, and anxiety. If itching is ever connected with libidinous drives it should be qualified as their equivalent and not as their concomitant. There is—in the unanalyzed—hardly ever an awareness of the sexual character of the sensation: itching. It is frequently easier to establish the sexual character of an action than that of a sensation.

Scratching and Other Self-Manipulations

More obvious is the connection between sexuality and the symptom of scratching which in its various forms is an important symptom in many dermatoses. It can assume violent proportions, e.g., in Sulzberger-Garbe's Syndrome (Schur, 1950b), in neurodermatitis, in pruritus vulvae and ani, in atopic eczema, etc. In some conditions such as "neurotic excoriations" it constitutes the leading symptom. Through secondary infection, lichenification, and probably through release of metabolites in the injured area scratching can create a vicious circle even on the somatic level.

Scratching may assume the role of sexual gratification.[18] Even dermatological observers were impressed by the orgastic character of the scratching spells of cases of "Chronic, Exudative, Discoid and Lichenoid Dermatitis" (Schur, 1950b), which proceed in a constant crescendo and end abruptly in a state of exhaustion. The gratification in scratching

18 See Fenichel (1945a), as quoted above.

exceeds the mere elimination of the displeasure of itching, and becomes in many cases the main or even the only way of sexual gratification. This regression to the autoerotic phase of skin erotism is in line with our knowledge of the increased cathexis of diseased organs. The destructive character of scratching lends itself especially well to the discharge of sadomasochistic drives.[19]

It stands to reason that a dermatosis acquired in infancy or childhood will profoundly influence the psychosexual development, and in such cases we will expect a prevalence of pregenital fixations. However, analysis of cases of certain dermatoses acquired much later in life reveals a similar structure.

Scratching then assumes the character of a masturbatory function. The satisfaction (relief) derived from it is of even shorter duration than the satisfaction derived from other pregenital masturbatory functions. The desire to repeat it is nearly constant, so that scratching frequently assumes a compulsive character. The patients we are discussing, are quick to lose any faculty for delay they might have possessed at the onset. Scratching assumes another significant similarity to masturbation. The patient knows it is bad for the skin; he feels guilty, humiliated, because he cannot abandon it. The battle against scratching takes over all the characteristics of the battle against masturbation. In the analysis of such cases we are faced with the difficulty of showing the patient the reality aspect that scratching is bad for the skin—but not because of its sexual character. Some patients can only give up scratching after having been enabled to scratch without guilt feelings. The damage inflicted by scratching is frequently accepted as punishment for masturbation and on a primitive level justifies further scratching. The scratching, especially after going to bed, is frequently accompanied by fantasies which may represent important analytic material. Exhibitionism and the defense against it play here an extremely important role, both as a partial instinct and as a primitive form of object relationship. Scratching away a lesion which "has to be seen" serves as a primitive defense and self-punishment at the same time.

This brings us to the relation of scratching to aggression. It can be observed in every case how scratching becomes an important expression of aggression. Even dermatoses in which itching is the leading symptom hardly ever *itch* during sessions. Yet if we observe the patient approach-

19 The discussion of the lesions and of their secondary elaboration, to follow later, will give us an opportunity for a presentation of further aspects of sexuality in dermatoses.

ing a hostility-arousing topic we will often notice his hands assuming a claw-like position, ready to tear someone to pieces. Frequently the patient "digs in" in his own flesh, or starts to scratch without itching. This occurs even more generally outside the sessions. Whereas frequently scratching represents "aggression turned against the self," in most cases this is an oversimplification. Analysis could show a stratification of meaning. While on one level it might express self-punishment, on a deeper level it means punishing an external object, usually the mother. One of my patients spent a major part of a session complaining about a physician who subjected him to some allergy tests. He finally said: "Of course, I scratched all night." Asked why, he answered: "I had to show him what he did to me." From here he proceeded to discuss the eating difficulties of his early childhood. It was like an infant punishing his mother by refusing food. On a still deeper level the skin, which is both a protective layer and an organ of perception,[20] had become part of the self and outer object. This may be paralleled by a refusion of self- and object representations. On all these occasions of scratching these patients manifest the previously discussed defect in their ability to neutralize aggression.

It is in such deep states of regression that the patients do the greatest amount of damage. Such regressive states may precipitate prolonged relapses. It can easily be seen that itching and scratching can become dangerous obstacles when used in the service of resistance. The anticipation of such difficulties will direct the technique. Daily sessions are imperative. Id material has to be approached with utmost care. Secondary process thinking has to be encouraged first on the periphery and in areas less involved in conflict. Occasionally it becomes necessary to hospitalize the patient and continue the analysis during that period. The co-operation of an understanding dermatologist is essential. (See pp. 160-161).

Scratching frequently occurs during sleep and can be connected with collateral dream material. In dreams of our sample case, scratching symbolized the elimination of her father's sperm from her skin; this could be linked to very early pregnancy wishes during and after her mother's pregnancies (at ages two and a half and five), to her amenorrhea after her father's death, and to the exacerbation of her symptoms during her own first pregnancy.

Other manipulations involving the skin include a host of actions which in turn may be paralleled by a whole scale of mental pathology.

---

[20] It is here interesting to note that the skin shares with the central nervous system its origin in the ectoderm.

Picking and squeezing of blackheads, follicular lesions, lesions of acne rosacea, of simple acne, etc., may be substituted or supplemented by the use of instruments—needles, scissors, etc. These manipulations have in common their compulsive character, the masturbatory background, the guilt feelings, the element of self-punishment, and frequently also the mechanisms of punishing others by self-destruction. These mechanisms are reminiscent of those described in scratching, except that the relief and direct satisfaction are less obvious. The results of the manipulations (secondary infection, scars, disfiguration) are being used both for the distorted satisfaction of instinctual, e.g., exhibitionistic aims, and for the defense against them. Projection accounts for the feeling which is so common among patients with dermatoses that "everybody must see such terrible lesions" (Schur, 1950b). This creates the well-known "Leper complex"—a term widely used in dermatological literature. It is in line with the ego defect of these patients that their countercathexis uses non-neutralized aggressive energy (Hartmann, 1953).

Nevertheless, in some cases such an interpretation is incomplete. Let me here quote Freud (1915b):

> A patient whom I have at present under observation has let himself withdraw from all the interests of life on account of the unhealthy condition of the skin of his face. He declares that he has blackheads and that there are deep holes in his face which everyone notices. Analysis shows that he is working out his castration complex upon his skin. At first he busied himself with these blackheads without any misgivings; and it gave him great pleasure to squeeze them out, because as he said, something spurted out when he did so. Then he began to think that there was a deep cavity wherever he had got rid of a blackhead and he reproached himself most vehemently with having ruined his skin forever by 'constantly fiddling at it with his hand.' Pressing out the content of the blackheads was clearly to him a substitute for onanism ... This substitute-formation has, in spite of its hypochondriacal character, considerable resemblance to an hysterical conversion; and yet we have the feeling that there must be something different in it, that we cannot believe such a substitute-formation possible in a case of hysteria, even before we can say in what the difference consists. A tiny little hole such as a pore of the skin will hardly be used by an hysteric as a symbol for the vagina, which otherwise he will compare with every imaginable object capable of enclosing a space. Besides, we should think that multiplicity of these little cavities would prevent him using them as a substitute for the female genital [pp. 131-132].

Freud uses this example to differentiate substitutive ideas in schizophrenia and in the transference neurosis and to illustrate what he calls hypochondriac language or "organ speech." While Freud's patient was a full-fledged schizophrenic, and his skin symptoms but one manifestation of a delusional system, we find with surprising frequency in patients who in their total behavior and symptomatology are far from psychotic, not too dissimilar attitudes toward their manipulations, toward the results of such manipulations, and toward their lesions in general.[21]

In the absence of lesions some of these manipulations are directed against the appendages of the skin, the hair, or the nails. They all carry long and complicated names (trichotillomania, trichocryptomania, dermatothalasia, onychotillomania, etc.). They all may share the compulsive, self-destructive character. Trichotillomania, the compulsive pulling of hair, frequently associated with swallowing the hair, occurs mostly in children. I could observe in *statu nascendi* its development in a little boy of one year. It started with a strong cathexis of his mother's hair. He insisted during a certain phase on being given one of her hairs before going to sleep. To hold the hair in his mouth supplemented or replaced thumb sucking. Later this procedure was in turn supplemented and then replaced by pulling and sucking his own hair. The mechanisms of incorporation of the object, of the merging of the object with parts of the self, the fusion of libidinous and destructive aims, is here quite evident. The symptoms disappeared when the boy entered a new developmental phase. In cases where this symptom persists or develops at a later stage, we can see a gradual prevalence of destructive aims. The understanding of the mechanisms underlying this syndrome might, as will be seen later, throw some light on the background of certain cases of alopecia generalisata and areata.

In the manipulations of cases of acarophobia—who constantly try to dig some insects out of their skin—the delusional character is undisguised. I could observe a pharmacist who used more and more powerful ointments and lotions to "destroy" an imaginary fungus infection of his face and extremities. This resulted in deep-seated burns and severe dermatitis. Such cases are beyond analytic help, yet may respond, at least temporarily, to "magical" devices. When our sample case tried to dig her father's sperm out of her skin, she came close to the mechanisms of acarophobia (see the symbolic relationship of children-insects-sperm), yet she had these associations on a dream and fantasy level only. In the delusion the primary process completely invades the system Pcs., especially the word representations (Freud, 1916; Lewin, 1954).

[21] I defer the discussion of this point to the section on the lesions and secondary elaboration (pp. 147-150).

The Specific Eruption as a Sample of Somatic Symptom Formation

Under what psychological conditions do we expect the eruption not of secondary lesions such as secondary infection, lichenification, but of lesions which are specific for the entity? Case histories indicate that the first outbreak or individual relapses may be closely related to a traumatic event or a particularly conflictual situation. To obtain such a history with any degree of accuracy is very difficult and meets with understandable skepticism of "organically oriented" physicians. Under the spotlight of day-to-day analytic observation such connections become more convincing.

If we have established the fact that a new eruption may be precipitated by "emotional" factors, can we now also describe in dynamic and economic, topical and structural terms the situation in which this occurs? How does such a situation compare with situations leading, e.g., "only" to itching?

These questions are not easy to answer. In our sample case the analysis showed that during periods of *frequent new eruptions* similar factors were responsible for itching as well as for new lesions. Do we then have to consider mainly quantitative factors? A possible answer was gained from the observations obtained during the analysis of cases of chronic, exudative, discoid and lichenoid dermatitis (for details, see Schur, 1950b). In these cases the first eruption came at the climax of an unbearable conflict. The climate of the precipitating situation may be compared, for instance, with the "obsessional delirium" in Freud's unsurpassed description of the "Ratman" (1909), except that the "Ratman" did not have a readiness for physiological regression.

One of my cases suffering from chronic, discoid, exudative and lichenoid dermatitis, developed a complete remission under treatment. Then, however, he met with an extremely traumatic experience which gave me an opportunity to observe what was comparable to an experimental situation. His father suffered a coronary thrombosis. The patient visited him in the hospital and had to hand him the urine bottle. He saw a catheter in the penis which was covered with blood. He went into a state of increasingly uncontrolled anxiety. In spite of the most concentrated effort on my part it was impossible for him to regain some degree of ego control. A series of dreams, besides indicating increasing regression, pointed to the need for desperate action and led me to predict a recurrence of his dermatosis. As a final last attempt he sacrificed his precious moustache, the object of great narcissistic pride. The following day he woke up with a lesion on his penis, a localization with which most of these cases begin, and which had also been the site of his initial lesion. His father died shortly thereafter and again he soon developed, as he had at the onset of his illness, a generalized eruption.

The first lesion is thus precipitated by a situation in which ego control has disintegrated. Primary process prevails in thinking, neutralization of affects[22] and instinctual drives have failed. The insoluble conflict demands some kind of defensive action which takes the form of a most primitive *organ action*. This term is here used as an extension of Freud's term (1915b) of *organ language*. In this case there was a symbolic sacrificial shedding of *pars pro toto,* i.e., part of the penis—to avoid the terrible fate of total castration. At the same time the lesion satisfied libidinous (e.g., exhibitionistic) and aggressive instinctual drives.

If we now come back to our sample case: the patient's past history also showed that after a period of considerable remission sudden new eruptions were connected with traumatic events. The last generalized eruption preceding treatment was precipitated by marriage and pregnancy. During the first two years of the analysis she was never free of lesions. It was during this period, that the differentiation between situations precipitating itch and/or lesions was so difficult. After some progress in her analysis the intervals between the eruptions of new eczema lesions increased.

During the third year of her analysis she still itched and scratched under circumstances similar to those described before. But it now became possible to differentiate the circumstances under which new *eruptions* would come up. In some instances they were due even then to a sudden, unexpected, intensive strain to the emotional equilibrium: e.g., a sudden breakthrough of unconscious material, when an illness of her son made her aware of her intense hostility against the boy who represented to her both her younger brother and the child given her by her father. It was therefore a combination of quantitative factors and of the suddenness of an impact which created a traumatic situation and broke through barriers of the ego, precipitating farther-reaching regression, and with it a change in the economic situation. Such a relapse was usually accompanied by stubborn, sulking resistance, by loss of insight, and by new doubts in the validity of the analytic approach to an "organic" condition.

Yet during this phase of her treatment eruptions occurred also under circumstances which were accessible to analysis. They were frequently reminiscent of situations in her adolescence. I have mentioned that she would get lesions, mainly on her face, before going to church or to a party. During a certain phase of her analysis she had transferred her full hostility toward her mother to her mother-in-law, who actually was not

22 Or more precisely: ability to use neutralized energy in affects.

an easy person to live with. She was faced with the deeply resented necessity of spending a part of the summer with her in a small bungalow, and most of her sessions were concerned with the analysis of this situation. A few days before the set date she broke out on her face.

We are used to describe such an occurrence in terms such as: "the defensive character of the lesion." For the following reasons this description is not satisfactory: Analysis revealed, as is to be expected with all symptoms, (1) that the eruptions were equivalents of libidinous (e.g., exhibitionistic) and aggressive instinctual drives; (2) they represented a defensive organ action; and (3) they were equivalents of affects.

For further clarification it will be helpful to consider certain formulations by Freud (1937), Hartmann (1950), Rapaport (1951b), and others. In "Analysis Terminable and Interminable" Freud (1937) stated:

> . . . each ego is endowed from the beginning with its own peculiar dispositions and tendencies . . . When we speak of "archaic inheritance" we are generally thinking only of the Id and apparently we assume that an Ego was non-existent at the beginning of an individual's life. But we must not overlook the fact that Id and Ego are originally one, and it does not imply the mystical overestimation of heredity if we think it creditable that, even before the Ego exists, its subsequent lines of development, tendencies and reactions are already determined.

While this paragraph mainly emphasizes the importance of genetic factors for ego development, it points also to the fact that the ego—and its functions—emerge from the id; hence, the ego as well as the id, has its innate qualities. The precursors of the ego must therefore in their characteristics be closer to the id. Hartmann (1950) elaborated on these concepts and suggested that defense mechanisms do not make their appearance as such, but are modeled after and develop from some form of instinctual behavior or reflex actions. Let us add here that such "actions" are not restricted to the motor system but find their expression in the inner environment such as, for instance, in electrolyte distribution and in the hormone level.

In his attempt to clarify the theory of thinking Rapaport (1951b) stresses the genetic aspect. Using as his conceptual model the infant's behavior at the breast with the sequence of restlessness; appearance of, and sucking action on, the breast; subsidence of restlessness—Rapaport develops what he calls the primitive models of action, thought, and affect. He calls action a discharge activity whose aim it is to re-establish equilibrium. The primary model of thought is mounting drive tension—absence of drive-object—hallucinatory image of it.

I have stressed the importance of ego regression in anxiety and its impact on the psychological structure of the anxiety situation and on the resulting discharge phenomena. We assumed that itching can represent an affect concomitant or equivalent. In the condition leading to the *first* eruption or the recurrence of an eruption after a prolonged interval we can see a regression to the precursors of thought, affect, instinctual drives and defensive action—expressed exclusively on the somatic level.[23] Let me stress specifically that in the use of the term "defense," what we actually mean are the precursors of defense. Then defense is not only cathexis but also primitive action and discharge.[24]

This interpretation pertains to eruptions which occurred after a symptom-free interval under the spotlight of the analytic observation which enables us to differentiate between the secondary symbolic elaboration to which any lesion or function may be subjected and the primary symbolism of these symptoms. Such observations during analysis make the *reconstructive* interpretation of similar mechanisms in the initial eruption of other cases more plausible.

RELATIONSHIP OF SYMPTOM FORMATION IN DERMATOSES TO CONVERSION: ANALOGIES AND DIFFERENCES

These considerations necessitate a discussion of the relationship of symptom formation in dermatoses[25] to conversion symptoms. It is beyond the scope of this paper to go into a detailed discussion of the hysteria problem. Let me just state that in this area we have to face an embarrassing truth. While Freud built psychoanalysis on the observations gained from hysteria, he obviously never got around to fully applying the knowledge of pregenital and ego development, of metapsychological and structural concepts, to the problems of hysteria. He alludes to this in *Inhibitions, Symptoms and Anxiety* (1926) and in his *New-Introductory Lectures* (1932). Fenichel (1945a) tried to fill some of this gap by his introduction of the term "pregenital conversion." In Freud's early writings, particularly in his letters to Fliess (1887-1902), and in the entire

---

23 It represents part of the fascination of an analytic study of dermatoses that one can really "see" certain responses. The simultaneous observation of somatic and psychic phenomena constitutes a unique experimental setting.

24 In my paper "The Ego in Anxiety" (82) I have tried to develop the concept of tension as the physiological counterpart of the ego attitudes of *Angstbereitschaft* or vigilance. The concept of the physiological equivalents of precursors of defenses may represent another step toward the eventual development of a "physiology and pathology of defenses." (See also pp. 129-130.)

25 I purposely restrict this discussion to the symptom formation in dermatoses, although it may also be valid for other "psychosomatic" disorders.

early analytic literature many somatic disorders have been described under the heading of "conversion hysteria" and also of "actual neuroses." In his paper on the psychogenic disturbances of vision Freud (1910) assumed that a neurosis can lead "through toxic modification" to structural changes, thus separating "neurotic" from "psychogenic" disturbances. In the first area of application of psychoanalysis to somatic medicine the concepts of "body language" and "organ symbolism" were extended to explain a host of functional and structural pathology. The reaction to this trend coincided with the development of "psychosomatic concepts." It also coincided with the relative disappearance of typical cases of conversion hysteria from our analytic material. This led to a certain restriction of the concept of conversion. While Fenichel (1945a) still defines conversion as "not simply somatic expressions of affects but very specific representations of thoughts which can be retranslated from their 'somatic language' into the original word language" (p. 216), the term conversion has later been restricted to "those neuroses in which somatization occurs through innervation of the voluntary nervous system and its muscles and sensory apparatus" (Grinker and Robbins, 1953, p. 74). Similar qualifications are expressed by Alexander (1950): ". . . symbolic expression of psychological content is known only in the field of voluntary innervations such as speech, or expressive movements, such as facial grimacing, gesticulation, laughter, weeping, etc." (p. 41).

It has been necessary for the progress of our understanding to stress the fact that altered function of the vegetative nervous system and the endocrines, and altered structure of our organs may be the somatic equivalents of affects, conflicts, and neuroses, and that these equivalents do not always express an idea. Yet I have the impression that for purposes of schematic presentation the demarcation between voluntary and autonomic innervation as criterion for the faculty of symbolic representation has been drawn too sharply. It impresses one as a remnant of the old strict delineation between the concepts functional and organic. It is interesting to note that we find both errors and specific exceptions in Alexander's presentation when he includes, e.g., weeping in the expressive movements or speaks of blushing as "possible exception." Grinker and Robbins (1953) become somewhat vague when they discuss vomiting. After stressing the difference between the symbolic nature of symptoms mediated through the voluntary nervous system and a "vegetative neurosis" where the symptom is, "the end result of a chain of physiological events intiated by the conflict," they state: "In the symptom of vomiting there is a more complicated pattern, because it is brought about in part by action of the voluntary musculature and in part by the involuntary musculature. In a given case one innervation or the other may be dominant and between these two poles there may be all grades of responses" (p. 188). They are still vaguer when in their discussion of the symbolic meaning of skin lesions they say: "The significance of these factors and the meaning to the patient can only be determined by careful unprejudicial study of the individual psychology. Psychoanalysts have frequently observed that the location of itching or skin lesions seems to have symbolic significance. Some of these observations indicate that eruptions on the forehead symbolize guilt; on the hands, prohibited sexual or aggressive activity; around the vulva or anus, prohibited sexual gratification, etc." (p. 270).

Vomiting in infancy frequently is an early expression of rejection of the mother and therefore symbolic in meaning. Should we deny the presence of such meaning in the neurotic symptom of vomiting? Vomiting as symptom of hysterical pregnancy fantasy was mentioned by Fenichel (1945b) who used this example to repudiate Alexander's too-narrow definition of conversion. More of such inconsistencies could be quoted. They indicate that in this, as in other areas, there are no rigid boundaries in the realm of the psyche. The ego and the id are not separated by an Iron Curtain. The whole concept of cathexis as related to the three systems, Cs, Pcs and Ucs indicates fluid transitions. This becomes even more transparent when we apply the genetic principle to all mental phenomena. The ego does not start on any particular day of our life span. Anxiety has no birthday on which it emerges from its precursors. Recognition and anticipation emerge very gradually, and so does speech. And even in the adult many intangibles give, for instance, an ideational meaning to facial expression which is beyond voluntary innervation. What gives our eyes a happy, or sad, or loving expression? It is in this context that the skin can assume the role of an organ of expression as well as of perception. The skin provides both separation from and contact with the environment. The skin which is the seat of the tactile and of temperature senses is also in its entirety a potentially erogenous zone, with the well-established zones of predilection. It therefore does not seem a fantastic assumption that in special constellations with deep ego regression the skin can serve as transmittor of primitive symbols of thought, speech and action. The bleeding skin as the stigma of hysteria was always considered a conversion symptom.[26] We may now add the initial lesions of certain

[26] See also the interesting observation on a wheal reaction in a tattoo by Graff and Wallerstein (1954).

dermatoses to this list of symbolic, archaic, organ language and of organ action as precursors of defense.[27]

These considerations illustrate the *similarity* between symptom formation in certain dermatoses and hysterical conversion. In both, instinctual drive and defense find an expression in the somatic sphere which can be "translated" into words and "make sense" on a conscious level. However, this similarity is limited to the structure of the symptom "eruption" which constitutes but one aspect of the variegated pathology of such cases. They frequently also show definite obsessive, compulsive and phobic symptoms, and symptoms reminiscent of true hypochondriasis. Libidinous regression goes much deeper, with prevalence of exhibitionistic and narcissistic tendencies. Differentiation between the self and the object is vague. The skin is being treated as both part of the self and as outer object. I have discussed in detail both the prevalence of regressive types of anxiety and inability of these patients to neutralize their aggression, which are analogous to the ego defects of schizophrenics.[28]

Let me add here the following observation made in a number of cases suffering from various dermatoses, among them three cases of psoriasis. Not only could one find the much more common confusion about the difference of the sexes and the parallel existence of hetero- and homosexual aims; they showed—long before the outbreak of their dermatosis— a deep-seated confusion about their own identity. This in turn was based on a primitive, extremely ambivalent identification with the mother. Such an identification is especially confusing to male patients and calls for specific defenses. The resulting split in the ego organization, which may vary in its impact, is reminiscent of Freud's description (1927) of the fetishist. I am referring here also to the papers by Greenson (1954a, 1954b) and Bychowski (1954). Once a lesion has been established, it can *add* to this confusion of identity by its localization, its character, or by its secondary symbolic evaluation. This applies also to certain cases of ulcerative colitis and gastric or intestinal fistulae. This increased confusion of identity is paralleled by a tendency to refusion of self- and object representation and by vagueness of self-boundaries.

[27] We can detect phylogenetic precursors of such organ defense in the "autotomia" of lower animals, who sever parts of their body after a painful stimulation, a fact which Ferenczi (1921) pointed out.

[28] For further discussion see pp. 150-154.

SECONDARY ("PATHONEUROTIC") REACTIONS AND THE CHRONICITY
OF THE SYMPTOM

An attempt to explain the tendency to repeated eruptions, which is crucial for the chronicity and incurability of these dermatoses, can be made on several levels. We can use the common cliché, borrowed from immunology, and say that once the "initial resistance" is broken, many factors can precipitate new eruptions. More in line with modern concepts of the stress reaction (Selye, 1950) is the explanation that a specific lesion can be precipitated by specific or unspecific stress. Even if the initial precipitating cause must be specific, once a lesion is established a multiplicity of then unspecific reasons can provoke similar specific reactions. Thus we see that in many dermatoses, once the lesion is established, such factors as localized and generalized infections, thermic influences (changes of season, heat, cold, humidity), nutritional, metabolic and many other factors can probably precipitate new lesions during certain phases. All these arguments are marshaled to discredit the possible implication of psychological factors, and they play a large role as source of endless resistance in the analytic treatment of such cases. We, however, are interested in the following question: can we find *psychological* factors explaining the chronicity of the disease?

Here we have to take another detour and first return to the example given by Freud in the "The Unconscious" (1915b) and quoted above (see p. 138). In quoting it, I mentioned that similar attitudes toward skin manipulations and their results can be found in an amazing number of patients who certainly would not be classified as schizophrenics. Yet these patients spend a great deal of time in front of the mirror to inspect their skin. Each tiny lesion, mostly insignificant and hardly noticeable, is registered and subjected to all kinds of treatments and manipulations.[29] The patients are convinced that everybody is bound to notice the "terrible" lesions or the "terrible" damage they have done to themselves. They have to get some substance out of their skin, pus, blackheads, often just blood or serum. All this is obviously symbolically overdetermined, and of undisguised compulsive-masturbatory character.

In such cases we discover characteristics which we find in true hypochondriasis: the narcissistic overvaluation of the symptom, in our cases of the whole skin. This syndrome is frequently encountered among highly

29 We find—as so frequently in other areas of human behavior—similar roots in the mass appeal of "beauty treatments" which is not limited exclusively to the female part of our population.

narcissistic beautiful women, whom Freud (1931a, 1932) described so convincingly. Exhibitionistic tendencies accordingly play a predominant
role. Punishment of others and of oneself plays a similar role as in
scratching. The ego regression which prevails in these states explains the
prevalence of primary process thinking in the symbolic elaboration of the
lesions and the manipulations. This is confirmed by another peculiar
phenomenon: such patients perform these manipulations in a state of
revery, under detachment of cathexis from the environment. The mirror
remains the sole object representation.[30] But this rather severe pathology
was usually restricted to this symptom. Such patients may function excel-
lently in life and may have a good faculty for sublimation. If I may use
a simile from somatic pathology, they have succeeded in encapsulating
their symptom. Or may we say, the greater part of their ego has not been
submerged and has retained its free mobility (Hartmann, 1939). Nevertheless such a "focus" is not without danger.

In these cases the "lesions" per se are actually quite insignificant and
their origin has little, if anything, to do with the underlying emotional
structure. *However, once the symptom is established, it acts as a focal
point for the convergence of diverse pathological mechanisms.* A similar
chain of events obtains in many "organic" diseases. Any diseased organ or
any alteration of function draws narcissistic libido. This always results
in changes in all structures. Any prolonged or chronic illness, or any permanent loss of an important function (crippling injury, amputation, etc.)
increases the strain, and requires complex adaptation with a shift from
object libido to narcissistic libido. The onus of the adaptation will be on
various ego functions. We see here a gamut of response determining the
outcome, which lies anywhere between a restoration of the status quo
to the development of a pathoneurosis or even, to follow a term of Meng
(1934), of a pathopsychosis. Thus we are dealing in every response to
organic disease with a temporary or permanent regression affecting all
psychic structures.

We know that the outcome will depend not only on the severity of
the organic disease, but to a large extent on the degree of mental health
at the time of onset. The same adaptation must take place in every skin
disorder, whatever its precipitating cause.

The response to "organic" disease depends among other factors also on
the meaning of an organ system and its function for the mental apparatus,

[30] "Mirror, mirror on the wall, who is the fairest of them all?" I point here also
to the role of the mirror in the symptomatology of the "Wolfman" during his
psychotic episode, which was also partly precipitated by and centered on a skin lesion
(Brunswick, 1928; Schur, 1950b). See also pp. 152-154.

and on the amount of sensory stimulation emanating from the diseased organ (pain, itching, etc.). Thus an itching dermatosis will precipitate different responses than one which causes pain and/or disfiguration. Any dermatosis will tend to increase narcissistic cathexes, and will increase and/or revive conflicts around exhibitionism. Itching will revive all the conflicts around masturbation (see p. 135). It puts particular strain on the adaptive functions, because in most cases we lack pharmacological agents which provide adequate symptomatic relief. Pathoneurotic reactions are frequent and create a vicious circle.

Next we have to consider the fact that ego reactions do not end with the establishment of a symptom. The fact that countercathexis may be directed against symptom and affects as well as against instinctual drives, has been stressed by Freud (1926), Fenichel (1939) and others. The nature of the countercathexes depends on the symptom, and may further constrict the "conflict-free area of the ego" (Hartmann, 1939). This in turn may give rise to new symptoms, as happens in severe phobias and obsessional neuroses.

After this detour, let us consider the state of affairs in the case of a dermatosis precipitated by a traumatic event in the manner described above (see p. 140). We are dealing with patients who even before the outbreak of their dermatoses have shown both neurotic symptoms and signs of a precarious equilibrium in many areas of adaptation. The initial eruption itself was both the result and the expression of a deep regression.

The established somatic lesion results in a far-reaching shift of cathexis to the lesion, the organ, the self. It becomes the focus of narcissistic regression. It may for the time being relieve the intolerable tension of a conflict which until then involved the environment representing oedipal and preoedipal objects.[31]

These patients react to the initial outbreak with an abundance of pathoneurotic reactions, much more so than patients with a dermatosis which was not precipitated by an emotional conflict. Such reactions may assume a phobic and/or obsessive character and lead in turn to similar

[31] Following the tendency for teleological formulations one frequently hears or reads: The psychosomatic symptom is a defense against a psychotic breakdown. I was myself guilty of similar formulations. This sounds as if the defensive aspect were directed against the "psychotic breakdown." We should say more precisely: The shift in cathexis and the narcissistic regression make conflicts centered around external objects lose some of their critical urgency. This may temporarily relieve an economic situation in which the ego is submerged by intolerable quantities of affects and which could have resulted in a psychotic break.

This explains also the widely reported—but not too frequent—cases where a sudden disappearance of a psychosomatic symptom has been followed by a psychotic episode or suicide.

consequences as other severe phobias and compulsions. I have mentioned before that these patients show a constant readiness for anxiety (*Angstbereitschaft*, "free-floating anxiety"), and that this ego attitude of constant vigilance also has its somatic manifestations and is probably the basis of what is commonly called "tension" (see p. 129). This is then the state in which the patient may respond with a new outbreak to any change in the economic situation and when the differentiation of circumstances precipitating either only itch or new lesions becomes impossible. Here the regression has reached the core of the psychosomatic continuum. Any resemblance to primitive symbolic organ language or organ action which we described for the *initial* lesion has been lost. However, the lesions may supply the basis for secondary symbolic elaborations. It is this vicious cycle, which accounts for the chronicity of such diseases. Unfortunately it is in this stage that the patients come for treatment which explains the tremendous technical difficulties encountered in these cases.[32]

Analogies and Differences Between Patients with Severe Dermatoses and Schizophrenics

On the height of the eruptions such patients are certainly deeply disturbed and the clinical impression may be reminiscent of a schizophrenic process. I have stressed before the similarity of the following ego defects of these patients with the defects of schizophrenics:

a) In both instances the prevalence of primary process thinking impairs the vital ego function of evaluation of danger. This results in regressive types of anxiety reactions in which ego control is either lessened, or abandoned as in uncontrolled anxiety. Such a deficiency constitutes the closest analogy to schizophrenia (see Mahler et al., 1949; Eissler, 1953; Hartmann, 1953).[33]

---

[32] The establishment of such a vicious circle may also play an important role in such entities as ulcerative colitis and bronchial asthma.

[33] I prefer this formulation to the one used by Eissler and Hartmann. Hartmann (1953) states: "While anxiety is a present and central phenomenon in schizophrenia, it appears that its use as a signal to announce and forestall danger is mostly defective" (p. 182). As I have discussed at length, we are dealing in the anxiety situation with a complex ego function which I have described as a biphasic response. In the first phase the ego perceives and *evaluates* the danger, while in the second the ego *responds* to this evaluation. Both phases, of course, occur nearly simultaneously. If the situation is one of potential danger, and the ego responds prevalently on the level of secondary processes, the whole process has a thought-like quality. This whole process corresponds to what Freud called signal anxiety. If the evaluation of danger is regressive (defective), the response to this evaluation may also be regressive. Eissler's and Hartmann's formulation does not emphasize the fact that "the anxiety which the ego cannot use as a signal" is already based on a defective ego function, while my formulation stresses

b) The impairment of ego functions extends to the ability to neutralize aggression, the failure of which is apparent not only in the somatization of responses, but in other instances where we assume the use of aggressive energy: in countercathexis and in the primitive punitive superego. Thus primitive defenses like "sacrifice," "talion principle" (see Fenichel, 1939; Menninger, 1954; Schur, 1950b) may also result in somatic phenomena and contribute to the initial and to recurrent lesions.

What, then, are the differences between these cases and schizophrenics? We can see them clearly when we first compare the case of one of my "ladies with the mirror" with such cases as Freud's (1915b) acne patient or my patient with acarophobia. The "lady with the mirror" was a narcissistic type (Freud, 1931b). She had her share of conflicts and symptoms. As far as her skin was concerned, she had hypochondriasis-like attitudes. Yet she had a well-structuralized and very effective ego. She was highly capable of complex abstract thinking. If not in front of the mirror and engaged in her skin manipulations, she had full insight. We can thus compare her ego impairment to one with an obsessional idea in contrast to the ego defect of a patient with a delusion. The differences become less striking when we proceed in our examination toward the cases with severe pathology, especially at the height of their eruptions. In the latter the combination of regressive types of affects, of the failure of neutralization, of the narcissistic regression, and the maze of symptoms and countercathectic mechanisms, results in severe constriction of many ego functions, which in turn may lead—to use a simile from somatic pathology—to an "atrophy" of certain ego functions. Nevertheless, in most of these cases, one has the impression of an ego which has been only paralyzed and immobilized. During the analytic session, for instance, when verbalization helped the reestablishment of secondary processes and anxiety resumed the character of controlled anxiety, one could see that this paralyzed and constricted ego, to use Eissler's (1953) terminology, was not only able to *form* structure but *had* structure. *It is the very capacity to restore secondary processes which probably represents a most significant difference.*

Accordingly, these cases even at the height of their eruptions fail to show the impairment of the function of language which is so typical for the schizophrenic thought disorder. To quote Freud (1915b): "In schizophrenia *words* are subject to the same process as that which makes dream-images out of dream-thoughts, the one we have called the primary mental

---

the biphasic character of the anxiety response and establishes the mutual interdependence of the impairment of several ego functions. These are the considerations which also led me to a somewhat different formulation of the signal concept (Schur, 1953).

process. They undergo condensation, and by means of displacement transfer their cathexes to one another without remainder; the process may extend so far that a single word, which on account of its manifold relations is specially suitable, can come to represent a whole train of thought. The works of Bleuler, Jung and their pupils have yielded abundant material precisely in support of this very proposition" (p. 131). In these cases the split between the "idea of the word" and the "idea of the thing" (Freud, 1915b, p. 133) is never so conspicuous (see also Hartmann, 1953).

While the inability to neutralize aggression is common both to the schizophrenic and patient with a psychosomatic disorder, we find only in schizophrenia states of nearly complete defusion of instinctual drives. The self-destructive results of the somatic process represent rather a by-product of the discharge phenomena than a primary aim.

We see more fluid transitions in the equally essential area of the type and level of identification. When one of my patients with chronic, exudative, discoid and lichenoid dermatitis developed the lesion on his penis he reacted to it and to the death of his father, which occurred a few days later, with increasing confusion of his identity. Homosexual aims were replaced by bisexuality, and on a still deeper level by complete acceptance of femininity, based on identification with the mother. This step may have been precipitated by the following mechanisms: "If my father not only can be castrated but can even die—then it is safer to be a woman."[34] In cases where a considerable confusion of identity had existed previously, such a mechanism may precipitate a regression to the most primitive types of identification (Jacobson, 1954a). The simultaneous tendency for refusion of self- and object representation and for vagueness of self-boundaries constitutes the greatest threat to the maintenance of reality—to females as well as to males. In the schizophrenic the defense against this most primitive identification can only result in feeble, repetitious and futile attempts to find the restitution of an external object.

The transition from confusion of the sexual aim and of identity to the most primitive levels of complete identification and thereby to the development of psychotic symptoms can best be studied in cases which were under analysis before this deepest regression had taken place, as for instance in my previously quoted case. We have a classic example of such a transition in this "best analyzed of all cases"—the Wolfsman (Freud, 1918). When he regressed to a complete primitive identification with his mother, he lost the contact with reality and developed his psychotic

---

[34] When I published this case in 1950 (b) I was not yet aware of this deepest meaning.

episode with prevalence of hypochondriacal and paranoic symptoms. The Wolfman did not act any more *like* his mother, he had become his mother (Brunswick, 1928, p. 121).[35]

To summarize the differences: The regression in schizophrenia and in psychosomatic disorders goes in different directions. In schizophrenics it culminates in a further dissolution of ego functions, especially in the sphere of thought processes, in a far-reaching defusion of instinctual drives and in the establishment of total primitive identifications. The regression in psychosomatic disorders results in a resomatization of various responses.

I have tried to describe in analytic terms the mechanisms operative in (1) the initial lesion in new eruptions following a prolonged interval; and (2) in chronic lesions of cases of atopic eczema and chronic, exudative, discoid and lichenoid dermatitis. I found such mechanisms operative also in certain cases of seborrhoic eczema and allergic contact dermatitis. Preliminary impressions would also put psoriasis in this category.[36] In

[35] While it is beyond the scope of this paper to discuss this topic in greater detail, it is necessary to point out that this formulation entails what I consider an essential complement to Freud's presentation (1911) of the Schreber Case and of Katan's (1949, 1950, 1952, 1954) numerous papers on that topic, and to Brunswick's interpretation (1928) of the Wolfman's psychotic episode. In my formulation the emphasis is not on the homosexual aim and the concomitant increased castration fear, but on the complete primitive identification with the mother. It is interesting to note that the importance of this identification was stressed by Freud (1915c, p. 158) in his paper on female paranoia and by Brunswick (1928), yet with the main emphasis on the homosexuality. We may speculate that the complete identification in the Wolfman was precipitated by a mechanism similar to that operative in my patient: to see the "castrated" father figure—Freud—and to anticipate his impending death. This made it safer for both to be a woman. Such an explanation seems more plausible than the interpretation of the revived passive homosexual transference feelings as the main precipitating factor. While the undisputed homosexuality explains some of the *content* of the fantasies, the break with reality can be explained with much greater pertinence by the complete primitive identification. To quote Jacobson's (1954a) patient: "Do you know the difference between closeness, likeness, sameness, and oneness? Close is close as with you; when you are like somebody, you are only *like* the other, you and he are two; sameness—you are the same as the other, but he is still he and you are you; but oneness is not two—it is one, that's horrible" (p. 251). Macalpine and Hunter (1953), in their interesting study of the Schreber Case, also criticized Freud's overemphasis on homosexuality as the precipitating factor of Schreber's psychosis. While their paper contains valuable hints to Schreber's complete identification with a woman, their emphasis is on the "pregenital archaic procreation fantasy." This emphasis adds greatly to the understanding of the *content* of the fantasies, but again does not explain the break with reality—especially not in cases of female paranoid schizophrenia. The procreation fantasies are the *consequence* of the complete identification and the resulting break with reality and not the cause of the latter.

[36] I am presently engaged in a study of psoriasis which is being conducted at the Psychoanalytic Institute of the New York State University with the collaboration of

their initial lesion cases of total and localized alopecia show a similar mechanism.

Careful analysis of other dermatoses might reveal that the symptom formation may follow similar lines.[37] In some of them even the initial lesion will be "averbal," the somatic *equivalent* of a certain economic situation accompanying deep regression. I have to emphasize once more that only very careful analysis can distinguish between primary symbolism and secondary symbolic elaboration.[38] Such important entities as pruritus ani and vulvae have been omitted in this category because, according to my experience, their development is different. The initial lesion is mostly an accidental local dermatitis which may be precipitated by a multitude of factors. Once established the lesion becomes the focus of a pathoneurotic reaction. The overcathexis of the organ, the intolerance for the itch, overmedication, and especially scratching with all its implications, create a vicious circle: any deterioration of the local lesion creates new regression. Such a pathoneurotic reaction takes place only in patients with a precarious mental equilibrium. If caught relatively early such cases benefit frequently from proper local treatment, particularly if combined with some "superficial" psychotherapy. Cases of long duration present severe pathology (Macalpine, 1953).

THE PROBLEM OF SPECIFICITY

It will be noted that I spoke of specific lesions, but not of specific conflicts, defenses, personalities, the specific kind of a mother, etc. I am referring, of course, to the old problem of the choice of symptom. There is a repetitious trend in the literature to link certain somatic diseases, usually listed among "psychosomatic disorders," with *specific* psychological causes. I will restrict myself to the field of dermatoses and quote

---

Drs. Coltrera and Dickes. A study of psoriasis seems to me very essential for the following reasons: not only is psoriasis a frequent dermatosis, but itching and therefore scratching are much less important factors in psoriasis. Therefore it lends itself especially well to the study of factors precipitating the *specific* lesions.

37 I do not feel entitled to make such claims on the basis of prolonged interviews and clinical impressions only. Among others, acne (simplex and rosacea) pompholyx, and certain cases of exfoliative dermatitis would warrant extensive study.

38 See, e.g., Sperling's (1953) observation on urticaria. For the importance of "emotional factors" in other dermatoses I refer to Wittkower et al. (1953) where the pertinent literature, especially the "dermatological," is adequately quoted. The authors approach the topic from a general clinical angle. Their psychological approach, as will be mentioned later, stresses mainly the "personality profiles" of various entities, claiming far-reaching "specificity" of personalities and conflicts.

only a few examples which I consider representative of a certain approach.[39]

Spitz (1951, 1954) claimed that mothers of children with early atopic eczema always avoided close physical contact in the necessary daily procedures (feeding, bathing, etc.). They were clumsy and frightened when they had to hold the infants. The author adds that such infants at birth had cutaneous reflexes markedly different from those of average children. Spitz's findings require careful consideration, but also controls.

Spitz's study approaches the problem of specificity from the angle of the highly significant early mother-child relationship. Completely different is the approach of other clinicians who try to correlate each entity with a specific "personality type" which will respond to a specific conflict with a specific lesion. Such generalized conclusions are drawn by some authors from statistics based on a few psychiatric interviews or on brief observation in superficial psychotherapy. They speak then of a "disguised or undisguised eczema personality," of a "rosacea personality," "weeping of the eczema," or finally of urticaria: "various writers have contended that urticaria eruptions are equivalent to a suppressed cry. This may be true. Yet the tears shed into the skin seem to be tears of fury rather than of sadness" (Wittkower et al., 1953, p. 147).

While Alexander (1950) sees the specificity in the prevalence of certain instinctual needs, the satisfaction of which is inhibited by strong specific defenses, other authors center on the importance of certain affects. Especially hostility (anger, rage) and its vicissitudes are made responsible for specific entities (Saul, 1939, 1941; Zaidenz, 1950).

In none of my own observations could I find specificity of personality, of conflict, or of defense against one phase of sexuality, or of aggression and the defense against it. All types of neurosis were represented in my material. Even among representatives of the same entity, differences were quite striking. However, without claiming any specificity, one may summarize certain characteristics, which these patients have in common. As far as reconstructive analysis can determine, many such characteristics are present before the initial outbreak, unless it occurred in early infancy.

1. The patients show a great variety of neurotic symptoms and character traits.

2. Their libido development shows a prevalence of narcissistic and pregenital elements, with intensive conflicts around exhibitionism (definitely present before the initial lesion!).

[39] For the discussion of the problem of "specificity" see Deutsch (1939a, 1939b, 1953), Grinker (1953), Kubie (1953) and Schur (1955).

3. They show a widespread impairment of ego functions (anxiety, aggression, identifications, etc.).

4. In line with their defective libido and ego development, the object relationships of these patients are tenuous, built around their narcissistic and pregenital needs, and are characterized by extreme ambivalence.

5. They all have suffered an unusual amount of early traumatization.

While the other characteristics can be found in a great variety of neuroses, the severe ego defects of these cases are reminiscent of what we now frequently call "borderline states." This corresponds to the fact that they frequently reveal "borderline types" of responses when subjected to psychological tests with projective techniques.

While all the cases whom I analyzed or who were studied by me or my collaborators in extensive interviews and in supervised psychotherapy showed these characteristics, it should under no circumstances be claimed that this combination of factors will be found in emotionally precipitated dermatoses only. I would therefore not dare to diagnose a dermatosis from reading the psychiatric history. Even knowing the diagnosis dermatosis, it would not be permissible to diagnose a specific entity. Here I can only report an impression, which would require confirmation through extensive observations: While certain cases of atopic eczema, urticaria, and dermatitis of the type of contact dermatitis have the above-mentioned characteristics in common, they are emotionally not quite as sick as, e.g., patients with Sulzberger-Garbe's syndrome or with total alopecia.

What accounts then (1) for the specificity of the organ choice, and (2) for the specificity of the lesions?

Nothing has changed in our general approach since Freud's formulations (1912). He summarized it in his statement: *"Daimon kai tyche* determine the fate of man; seldom, perhaps never, one of these powers alone. The relative aetiological effectiveness of each is only to be measured individually and in single instances. In a series comprising varying degrees of both factors extreme cases will certainly also be found. According to the knowledge we possess we shall estimate the parts played by the forces of heredity and of environment differently in each case, and retain the right to modify our opinion in consequence of new knowledge" (p. 312, footnote 3). In "Analysis Terminable and Interminable" (1937) he elaborated on the relative importance of genetic and environmental factors. He introduced the genetic factor as a quantitative consideration. The more pathologic the genetic endowment—and he stressed that this applies to the ego as well as to the id—the less environmental traumatization will be necessary to produce a neurosis. I have compared the consideration of genetic factors to the introduction of economic factors in the etiology of neurosis (Schur, 1955); Bergman and Escalona (1949), Fries and Woolf (1953) and others have tried to establish certain innate factors in the responses of the newborn and in early infancy. Greenacre (1952) has stressed that, apart from genetic factors, we have to consider intrauterine and very early infantile traumatization in the predisposition to anxiety or, as I would say, to regressive types of anxiety reactions. Freud (1913) had originally tried to establish a connection between certain types of neurosis and certain phases of libidinal development. He then saw the genetic factor in the choice of neurosis in certain "libidinal types" (1931b). Yet he recognized soon that ego development participates in the determination of the type of neurosis. Later he recognized the importance of genetic factors for the ego (1937). Anna Freud (1936) stressed the crucial role of the phase of the id and ego development in which the child was subjected to traumatization. This factor was also stressed by many other authors, e.g., by Greenacre (1952) in its significance in reconstructive analysis, and by Kris (1950) in longitudinal studies. The entire clinical picture of our cases points to a combination of innate and very early environmental factors in the etiology. That here early interrelationships between infant and mother enter as an important variable is therefore undisputed. It has been stressed by Grinker (1953) and Kubie (1953) that the sum total of these factors may account for the specificity of responses.

All this means that we have to learn to deal more and more with what we may call "constellations" (Schur, 1955) as a causal factor, both in general and in specific etiology.[40] This means we have to consider certain types of libidinal and ego endowment and development, a certain genetic and developmental setup of organs and organ systems, related to certain environmental influences.[41] Freud stated that with more pathological endowment less environmental traumatization will result in a neurosis. We may establish a similar, but somewhat more complicated ratio in "psychosomatic" disorders. Here the innate factor influences the development of a neurosis in a similar way. But it must influence also the readiness to respond with a specific organ or organ system. The neurosis is here in a way interpolated between environmental traumatization and the responding organ.

The ratio would then be: The more a certain way of organ response is

[40] I tried to apply this approach to the problem of obesity (1955).

[41] The stability of homeostatic regulation varies greatly in early infancy. Instability may manifest itself at any time of life in such entities as "neurocirculatory asthenia" or for instance in the tendency to multiple involvement of the endocrines (see J. Bauer, 1945; and Bergmann, 1932).

genetically determined, the less is the relative importance of the neurosis. The relative importance of genetically determined organ responses differs not only with different entities but may show considerable variation within the same entity. This can be exemplified in the field of dermatoses, for instance, in the allergic dermatoses and in psoriasis. In some cases the "organic" factor may be prevalent. Such cases, if they are representatives of the allergic state, usually show multiple hypersensitiveness. Here a neurotic conflict may occasionally act as a trigger, substituting as it were for an allergenic substance (e.g., in certain cases of contact dermatitis). In other cases the genetic factor (of great importance in atopic eczema, psoriasis, seborrhoic eczema, rosacea, etc.) will determine the *type* of response, yet in the entire constellation the emphasis will be on the neurotic conflict.

We may now say: In all these entities the specificity, which in turn is determined by a constellation of factors, lies in the readiness for certain specific organ responses. In some representatives the readiness for response is such that the dermatosis will be precipitated by a multitude of causes. In others—and it seems to be at least a high percentage—it requires a specific constellation involving all the psychological characteristics. All these possibilities can be represented in a scheme which proved to be useful not only for the interpretation of clinical entities, but also of individual representatives of such an entity.

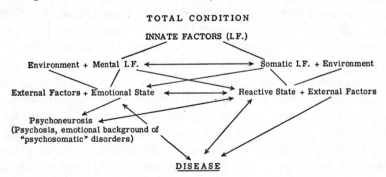

TOTAL CONDITION

INNATE FACTORS (I.F.)

Environment + Mental I.F.   Somatic I.F. + Environment

External Factors + Emotional State   Reactive State + External Factors

Psychoneurosis
(Psychosis, emotional background of
"psychosomatic" disorders)

DISEASE

We see on the first line the innate factor which may be manifested in the somatic and mental sphere. The arrows indicate their mutual interdependence. The interaction of somatic genetic factors and the environment, under the influence of emotional factors (again indicated by arrows) creates what, in analogy to the allergic state, I have called the reactive state, indicating the readiness for reacting in the somatic sphere. Similarly, the term "emotional state" indicates the readiness to respond with neurosis, psychosis, or to supply the emotional background of "psychosomatic disorders." The arrows indicate the mutual interdependence of these variables.

The only two entities in which, according to my observations, genetic factors are either negligible or at least not discernible, and in which correspondingly the neurotic conflict seemed to be the sole etiological factor, the total alopecia and chronic, exudative, discoid and lichenoid dermatitis.

In these cases the reconstruction in the analysis brought up certain points suggesting that the organ choice might be explained by the life history. In two cases of total alopecia the hair was hypercathexed, in both cases the hair of the patients, in one of them also that of the mother. One of my patients with chronic, exudative, discoid and lichenoid dermatitis had been a very skinny child. A large part of his symptoms revolved around an obsession with thinness. His nickname since early childhood had been "Skinny." Following the language of the primary process he then really became skinny. In another case of the same entity, the patient's most important infantile traumatization occurred during an episode of scarlet fever at the age of four. He also had a severe burn at the age of two. In his adolescence he developed a painful excoriation on his penis after masturbation. His first lesion developed on the same spot. Our sample case developed her first eruption at the age of one. As was guessed from her analysis and confirmed by her mother, she had pneumonia at that time. She developed first a severe diaper rash and then the first signs of her atopic eczema.[42]

TECHNICAL PROBLEMS

I now shall resume the discussion of this patient's analysis. In the fourth year of her analysis she entered into a phase which was not very different from that of our common neuroses. She brought early infantile material of the kind we are used to getting in other cases. She gradually learned to express affects and transference phenomena on a more advanced level. She no longer talked and acted with her skin. Her early hatred for her mother, rooted in her earliest, infantile relationship, proved to be at least as important as her traumatization by her father. Her mother had not satisfied her needs on any level. Correspondingly she was unable to develop object relationships beyond the level of a need-satisfying object (Anna Freud, 1954a, 1954b). Only after the relationship with her mother,

[42] These last two cases would confirm the opinion expressed by Deutsch (1939b) that organs early afflicted by "organic" disease may later be selected for symbolic expression.

her sibling rivalry, and her penis envy were worked through, could she develop an accepting attitude toward her husband. She became capable of normal orgasm. She became pregnant again, and this pregnancy brought a lot of material into the analysis. She learned, partly in identification with her analyst, to see the behavior of her mother as the manifestation of weakness and neurosis rather than of viciousness. She developed a somewhat forgiving attitude toward her, and with it she could accept femininity and motherhood. During this time her skin cleared completely, and her complexion could have served as advertisement for any "beauty cream." She terminated the treatment toward the end of the pregnancy. Her skin has remained clear ever since.

I discussed this sample case in greater details because it presented the opportunity to study the factors involved in symptom formation with special emphasis on ego regression. It also exemplified problems of technique and methodology of research.

I have already referred to several of the technical difficulties, which obviously become particularly significant, when the patient seeks treatment because of his dermatosis. When I started to treat such patients I had no idea of the importance of emotional factors in the etiology and was, so to say, at least doubtful about a potential therapeutic result. My doubts were reinforced during the course of the treatment with its stormy relapses. I had to tell the patients that they were being treated for their general emotional problems; no promise could be made that the skin would improve.

What factors account for the therapeutic results? If regressive reactions which accompany affects and instinctual drives can produce symptoms, *anything* counteracting such regression should be beneficial. That patients rarely itch during sessions cannot be explained only with alleviation of anxiety by the analyst. The explanation seems to be that verbalization is, in the scale of ego responses, counteracting ego regression. Verbalized thoughts are closer to the secondary process than fantasies, daydreams, etc. Thus verbalization has more than cathartic value. Any improvement by "organic" methods can also counteract regression and help break a vicious circle.

Hence patients suffering from the dermatoses enumerated above, may occasionally profit from less intensive psychotherapy, e.g., group therapy.

We usually distinguish intellectual and emotional understanding in the responses of our patients. We also know that intellectualization may be a type of troublesome resistance. Yet in these cases intellectual understanding may, especially in the initial phase, represent progress as compared to the deep preverbal regression.[43] To use it as a proper tool is one of the intricacies of the treatment. As the analysis proceeds in the uncovering of the unconscious conflicts, the predominance of primary process thinking recedes and simultaneously patients who used to think, feel, and act with their skin, learn to use normal channels of expression.

Consequently, I consider it possible to submit such cases to the full process of analysis. The criteria for selection follow those in other severe neuroses and "borderline cases" (Anna Freud, 1954a; Stone, 1954). The analyst should be familiar with the special difficulties of such cases and be prepared to continue the analysis during periods of hospitalization if necessary. Only desperate cases may require what Kaufman (1953) and Margolin (1953) have described as "anaclitic" therapy. In others analysis must be preceded by a preparatory stage of medical treatment and supportive psychotherapy. A majority of cases will tolerate analysis, especially if treatment is begun comparatively early.

I feel strongly that the proper methodological approach to the understanding of various dermatoses—and this applies to all fields of "psychosomatic" research—is the analysis of representative sample cases of each entity. It would be highly desirable to extend this method to all dermatoses which potentially belong to this group. Any insight gained by sample analysis can then be supplemented by observations gained through extensive diagnostic interviews backed up by projective techniques, by analytically oriented psychotherapy, and by longitudinal observations.

The main purpose of this paper was to demonstrate in what way the pure analytic approach can contribute to the understanding of certain physiological mechanisms. Special emphasis was given to the importance of ego regression for economic considerations.

BIBLIOGRAPHY

Alexander, F. (1950), *Psychosomatic Medicine*. New York: Norton.
Bauer, J. (1945), *Constitution and Disease*. New York: Grune & Stratton.
Bender, L. (1950), Anxiety in Disturbed Children. In: *Anxiety*, ed. P. Hoch and J. Zubin. New York: Grune & Stratton.
Bergman, P. and Escalona, S. K. (1949), Unusual Sensitivities in Very Young Children. *This Annual*, III/IV.
Bergmann, G. von (1932), *Funktionelle Pathologie*. Berlin: Springer.
Binger, C. A. L.; Ackerman, N. W.; Cohn, H. E.; Schroeder, H. A.; Steele, J. H. (1945), *Personality in Arterial Hypertension*. New York: American Society for Research in Psychosomatic Problems.
Bonaparte, M. (1952), Some Biopsychical Aspects of Sado-Masochism. *Int. J. Psa.,* XXXIII.

43 The therapeutic result which Freud (1909) obtained in the case of the "Ratman" might be significant in this context.

Brunswick, R. M. (1928), A Supplement to Freud's "History of an Infantile Neurosis."
In: *The Psychoanalytic Reader,* ed. R. Fliess. New York: International Universities Press.

Bychowski, G. (1954), The Structure of Homosexual Acting Out. *Psa. Quart.,* XXIII.

Cannon, W. B. (1920), *Bodily Changes in Pain, Hunger, Fear and Rage.* New York:
D. Appleton & Co.

Coleman, R. W.; Kris, E.; Provence, S. (1953), The Study of Variations of Early
Parental Attitudes. *This Annual,* VIII.

Deutsch, F. (1939a), *The Production of Somatic Disease by Emotional Disturbance.*
Baltimore: Williams & Wilkins.

—— (1939b), Choice of the Organ in Organ Neurosis. *Int. J. Psa.,* XX.

—— (1953), Discussion. In: *The Psychosomatic Concept in Psychoanalysis,* ed. F.
Deutsch. New York: International Universities Press.

Eissler, K. R. (1953), Notes upon the Emotionality of a Schizophrenic Patient and Its
Relation to Problems of Technique. *This Annual,* VIII.

Fenichel, O. (1939), The Counter-Phobic Attitude. *Int. J. Psa.,* XX.

—— (1945a), *The Psychoanalytic Theory of Neurosis.* New York: Norton.

—— (1945b), The Nature and Classification of the So-Called Psychosomatic Phenomena. *Psa. Quart.,* XIV.

Ferenczi, S. (1921), Psycho-Analytical Observations on Tic. In: *Further Contributions
to the Theory and Technique of Psycho-Analysis.* London: Hogarth Press, 1950.

Flescher, J. (1955), A Dualistic Viewpoint on Anxiety. *J. Am. Psa. Assn.,* III.

Freud, A. (1936), *The Ego and the Mechanisms of Defense.* New York: International
Universities Press, 1946.

—— (1954a), The Widening Scope of Indications for Psychoanalysis. Discussion. *J. Am.
Psa. Assn.,* II.

—— (1954b), Psychoanalysis and Education. *This Annual,* IX.

—— (1954c), Problems of Infantile Neurosis. A Discussion. *This Annual,* IX.

Freud, S. (1887-1902), *The Origins of Psychoanalysis.* New York: Basic Books, 1954.

—— (1909), Notes Upon a Case of Obsessional Neurosis. *Collected Papers,* III. London:
Hogarth Press, 1950.

—— (1910), Psychogenic Visual Disturbance According to Psycho-Analytical Concep-
tions. *Ibid.,* II.

—— (1911), Psycho-Analytic Notes Upon an Autobiographical Account of a Case of
Paranoia (Dementia Paranoides). *Ibid.,* III.

—— (1912), The Dynamics of the Transference. *Ibid.,* II.

—— (1913), The Predisposition to Obsessional Neurosis. *Ibid,* II.

—— (1914), On Narcissism: An Introduction. *Ibid.,* IV.

—— (1915a), Repression. *Ibid.,* IV.

—— (1915b), The Unconscious. *Ibid.,* IV.

—— (1915c), A Case of Paranoia Running Counter to the Psycho-Analytical Theory of
the Disease. *Ibid.,* II.

—— (1916), Metapsychological Supplement to the Theory of Dreams. *Ibid.,* IV.

—— (1917), *Introductory Lectures on Psychoanalysis.* London: Allen & Unwin, 1929.

—— (1918), From the History of an Infantile Neurosis. *Collected Papers,* III.

—— (1926), *Inhibition, Symptoms and Anxiety.* London: Hogarth Press, 1948.

—— (1927), Fetishism. *Collected Papers,* V.

—— (1931a), Female Sexuality. *Ibid.,* V.

—— (1931b), Libidinal Types. *Ibid.,* V.

—— (1932), *New Introductory Lectures on Psychoanalysis.* New York: Norton, 1933.

—— (1937), Analysis Terminable and Interminable. *Collected Papers,* V.

—— (1938), Splitting of the Ego in the Defensive Process. *Ibid.,* V.

Fries, M. and Woolf, P. J. (1953), Some Hypotheses on the Role of the Congenital
Type in Personality Development. *This Annual,* VIII.

Graff, N. I. and Wallerstein, R. S. (1954), Unusual Wheal Reaction in a Tattoo. *Psychosom. Med.*, XVI.

Greenacre, P. (1952), *Trauma, Growth and Personality*. New York: Norton.

Greenson, R. R. (1953), On Boredom. *J. Am. Psa. Assn.*, I.

—— (1954a), On Moods and Introjections. *Bull. Menninger Clin.*, XVIII.

—— (1954b), The Struggle Against Identification. *J. Am. Psa. Assn.*, II.

Grinker, R. R. (1953), *Psychosomatic Research*. New York: Norton.

Grinker, R. R. and Robbins, F. P. (1953), *Psychosomatic Case Book*. New York: Blakiston.

Hartmann, H. (1939), Ich-Psychologie und Anpassungsproblem. *Int. Ztschr. f. Psa. u. Imago*, XXIV. Translated in part in: *Organization and Pathology of Thought*, ed. D. Rapaport. New York: Columbia University Press, 1951.

—— (1950), Psychoanalysis and Developmental Psychology. *This Annual*, V.

—— (1953), Contribution to the Metapsychology of Schizophrenia. *This Annual*, VIII.

—— Kris, E.; Loewenstein, R. M. (1949), Notes on the Theory of Aggression. *This Annual*, III/IV.

Jacobson, E. (1954a), Contribution to the Metapsychology of Psychotic Identifications. *J. Am. Psa. Assn.*, II.

—— (1954b), The Self and Object World. *This Annual*, IX.

Katan, M. (1949), Schreber's Delusion of the End of the World. *Psa. Quart.*, XVIII.

—— (1950), Schreber's Hallucination about the "Little Man." *Int. J. Psa.*, XXXI.

—— (1952), Further Remarks about Schreber's Hallucination. *Int. J. Psa.*, XXXIII.

—— (1954), The Non-Psychotic Part of the Personality in Schizophrenics. *Int. J. Psa.*, XXXV.

Kaufman, M. R. (1953), Problems of Therapy. In: *The Psychosomatic Concept in Psychoanalysis*, ed. F. Deutsch. New York: International Universities Press.

Kris, E. (1949), On Preconscious Mental Processes. In: *Psychoanalytic Explorations in Art*. New York: International Universities Press, 1952.

—— (1950), Notes on the Development and on Some Current Problems of Psychoanalytic Child Psychology. *This Annual*, V.

Kubie, L. S. (1941), A Physiological Approach to the Concept of Anxiety. *Psychosom. Med.*, III.

—— (1953), The Problem of Specificity in the Psychosomatic Process. In: *The Psychosomatic Concept in Psychoanalysis*, ed. F. Deutsch. New York: International Universities Press.

Lewin, B. D. (1954), Sleep, Narcissistic Neurosis and the Analytic Situation. *Psa. Quart.*, XXIII.

Liddell, H. S. (1949), The Role of Vigilance in the Development of Animal Neurosis. In: *Anxiety*, ed. P. Hoch and J. Zubin. New York: Grune & Stratton.

Macalpine, I. (1953), Pruritus Ani: A Psychiatric Study. *Psychosom. Med.*, XV.

—— and Hunter, R. A. (1953), The Schreber Case. *Psa. Quart.*, XXII.

Mahl, G. F. (1950), Anxiety, HCL Secretion and Peptic Ulcer Etiology. *Psychosom. Med.*, XII.

Mahler, M. S.; Ross, I. R., Jr.; de Friess, Z. (1949), Clinical Studies in Benign and Malignant Cases of Childhood Psychosis (Schizophrenia-like). *Am. J. Orthopsychiat.*, XIX.

Margolin, S. G. (1953), Genetic and Dynamic Psychophysiological Determinants of Pathophysiological Processes. In: *The Psychosomatic Concept in Psychoanalysis*, ed. F. Deutsch. New York: International Universities Press.

—— Orringer, O.; Kaufman, M. R.; Winkelstein, A.; Hollaender, F.; Janowitz, H.; Stern, A.; Levy, M. H. (1950), Variations of Gastric Functions During Conscious and Unconscious Conflict States. *Proc. Assn. Res. Nerv. & Ment. Dis.*, XXIX.

Meng, H. (1934), Das Problem der Organpsychose. *Int. Ztschr. f. Psa.*, XX.

Menninger, K. A. (1954), Psychological Aspects of the Organism under Stress, Parts I and II. *J. Am. Psa. Assn.*, II.

Rapaport, D. (1951a), The Conceptual Model of Psychoanalysis. *J. Personality*, XX.
—— (1951b), *Organization and Pathology of Thought.* New York: Columbia University Press.
—— (1953), On the Psycho-Analytical Theory of Affects. *Int. J. Psa.,* XXXIV.
Saul, L. J. (1939), Hostility in Cases of Essential Hypertension. *Psychosom. Med.,* I.
—— and Bernstein, C. (1941), The Emotional Set-up of Some Attacks of Urticaria. *Psychosom. Med.,* III.
Schur, M. (1950a), Basic Problems of Psychosomatic Medicine. In: *Elements of Psychoanalysis,* ed. H. Herma and G. M. Kurth. New York: World Publ. Co.
—— (1950b), Exudative, Discoid and Lichenoid Dermatitis (Sulzberger-Garbe's Syndrome): Case Analyses. *Int. J. Psa.,* XXXI.
—— (1953), The Ego in Anxiety. In: *Drives, Affects, Behavior,* ed. R. M. Loewenstein. New York: International Universities Press.
—— (1955), Constitutional Aspects of Psychosomatic Medicine. *Samiksa,* VIII.
Selye, H. (1950), *Stress.* Montreal: Acta, Inc.
Sperling, M. (1953), Food Allergies and Conversion Hysteria. *Psa. Quart.,* XXII.
Spitz, R. A. (1951), The Psychogenic Diseases in Infancy: An Attempt at Their Etiological Classification. *This Annual,* VI.
—— (1954), *Genése des premières relations objectales (observations directes sur le nourrisson pendant sa première année)* (in print).
Stern, M. M. (1951), Anxiety, Trauma and Shock. *Psa. Quart.,* XX.
Stone, L. (1954), The Widening Scope of Indications for Psychoanalysis. *J. Am. Psa. Assn.,* II.
Varendonck, J. (1921), The Psychology of Daydreams. In: *Organization and Pathology of Thought,* ed. D. Rapaport. New York: Columbia University Press, 1951.
Wittkower, E.; Russell, B.; et al. (1953), *Emotional Factors in Skin Diseases.* New York: Paul B. Hoeber.
Zaidens, S. H. (1950), Three Cases Illustrative of Emotional Factors in Dermatology. *Psa. Rev.,* XXXVII.

SIMULTANEOUS ANALYSIS OF MOTHER
AND CHILD[1]

DOROTHY BURLINGHAM (London)
in co-operation with
ALICE GOLDBERGER (London) and ANDRÉ LUSSIER, Ph.D.
(Montreal)

I. INTRODUCTION AND PREHISTORY

The case of Bobby is one of those on whom much effort by psychiatrists, analysts, child guidance workers, etc., is spent, often with the disappointing result that the child falls back into his former abnormalities after the contact with and effort of the respective workers have been withdrawn. Though there seems to exist in the child a good potentiality for improvement or even complete recovery, another force seems to be at work which counteracts constantly the therapeutic efforts which are made. Analysts have recognized for some time that this force emanates from the mother, usually in spite of the mother's conscious efforts to co-operate in treatment. In child guidance work where dealings with the mother are by necessity of a more superficial nature, her pathogenic influence on the child is ascribed mostly to her hostile feelings toward it, i.e., her rejection, or to her seductive behavior, or to the abnormalities of her own object relationships, or to her psychotic traits. It seems to us that nothing short of an analysis of the mother can reveal in detail which influences are at work and what the more intimate relations are between her unconscious fantasies and attitudes and her child's disturbance.

(i) *Bobby in Child Guidance Treatment* (age 2½)

Bobby was first brought to a child guidance clinic (Hornsey Infant Welfare Centre) at the age of two and a half, his symptoms then being feeding difficulties, wetting and soiling, retardation of speech, biting attacks on the mother and clinging to her. The case was assigned to Miss Ruth Thomas, then the visiting psychologist.

The mother attended for the period of one year, once weekly. She seemed a simple woman, somewhat slow in understanding, but co-operative. She followed

[1] This investigation has been carried out in the Hampstead Child-Therapy Clinic, London, which is maintained by the Field Foundation, Inc., New York. It has been aided by a grant from the Foundations' Fund for Research in Psychiatry, New Haven, Connecticut.

the advice given with regard to the handling of feeding and habit training and the child improved. His eating increased, and wetting and soiling disappeared after two months. In connection with Bobby's separation anxieties, the mother was instructed not to expose him to shocks. She showed her understanding of this by preparing Bobby well for a half day's separation from her when she had to go to hospital for an examination. When urged there to remain for treatment she refused, remembering her promise to Bobby to return on the same day and Miss Thomas's advice. She co-operated equally well where Bobby's castration fears were concerned. The only point where she proved adamant was in her allegedly hygienic attitude toward handling and cleaning his penis.

In spite of the mother's helpfulness, Miss Thomas distrusted the stability of the improvement, and when Bobby developed the new symptom of breaking away from his mother to run into the street traffic she advised child analysis.

(ii) *Bobby's First Analysis* (3½-4½ years of age)

At this time, at the age of three and a half, Bobby was taken in analysis by Dr. Martin James, then an analyst in training at the London Institute of Psycho-Analysis. Again the mother co-operated to the fullest extent to which her own difficulties permitted. The analytic material developed in an orderly fashion by means of fantasy play, a primal scene being uncovered finally at the end of the first year. Again the child improved. The analysis was broken off when the analyst had to leave London. It was a striking point in Dr. James's observations that the mother had forgotten whatever interpretations and advice she had been given during the first child guidance treatment.

Dr. James managed to keep contact in occasional interviews to watch the child's progress. When the situation deteriorated once more, Bobby was referred to the Hampstead Child-Therapy Clinic where, for the reasons mentioned above, his case was selected for inclusion in our project of "simultaneous analysis of mother and child."

(iii) *Bobby and his Mother in Analysis* (Bobby aged 4 years 10 months)

The analysis of Bobby and his mother now became the concern of a team of workers. The mother's analysis was undertaken by Dr. André Lussier of Montreal, Canada, then in training at the Institute of Psycho-Analysis in London. The analysis of Bobby was carried out by Miss Alice Goldberger, an analytic child therapist trained in the Hampstead Child-Therapy Course. For the purpose of keeping the analytic work of the two therapists independent and uninfluenced by the material of the other partner, Mr. Lussier and Miss Goldberger were instructed not to communicate with each other. Instead, both reported their material to me at weekly intervals for purposes of integration. The analytic material is therefore theirs, my part being that of supervising or controlling analyst. I have received permission from both to use it in the communication which follows.

II. Feeding Problems

(i) The Child's Behavior

As in every child's analysis, the first account of the early feeding problems was given by the mother; in Bobby's case it was only to be expected that her reports might be even more colored by her own disturbances than happens usually. Her first description of Bobby was that of a perfect baby. It took some time until she remembered that she herself did not have enough milk, that accordingly there was difficulty in breast feeding and that the child had to be weaned at the age of twelve weeks. As regards his own activity in the feeding process, she described that he would not grasp a rusk to chew, that she had to hold it for him, that he would not attempt to hold a spoon to feed himself. According to her, this passive attitude toward food had outlasted babyhood and persisted up to the time she brought him to analysis. When he was four and a half, she would still sit beside him at mealtimes, feed him like a baby and urge him to eat more than he wanted to take voluntarily. By that time he had acquired many food fads and would ask her for special dishes which he would then refuse.

According to the mother, Bobby's feeding difficulties had reached a peak at the age of one year when he suffered from a severe attack of diarrhea, retained no food, cried, whined and hardly slept. This condition seems to have lasted for eight months when he was finally put on a strict diet which she kept up for six months. When Bobby was two years old, the mother had to go to hospital and Bobby was sent to a residential nursery. According to the mother, he fell ill there and returned severely constipated. The mother blames his further difficulties on this time of separation. When Bobby went to school, the mother distrusted his eating the school meals and insisted on having him home to feed.

In contrast to this behavior with the mother, his father reported that Bobby ate well when with him. The same was reported from school when the teacher finally insisted on his remaining for meals. In his sessions with the therapist Bobby would show greed for food, would demand quantities of drinks and eat by himself without any difficulty when given food. There seemed to be no doubt that his attitude to eating varied with his moods. Periodically he had states of depression when he felt unloved and unworthy of love. Once, when he had been moved to a lower form in school and had fallen into such a mood, he told his therapist that he ate too much, but that he felt all the time as if he were starving. In this and similar sessions he demanded not only food but other signs of affection. It was characteristic of his oral greed that he could not bear frustration at such times but had to have his wishes fulfilled immediately or fall into a panic.

This evidence given by the father and the teacher as well as Bobby's behavior in the analytic session showed that he was able to have a normal or even increased appetite with perfect ability to be active in feeding himself. His abnormal behavior in the feeding situation was reserved for the mother whom he controlled and tortured by his passivity and his refusal to eat. She reacted to this by taking the active part and forcing food on him.

Seen from the point of view of this child's analysis, we would say that, through his behavior, Bobby forced the mother to react toward him as she did. Seen from the aspect of the mother's analysis, as will be shown below, Bobby's behavior takes on a different connotation. There is, in the mother's analytic material, ample evidence that in handling the child's feeding situation she was herself under the domination of powerful unconscious fantasies which determined her attitude. In this light the child's behavior will be seen as a reaction to the mother's provocation.

(ii) *Material from the Mother's Analysis*

The Mother as an Unwanted Child.—Bobby's mother had been told in childhood that she had been unwanted and that her mother, when pregnant with her, had taken quantities of pills in order to abort. When she grew older she was not considered normal, but queer, odd, strange. It is this image of herself as a child which she projected later onto Bobby in forming the idea that he could not be normal either. In spite of his having been a healthy baby she could not trust herself to have produced a normal child. This particular remnant from her own childhood created a need in her to have an abnormal, queer child herself.

Analytic Material Underlying the Difficulties of Breast Feeding.— In the mother's analysis the simple fact told to the child's therapist that she had had insufficient milk to feed Bobby proved to overlay a very different state of affairs. Actually, her milk had not been insufficient, it had flowed freely but dried up always as soon as she put the child to the breast. The fantasy material which she revealed was the following. She had learned early (before the age of five) that she had been breast-fed herself, but that her mother developed cancer of the breast soon after. The mother died of this cancer before Mrs. N. was six years old. The child conceived the idea, which persisted for ever after, that the mother's illness was due to injury which she as a suckling infant, had done to the breast. She took this as a confirmation that she was born a bad child and that her fate was to destroy the people she loved. The idea that she had killed her mother became conscious, remained in her mind, and served as reinforcement of her masochistic inclinations.

These partly conscious, partly unconscious fantasies were not the only barrier to breast feeding. There was, further, the idea in Mrs. N.'s mind that breast feeding was disgusting and degrading, fit only for animals such as cows. Analysis traced this back to observation of cows being milked or suckled by the calf and the equation of breast and penis. Nursing Bobby, therefore, became for her the act of permitting him to commit fellatio with her.

There was the further idea in her unconscious that by taking her milk Bobby would empty her out, being empty equalizing for Mrs. N. a state of deep depression. The feeling of emptiness was connected in her mind with hunger, i.e., the lack of food which she had experienced before as well as after her own mother's death. Mrs. N.'s family had been poor, they had often gone hungry and her mother in the time of her illness had become a bad manager, failing to provide proper nourishment for her children. When Mrs. N. was taken to hospital once as a child because of skin trouble, malnutrition had been diagnosed. For Mrs. N. as well as for Bobby food and love, being unloved or starved, were synonymous.

So far as Mrs. N.'s conscious intentions were concerned, she had meant to give Bobby a better childhood than she had had herself. Where she had been hungry, she wanted to satisfy him; where she had been empty, she meant to keep him full and loved. But her unconscious fantasies and anxieties prevented her from realizing this aim. Her defenses against being given a cancer by him (as she had given to her mother), her defenses against fellatio fantasies and the warding off of emptiness and depression stopped her milk from flowing for the child and forced her into making him repeat her own experiences of deprivation. What Bobby actually experienced was her withdrawal from him, her refusal of satisfying nourishment, i.e., her rejection.

Further Material Concerning Feeding.—At a later term of her analysis Mrs. N. was deeply concerned with her guilt feelings toward Bobby, not only for having deprived him of her milk but also for failing to feed him properly at the succeeding stages. She blamed herself for the attack of severe diarrhea at the age of one which she ascribed to giving him meat that was not fresh and insufficiently cooked by her. According to her, he was ill for months without interruption, and it seems that during this time she tried unsuccessfully to convince several doctors of the severity of his state and of her own part in it. Finally she found one doctor onto whom she could project her own feelings of self-accusation. She felt that after examining the child this doctor looked at her accusingly as if he wanted to condemn and kill her for neglect. These self-accusations were projected equally onto Bobby himself. She was convinced that he blamed her and that from the beginning of the diarrhea he ceased to smile at her.

During the illness, and on doctor's advice for four months after, she kept Bobby on a severe diet, evidently on a starvation diet. During day and night the child continued to cry and shout "dinner, dinner." According to Mrs. N., she never slept during that period, spending the night by the child's bed. Mrs. N. felt certain that in some magical way her thoughts had produced his illness and with it the child's further abnormality, greed, impatience and aggressive behavior toward her.

It was possible in the analysis to trace back also the story of the uncooked food to the period in Mrs. N.'s life when her own mother had become incapacitated by illness and ceased to cook. The analysis unearthed Mrs. N.'s fantasies of revenge, her death wishes against her mother and the memory of spiteful and hurtful acts committed against her. There seems no doubt that it is this hostile attitude toward her own mother which affected her relationship to Bobby and induced in him a behavior which tyrannized and controlled her in return. The suffering caused in her by Bobby's naughtiness and uncontrollable behavior served to assuage the unconscious guilt which stemmed from the relationship to her own mother.

III. Anal Problems

(i) *The Child's Behavior*

The mother's description of Bobby's anal problems was as dramatic as that of the oral ones. Here too she described an initial easy phase with training from birth, with few soiled napkins after the age of eight months. Trouble began with the diarrhea at twelve and a half months when she gave up potting, and with the severe constipation after the return from the nursery when he would hold back his motions for four to five days. Her description of his anal behavior sounded most odd. When unable to hold back defecation any longer, he would stand at a window, look out and dirty his trousers in this position unless his mother took off the trousers beforehand. In the nursery he had learned to run on tiptoe and from his mother he had picked up songs. He used both in a curious ritual which was still in force in the beginning of his second analysis. When he could no longer hold back his motions, he would rush up to his mother, order everybody out of the room and without trousers, wearing soft slippers and a vest only, he would run on tiptoe around the room, the mother singing a special song: "Tiptoe through the tulips." He then hung on to his mother, crouched down and she had to catch the feces in the pot. This ritual had to be repeated many times until, in small portions, he had finished. The mother had to empty the pot for every separate piece of feces. He did not look at his feces.

Bobby never used the lavatory, feared even to enter it. He was afraid to pull the chain or watch the water rushing down. Connected with his anal messiness was a general untidiness and messiness which provoked the mother in the highest degree. His anal obstinacy revealed itself also in firm refusals to do whatever she demanded of him. On such occasions he would fly into uncontrollable tempers. This revolt against the mother was all the more exhausting for her as he was extremely clinging and refused to let her out of his sight.

(ii) *The Child's Analytic Material*

In contrast to the oral symptoms, Bobby's stubbornness, obstinacy and ambivalence were transferred fully to the analytic session and his relationship to the therapist. His strict early habit training coupled with the later inability to hold back his feces at the time of the diarrhea had left him with a feeling that he could not accomplish anything. The mother played on this conviction by assuring him constantly that there was nothing he could do right and by treating him like a baby. He expressed this in the analytic hour by refusing to undertake any play activity; he was convinced before starting that he would fail.

He soon revealed two major anxieties which dominated his behavior in feeding and in defecation: the fear of emptiness and the fear of being full. On the one hand, emptiness, i.e., the idea of being starved, unloved, deprived of all good things inside, made him greedy. It also made him retain his feces since he felt empty and deprived of good body contents when they left his inside. On the other hand, the content of his bowels was called bad by his mother and regarded by Bobby himself as such. The more he ate, the more it would accumulate in him and, due to constipation, turn him into something altogether bad. Therefore he had to refrain from eating and had to try and defecate to keep empty.

This preoccupation with the inside of his body based on the alternating events of diarrhea and constipation in his infancy was expressed in his analytic hours in a symbolic play, the symbol owing its existence to an actual event. At the age of four Bobby had been in an underground train when it was held up in a tunnel for half an hour. He was much impressed and badly frightened by this incident. Following it he played in the analysis that he himself was the underground train and in this identification rushed about the room excitedly producing noise and, as he called it "stink." Still in the role of the train, he would get painfully stuck in the tunnel, frightening himself and his imaginary passengers. When not playing this game, he drew underground trains, scribbled over them, called them dirty and remarked "the underground has a funny bottom." There was no doubt about Bobby's identification with the train, nor of the identification of his intestines with the tunnels where the dirty, stinking, bad body contents were arrested.

Other meanings of his body contents and the act of defecation filled many other analytic sessions. His excrements were "good," precious, because his mother stressed their value so highly. Bowel movements signified the loss of this precious substance which was accompanied by a feeling of his whole inside getting emptied, running out. In defense against this feeling of loss, he invented a dolls' play in which the doll (representing himself) was put on the pot, the pot afterwards having to be placed either on his own or the doll's head in an attempt to pour back the precious content into the body. Sometimes the doll's hat was used in the same manner in the place of the pot.

In another symbolic play Bobby represented his fear of falling into the lavatory and being washed away, as the feces were. In this play his dolls were pushed into the lavatory head first. He accepted the therapist's interpretation of this action by saying: "You didn't know, it is me. It is Bobby, I." Another symbolic game served to dramatize Bobby's fantasies of anal birth. This was staged with teddy bears, the baby teddy being born out of the father teddy's anus. It was also acted out with dolls which either fell or were pushed by him to drown; then he lifted them out of the water and they were born. At other times he himself took the role of the baby, threw himself on the floor (calling it water) and urged the therapist to bend over him and slowly to lift him out of the water through a narrow gap between the table and the wall. He made it quite clear that also the feces were babies who were drowned and who had to be reborn. His wish for reassurance that babies could be reborn determined some of his defecation ritual, namely the need to pass his feces in small pieces, and to have each piece thrown separately into the lavatory. By keeping his anal babies separate he proved to himself that he was not empty and that he could produce a multitude of children. Other games of falling and losing, although closely connected with the anal ones, had a phallic meaning. He opened a paper lantern and called it full; he folded and closed it and called it empty or dead, asking anxiously whether he would have to die too. This was accompanied by his falling down on the floor, stretching himself to his full length or holding a broom on his head and falling down with it. Here the falling was equated not only with the losing of the feces in the lavatory but with the "falling down" (limpness) of the erect penis which Bobby represents here by his whole body. Falling, losing, emptiness were connected in his mind with death.

(iii) *The Mother's Analytic Material*

Constipation.—With Mrs. N. constipation was a lifelong symptom beginning very early during her mother's lifetime when she forced her mother to remain with her during defecation and wait for her to perform. To keep her feces inside came to represent the only means to get attention and not to feel lonely. They became highly valued, a very precious possession. The analysis demonstrated that the emptying of her bowels was the signal of emotional emptiness and subsequent depression. She remembers vividly that as long as she was constipated and obstinate, there was human presence around her, there was pressure, there was a high degree of attention paid to her for what she had inside; but as soon as she had complied with the demands of the mother, there was no fuss made anymore about her, nobody around, no pressure, just the feeling of emptiness inside and outside, the feeling of loneliness. The strongest imprint in her feelings was the connection between the losing of feces and the losing of attention, with the simultaneous equation between keeping the feces inside and keeping hold of the mother.

Since the mother was ill already at this time she was made to understand that her behavior would tire her and make her die. Thus her constipation assumed a double meaning. On the one hand, it served as a reassurance that her mother was at her side, that is, not dead; on the other hand, it was an expression of her death wishes against her mother, a means of killing her. It was this ambivalence toward the mother which turned Mrs. N. into a clinging child who could not be separated from her mother even for a few minutes and had to hold her hand continually. The mother tried to cure her constipation by means of enemas which were experienced by her as a sexual attack and resulted in permanent sadomasochistic fantasies and attitudes.

At this time Mrs. N. also projected the fantasy of her own dirty inside onto the mother. In the last phase of her life the latter appeared to the child to lose her mind, to become negligent and forgetful, the state of the whole house becoming one of dreadful disorderliness and dirtiness. According to Mrs. N., her mother accumulated possessions and secured all sorts of food, rotting fruits, sweets, etc., in her drawers where they were found after her death. The horror with which the patient described the emptying of these drawers after the mother's death showed convincingly that these places represented to her the dirty inside of her mother's body. Later she developed a phobic attitude toward her own drawers which represented her own dirty inside. Any preoccupation with these drawers assumed the significance of anal masturbation. This attitude continued until the mother's death, the constipation now (in addition to her behavior at the breast) being used as a basis for her guilt feelings. Several years after the mother's death at the age of nine she was sent to hospital where her constipation was treated again by means of enemas.

Anal Birth Fantasies.—When Mrs. N. became pregnant with Bobby this ended for her, for the time being, the dread of emptiness and brought back the happy feeling of keeping the mother alive within her. This led to the wish to prolong her pregnancy indefinitely, and she actually succeeded in delaying delivery. She experienced the birth of the child as a loss of the feces which the outside world wanted her to give up and reacted to it with a deep and frightening feeling of emptiness with severe depression and suicidal thoughts. She refused to defecate for two weeks after the birth and when forced by necessity to do so, she had the terrifying fantasy that she was actually defecating a baby.

On the other hand, her feces as well as the baby inside her also represented the penis which she had desired to possess all her life. From this aspect pregnancy was for her the denial of castration, and the birth of the child the repeated loss of the penis to which she reacted with depression.

Anal Union.—When comparing the anal histories of Bobby and his mother, we are struck by the many similarities in behavior and fantasy content. Both Bobby and Mrs. N. as a child used their toilet training to secure their mothers' presence and attention and fought out a struggle with the mother over it, which assumed sadomasochistic proportions. With both, these struggles resulted in a hostile attitude and death wishes against the mother which in their turn were superseded by compulsive clinging. With both, this led to the symptom of constipation and subsequent treatments, enemas, etc.

It is of interest to note that there is no similarity of external life circumstances to which this almost identical pathological result can be ascribed. On the contrary, Bobby and his mother developed under completely different family circumstances. Bobby was an only child on whom his mother's attention was lavished excessively from the beginning; Mrs. N. was the youngest of many children, and had to fight for her mother's attention which was withdrawn from her increasingly when her mother fell ill. Her mother's deterioration and her early death were powerful pathogenic factors in Mrs. N.'s development and psychopathology.

It is open to speculation by which paths the mother's fantasies concerning the equation of body content and the mother image reached Bobby. We may assume that he developed a heightened sensitivity for the mother's excitement when she handled him on the pot. While she waited for him to pass his motions, she identified with him and projected onto him her own early wishes connected with her own mother. She had to remain with him as she had forced her mother to remain with her during defecation. As she had enjoyed the presence of her mother outside as well as inside on these occasions, she felt a special union with her own child when performing the same services for him. Bobby answered with his anal ritual to this sexualized attitude of the mother toward his bowel movements. Under the light of analysis, this ritual assumed the aspect of a *folie à deux*. As described before, the ritual consisted of tiptoeing round the room, standing by the window while making the mother sing and hold the pot under him. The song chosen is a love song and the complete wording of the refrain in question is the following:

Tiptoe to the window, by the window,
That is where I'll be, Come tiptoe thro' the tulips with me.

Bobby's act of defecation thus becomes a moment of perfect loving union between the two partners.

Projection of Separation Anxiety.—Another symptom connected with the child's anal behavior, namely separation anxiety, does not seem to be as evenly distributed between mother and child. In overt behavior Bobby clung to his mother as she had clung to hers. On the other hand, it soon became evident that, as with eating, Bobby was well able to behave differently when not under his mother's direct influence. He enjoyed his independence when with his father, with his analyst, in school, and he reacted well to a separation from the mother when the Clinic helped to find a summer holiday place for him. It was the mother who, for two reasons, could not allow Bobby to enjoy such independence. Her feeling of freedom when she was without him was felt by her as a proof of her hate for her child and her death wishes against him. When the child showed pleasure in being without her, he symbolized for her her own mother who had withdrawn from her. To blind herself to her inability to part from Bobby, she projected her feelings onto him, felt the separation anxiety to be his and provoked its manifest expression in every way. When mother and child met again after separation, the anal scene was taken up immediately. Thus, when the mother fetched Bobby from the holiday home after the vacation, he informed her immediately that he had had no motion during the whole fortnight, which of course was not true.

Projection of Body Processes.—There was another striking incident in the mother's history which gave evidence of the identification of her own body processes with the child's. During Bobby's period of diarrhea at twelve months the mother suffered simultaneously from what she described as an "accumulation of stuff in the fallopian tubes" (according to the medical report organic effect of permanent constipation). On the day when Bobby was pronounced cured of his diarrhea, she went to hospital herself for an examination and remained for an immediate operation. To her mind this was a necessary general clean-up of her dirty inside. She experienced the operation as a mixed anal and oedipal event. In her description, her feelings when entering the operating room were those of a young girl going to her wedding; she was all excited. After the operation her interpretation of the event changed. She felt that something had been taken away from her by force and, in her own words, that "she would never know what it was." The fantasies concerning this operation linked the anal deprivation by means of enemas with a phallic deprivation (being deprived of a penis). There was also the contrasting unconscious fantasy that the doctors left something hard and stiff inside her, which took the alternating significance of penis, feces, the mother inside her. In retrospect it could be shown in the analysis that when her fantasies of fullness and emptiness ceased to be concerned with the child's body, they turned immediately to her own body where they were lived out instead.

Anal Birth.—For both mother and child the act of defecation represented a symbolic birth, although in this respect there are some significant differences between their fantasies. In the mother's unconscious the size of the big feces played a special part. Especially immediately after Bobby's birth she felt her excrement to be "as big as a baby." According to the analysis, in her case the equation feces-baby had secondary significance to the equation feces-mother. Therefore the expulsion of the feces is followed by emptiness, depression and suicidal thoughts. It is difficult to say on the evidence of Bobby's material whether or not he was affected by this part of the mother's psychopathology. His fantasies of anal birth rather had the quality of the normal infantile birth fantasies of the anal stage. He himself was the anal baby, identified with his own bowel content; therefore he experienced anxiety when the mother did not cherish his anal products but "drowned" them in the lavatory. As a defense against his fear of being thrown away and drowned by the mother he developed the compulsive play dealing with the rebirth (the lifting out of the water) of himself, his dolls, his teddy bears. This is perhaps the point where the material of mother and child is furthest apart. Where the child experienced anxiety, the mother developed states of depression.

IV. Oedipal Phase—Phallic Strivings and Symptoms

(i) Mother's Description of Bobby's Behavior

The mother's complaint about Bobby's behavior in the oedipal phase was no less dramatic than that concerning earlier attitudes. As mentioned before, she described that he could do nothing for himself and forced her to do everything for him; that he would stand by limply to let her dress him, to the extent that she had to push his arms into the sleeves of his clothes; that he said continually, "I can't do it, you do it."

According to her, this passive behavior alternated with his controlling her, his insistence that she had to do as he ordered, accompanied by temper tantrums when she kept him waiting or did not do as he required of her.

She described him as extremely provocative. When she wanted him to be quiet, he made a great deal of noise, shouted and screamed. He would run aimlessly around the room, crashing into the walls. One of his favorite games consisted of running from one wall to the other with a toy bus held in front of him, imitating the noise of an engine.

He was "rude" to her, lifted her skirts and showed her his penis. By this she would be provoked to the degree of hitting him.

His provocations included dangerous actions by which he frightened her, such as jumping down from great heights. This behavior reached its climax in the symptom which led to his referral: namely his tearing himself from her in the street when he would run in front of cars and buses.

Finally she complained about his difficulties in falling asleep and his night terrors from which he would awake screaming. When this happened she would go to his bed to comfort him and when unsuccessful take him to bed with her.

(ii) The Child's Material

Passive Actions.—It was possible during the child's treatment to witness his quick transformations from a manly active child to a frightened, helpless and passive one. These changes occurred when he caught sight of his mother at the end of the hour. When alone with the therapist, he would soon put his coat on without assistance, but if the mother arrived before he did this, he would be seen standing limp and helpless, arms hanging down by his side while the mother would attempt to dress him.

At other times, of course, as reported before, his passivity was transferred into the sessions, when he became unable to play and insisted that he could do nothing for himself.

Ambivalence.—Much of his material was acted out in the analytic hour with the help of doll play, the dolls being called girls, and babies, representing his mother and himself. Or he would himself take the role of the mother and act out with dolls the sadomasochistic behavior which his mother displayed in her handling of him. He tortured the dolls, asking them at the same time whether they loved him. He would, for instance, tell his favorite doll, called Mary, that she need not be afraid, that he would merely wash her hands and face. Then, disregarding his promise, he would undress her completely, push her into the water viciously, splash her and leave her alone lying in the bath. Again he would ask her whether she loved him. Similar behavior was transferred directly onto the therapist whom he tantalized and provoked, simultaneously begging for signs of love and affection.

Castration.—The dolls were used further to act out castration fears and his defense against them. Again Bobby reverted to the use of the dolls' hats which, during his anal play, had symbolized the pot. Hats took on the new role to represent the penis, or part of it, especially the father's penis with its magical power. When representing the mother's castrated genital or the castrated male, the same hats were used as receptacles. Hats were also a symbol to represent departure. To take the hats off meant that either the penis or the whole person disappeared. While acting out his fears and fantasies he would, for example, pull off the hat of the doll Mary which represented himself (castrate himself); then tear off all the hats of all the dolls or exchange the hats of the male and female dolls (change sex with his mother).

Analysis showed that he was very much aware of his mother's genital which he considered castrated. Incidents were uncovered when he had the opportunity of making observations of her body. Once she had opened the door to him to let him into her room when she had a severe hemorrhage and her nightgown was covered with blood.

Much of Bobby's peculiar behavior and symptoms could be traced to his castration fears. In his behavior toward his own body he identified with the sadistic, castrating mother image and developed tendencies of self-injury: he would bang his head when thwarted, pick the skin of his lips, bite his nails until he drew blood. This also served as punishment for his sadistic wishes toward the mother. He developed a fear of proximity to females, refused to sit next to girls at school and either cried on such occasions or threatened to break them up. He also threatened his mother to "break her up," castrate her. He would refuse to let her sit next to him at mealtimes. He distinguished his father and himself as men, on the one hand, and his mother as a damaged person, on the other hand: he and his father had to have the same kind of good dinner plates while his mother was assigned a damaged plate with the pattern worn off. His father and himself were not allowed to use a broken chair on which he made his mother sit.

Intercourse Fantasies.—Bobby's oedipal jealousy was brought to the fore when Bobby's mother started her own analysis with a male analyst. This was acted out in the transference in a wild manner by Bobby throwing himself on the couch, taking a cushion between his legs, attacking the therapist with it, etc. He began to masturbate in the hour, became excited and noisy, ending up the scene by falling down, having an accident, being broken and killed. He invited his therapist to ride on a horse with him, to go alone with him to "the Silly Islands" and to drown with him. It is easy to see that Bobby's fantasies of intercourse with himself in the male role end invariably in his own downfall, injury, humiliation, death (castration).

Defenses Against Castration Fears.—Bobby used a variety of mechanisms to ward off his castration fears, wishes and fantasies. When his castration fear was too great he regressed to anal-passive behavior which accounts for many of his character traits and behavior patterns described before.

A lesser amount of anxiety was dealt with by means of other mechanisms. As expressed in the doll's play, he would *reverse* the masculine and feminine roles (putting girls' hats on the boys and vice versa). When playing intercourse with the dolls he made his female doll jump on the male one. He modeled ice-cream cones out of plasticine, saying that boys have lovely brown ones, girls nasty red ones (this last information only whispered); this was immediately altered into girls doing brown big jobs and boys red ones. The tendency to reverse was shown also by putting on his coat front to back.

He *reassured* himself as to the intactness of his penis on the one hand by exaggerated exhibitionism to his mother, on the other hand by taking over the activity of the erect penis with his whole body. The latter defense explained much of his restlessness, wriggling, running about and crashing into walls. When hurling himself bodily against an obstacle he imagined himself acting out a masculine attack on the mother. He also fantasied himself into the role of the strong protective male who rescues the female from dangers.

In his transference behavior he demonstrated many of his frightening experiences turned from *passive* events into *active* ones. Pencils in a box represented the teachers of whom he was afraid and who were punished in their turn by being locked in their box. His game of being an underground train and frightening others represented his own fear in the underground. He took the castrating role toward the therapist, threatening to pull off her arms, legs and nose. Most revealing were his attempts to push back her sleeves in a very rough manner. This represented what he experienced as his mother's attack on his penis when she pushed back his foreskin. In the transference he repeated the wild excitement which he felt on these occasions accompanied by the going limp in the presence of the mother. (Incidentally his refusal to put his own arms into the sleeves of his coat was traced back to the same situation.)

(iii) *Mother's Material with Its Implications for the Child*

As in Bobby's case, the mother's anal fixation colored her oedipal strivings. Her conscious and unconscious conflicts over defecation coincided with her penis envy which had dominated her relationship to father and brother. For her unconscious the making of big stools was to possess a penis. All her life she had had the fantasy that something was missing on her body, something had not been completed, and it would grow some day while she slept. During her oedipal phase her equation feces-penis was linked with her intense wish for a child from the father and this formed in her unconscious the usual symbolic equivalent: feces = penis = child. The anal-phallic meaning of the child was most conspicuous during the time of pregnancy and birth. Her happiness during this period was due to the threefold symbolic meaning of the foetus as the good body content (anal); the possession of the penis (phallic), and the re-creation of the mother inside her body.

Bobby as the Mother's Penis.—Fantasies about the secret possession of a penis and of its dreaded loss filled her analysis. From the moment when she had born a male child, these were projected on Bobby and molded her relationship to him. Bobby personified for her the brother's penis which she had wanted for herself. In this role he was for her a highly exciting, erotic influence, fascinating as well as frightening. When Bobby himself was excited, she felt increasingly unable to control him, helpless and powerless. Bobby's wild antics had for her the meaning of an erection of her own. Although she felt consciously that his exhibitionistic tendencies were intolerable to her, unconsciously she provoked them and felt thoroughly overwhelmed by them. Her analysis left no doubt that Bobby's exhibitionism meant to her the realization of her own unconscious wish to have a penis which she could exhibit. No wonder that she felt powerless in helping him to control himself. Although so far as Bobby was concerned, his exhibitionism originated from his need to reassure himself about his masculinity, the meaning it assumed for the mother perpetuated the symptom and gave it an important place in his relationship to his mother. By exhibiting himself to her he established a new union between her and himself, offering his penis to her as the cherished completion of her own body.

Bobby as the Father's Penis.—Bobby's masculinity represented to the mother also another and more sinister aspect of her penis envy, namely the father's dangerous masculinity. When overwhelmed by these fantasies she felt him to be a man, a grownup, his penis becoming a threat to her, paralyzing and dominating her. According to her own description in the analysis, all Bobby had to do to dominate her was to exhibit himself. The more excited he became the more she lost control of the situation, the smaller she felt and the bigger he seemed to her. The analysis related her dread of him to observations during the primal scene which she had made in the parents' bedroom. The sight of her father's penis had had a deep and dramatic effect on her. These experiences were revived later in her adolescence when she felt the compulsion to look at exhibitionists and when she imagined "the worst" in connection with some workmen, i.e., when she imagined them coming toward her with erected penis to seduce her. The violent feelings which were aroused in her by such memories directed themselves against the child's penis and did not remain without effect on him. We remember in this connection that Bobby could never exhibit to his mother without the scene ending in his literal and symbolic "downfall." What began usually as a love play between child and mother ended with the mother's violent rejection of the boy's masculinity.

Bobby as an Incestuous Child.—It was unfortunate for Bobby that he represented for the mother not only the father's seducing masculinity but also its imaginary result. At the period when the analysis dealt with her oedipal conflicts she would talk of Bobby in the most violent manner as a filthy creature, a filthy monster who would be the shame of her life. She was disgusted by the idea of ever having wanted a child, only a degraded and depraved woman would have such a wish, she would have to pay for it by being ashamed all her life, the child being bound to be a curse for her; she would never pay enough for her guilt. The analysis traced back this guilt to a fantasy in which Bobby represented the realization of her wish to have a child from the father.

Sadistic Conception of Intercourse—"Cat and Mouse" Fantasy.—Mrs. N.'s conception of intercourse was a sadomasochistic one. Her childhood was dominated by the wish to be beaten by her father which expressed itself consciously in the usual beating fantasies. Her fear of the father was stimulated further by seeing him drunk repeatedly and by watching him on such occasions beating a horse. In her unconscious she identified with the horse, wishing to be treated likewise. Unconsciously she attributed the mother's death to the father's brutal attack on her in intercourse. Every sexual relationship was understood by her as a rape, as a sadistic attack on a defenseless woman.

In her childhood she had an obsessive conscious fantasy which represented these unconscious ideas. In this fantasy a cat took sadistic pleasure in letting a mouse hope for freedom and escape and then to pounce on it. Her own identification alternated between the sadistic role of the cat and the masochistic one of the mouse. This "cat and mouse" fantasy was repeated in the transference relationship in which she played the role of the victim and assigned the role of sadistic attack to the analyst. She expected the analyst to feel "like murdering her" when she provoked him. Every detail of the analytic setting became invested with sadistic meaning, such as "forcing words, speech, dreams out of her," watching her and waiting for the first occasion to abuse her. In her own words the analyst was "a vulture watching for the occasion to pounce on her." Especially when she left the room at the end of the hour, she would expect the analyst to force her back to the couch, because she had not yet endured enough.

But this "cat and mouse" fantasy was transferred no less compulsively onto Bobby, the child and herself representing sometimes one, sometimes the other partner. At times Bobby symbolized herself in the role of helpless victim. At other times she herself was the victim, ascribing to Bobby the controlling and dominating role. She would provoke scenes with him in accordance with this fantasy and work them up until a specific intensity and peak of excitement was reached. This done, she suddenly reversed the roles and felt very much like "murdering Bobby," like "knifing him." Scenes of this kind ended usually in a beating which she administered in a compulsive and uncontrolled manner.

This part of the mother's analysis threw light on the child's symptom of "unruliness," being "out of control." It is to be assumed that his behavior was the answer to the intense provocation emanating from the mother's conscious and unconscious fantasy.

Acting out on the Street.—Mrs. N.'s sexual excitement which was stimulated by her sadomasochistic interpretation of the analytic setting was acted out partly in the sessions themselves partly on the street. The more her transference feelings increased, the more afraid she became of the traffic until her attitude approximated an agoraphobic one. She did not feel safe in the street any more and felt that she could not control her movements. Lorries and buses took on a frightening aspect, waiting to hit her and to run over her. She felt as if the radiators of the oncoming big lorries were alive and human; she felt the lorries to be driverless. This material was interpreted to her as displaced erotic excitement (radiators = erect penis, fantasy of intercourse = being run over). Again she remembered the threatening men of her adolescence coming with erected penis ready to rape her.

This insecurity in the street showed occasionally already in the analytic room when leaving the session. When she stumbled and hit herself against the wall under the analyst's eye, she felt like a prostitute.

There is a definite link here between Mrs. N.'s sexualization of the traffic and the symptom of running into the traffic which had led to Bobby's referral to analysis. For mother and child, the buses were phallic symbols. What appeared as a phobic attitude in the mother appeared in the child as an almost compulsive play with the toy buses which he held in front of him when dashing himself against the walls of the room and further in the irresistible attraction which the traffic held for him. Mother and child acted, although in a different manner, under the domination of an identical fantasy.

Manipulation of Bobby's Penis.—Mrs. N.'s analysis provided some information why she had been unable in the first instance to follow Miss Thomas's advice regarding the handling of the child's penis and why she had forgotten all the conversations dealing with the matter. Since then she had been repeatedly advised that pushing back the foreskin was not only superfluous but positively harmful to the child, but had never altered her behavior. In a late stage of her analysis she produced a dream which was related to this problem. "There is something like a clock; she feels she has to touch it, she has to see if it functions well. In handling it she breaks it, it stops functioning properly, she feels so guilty that if anybody asks her if she has touched the clock, she will say no." The associations to this dream and the symbolic elements led back to the idea that she had damaged herself when masturbating. Usually this creates in a child the compulsion to touch the genital, to masturbate again, to find out whether it was intact still or had stopped to function. In Mrs. N.'s case this compulsion had been transferred onto her child. Her worry about her own castrated genital had changed into a worry about the state of Bobby's penis. She felt obsessed by the idea that there was something wrong with it and she had to check up on it. The compulsion contained both sides of her ambivalence toward his penis, her wish to have it

healthy and intact (as her own) with the counterwish to have it damaged
and destroyed (her father's, her brother's and her own) in retaliation. The
handling of Bobby's penis thus served several purposes: it provided her
with sexual excitement in a masturbating act carried out on him; it
created an outlet for the aggressive and masochistic side of her penis
envy; and finally it gave her control over his masculinity which she experienced as an uncontrollable force. It is not surprising that no amount
of advice coming from the environment could have any influence on this
particular piece of her behavior. It is equally understandable that Bobby
reacted to this constant threat to his masculinity with anxiety, regression
and passivity.

V. Summary and Conclusions

The comparison between Mrs. N.'s and her child's psychopathology,
as it emerged in their respective analyses, is not complete. There is a mass
of material on both sides which has not been used in the foregoing study
in which I have set myself the aim of high-lighting only the most vital
points of interaction.

But even within these limitations it seems possible to show that the
influence of the mother's actions, her manifest attitude, her conscious
and, above all, unconscious fantasies and anxieties, is neither straight-
forward nor uniform. The following types of interaction seemed to me the
most important ones:

(a) There are examples where the mother's inhibition of function,
due to unconscious anxiety, has a lasting pathogenic influence on
the whole life and development of the child. Such an instance is
the mother's attitude to breast feeding. As described above, she
repeats her own death wishes against her mother, projecting the
role of attacker on Bobby who, she fears, will suck her dry, empty
her out. To protect her own life she has no milk for him, and this
fact turns him from a potentially happy and satisfied into a
querulous and dissatisfied infant. Here her unconscious fears
play the role of active pathogenic environmental agents.

(b) The same is true where her fantasies of emptiness and fullness
are concerned, although the outcome is different in this case.
These not only determine his feeding situation, playing a large
part in the mother's evaluation of his digestive upset and enforce-
ment of the diet, they are also taken over by Bobby and turned
thereby from an external agent into an internal one. It is impossible to say in which way Bobby was reached by the mother's

fantasies concerning the body content and its relation to the mother image; this may have happened through observation of her attitudes or—since this seems to happen between mother and child—by direct communication between their unconscious. However that may be, the idea of the good and bad body contents becomes an integral part of Bobby's own fantasy life and determines his later feeding troubles and his constipation.

(c) Where Bobby's exhibitionism is concerned we have described the mother's influence as a secondary, not a primary factor in his development. Bobby's exhibitionism seems to arise normally, determined on the one hand by his phallic wishes and strengthened on the other hand by his need for reassurance against castration fears. But this typical occurrence in the child meets with the mother's overvaluation of his penis, her conflicting desires for it and hostile impulses directed against it. What might have been a transitory phase in Bobby's life is turned thus into a permanent symptom by the mother's response. Bobby cannot fail to notice that, to quote the mother, he need only show his penis to dominate her completely.

(d) Again, Bobby responds to the mother's sexualization of the traffic. In this case the mother defends herself against the sexual threat embodied in the cars and lorries by a near-phobic attitude. Bobby reacts to the same symbolization in the opposite manner. Where the mother avoids the traffic, he tears himself from her to run right into it, i.e., by a positive fascination, and provocation of his passive masochistic attitudes.

(e) Mother and child meet most intimately in the two following symptoms which amount to a *folie à deux* in the intensity in which they are enacted: the "cat and mouse" fantasy and the anal ritual. Here, Bobby enters fully into the sadomasochistic arrangement of the mother, letting himself be provoked by her and provoking her in turn until the whole scene ends in the act of her beating him (an acting out of her own beating fantasies directed toward her father). Mother and child take it in turn to be aggressor and victim, exchanging roles usually in the middle of the scene.

The acting out of a fantasy with the roles divided between them is more impressive still in the anal ritual when mother and child enter into the most intimate partnership, the child moving his body to the mother's singing, his defecation being timed to her co-operation.

It needs no further explanation why Mrs. N.'s difficulties with Bobby were not improved lastingly by child guidance treatment; her problems were much too deep-seated and severe to be accessible to advice and guidance. Even under analysis she proved a most difficult patient with violent mood swings which were acted out in the transference and in her home surroundings. Even where insight was achieved, improvements alternated with relapses at the slightest provocation.

In Bobby's analytic treatment it became possible to differentiate between two different ways in which he responded, on the one hand to the mother's fantasies, on the other hand to her behavior. So far as he was under the influence of her fantasy life, analysis was able to set him free by lifting his reactions to consciousness and working through them. Although originating in the mother's unconscious, this fantasy content had become his own, could be treated as such, and analysis of it was followed by the usual relief. In many instances analysis had to deal also with a second outcrop of fantasies overlaying what had been initiated by the mother. The material of the good and bad body content overlayed by the birth fantasies of the anal babies, their drowning, their being saved out of the water, etc., is a case in point. This was slow work but satisfactory since Bobby made definite advances toward normal behavior and independence of his mother. He became able to eat and defecate without her help even in her presence, he attended school without difficulty, reacted well to other children and even enjoyed a holiday period away from his mother.

So far as his reactions to the mother's behavior, i.e., her violent acting out of her fantasies was concerned, the outcome was less favorable. Her behavior such as the "cat and mouse" provocation and above all her constant handling of his genitals acted on him as permanent seductions. Such seductions served to renew continually his close tie to her and thus to outweigh the influence of analysis which worked in the opposite direction.

This last reflection may be helpful whenever we have to assess the chances of freeing a young child by analysis from the pathogenic influence of the mother's disturbance. The child who is seduced by the mother's fantasies only, can be freed from this grip more effectively than another who has to contend also with manifest actions on the mother's part and therefore with the actual bodily stimulation and excitement which are aroused by them.

FURTHER CONSIDERATIONS REGARDING FETISHISM[1]

PHYLLIS GREENACRE, M.D. (New York)[2]

In a paper on fetishism (1953) I made an effort to organize the clinical picture and life-historical findings of such cases as I had observed, in relation to the development of the body image, since the fetish itself so clearly acts as some kind of stabilizer or reinforcement for the genital functioning of the patient. From this angle, my clinical material indicated rather clearly, I thought, the nature and timing of the special faults in the body image, which were patched up by the use of the fetish in later life. This was a limited presentation, but for me a useful one, since it offered a frame of reference for organizing clinical material, which at the very least is complex and confusing.

The main points of that paper were as follows: The disturbance of the fetishist appearing clinically as an unusually severe castration fear comes essentially from disturbances of pregenitality which render the child structurally unsound and insecure to meet genital-oedipal problems and especially to meet the normal castration threats of this period. In those cases which I saw these threats were already overwhelming, having appeared before the full oedipal development in unusually severe actual traumata of a specifically castrative type—threats not merely by seeing the mother's genital and observing her apparent castration at a time of special masturbatory arousal, as was first postulated by Freud (1927), but much more than this by witnessing or experiencing bloody mutilating attacks in the form of operations (on the self or others), childbirth, abortions, or accidents. These traumatic events, although unknown to the patient early in the analysis, have generally been accessible to validation after they have been brought to consciousness through analytic reconstructions.

[1] Read at the International Psychoanalytic Congress, at Geneva, Switzerland, July, 1955.

[2] From the New York Hospital and the Department of Psychiatry, Cornell University Medical College, New York.

Such traumatic events seemed to occur at two specially vulnerable times: in the last half of the first year or first half of the second, and at the time of the early phallic phase. Sometimes the disturbances of the two eras were remarkably similar, the second seemingly reinstating the disturbances of the first with greater specificity—this being commensurate with the clearer perceptiveness combining with the special body sensitivity of the phallic period. In the first period, however, the occurrence of "internal traumas," as in attacks of infantile rage, spasms, fevers, anesthesias, also created severe disturbances of body sense of self, apparently with feelings of imminent dissolution. The traumas of the anal-phallic period were more consistently genital castrative threats. The effect of the disturbances of the first period was to increase the clinging reaction, and prolong the primary identification tendency. This meant that the fetishist, who is characteristically male,[3] identified in infancy with the mother or even with a sister (if there was one close in age and in constant contact with the patient). The bisexuality of later life was derived in part from this, and from the continued activity of primary identification, and not so completely from postoedipal female identifications, as is true in neurotic cases. The mediation of primary identification through vision, which substitutes for or combines with oral incorporation in some situations, could be seen in its reactivated form in the vicissitudes of foreplay and sexual intercourse in the fetishistic patient, who can then only stabilize his basic sexual identity through the use of the fetish, which can be felt as well as seen. The fetish is a further safeguard against the anxiety due to feelings of change of body size, resulting primarily from body-phallus problems, and to dissolution anxieties which may have further become attached to fear of the orgasm.

The present rather brief communication must be devoted to taking up some of the considerations omitted in the earlier paper and making further suggestions, rather than drawing new conclusions. I have not added to my clinical experience since that study except for the two posthumous analyses of Swift and Carroll recently attempted by me (1955). The amassing of material for clinical study is particularly difficult

---

[3] It is only fetishism at a clearly genital level that is restricted to males. This is probably due to the fact that the exposure of the male organs and the consequent visibility of achievement or failure of potency and orgasm constitute a special narcissistic hazard to the male. The sense of failure due to frigidity in the female is softened by the possibility of concealment. Forms of fetishism which are not always clearly linked to the genital functioning (such as certain drug addictions, kleptomanias, special religious practices, the use of lucky charms)—and even those linked to the genital activity but not demanding the objective fetish—such as set fantasies or rituals preparing for masturbation or intercourse, seem to occur in female as well as male.

in these cases, as relatively few patients suffering from perversions come to analysis, although one gets the impression that they are not so infrequent in the population at large. When the perversion works successfully, the person does not seek help unless he gets into social or legal difficulties. In analytic practice the perversion is likely to turn up as one of the complications of some other condition. Such analyses are long and tedious. One cannot accumulate many in a lifetime.

The main topics which I would like to bring out now have to do with (1) the interrelation between different types of perversion; (2) certain problems of body reality and their relation to the general sense of reality; and (3) aggression and acting out in relation to the reality sense.

It is hard to estimate the frequency of the "pure" monomorphous perversion. Fenichel (1954) said, "The typical pervert has one way only of gaining sexual pleasure. All of his sexual energies are concentrated on one particular partial instinct, the hypertrophy of which competes with his genital primacy—The capacity for genital orgasm is blocked by some obstacle that is more or less overcome by the perverse act" (p. 325). While this concept of such pure forms of perversion is undoubtedly useful in understanding the differentiation of the perversions from unorganized polymorphous perverse infantile states and from the earlier concept that the perversion represented the negative of the neurosis, still it is doubtful whether it states the general situation in perversions. In my own clinical experience it has generally been true that while there was one preferred perversion, other perverse activities might be instituted at different times in life or even concurrently with especially active periods of the perversion of choice. Bisexuality especially seems to be ubiquitous; and homosexuality nearly always breaks forth in some overt form, not merely being represented in nongenital activities and attitudes.

This combination of various perverse forms in the individual life seems to be understandable. Severe disturbances in the period from six to eighteen months of life which produce the need for a strengthening of the clinging dependent relationship to the mother, are generally severe, permeating, and sometimes repeated. I believe it is of particular importance that these severe disturbances occur at a time of the gradual transition from dominance of the primary process to that of the secondary process. They constitute an enormous stimulation of aggression (with which the infant is more liberally supplied than at any time later in life) which affects all of the developing libidinal phases and tends to make for some confluence of discharge routes, or at least the ready availability of alternate routes. I have referred to this condition in earlier papers (1954), as occurring in some extremely severe neuroses or so-called borderline cases, but I have come to consider it as contributing especially the ground work for the development of perverse organizations of the aggressive and libidinal components of the development. Incidentally, I am not impressed by the constitutional inferiority of perverse patients or by selective inferiorities and hypertrophies in them. In these respects they seem to me to contrast with malignant schizophrenics, many of whom show irregularities of development which are apparent or foreshadowed at or soon after birth. The earliness and the sweeping character of the first group of infantile disturbances probably contribute the stamp of the combination of tendencies to action and to body-grounding (or reflection in physical symptoms) which is characteristic of many perversions.

It is the traumatic disturbance of the phallic period, however, which leaves, I believe, the deposit of the specific content, compulsively repetitive or ritualistically acted out in the search for sexual relief in fetishists. In this connection it is to be noted that the perverse fetishist may have a real problem of establishing a tender sexual relation with his loved one. He may feel tenderness for her and the wish for an active yet tender consummation: yet the sexual act, once approached, is too aggressivized, and the fear of castration fits too readily with the identification through vision and with the fantasy of punishment for killing, so that continuation of intercourse becomes a struggle for relief and to preserve some sense of body integrity rather than to achieve much positive pleasure or to give any. Indeed, it may be suspected that perverse individuals do not readily achieve a high degree of object relationship with their partners, who are used rather for narcissistic than for mutual gratification, especially at the genital-sexual level. When there is a fair degree of object relationship otherwise, it is jeopardized rather than supported by the sexual act.

W. Hoffer (1950) has described clearly the special significance of the latter part of the first year (from about four months on) in the development of the body ego, and the necessity for the integration of the visual and tactual sensory explorations in appreciating the self-body as separate from the outer world. Winnicott's article (1953) on transitional objects and transitional phenomena clarifies the development of this period further. He shows that in the nearly ubiquitous infantile fetish there is normally a transitional preferred object, usually a toy or something else closely associated with the infant, used in the development of secure relationship to the objects of the outer world. It is an object which is both a me-object and a not-me object, until the not-meness can be thoroughly accepted. The route of the early possible derivation of this transitional object—from the genital as well as from the breast and the behavior of the infant in relating the own body to the transitional object—is described in an anecdote told by Loewenstein (1950). He writes of a ten-month-old child who caught sight of his own penis, touched it with seeming pleasure, and then lost it again due to his "letting out" his own protuberant abdomen which then hid it. He succeeded in rediscovering his penis by pulling in his abdomen. But in the course of his maneuvers of repetitive rediscovery, he would crawl away from where he had been at the time of the loss, and look back over his shoulder to see if the penis, like a toy, had been left behind. Only after repetitive game-playing did he learn consistently to pull in his abdomen in order to find his penis. In the same article Loewenstein concluded, on the basis of additional clinical material, that "processes of the phallic phase such as fear of losing the penis under the pressure of castration anxiety, might indeed follow or reactivate traces of that period of formation of the body image, however short it may be, in which there remains an uncertainty as to the penis belonging to one's own body." These eras of development pointed out by Loewenstein are those of special biological and pathological significance in the pre-fetishist.

It is exactly the period of the transitional object which is the first disturbed one in the fetishist. I suspect that at this time the integration of visual (and/or oral) aggression with its accompanying libidinal component and tactual sensorimotor drives does not occur adequately. Clinically the visual-oral aggression remains overly strong and the assumption of tactual support does not occur automatically but has to be specially maneuvered in the construction of the fetish of adult life. I have dealt with these same clinical phenomena in my earlier paper (1953) in speaking of continued primary identification through vision.

The sense of identity and object reality of the self as a separate individual is further naturally much influenced by the clearness of the sense of sexual identity. This depends in a fundamental way on the clear awareness of the own body, especially the genital organs, and on the reciprocal awareness of their differences from those of certain other individuals. It is the vulnerable phallic phase which is the second period of traumatic disturbance in the fetishist, of a nature to undermine the child's appreciating his own organ appropriately. Since, as pointed out by Loewenstein, this is a time maturationally linked to the first period, the whole sense of separateness from the other and especially from the *other sex* is impaired, but in a characteristic way. There is not a fusion with the other or continuous confusion. (Again, I would contrast with some schizophrenics). But there is an oscillation in sense of body-self with quick identifications with others, mediated largely through vision, especially in sexual situations. The changeability from feelings of possessing a strong penis to feelings of not having any, occur with great rapidity. These changes in sense of body image seem to be concentrated chiefly on the genitals but affect the whole body secondarily.

Anyone who has followed closely in an analysis the premenstrual states of young women who have maintained a strong illusory penis fantasy until puberty, is aware how much the subjective reaction to the state of the genitals is regularly reflected in feelings concerning the whole body—and that the impact of two opposing images may contribute to a feeling of body unreality or even more generalized confusion (Lewin, 1948).

Not only is the whole body of the fetishist more than ordinarily equated with the phallus, but every part of it may become genitalized. It suffers *in toto* or in its various parts all of the distresses of castration anxiety in anticipation of intercourse or when the sexual performance has not been successful.

The body is clearly the arena of playing out fantasies and memories which are expressed as body sensations and even body imagery, rather than by thought imagery. In some instances, the fetishist expresses in his body symptoms the same forms which he characteristically reproduces in the fetish or in fetishistic rituals. Thus a patient of mine with a foot and shoe fetish involving the requirement that a girl should wear certain forms of strapped or buckled shoes, binding her around the ankle, or that the slipper be supplemented by a slave anklet, would, in the absence of the fetish, feel these same sensations around his own arms and legs, described as tourniquet-like sensations, or feelings of wearing leggings which bound him around ankles and knees and made his legs exquisitely tender. These were multiply determined, derived in part from observation of beatings of the mother at the hands of the father in sadistic sexual scenes and from witnessing or overhearing abortions performed at home at least twice in his early childhood and again at prepuberty. In his latency period he had acted out rather set fantasies of being the fascinated slave of his girl cousin who impersonated Cleopatra. As part of the mutual mirroring identification between the two, he played the part of the enslaved one and she wore an array of slave jewelry. It was an interesting thing with this patient that the external traumata suffered in the early phallic period combined more or less with a very bloody tonsillectomy which he himself suffered; but especially in connection with the physical grounding of the symptoms, that each period of stress following the mother's abortions was followed after some time by an illness in the patient which was diagnosed as rheumatic fever and once was sufficiently severe to require hospitalization. Whether or not the emotional reaction of witnessing the mother's operation aroused the response in the boy's body which contributed to the rheumatic fever symptoms cannot be said, but it seems quite certain that, at any rate, the boy's illness took over the picture of the mother's and the bandaging of his own legs during these illnesses became amalgamated with the seeing of the mother covered with a sheet for the operation which was done at home. Back of this was the sadistically exciting primal scene.

The limited nature of the fantasies of the fetishist has further impressed me. These tend under most circumstances to be stereotyped and to be expressed either in body terms and symptoms; in set repetitive thought imagery associated with masturbation or anticipation of intercourse; or in ritualistic acting out. The fantasy life is neither so extensive, so rich, nor so widely invading of life as may be true in the schizophrenic. Neither is it so available for intellectual pursuits. The tendency of the fetishist to express through his body or to act out through it his sado-masochistic fantasies has additional importance in that it adds therapeutic obstacles through the ever-present tendency to resort to this rather than to use language; and to the great hypertrophy of the secondary gain.

Tendencies to action and acting out seem implicit in the character of fetishists and possibly in all perverse characters. This may find its base in the physical soundness of the earliest infancy. But it is probably largely influenced by the preverbal and extreme stimulation of aggression in such infants as the results of strong, sweeping and early actual traumas. There is then a suffusion of the entire body with aggressive stimulation. When this is severe and diffuse, the effect may be compared to that of shock, panic, or horror of later life: direct defense is impossible, running away equally so—and the very diffusion of the aggression results in frozen immobility, but with a susceptibility to active irritability when the crisis is past.

There is accompanying this immobility a psychic state of unreality, since the stimuli cannot be adequately responded to. This corresponds to the *topical* unreality state of the later perverse patient, as in contrast to the more diffused unreality perplexity, or depersonalization of the schizophrenic. When the later, and usually specific, traumata of the phallic phase occur, there is a definite patterning of the activity content, which partakes then of something like the rigid repetitive action tendencies of the traumatic neurosis of later life. These would seem to fulfill the dual need of unconscious efforts to verify the reality of the earlier experience and to master it. But through all this, the full pleasure of the libidinal maturation has been vitiated by the tensions of the too strong aggressive components.

Moreover, the early suffusion of the infant with aggression, with its resultant paradoxical immobility has established a kind of automatic reversal of reaction at a psychophysiological level, which contributes to and may be the paradigm of later forms of quick denial and reversal (as well as to the topical unreality already mentioned), which are so characteristic of the fetishist, and to a lesser extent of other perversions and of some impulse disorders. (Incidentally, it has seemed to me that this kind of infantile reaction is beautifully illustrated in the Wolfman scene of the Christmas tree with the immobilized and staring little wolves, reflecting the primal scene.) This kind of quick denial is characteristic of the fetishist's sense of reality and so complicating in the treatment that the analyst sometimes feels as though he were working between two mirrors: wherever he looks, the patient is at once absorbed in the view in the opposite direction, and the two views really reflect the same thing. In addition, the acting-out tendencies of the patient have generally led him into reality complications in life, increased his load of reality guilt, and favored an increase in defense by denial, as well as the flowering of of protective screen memories.

BIBLIOGRAPHY

Fenichel, O. (1945), *The Psychoanalytic Theory of Neurosis*. New York: Norton.

Freud, S. (1927), Fetishism. *Collected Papers*, V. London: Hogarth Press, 1950.

Greenacre, P. (1953), Certain Relationships between Fetishism and the Faulty Development of the Body Image. *This Annual*, VIII.

—— (1954), Contribution to the Discussion: Problems of Infantile Neurosis. *This Annual*, IX.

—— (1955), *Swift and Carroll: A Psychoanalytic Study of Two Lives*. New York: International Universities Press.

Hoffer, W. (1950), Development of the Body Ego. *This Annual*, V.

Lewin, B. D. (1948), The Nature of Reality, the Meaning of Nothing; with an Addendum on Concentration. *Psa. Quart.*, XVII.

Loewenstein, R. M. (1950), Conflict and Autonomous Ego Development During the Phallic Phase. *This Annual*, V.

Winnicott, D. W. (1953), Transitional Objects and Transitional Phenomena. *Int. J. Psa.*, XXXIV.

ON SYMBIOTIC CHILD PSYCHOSIS

Genetic, Dynamic and Restitutive Aspects[1]

MARGARET S. MAHLER, M.D. and BERTRAM J. GOSLINER, M.D.
(New York)

It was not until many years after ego psychology had gained its proper place within the framework of psychoanalytic theory that psychoanalysts began to scrutinize the available data of the first fifteen to eighteen months of life (Ribble, Fries, Spitz, and others). Even then the beginnings of the verbal stage of development, the period from eighteen months onward, were little studied, except by Anna Freud, Burlingham, and Bowlby. However, Ernst Kris and his co-workers at Yale are now engaged in systematically studying this period of life.

In the second year of life the infant gradually changes from an almost completely vegetative being, symbiotically dependent on the mother, into a separate individual. He still commands, and obtains, the executive services of this external ego (Spitz, 1951). But he becomes increasingly aware of his own capacities as well as of his own separateness. This apperception is, however, still a very precarious one at twelve to thirty months of age.

During the second year of life it is the maturational growth of locomotion which exposes the infant to the important experience of deliberate and active bodily separation from and reunion with the mother. Furthermore, the normal toddler of one and a half to two and a half years, delights in exploring his environment, however indiscriminate his efforts. From so doing he derives sound narcissistic satisfactions. He discovers and masters ever-increasing segments of his physical surroundings, provided he feels his mother's encouragement and availability. This is that second eighteen-month period of life in which pregenital libidinal phases

[1] Some parts of the material used in this paper refer to cases of The Children's Service of the New York State Psychiatric Institute and Columbia University.

Paper given on February 22, 1955 at the New York Psychoanalytic Society, and later at the Philadelphia Psychoanalytic Society; also at the Austen Riggs Center, Stockbridge, Mass.

progress in a rapid and overlapping procession. Yet, this same period is
no less fateful as far as the infant's ego development and object relationships are concerned.

Let us, for the sake of brevity, call the period from twelve-eighteen
to thirty-six months the *separation-individuation phase* of personality
development. It is our contention that this separation-individuation
phase is a crucial one in regard to the ego and the development of object
relationships. It is also our contention that the characteristic fear of this
period is separation anxiety. This separation anxiety is not synonymous
with the fear of annihilation through abandonment. It is an anxiety
which is less abruptly overwhelming than the anxiety of the previous
phase. It is, however, more complex, and later we hope to elaborate on
this complexity. For we need to study the strong impetus which drives
toward separation, coupled with the fear of separation, if we hope to
understand the severe psychopathology of childhood which ever so often
begins or reveals itself insidiously or acutely from this second part of
the second year onward.

This separation-individuation phase is a kind of second birth experience which one of us described as "a hatching from the symbiotic mother-
child common membrane." This hatching is just as inevitable as is
biological birth (Mahler, 1954).

In animals the absolute dependency on a mother animal is brief.
Yet one can observe that pups prematurely taken from the mother are
insecure and are considered somatically and dispositionally less stable.
Dog breeders furthermore advise that if one has the choice of the litter,
the procedure by which he can be sure of getting the best pup, is to
watch the bitch with the litter and pick the preferential pup. However,
even with her preferential pup, as with all the others, the most motherly
and devotedly nurturing bitch seems to get bored and obviously annoyed
by the nursing process in a comparatively short time. She still plays with
her pups for a while longer, and seems to enjoy them, but will soon leave
them to their own devices. If she happens to be a hound, for example,
she will leave them in favor of her phylogenetically inherent individual
instinct gratification, her hunting, for long stretches of time. As for the
pups, they will follow her in hunting when they are good and ready.

This rapid individuation process of the pup is duplicated in the case
of the human infant with his mother, as in a slow motion picture. Both
the symbiotic and the individuation phases are greatly prolonged. However, in humans some emotional tie to mother persists "up to the grave."

A strong and adequate symbiotic phase is a prerequisite for subsequent successful disengagement of the human infant as well. Only if

symbiosis has been adequate, is he ready to enter the phase of gradual separation and individuation. The aim and successful outcome of this individuation process is a stable image of the self. As Edith Jacobson (1954) has described, the stable image of the self depends upon successful identifications on the one hand, and distinction between object- and self-representations on the other.

We shall discuss neither the normal symbiotic nor the normal individuation phases in full. However, we cannot avoid giving a brief resumé of those events in the two phases, which we believe are essential to understanding the psychotic breakdown, the prepsychotic phase, and remissions in symbiotic child psychosis.

The newborn's waking life centers around his attempts to reduce tension. To ameliorate his unpleasure the infant has two avenues: his own body (Hoffer, 1949), and his mother's ministrations. The effect of his mother's breast and ministrations in reducing the pangs of need-hunger cannot be isolated nor differentiated by the young infant from tension-reducing attempts of his own, such as urinating, defecating, coughing, sneezing, spitting, regurgitating, vomiting, all the ways by which the infant tries to rid himself of unpleasurable tension. The effect of these expulsive phenomena as well as the gratification gained by his mother's ministrations help the infant, in time, to differentiate between a pleasurable and good quality and a painful and bad quality of experiences.

When the mother is a source of satisfaction, the infant responds positively to her, as may be observed by tension reduction manifested by quiescence and sleep. When body tension or mothering manipulations are a source of pain and displeasure, the infant deals with it as he deals with noxious stimuli in general: he draws away from it, tries to expel it, to eliminate it. In other words, the infant's first orientation in his extrauterine life is according to "good-pleasurable" versus "bad-painful" stimuli. Since hunger is the most imperative biological need, these qualities of "good" and "bad" seem to become equated with "edible" versus "inedible" substances.

Through the inborn and autonomous perceptive faculty of the primitive ego (Hartmann, 1939), deposits of memory traces of the two primordial qualities of stimuli occur. We might visualize that these scattered foci of memory deposits form little islands within the hitherto oceanic feeling of complete fusion and oneness with the mother, in the infant's semiconscious state. These memory islands, containing imprints of "pleasurable-good" or "painful-bad" stimuli, are not yet allocated either to the self or to the non-self. We further may assume that these primitive memory deposits are cathected with that primordial undifferentiated drive energy, which Fenichel and Edith Jacobson (1954) have described. The young infant is exposed to one rhythmically and consistently repeated experience, namely, that hunger and other need tensions arising inside the body cannot be relieved beyond a certain degree unless relief is supplied from a source beyond his own orbit. This repeated experience of a need-satisfying good outside source to relieve him from a bad inside tension eventually conveys to him a vague affective discrimination between "self" and "non-self." It is at this point of differentiation that the predominantly "good" and predominantly "bad" memory islands become vaguely allocated to the self and non-self. The qualities of "pleasure-giving" or "pain-inflicting" become anchored to the mother, but also to the primitive memory islands formed through "pleasurable" and "unpleasurable" sensations from wtihin his own body. This seems to be the beginning of the formation of scattered part images of the object and part images of the body self as well (Jacobson, 1954). We wish to emphasize that the self-images are endowed with the same qualities of prevailingly "good" and predominantly "bad," as are the scattered part images of mother.

We would propose that from the primordial undifferentiated drive energy, libido and aggression differentiate *pari passu* with the infant's primitive reality orientation according to the above-described differentiation of the "good" and "bad" scattered part images of mother and self. "The mother in the flesh," as Bowlby (1952) calls the real mother, is both a source of pleasure and a source of unpleasure, just as the own body is both. To "bad" stimuli coming from inside or outside, the infant reacts with impetuous aggression, by ridding and ejective mechanisms; to "good" stimuli coming from inside or outside, the baby reacts with quiet bliss, and later on, with reaching out. Both pleasure and unpleasure manifestations, however, are overshadowed by the still more undifferentiated and unneutralized impetuous drive of aggressive and indiscriminate incorporation of good and bad, which reaches its peak at the period of oral aggression.

The infant has the tendency to suck in, to mouth, to incorporate, to devour, as much of the outside object as possible. His expulsive, ejective, ridding tendencies alternate with this tendency to engulf.

The vicissitudes of primitive aggression are of particular importance, as Hartmann (1939, 1953), Hartmann, Kris and Loewenstein (1949), Anna Freud (1949), Hoffer (1950a), Bak (1954), and Mahler (1948) have emphasized. The generally accepted psychoanalytic hypothesis that the infant relegates unpleasurable feelings to the non-self, to the outside world, is difficult to demonstrate. Negative hallucination in the infant is even more difficult to observe than its positive forerunner. What we can observe are the two distinct groups of phenomena just described. The infant tries to expel, to sever from his own body orbit, all painful stimuli, irrespective of whether the painful stimulation has originated from the outside or from the inside. Secondly, we can also observe, particularly from five to six months on, an indiscriminate incorporative tendency, which is familiar to all of us. In both observable groups of phenomena the surplus of unneutralized aggression versus libido seems evident.

Hoffer (1950b) drew attention to the fact that deflection of the surplus unneutralized aggression from the body ego is of utmost importance for normal body ego development.

Libidinal cathexis, on the other hand, should gradually shift from the visceral, particularly abdominal, organs in cranial and peripheral direction (Ribble, 1941; Greenacre, 1945; Mahler, 1951). With the libidinal shift of cathexis to the sensory perceptive system, great progress is achieved, and clearer demarcation of the own from the mother's body thus evolves.

We may assume that confluence and primitive integration of the scattered "good" and "bad" memory islands into two large, good and bad part images of the self, as well as split good and bad part images of the mother, do not occur before the second year of life. This is attested to by the normal emotional ambivalence which is clinically discernible at this age.

Only now, from twelve-eighteen months on, in the subsequent eighteen-months period of separation-individuation, are the rapidly alternating primitive identification mechanisms possible and dominant. We owe their description to Melanie Klein (1939).

In the further course of normal development there is unification of the split images of objects and of the self, and a unified object representation becomes demarcated from a unified self-representation.

Solid integration, in which there is a blending and synthesis of "good" and "bad" mother images, even in normal development, is not achieved either during the symbiotic phase of mother-child relationship, nor is it completed in the next eighteen-months period of life, during the separation-individuation phase. If the symbiotic and the separation-individuation phases were normal, however, from three or three and a half years on, the child should increasingly be able to respond to the "whole mother," to realize that one and the same person can both gratify and disturb him. With the advent of the latency period the child should not only clearly perceive and recognize that mother is separate and complex, but that other important love objects and he himself are separate and complex as well. He should also begin to be able to modulate feelings within himself, appraise good and bad by trial acting (i.e., thinking).

We could not help delving into these descriptions because during the disorganization-regression process of symbiotic psychosis all these earlier stages again become dominant.

For purposes of understanding our points, we propose focusing on the position of defense of the eighteen- to thirty-six-month infant, to defend his own evolving, enjoyable and jealously guarded self-image from infringement by mother and other important figures. This is a clinically important and conspicuous phenomenon during the separation-individuation phase. As Anna Freud (1951) has pointed out, at the age of two and three a quasi-normal negativistic phase of the toddler can be observed. It is the accompanying behavioral reaction marking the process of disengagement from the mother-child symbiosis. The less satisfactory or the more parasitic the symbiotic phase has been, the more prominent and exaggerated will be this negativistic reaction. The fear of re-engulfment threatens a recently and barely started individual differentiation which must be defended. Beyond the fifteen- to eighteen-month mark, the primary stage of unity and identity with mother ceases to be constructive for the evolution of an ego and an object world (compare Loewald [1951].) In boys as well as in girls, around eighteen months (in some cases even much earlier), the father has become an important object. This relationship ordinarily has the advantage that the inner image of the father has never drawn to itself so much of the unneutralized drive cathexis as has the mother's, and therefore there is less discrepancy between the image of father and the real father. (See also p. 207; and Bowlby, 1952).

From the very beginning, the infant creates the world in his own image, wherein the symbiotic partner is the indispensable catalyst and beacon of orientation. Early painful or distressing bodily injuries, traumata or illness disrupt this process of self-differentiation and object creation. In his paper on "Repression," Freud (1915) gave us a description of how such disruption comes about. The infant is unable to eject, or later on repress; in other words, to eliminate too massive or continually harassing painful noxi. His impetuous ridding mechanisms may merely lead to exhaustion and apathy. Then regression to a more archaic stage occurs in which the budding self-awareness as well as apperception of the "good" part image of the mother is drowned (Mahler and Elkisch, 1953). Inasmuch as all happenings in the symbiotic phase are dominated by orality, the infant furthermore loses the necessary and normal delusional experience of incorporating and thus having the good mother in himself, restoring the blissful state of omnipotent fusion with the mother (Lewin, 1950). Instead, he struggles in impotent rage and panic, with the catastrophic fear of annihilation, by introjected bad objects, without being able successfully to invoke the good part object, the soothing breast, or the ministering mother. (Compare p. 206.)

It is obvious that such factors as early and prolonged illnesses or pain interfere with the fusion and blending of good and bad images of objects and self. Instead, fused and confused faulty couplings of part images of self and object occur. These hinder reality orientation. In constitutionally oversensitive and vulnerable infants the pathogenic effects of the described intrapsychic events are enhanced and a pre-psychotic stage may be set, if fixation to the symbiotic phase is reinforced during the individuation phase. These auxiliary events occur in the case of mothers who are overstimulating, overprotective, anxious or emotionally unavailable symbiotic partners.

The children suffering from symbiotic child psychoses described in this and previous papers (Mahler, 1952) are not to be thought of as normal children in whom a psychotic process is induced by an emotionally disturbed mother. These children are constitutionally vulnerable and predisposed toward the development of a psychosis. It is the very existence of the constitutional ego defect in the child that helps create the vicious circle of the pathogenic mother-child relationship by stimulating the mother to react to the child in ways that are deleterious to his attempts to separate and individuate.

The pathogenic effect of the attitude of the symbiotically overanxious mother is particularly increased if that mother's hitherto doting attitude changes abruptly at the advent of the separation-individuation phase. Coleman, Kris, and Provence (1953) have drawn attention to the important fact that the attitude of mothers to the same child in different phases of his development may undergo radical changes. A complementary pathogenic factor is the well-known parasitic, infantilizing mother who needs to continue her overprotection beyond the stage when it is beneficial. This attitude becomes an engulfing threat, detrimental to the child's normal disengagement and individuation from his second year of life on. Another type of symbiotic parasitic mother cannot endure the loss of her hitherto vegetative appendage, but has to, emotionally at least, slough him off abruptly.

A case in point was that of Aro, who was brought by his pediatrician for consultation at the age of nine and a half, because of his incapacitating seizure-like paroxysms of generalized tics. He had been having tics with intermissions since the age of six. The referring pediatrician stated that Aro had been hypertonic and hyperkinetic from birth on. He had suffered from pylorospasm. Yet he is said to have been a happy, outgoing infant till the age of about two and a half. As an infant he smiled at people, cooed, played pat-a-cake, how big, etc., which is noteworthy as differential diagnostic criteria to rule out early infantile autism (Mahler, 1951). At closer questioning the mother recalled, however, that Aro never could tolerate frustrations. He insisted that the mother or the nurse be closely at hand at all times. When, at the age of one and beyond, Aro was put into a playpen, he would throw a temper tantrum. In retrospect this was the first manifest sign—we believe—of a progressive disturbance in the neutralization of aggressive drive energy. This assumption is borne out by subsequent disturbed behavior: as soon as Aro could stand on his feet and walk, he manifested a "deadly" hostility toward his five- and seven-year-older siblings. He threw forks and knives and spit at them. This behavior, in turn, brought about a radical and abrupt change in the mother's attitude toward Aro. She was indignant and completely intolerant in the face of the small boy's bold, and what seemed vicious attacks upon his so much older siblings. The mother unhesitatingly and completely sided with the older siblings. Aro was often severely restrained, reprimanded and ostentatiously left behind. But there were objective signs and symptoms of constitutional vulnerability of the ego, such as hypertonicity, in Aro's case.

At ten weeks Aro developed a severe pyloric stenosis. He would eagerly take his bottle and keep the milk down for a few moments. Then there would be contractions of the stomach, observable through the abdominal wall. Unmistakable expressions of pain accompanied these contractions, and the milk was expelled by violent projectile vomiting. Very soon after the vomiting Aro would be given another bottle; and if he vomited again, this was followed by forced feeding. He was weaned from the bottle to a cup at five months. From that moment to the present he has put fingers, toys, and various objects indiscriminately into his mouth.

Attempts at toilet training were started unbelievably early by a strict nurse. About the age of four Aro began to retain his feces for a week at a time, complaining that it hurt to defecate. The mother gave the boy frequent enemas against his struggling protests.

Aro began school at five and a half; a year after this, his tics began. At this time, the mother's father, who was devoted to the boy and to whom Aro was most responsive, died. A short time after the grandfather's death, Aro became depressed, his tics became violent. Most disturbing to the family was a loud yelling tic. (Later during a psychotic break Aro was to say that he had a yell that could be heard around the world, that could bring the dead to life.)

At school Aro was unable to work up to grade, in spite of his normal I.Q. At nine Aro suffered his first psychotic breakdown which lasted six weeks. Aro insisted that he would not leave his room until his tics stopped. He would shriek prayers to God and announce that he and his daddy had a secret. "I'm practicing the loudest yell in the world. When I give that yell everything will come to life—even the pictures in the room." Later, in his analysis, Aro elaborated this fantasy. In addition to the obvious wish to revive the dead grandfather, Aro fantasied that in response to his yell the most ferocious tigers in Africa would come to Aro, protect him, and kill Aro's enemies.

The details of the onset of the psychotic breakdown are revealing. It happened in the midst of psychotherapy with a therapist Aro shared with his mother. The morning of the onset Aro was to be taken to the psychiatrist, and the mother noticed that Aro was crawling like a baby on the front lawn and that he was masturbating. She harshly reprimanded him. They then waited in their car for a friend. She remembers fearing an accident. Aro, who always was affected by his mother's moods, appeared tense and worried. The friend, a teacher, finally arrived and dramatically explained the reason for being late. One of her pupils badly cut her knee and they had to stop the bleeding. At that moment Aro slumped to the floor of the car, writhing about and uttering inarticulate cries and groans. His body appeared completely out of control and his clothes were drenched with sweat. The psychiatrist gave Aro a sedative which was ineffective, and following this Aro refused to leave his room. The friend's tale of the bloody accident that happened to the child, triggered Aro's psychotic breakdown. At that time the child was suffering with intense castration anxiety. His excessive masturbation indicated that repression of his oedipal strivings had not been successful. The mother's harsh reprimand, the fear of an accident, the bleeding accident of the pupil, and particularly the impending visit to the psychiatrist who belonged to mother and represented the punishing father, added to Aro's mounting terror. His psychotic breakdown represents a refuge for his disorganized ego from castration anxiety, a reunion with the good object on a regressive level. The almost totally disorganized child sought to obtain strength and nourishment from the higher good powers (God, father, etc.). Only the good objects are ego-syntonic and can be tolerated within. Only by constant alternation of ejection of the bad and incorporation of the good object, can Aro succeed in replenishing his empty and disorganized self. It seems that during his psychotic episodes Aro's regressive behavior, entailing alternating primitive introjection-projection mechanisms, is similar to the patterning of the relationship between the normal symbiotic infant and mother, in which incorporative and ejective mechanisms alternate. The autism with its attendant megalomania connotes union and fusion with the good mother, the tic paroxysms signify the loss of control in the struggle to eject the incorporated bad object.

Aro, an emaciated child of about ten, usually was brought to the office by his mother, who sat down in the waiting room with an apologetic smile. Aro would sit as far away from her as he could get, and gaze away from her at the ceiling or wall. Frequently he would dart a look at her and then quickly avert his gaze.

His body was racked with involuntary movements of arms, torso, neck and face. The movements were particularly predominant in the mouth and jaw. We will not give a detailed description of his tic paroxysms. Frequently loud, guttural vocalizations accompanied the tic movements. The boy would appear terrified and anguished during these episodes. At the completion of the tic paroxysm Aro would repeat it volitionally in an abbreviated form, with a look of nonchalant mastery. He might, during this purposive repetition, hum a little tune and move his body, as if in response to the rhythm. At these times he would attempt to maintain a contemptuous, mocking attitude which he would preserve until he was overcome by the next attack.

Applicable to Aro's tic syndrome is the description by Mahler and co-workers (1945, 1949) of the tic syndrome as a loss of control of and struggle against introjected objects, ego-alien demoniacal inner powers. To our patient it was as if these powers gained possession and reduced the self to the status of a puppet. The voluntary repetition of the tic seizure indicates that ejecton of the demon has been successful and that the ego-alien inner force has been banished. The child for the moment is once again in command. His air of mastery during the volitional repetition of the tic movements, the rhythmic response of his body to his humming, indicates that his self-mastery is dependent upon the introjection of the good mother; he rocks and soothes himself.

Aro's defective ego alone is incapable of dealing with his inner needs. He constantly attempts to obtain strength and gratification from the outside by means of incorporation. His regressed patterning is that of an infant indiscriminately sucking in supplies from the outside. A consequence of this avid incorporative striving is that the bad and painful as well as the good and pleasurable are ingested and introjected.

This cycle in the tic paroxysm—need, inner turmoil, loss of body control, on the one hand, and the attainment of gratification and quiescence through introjection, on the other—brings to mind Aro's experiences with his pylorospasm. Then at ten weeks the ingested food caused actual pain and culminated in expulsion through vomiting. The vomiting was invariably followed by a fresh bottle until the infant attained satiety, even though at the expense of forced feeding. Or else quiescence through exhaustion ensued.

The fear of re-engulfment on the one hand and separation anxiety on the other is graphically demonstrated by the relationship of Aro and his mother. It was the mother who would ring the office and elevator bells, open the doors, greet and say good-bye to the analyst. There was never conversation or physical contact between mother and son. On occasion, when the mother came too close to him, Aro would suddenly lash out with his fist, striking her sharply on the breast.

Although mother and child did not converse, there was much communication by means of gestures, body movements and facial expressions. The mother was particularly adept at remaining at, what for Aro was an optimal distance from him. He would indicate by tics or mouth-fingering, etc., when she was too far away and, as mentioned before, would strike her when she came too close.

The communication without words between Aro and his mother is illustrated by the following: In the waiting room on one occasion Aro lurched to his feet, looked over at his mother, then looked toward the bathroom. He made a gesture toward his penis. His mother quickly arose, opened the bathroom door, and switched on the light. Aro urinated with the door open, looking back at his mother and chuckling happily. The mother flushed the toilet.

From the first, Aro willingly came into the consultation room alone. Without a sign of recognition he would move past the analyst with a curious propulsive gait and run through the open doors to the playroom. The social amenities were never responded to. He would cringe and shrink away from the slightest physical approach on the part of the analyst. Often Aro would look to the side, mutter to himself and then laugh wildly, without contagion. At such times he appeared to be responding to purely inner ideas or stimuli. His being out of control, violently hitting at the chair or the wall, his body being thrown about by his paroxysms of laughter, appeared frankly psychotic.

Aro would listen intently to the sound of the elevator taking his mother down. As soon as the noise would cease, Aro would roam about the room investigating its contents. He would look, touch and retouch, smell and mouth the objects and compare their weight. He would both taste and bite them.

He would question the analyst: "What is it?—How long have you had it?—How old is it?—What's it for?—Which is best?" etc. Such questions were repeated over and over again, in a nagging querulous voice. Attempts to answer them were drowned out by Aro's loud vocal tics and by Aro repeating the first few words of the answer. When an answer was finally completed, Aro would repeat the answer over and over again, each time with a different tone and inflection so that the answer would range the gamut from a simple statement to puzzled, disbelieving, astonished, angry, scornful affects.

Aro's restitutive attempts to orient himself in the environment are successful with inanimate objects. Because of their stability and constancy, and because he can explore them at his own speed, he can make them a part of his own experience. He is able to categorize them as to good or bad. Aro is unable to blend, modulate or synthesize. There is no grey— only black or white. Cars made by General Motors are good—all others are bad. Aro cannot discriminate or grade within either group. There is no difference between Cadillac and Chevrolet. They are both General Motors and hence both good. Unlike himself, inanimate objects do not change rapidly in an unpredictable way and thus serve as a frame of reference to the child struggling to control in a chaotic world.

Aro's attempt at orientation by means of questioning succeed less happily. The answer provoked by his question is not predictable, either in terms of its final form, its ultimate meaning or its effect on him. Aro, constantly threatened with loss of self-identity through ego-alien powers gaining ascendency, must maintain a dominance and control over the answers his questions provoke. His interruptions, mimicry, etc., serve this end. He is careful not to be taken by surprise and not to be emotionally stirred. An emotion which arises unbidden and which takes an unpredictable course is experienced by Aro as if it were a foreign body, threatening the integrity of his ego. Because he cannot synthesize and modulate, Aro has to employ the above-mentioned maneuvers—to "tame," as it were, the answer and thus to achieve mastery over it. He makes it his own through a process of alternating ejection and incorporation.

The transition from one situation to another was very difficult for Aro. This was demonstrated by his behavior when he heard the elevator's noise, indicating the return of his mother. He would tic violently, run to the door, run back to the center of the room, repeat this several times, and ask repeatedly, "Is it time—is it time?"

Most striking in Aro's relationship to his mother is his endeavor to remain at an optimal distance, spatially and emotionally, from her. The boy seeks to attain an equilibrium between the need of his weakened ego to obtain constant supplies from her and the threat of being engulfed and losing his self-identity to her.

He is unable to go more than a few blocks from home. He will scream in protest if she plans to leave the house and if she persists he will gag himself and retch. The father who, particularly in the preanalytic period, used to baby sit with Aro, relates that shortly after the mother would leave, Aro would stuff himself with food. He would eat an inordinate number of hot dogs and gulp down unbelievable amounts of soda pop. He would then, in great distress, turn to his father, and through frantic gestures implore help in getting rid of the ingested pain-producing food.

Aro will permit no intimacy. He will not suffer his mother to kiss or get close to him. He is abusive and hostile to her and takes a particular delight in uttering obscenities in her presence. He hits her, tells her she is ugly, and frequently orders her to leave the room. His fear of engulfment and his separation anxiety are dramatically illustrated by a frequent occurrence.

Aro will call to his mother in a piteous and pleading whine, "Mommy, Mommy," and will start toward her. He will then stop but continue to call, entreating her to come to him. When she comes to him he lashes out, hits her and screams, "Get away, bitch." If she retires, he calls her back. When she finally refuses to come to him, he implores her, breaks into sobs, sticks his fingers down his throat until he gags or retches.

It appears that Aro's ambivalent behavior is a result of his inability to create a fused and blended representation of his mother, as well as of his own self. Because of an inner need, it is toward the good mother he moves and it is she whom he so imploringly calls. The mother who comes cannot be reconciled with Aro's idealized mental image of the all-good mother. Aro reacts to the actual mother who comes to him with violent warding off, reminiscent of the primitive ridding mechanism of the baby in the symbiotic phase—the gesture with which that baby tried to expel the introjected painful stimulus.

As Aro undoubtedly entered the oedipal phase (the passive negative aspects of which were prominent in the analytic material), the father somehow became the helping, glorified figure—basically a "good object." On the other hand, Aro's oedipal strivings toward the mother maintain his image of her as mainly bad and threatening. Because of castration anxiety, the "ugly, castrated" mother must not come too close physically or emotionally; i.e., she must sit in the back of the car when he sits in front with his father, etc. Intimacy with the bad mother would result in re-engulfment, in a shattering of Aro's ego organization. The fear of being eaten and castration anxiety receive additional impetus from the boy's terrifying tic seizures. The involuntary movements are a loss of control of a part of the body and a loss of that part of the body from Aro's self-representation to an evil and stronger force, the bad mother and perhaps the oedipal father.

In Aro's case the psychotic mechanisms exist side by side with neurotic ones. By virtue of appersonization of the mother's executive functions as external ego (Spitz, 1951), Aro is still able to function on a regressed and constricted level. Though he has had several frankly psychotic episodes, his break with reality is not final and not complete. The main difference between cases like Aro's, where remissions are predominant, and others where the loss of reality seems permanent and irreversible, is whether or not representations of outside love objects remain partially cathected or whether cathexis has been completely withdrawn.

Bowlby (1952) has described that in the course of actual separation of the small child from his mother, both the good and the bad image of the mother undergo rapid changes. The good mother becomes glorified and the bad mother a hateful image. He has documented in his well-known film that, at reunion after separation, even the normal two-year-old temporarily has some difficulty in identifying either of his inner images with the real mother. Bowlby's case displayed a fleeting blank response when confronted with the "mother in the flesh." (Significantly, with the father the girl's reactions even at a second separation within half a year showed practically no lasting adverse effects—unlike the disruptive near-detrimental effect which the second separation had on the mother-child relationship.)

An effect similar to that produced on the normal two-year-old by actual repeated separation from the mother occurs, even without actual separation, with a symbiotic child for whom, through the factors previously enumerated, the prepsychotic stage had been set. A psychotic break may occur in response to any additional trauma, during the relative strain of the process of individuation. Experiences of disappointments in the course of the oral, anal, but particularly the oedipal phases of psychosexual development, harbor the threat of castration which in turn reinforces the threat of oral attack, in those children. The fantasies of being robbed of the contents of the body and finally of being engulfed and eaten up dominate. This latter, we repeat, is the projected counterpart of the avid tendency of these children to suck in, to gulp—good and bad objects alike.

We know, in retrospect, that integration of the good and bad mother images, as well as clear differentiation of representations of the part objects in the outside versus the part images of the self, has been defective in the cases in question. Hence, at the point when fear of re-engulfment, a fear amounting to fear of dissolution of identity, accumulates simultaneously with its apparent opposite, i.e., separation panic—the two overwhelm the ego. This occurs with such intensity that the progressive integration and gradual unlocking of couplings of scattered part-image representations of the self and object are prevented. There is regression to the stage in which unneutralized libido and aggression were vested in the symbiotic system within the child's inner delusional reality. At this point the real mother ceases to exist as a separate entity. The introjected split objects dominate the psychotic child's world. These are then the extreme cases which do not seem to respond to ouside stimuli but which seem to be continuously in communication with the introjected objects, as shown by bizarre posturing, giggling and stereotyped activities. Very often the introjected objects gain symbolic personification by means of exclusive preoccupation with a piece of cardboard, hallucinated bell, an adored extremity, a toy animal, and the like, to which the patients address passionate endearments. If they are told that the psychotic fetish is in danger, or if it is symbolically removed, they fall into an abysmal panic. At such a stage the patient may no longer show any signs of missing his real mother. It is at this stage that these children are routinely misdiagnosed as autistic cases.

To illustrate the genesis and dynamics of a complete psychotic break with reality we should like to sketch, in addition, very briefly the following case. B. S. was six years old when he was admitted to the Children's Service of the New York State Psychiatric Institute. He was extremely hyperactive and destructive. He not only displayed blind aggression toward other children but mutilated himself by biting and scratching, so that big brown calluses covered his two forearms and his left hand.

His illness began at two years of age. B. S.'s first year of life was marred by illness, chronic diarrhea. He was so weak and debilitated that his early maturational growth was gravely delayed. He would lie quietly by himself, flat on his back, and make no demands on his mother who attended to his physical needs. He made no response to his brother or father; he did not seem to know them. When he was two years old, his mother developed pleurisy and was hospitalized. The child's reaction to this was not recorded, but when at two and a half the child did start to walk the hitherto overly placid child became hyperactive, would bang his head against the crib, tear his hair out in bunches, and displayed increasingly bizarre behavior. He would withdraw from people but would use his carriage blanket as his constant companion. He rolled it up and talked to it and appeared to be "in a different world." He continued to be a grave feeding problem and took no food unless his mother spoon fed him. He attacked younger children and when prevented, bit and scratched himself.

On the ward he would talk only to his fetish in a continuous babble, frequently simulating his mother's talking to him. In this monologue with the fetish, it obviously represented himself.

B. S., like Aro, seemed possessed by unneutralized, destructive aggression which manifested itself, at times, in catatonic agitation and violence toward objects and his own body.

The actual break with or withdrawal from reality rarely occurs before our eyes. Such observation as described by Kubie in his beautiful communication, "Say You're Sorry,"[2] is exceptional. In Kubie's case the little girl's acute psychotic regression was triggered by the loss of the good substitute mother figure, represented by the supportive houseworker concurring with severe corporal punishment by the good father.

We believe the stable image of a father or of another substitute of the mother, beyond the eighteen-months mark and even earlier, is beneficial and perhaps a necessary prerequisite to neutralize and to counteract the age-characteristic oversensibility of the toddler to the threat of re-engulfment by the mother.

We have mentioned the dread of re-engulfment versus separation panic in the phase of individuation. We tend to think of the father too one-

2 See pp. 289-299.

sidedly as the castrating figure, a kind of bad mother image in the pre-oedipal period. Loewald (1951), to our knowledge, was the first to emphasize that, "Against the threat of the maternal engulfment the paternal position is not another threat of danger, but a support of powerful force." If there is a relative lack of support on the part of either parent (or the "uncontaminated" mother substitutes[3]), a re-engulfment of the ego into the whirlpool of the primary undifferentiated symbiotic stage becomes a true threat.

The toddler in the second eighteen months of life, whose ego is constitutionally vulnerable, symbiotically fixated, and now during the separation-individuation phase is additionally traumatized, may regress to even earlier archaic stages of personality development. A lapse into the archaic object-less, autistic stage may be the only solution. The child may suddenly or gradually lose his individual identity and his contact with reality.

This occurred to five-year-old M.C., for whose mother "All my children seemed to be the same." Although there are no detailed data of the symbiotic stage of M.C.'s development, from the mother's actual behavior at the time of M.C.'s hospitalization when five and a half years old, we can readily reconstruct it. At this time he was still exclusively on bottle feedings. The mother had made no attempt to foster the growth of independence in other areas either. M.C. was never permitted or encouraged to dress himself, nor to develop any spontaneity.

Shortly after M.C.'s birth, the father began to indulge in alcohol, at first only moderately, but gradually to an ever-increasing degree. During the earlier phase, well beyond M.C.'s second birthday, the father remained a moderately devoted father, caring for the infant and tending to his needs. In time, however, the father's behavior came to be more and more unpredictable. When intoxicated, he was frequently physically abusive toward the mother. This eventually culminated in a particular episode when the patient was four and a half years old. The father's behavior was so threatening toward the mother that she called the police, who then proceeded to arrest the father. M.C., who had witnessed the entire episode, was extremely disturbed, not only about the father's physical abuse of the mother but particularly about the rough treatment which the father received at the hands of the policemen. When the father was subsequently removed by the police, M.C.'s agitation and distress were very great. He cried repeatedly, "Where are they taking my Daddy?" His mother was obliged to take M.C. to the police station and there obtain her husband's release. It was following this experience that M.C. gradually regressed: his speech, which had been age-adequate, eventually became limited to two words. He reverted to urinating

---

[3] As Dr. Ernst Kris pointed out in his discussion remarks.

wherever the urge overpowered him, and defecated in closets. An earlier phase of father-child communication was used as stereotyped patterned behavior. The father's throwing the child, half angrily, half playfully, to the bed or ground, became a pattern of behavior in which M.C. would slump to the floor and lie there quietly and unresponsively with vacuous stare. This was only one evidence of his withdrawal from reality into his self-created inner world.

We have seen that Aro is functioning (to a great extent) on the level of the symbiotic infant and the toddler between eighteen and thirty-six months. He uses his mother as his external ego. He also wards her off with autistic defenses for fear of complete dissolution of his individual entity. Aro's case as well as the complete autistic withdrawal into a self-sufficient autistic inner world in cases as B.S.'s and M.C.'s, we feel, show that autism, this psychotic form of negativism, is an attempt at reactive restitution. When the good images in the outside world are insufficient or unusable to counteract the menace of demoniacal inner powers that harass, attack and almost annihilate the ego from within, as in the case of tiqueurs; or if both parental images become completely deflated and useless against castration threat (Jacobson, 1953); if, against consuming introjected bad objects and the hostile world (police, dangerous psychotherapist, death of grandfather, etc.), no object image in the outside world can be depended upon—then the break with reality and withdrawal into an inner world serve the function of survival. We designated this per se regressive psychotic defense, this secondary autism, a reactive restitution, because the ego thus restores, albeit regressively, the blissful oceanic feeling, the oneness with "the object," which seems the delusional substitute for that child whose ego is unable to endure the second hatching process, the actual separation from the good object.

BIBLIOGRAPHY

Bak, R. C. (1954), The Schizophrenic Defense against Aggression. *Int. J. Psa.*, XXXV.

Bowlby, J.; Robertson, J.; Rosenbluth, D. (1952), A Two-Year-Old Goes to Hospital. *This Annual*, VII.

Coleman, R. W.; Kris, E.; Provence, S. (1953), The Study of Variations of Early Parental Attitudes. *This Annual*, VIII.

Freud, A. (1949), Notes on Aggression. *Bull. Menninger Clin.*, XIII.

—— (1951), Negativism and Emotional Surrender. Read at the International Psychoanalytic Congress, Amsterdam.

Freud, S. (1915), Repression. *Collected Papers*, IV. London: Hogarth Press.

Greenacre, P. (1945), The Biologic Economy of Birth. *This Annual*, I.

Hartmann, H. (1939), Ichpsychologie und Anpassungsproblem. *Int. Ztschr. Psa.*, XXIV. Translated in part in: *Organization and Pathology of Thought*, ed. D. Rapaport. New York: Columbia University Press, 1951.

—— (1953), Contribution to the Metapsychology of Schizophrenia. *This Annual*, VIII.

——; Kris, E.; Loewenstein, R. M. (1949), Notes on the Theory of Aggression. *This Annual*, III/IV.

Hoffer, W. (1949), Mouth, Hand, and Ego-Integration. *This Annual*, III/IV.

—— (1950a), Oral Aggressiveness and Ego Development. *Int. J. Psa.*, XXXI.

—— (1950b), Development of the Body Ego. *This Annual*, V.

Jacobson, E. (1953), Contribution to the Metapsychology of Cyclothymic Depression. In: *Affective Disorders*, ed. P. Greenacre. New York: International Universities Press.

—— (1954), The Self and the Object World: Vicissitudes of Their Infantile Cathexes and Their Influence on Ideational and Affective Development. *This Annual*, IX.

Klein, M. (1939), *The Psycho-Analysis of Children*. London: Hogarth Press.

Lewin, B. D. (1950), *The Psychoanalysis of Elation*. New York: Norton.

Loewald, H. W. (1951), Ego and Reality. *Int. J. Psa.*, XXXII.

Mahler, M. S. (1948), Contribution to Round-Table Discussion, On Aggression. Annual Meeting of the American Psychiatric Association, Washington, D. C.

—— (1949), Psychoanalytic Evaluation of Tic: A Sign and Symptom in Psychopathology. *This Annual*, III/IV.

—— (1952), On Child Psychosis and Schizophrenia: Autistic and Symbiotic Infantile Psychoses. *This Annual*, VII.

—— (1954), On Normal and Pathological Symbiosis. Read at the Baltimore Psychoanalytic Society.

——, Elkisch, P. (1953), Some Observations on Disturbances of the Ego in a Case of Infantile Psychosis. *This Annual*, VIII.

——; Luke, J.; Daltroff, W. (1945), Tic Syndrome in Children. *Am. J. Orthopsychiat.*, XV.

Ribble, M. S. A. (1941), Disorganizing Factors in Infant Personality. *Am. J. Psychiat.*, XCVIII.

Spitz, R. A. (1951), The Psychogenic Diseases in Infancy: An Attempt at Their Etiological Classification. *This Annual*, VI.

PROBLEMS OF PSYCHOSEXUAL DEVELOPMENT

THE PRIMAL CAVITY

A Contribution to the Genesis of Perception and Its Role for Psychoanalytic Theory

RENÉ A. SPITZ, M.D. (New York)

In recent years two forms of psychoanalytic approach to the phenomenon of sleep have claimed our interest. I am referring to Lewin's (1946) interpretative and reconstructive work on the dream screen, on one hand, and to Isakower's (1938) clinical observations on the psychopathology of going to sleep, on the other. It is my belief that these two studies cover two aspects, and, beyond this, two stages of a regressive phenomenon, which has its counterpart in ontogenetic development. The regressive phenomena described by Lewin and by Isakower fall into the area of "normal" psychological functioning. The developmental data which I shall present in what follows, will serve to retrace the same process in the opposite, in the progressive direction. I hope to show that the dream screen hypothesis of Lewin and the clinical observation of Isakower have their parallel in the independent findings of direct infant observation and in the neurophysiology of perception. The convergence of the three lines of research, Isakower's, Lewin's, and my own, is noteworthy. Each started from a different point and, using different approaches, yields findings which are mutually explanatory. I have first spoken of such convergences in a communication on "Experimental Design" (1950b) and stated that in psychoanalysis such a convergence can occupy the place which validation has in experimental psychology.

THE DREAM SCREEN AND THE ISAKOWER PHENOMENON

Lewin's hypothesis takes as its starting point Freud's statement that the dream is the guardian of sleep. The fundamental wish-fulfilling nature of the dream ensures the continuation of sleep. In this function the dream is the manifestation of a regression to the emotional state of the infant when it goes to sleep at the mother's breast after having drunk his fill. Certain of his patients' dreams appeared as if projected onto a screen which, Lewin holds, is the visual memory of the breast. He further assumes that this dream-screen-breast is always present in dreaming; that in the "blank dream" it actually is the dream content. He connects these findings with his other proposition, that of the oral triad of the wish to eat, to be eaten, to sleep (to die).

Isakower's contribution is the clinical observation that some of his patients, when in the reclining position, particularly when subject to elevation of temperature, or in the predormescent state, have certain sensations which partake of the mouth, of the skin surface and of the hand sensitivity. The somewhat vague sensations are of something wrinkled, or perhaps gritty and dry, soft, filling the mouth, being felt at the same time on the skin surface of the body and being manipulated with the fingers. Visually the sensation is perceived as shadowy, indefinite, mostly round, approaching and growing enormous and then shrinking to practically nothing.

Lewin's and Isakower's observations have proved extraordinarily fertile both clinically and theoretically. The clinical observations of numerous analysts, including myself, have confirmed their findings.

When, however, I confronted Lewin's hypothesis with the findings of my own research on perceptive development, a difficulty arose. Lewin's description of the dream screen has a perceptive aspect and an affect aspect. We will begin with the discussion of the perceptive aspect, for since Freud's earliest writings perception has been rarely explored by psychoanalysts.

THE BEGINNINGS OF PERCEPTION

Both Lewin and Isakower state that the phenomena described by them are based on the memory of what they consider to be the first visual percept, namely, the mother's breast. My own work on the earliest stages of perception, conducted by the method of direct observation on infants, led me to experimental findings which at first appear to contradict their conclusion. In agreement with the statements of the academic psychologists Volkelt (1929), Hetzer and Ripin (1930), Rubinow and Frankl (1934), and Kaila (1932), I came to the conclusion that the first visual percept is the human face; to be more exact, it is a Gestalt configuration *within* the human face.

This first visual percept cannot be achieved at birth. It is progressively developed in the course of the first three months and is reliably perceived, and reacted to as such, in the course of the third month of life. I have elaborated these findings in my experimental study "The Smiling Response" (1946, 1948), in which I have also shown experimentally that at this period no other visual percept is recognized or reacted to in the same reliable manner as the human face.

This is a decisive turning point in the development of the psyche during the first year of life. It is the turning from passive reception to active perception, and accordingly I have called it, in analogy to an embryological concept, an "organizer" of psychological development. We will come back later to some of the details of this phenomenon.

The period prior to the crystallization of this first visual percept has been described by Hartmann (1939) and Anna Freud (1952) as the period of *undifferentiation,* by myself as that of *nondifferentiation.* The term nondifferentiation should be understood in a global, total sense: on one hand, the infant does not distinguish what is "I" from what is "non-I," the self from the non-self, let alone the constituent elements of his environment. On the other hand, his own faculties, be they modalities of feeling, of sensation, of emotion, are not differentiated from one another; finally, no differentiation within the psychic system or even between the psyche and soma can be demonstrated. A case in point is the phenomenon of the so-called "overflow" in the newborn.

The subsequent differentiation is a progressive one, maturational on one hand, developmental on the other. It is in the course of the first three months, more or less beginning after the sixth week, that we can detect experimentally certain areas in which the infant begins to distinguish visual percepts. The first such percept to which it reacts is the human face. Toward the middle of the second month of life, the infant begins to follow the movement and displacement of the human face. Later, after about ten weeks, he responds to the human face with a differentiated manifestation of emotion, that of smiling.

With these observational facts in mind, let us now imagine the perceptual world of the infant before differentiation has begun; to achieve this, it is well to project ourselves backward to the memories of our own childhood and to realize how gigantic every remembered street, house, garden, piece of furniture appears in our memory; and how, if we happen to see it again twenty years later, it seems, surprisingly, to have shrunk.

This shrinkage of remembered impressions is due to the increase of our own size, for man is the measure of all things. Considering that the infant's face is one third the size of the adult's face, and that the infant's whole length at birth is little more than one quarter that of the adult, one begins to realize how gigantic the adult appears to the infant.

Swift illustrates this in *Gulliver's Travels,* a point mentioned by

Freud (1900, p. 30); Lewin (1953a) refers again and again to this distortion of the infant's perception. The distortion is even more accentuated through the fact that the perceptive angle of the infant's vision, when approached by an adult, has to be an extremely wide one—we do not usually see people as close as the infant sees them. Lewin did not overlook this; he speaks of the "diplopic, amblyopic baby, with its weak powers of accommodation and its confused depth and color perceptions (1953a, p. 183). (See also Margolin, 1953.)

We can assume that the baby, if indeed it perceives anything, perceives moving, shifting, gigantic, vaguely colored and even more vaguely contoured inchoate masses. In the midst of this chaos certain of these shifting masses reappear periodically and are associated with certain recurrent sensations, feelings, emotions. They become associated, in short, with need satisfaction.

It is at this point that my observations on infants appear to contradict both Lewin's and Isakower's assumptions. The reason for this divergence is a twofold one; one has already been mentioned: namely, that the first percept to be crystallized out of the shifting nebular masses in the world of the baby is the human face. The second is an easily demonstrable fact which can be checked by anyone who takes the trouble to observe a nursing baby. The nursing baby does not look at the *breast*. He does not look at the breast when the mother is approaching him, nor when she is offering him the breast, nor when he is nursing. He stares unwaveringly, from the beginning of the feeding to the end of it, at the mother's face.

Therefore, I offer the proposition that the Isakower phenomenon does not represent the approaching breast—at least not from the visual point of view. In my opinion it represents the visually perceived human face. All the phenomena, all the details described in Isakower's and Lewin's examples, as well as in those provided by other analysts, are to be found in the human face. The cracks, the wrinkles, the roses, the spots—but let Gulliver in Brobdingnag speak: "Their skins appeared so coarse and uneven, so variously colored when I saw them near, with a mole here and there as broad as a trencher, and hairs hanging from it thicker than pack threads, to say nothing further concerning the rest of their persons" (Swift).

It would seem that the facts of perceptive development cannot be reconciled with either Isakower's or Lewin's assumptions. Such is not my opinion; on the contrary, I believe that my findings, and the observable data of perceptive development, actually form the bridge between the Isakower phenomenon and the Lewin propositions, and round them off in certain aspects. The real point of juncture is to be found in the observation that the infant, while nursing at the breast, is at the same time staring at the mother's face; thus breast and face are experienced as one and indivisible.

It should be remembered that at birth the newborn perceives only sensations originating *within* his body. He is protected from outside perceptions by the stimulus barrier. How, then, does the turning from inner stimuli to outer perception, be it even of the inchoate kind described earlier, come about? It seems to me that the present state of our knowledge permits the following proposition:

We possess one localized perceptual zone which includes in itself both the characteristics of interior and exterior perception. From birth on and even before (Minkowski, 1925, 1928; Davenport Hooker, 1942, 1943), a readiness for response to stimulation can be demonstrated in and around the mouth. This behavior is of an aim-directed nature. We may, with Konrad Lorenz (1950), call the readiness underlying this response an *innate releasing mechanism,* an IRM. Like all IRM's, it has survival value.[1] The resulting behavior consists in the following: The whole outside part of the mouth region, of the "snout" (nose, cheeks, chin and lips), responds to stimulation by a turning of the head toward the stimulus, combined with a snapping movement of the mouth. The function of this response is to take the nipple into the mouth.

We call this behavior the sucking reflex. Though it can be elicited by appropriate stimulation in the fetus and even in the embryo, at birth it is unreliable like all innate behavior in man. In reflexological terms, it is neither stimulus-specific nor response-specific; that means that it does not *always* take place in response to the stimulation of the snout, nor does it *only* take place in response to the stimulation of the snout.

But despite this comparative unreliability it is one of the most reliable responses at birth. Its reliability is second only to that of the clutch reflex, which is the closing of the hand on palmar stimulation; in the same order of reliability as the clutch reflex is its antagonist, described by me under the name of the *digital stretch reflex* (1950a) which consists

[1] IRM (innate releasing mechanism) is a concept introduced by animal ethologists (Uexküll, Lorenz). The concept has hardly ever been defined in the literature, except in terms of the releasing stimulus. An exception to this is an attempt made by Tinbergen (1950, p. 309). The approximate definition given by Tinbergen elsewhere (1951) will suffice: "There must be a special neurosensory mechanism that releases the reaction and is responsible for this selective susceptibility to a very special combination of sign stimuli. This mechanism we will call the Innate Releasing Mechanism (IRM)" (p. 42). We may complete it by a definition given by Baerends (1950): "The mechanism beginning at the sense organs, ending at the center released and including the sensitivity for characteristics of the object, we will call the releasing mechanism" (p. 338).

in the stretching of the fingers on dorsal stimulation of the phalanges. It is noteworthy that sucking and clutching—the two archaic responses which show directed behavior and which are far and away more reliable than all others at this period—are to be found in connection with the hand and the mouth; and, moreover, that they are both directed to an action of "taking into," as it were. It is surely significant that the regression in the Isakower phenomenon concerns the selfsame organs, the hand and the mouth.

One may speculate on the question whether the unreliability of these responses may have its cause in the fact that they are provoked by stimuli originating on the outside of the body, so that they impinge on the sensorium, which at this stage is not yet cathected. But, as we have stressed before, reception of inner stimuli is already present at this stage. Accordingly, we have next considered a stimulation which involves simultaneously both the outside and the inside. Such a stimulation takes place when the nipple is placed *inside* the newborn's mouth. In view of what we have said above, it is not surprising that this stimulation elicits a much more reliable response at this period; the response consists in sucking and in the concomitant process of deglutition.

What appears to me significant in this phenomenon is that the *inside* of the mouth, *the oral cavity,* fulfills the conditions of partaking for perceptive purposes both of the inside and of the outside. It is simultaneously an interoceptor and exteroceptor. It is here that all perception will begin; in this role the oral cavity fulfills the function of a bridge from internal reception to external perception.

Both Isakower and Lewin have included some of these ideas into their reconstructive approach to the problem. Isakower has assumed that the combination of the oral cavity with the hand corresponds to the model of what he defines as the earliest postnatal ego structure, and that the sensations of the oral cavity are probably unified with those of the external cutaneous covering.

Lewin (1953a) in his "Reconsideration of the Dream Screen," quotes Dr. Rogawsky to the effect "that the original cavity might well be the inside of the mouth, as discovered and perceived by the suckling's finger. Accordingly, the earliest impression of the mouth would serve as a prototype of all later ideas of body cavities."

I would agree with this formulation, but would make it more specific. It is misleading, in my opinion, to speak of the suckling's finger discovering or perceiving anything. At this early stage (the first weeks of life) the organ in which precursors of perceptions are received is the oral cavity and not the finger. We have, therefore, to consider rather what the oral cavity perceives when something—in the case suggested by Dr. Rogawsky, the finger—is introduced into it. Even earlier than this, the nipple, and the jet of milk coming from it, have acted as the earliest postnatal liberators from thirst. How enduring the memory of the unpleasure of thirst is can be seen from the repetitive mentioning of the gritty, sandy sensation in Isakower's examples.

To me this finding is not surprising. I have stressed again and again in the last twenty years that speaking of hunger in the newborn and infant is a misnomer. The sufferings of hunger are not comparable to thirst, nor do they occur in response to as brief a deprivation as those of thirst. We are all too prone to forget that at birth the infant shifts from the life of a water dweller to that of a land animal. During the intrauterine period his mouth cavity, larynx, etc., were constantly bathed in the amniotic liquid. After delivery a continuous stream of air will dry out the mucosa with great rapidity, particularly since the salivary glands begin to function only many weeks later. This drying out of the mucosa will cause all the discomfort sensations of a dry mouth, throat, nasal passages, etc., connected with thirst; and not with hunger. Thirst, or rather dryness of this area, will therefore be one of the first experiences of discomfort in the infant.

But the experience of relief from unpleasure through the nipple which fills the newborn's mouth (remember the disparity of sizes!), and the milk streaming from it, is only one part of the picture, a passive experience. The act of sucking and of deglutition is the infant's first active co-ordinated muscular action. The organs involved are the tongue, the lips and the cheeks. Accordingly, these are also the muscles which are the first ones to be brought under control, a fact which makes the later smiling response possible.

Similarly these will be the first surfaces used in tactile perception and exploration. They are particularly well suited for this purpose because in this single organ, the mouth cavity, are assembled the representatives of several of the senses in one and the same area. These senses are the sense of touch, of taste, of temperature, of smell, of pain, but also the deep sensibility involved in the act of deglutition. Indeed, the oral cavity lends itself as no other region of the body to bridge the gap between inner and outer perception.

True, the quality of this perception is a contact perception, not a distance perception like the visual one. Hence, a further transition has to occur from tactile to visual perception.

I have already mentioned one factor in this transition: the fact that the nursing infant stares unwaveringly at the mother's face as soon as his

eyes are open. We have to add to this a second factor, namely, the maturational and developmental level of the infant's sensory equipment, including the central nervous system on one hand, the psychological development on the other, during the first weeks and months of life, previously
characterized as the stage of nondifferentiation. Stimulation occurring in
one system of the body is responded to in others. Overflow is the rule of
the hour. We may again advance a hypothesis: when the infant nurses
and has sensations in the oral cavity while staring at the mother's face,
he unites the tactile and the visual perceptions, the perceptions of the
total situation, into one undifferentiated unity, a situation Gestalt, in
which any one part of the experience comes to stand for the total
experience.

THE MODALITY OF PRIMAL PERCEPTION AND ITS THREE SUBSIDIARY ORGANS

It has become evident in the course of this discussion that this first
experience of the baby is not a simple one. We had to expand our approach to the genesis of perception by including in it emotional qualities,
those of pleasure and unpleasure, as well as dynamic qualities, namely
activity and passivity. That, however, is inevitable in all developmental
research, as I have shown elsewhere (1946, p. 65), because affects are the
initiators of all perception, emotional development its trailbreaker, indeed
the trailbreaker of development in all sectors, hence also dynamic development.

Obviously the source of these affects of the infant is a physiological
one, a need. As Freud (1915b) stated, the drives originate at the dividing
line between the soma and the psyche. It is the need which produces the
tension that is expressed by the affective manifestations of unpleasure.
It is the need gratification which leads to tension reduction and quiescence. This dynamic process activates the first intraoral perceptions,
which take place on a dividing line again, that between inside and
outside.

The site of the origin of perception and of psychological experience
has far-reaching consequences. For it is here that the task of distinguish-
ing between inside and outside has its inception; this discrimination becomes established much later and will lead in an unbroken development
to the separation of the self from the non-self, of the self from the objects,
and in the course of this road to what is accepted and what is rejected
(Freud, 1925). I might mention in passing that the time necessarily
elapsing between the arising of the need and the reduction of tension
introduces a further element into our picture, that of the capacity to

wait, the capacity to tolerate tension or, in a term recently become fashionable, that of frustration tolerance.

The particular anatomical location and physiological function of the oral cavity enables it to distinguish the outside from the inside. This leads us to a qualification of a generally accepted psychoanalytic proposition stressed by both Isakower and Lewin. It is correct that the breast is the first object; it is probable that the breast, or rather the nipple, forms a part of the first percept; but direct observation proves that the breast definitely is not the first *visual* percept.[2] This is because at this earliest stage of life *distance* perception is not operative, but only *contact* perception. It is of special interest to our discussion to examine what organs besides the oral cavity are involved in the contact perceptions of the nursing situation. Three such organs are in evidence from birth.

1. Of the three, the most evident is the hand. Its participation in the nursing act is obvious to every observer. At birth this participation is in the nature of overflow; the sensorium of the hand is not cathected as yet, as shown by Halverson's experiments (1937). He found that the clutch reflex on palmar stimulation is reliably elicited when tendons in the palm are stimulated—a stimulation of deep sensibility—and was unreliable on cutaneous stimulation. The activity of the hands during nursing, when both hands find their support on the breast, consists in a continuous movement of the fingers which clutch, stroke, claw and scratch on the breast. This activity will accompany the nursing process consistently during the subsequent months. It will become more and more organized, probably as a function of the progressive cathexis of the hand's sensorium. We can imagine the development as beginning with an activity of the mouth, overflowing into the hand; at a somewhat later stage this is proprioceptively perceived and, when the sensorium is cathected, also exteroceptively. This early co-ordination of mouth and hand function and its progressive development is in agreement with the embryological and neurobiological finding that maturation proceeds in a cephalocaudal direction.[3]

2 Percept, the thing perceived (Hinsie and Shatzky), should be clearly distinguished from object (libidinal); the latter originates through the focusing of a constellation of drives onto a percept. Perception of the percept is the prerequisite of object formation.

3 Hoffer discusses the relationship between hand and mouth in two articles. In the first (1949) he investigates the function of the hand in ego integration and in the development of early ego functions. His conclusions are in accordance with the above statements; but they deal with a later stage than the cavity perception described by me. In his second article (1950), he introduces a new concept, that of the "mouth-self" which is progressively extended to the "body-self" through the activity of the hand which libidinizes various parts of the body. This process also occurs at a later stage than the one discussed in my present article.

2. The second organ which participates in the nursing situation is less evident. It is the labyrinth. Both Isakower and Lewin speak of the frequent presence of dizziness, murmur and noise in the phenomena they describe. This finding is supported by direct observation on the newborn. It has been shown experimentally that the stimulus which leads to the earliest conditioned response in the newborn is a change of equilibrium. The experiment consists in the following: If, after about eight days of life, the breast-fed infant is lifted from his cot and placed in the nursing position, he will turn his head toward the person holding him and will open his mouth. It is immaterial whether the person in question is male or female. What does this experiment show, what is the sensory organ involved in this reaction of the newborn?

When we lift the newborn from his cot and place him in the nursing position, we set in motion in the labyrinth a neurophysiological process of a very special nature. This process is a gravity-induced shift of the endolymph within the labyrinth, resulting in two sensory stimulations of a completely different nature in two spatially separate parts of one and the same organ. The pressure of the endolymph on the lining of the semicircular canals results in changes of the equilibrium sensation; the same pressure will simultaneously provoke auditory sensations in the organ of Corti in the cochlea. The morphological difference between the lining of the semicircular canals and that of the cochlea is responsible for the difference between the two resulting sensations. The sensations connected with the stimulation of the semicircular canals will be dizziness and vertigo, those connected with the stimulation of the Corti organ will be auditory, probably vague, rushing, murmuring, roaring noises which may be similar to the sensations described by Isakower and Lewin (see also French, 1929; Rycroft, 1953; Scott, 1948). We can then envisage that the newborn experiences the being lifted into the nursing position as an interoceptively[4] perceived experience with all the vagueness, diffuseness and absence of localization that is characteristic of prothopathic sensation.

3. The third organ involved is the outer skin surface. Isakower's as well as Lewin's descriptions emphasize the vagueness of the localization. Isakower speaks of the big and then again small "something," gritty, sandy, dry, which is experienced both in the mouth and on the skin surface, simultaneously or alternately; it is experienced like a blurring

---

[4] In the following I will speak of interoceptors and interoceptive systems, using the definition given by Fulton (1938) and Sherrington (1947): "The interoceptors are divided into two groups: (1) the proprioceptors (muscles and labyrinth) and (2) the visceroceptors (gut, heart, blood vessels, bladder, etc.)."

of widely separated zones of the body. I believe that we do not have to postulate intrauterine memories here. It seems to me rather that this is the echo of an experience that is analogous to that of thirst in the mouth—only that it involves the skin surface instead. Up to delivery the skin surface had been in the least irritating and most sheltering environment imaginable. It was surrounded by liquid and protected even against this by vernix caseosa. After delivery it is exposed to the roughness, unevenness, dryness of the textiles into which we wrap babies. It is inevitable that the stimulation due to these textiles will be infinitely sharper than we adults can imagine; that it will take quite a long time, weeks and months, until the newborn's skin has adjusted to these stimuli and toughened sufficiently to relegate them to the normal environmental background.[5]

It might be assumed that to the newborn the sensations of skin discomfort are indistinguishable from discomfort in the passages of mouth, nose, larynx and pharynx. From our knowledge of the nondifferentiation in the perceptive sectors (and all others) this must indeed be so.

The sensations of the three organs of perception—hand, labyrinth, and skin cover—combine and unite with the intraoral sensations to a unified situational experience in which no part is distinguishable from the other. This perceptive experience is inseparable from that of the need gratification occurring simultaneously and leading through extensive tension reduction from a state of excitement with the quality of unpleasure to quiescence without unpleasure. We do not postulate any memory traces, be they even unconscious, of this situational percept of the newborn. Whether engrams are laid down at this stage also remain unanswerable.[6] But this selfsame situational experience, repeated again and again, will many weeks later eventually merge with the first visual percept and be present simultaneously with it, remaining attached to it in first unconscious and later conscious visual imagery.

[5] Two highly pertinent papers of M. F. Ashley Montagu (1953, 1950) came to my attention too late to incorporate his findings into the present paper. Basing himself on some theoretical considerations, and on a series of observations on nonhuman animals (Reyniers, 1949; Hammett, 1922), he concludes that the skin as an organ has a hitherto unsuspected functional significance for physiological and psychological development. Laboratory evidence indicates that in the nonhuman mammals the licking of the young by the mother activates the genitourinary, the gastrointestinal and the respiratory systems. Some evidence is offered that matters may be, if not similar, at least analogous in man (Drillien, 1948; Lorand and Asbot, 1952).

[6] It is perhaps useful to remind ourselves in this context (and also in reference to the dream screen and to the Isakower phenomenon) that from the beginning Freud (1900) stated that the first mnemonic traces could only be established in function of an experience of satisfaction which interrupts the excitation arising from an internal need. This experience of satisfaction puts an end to the internal stimulus (p. 565).

The cluster of factors which go into the nursing experience of the newborn therefore can be enumerated as follows:

1. The psychophysiological factors of unpleasurable tension and its reduction through nursing;

2. A factor which in due time will become a psychological one, that of activity;

3. The neurophysiological perceptive factors of the oral experience of sucking and deglutition involving a number of proprioceptive sense organs situated within the mouth;

4. Simultaneous sensory experiences of the hand and of the outer skin;

5. Simultaneous interoceptive experiences in the labyrinth.

THE ACHIEVEMENT OF DISTANCE PERCEPTION

On reflection it must be evident that the majority of these factors—with the one exception of skin discomfort—belong to, or at least are very close to, perceptions of changes going on in the inside of the neonate, that is, proprioceptive perceptions. Even in regard to the hand we may assume that the movements do not represent a response to a tactile sensation, but an overflow into the hand musculature of the innervation of the nursing and deglutition activity. As for the labyrinth sensations, these belong patently to the coenesthetic (protopathic) system and share with this the diffuseness, vagueness and lack of localization.

We have to stress again that the whole experience with all its percepts and sensations is centered inside or linked up with the oral cavity and belongs to the modality of contact perception. That modality must also be postulated for the perceptions of the labyrinth which originate on the inside of the body. This contact perception, taking place *inside* of the body, is the crystallization point for the first modality of the perceptive process and is secured with the help of the endlessly repetitive experience of the unpleasure-pleasure cycle.

In the course of maturation, a second modality appears—distance perception in the form of the first visual percepts. Through the baby's unwavering stare at the mother's face during nursing the visual experience is merged into the total experience. The infant still does not distinguish inside from outside, what he sees with his eyes from what he feels with his mouth.

A large number of disappointing experiences—namely, waiting periods intruding between the perception of mother's face and the lowering of need tension through food in the mouth—are required before a differentiation between the two can take place. Until that occurs, mother's face—not the visual percept of mother's breast!—will mean "food in the mouth" and relief from unpleasure. It can be experimentally proved that at this stage—the third month of life—the visual percept of the maternal breast produces no change whatever in the hungry baby's behavior.

That much of this applies to the hand and its sensations, is obvious. After all, the simultaneous activity of the baby's hand during nursing is familiar to every mother. We may assume that also in the hand it is not so much the tactile percept which is connected with the intraoral experience, but rather a proprioceptive percept, that of the contraction and relaxation of the hand muscles which is perceived in the same manner as the contractions of the oral muscles in sucking. That something of the kind must be taking place can be shown in motion pictures, where it is amply evident that in the nursing baby the closure of the hand is performed in the same rhythm as the sucking movement of the mouth. The "taking into" quality of these hand movements appears to me to justify the proposition that they are experienced by the infant as belonging to the sucking movements of the mouth. Perhaps we are justified in expanding this proposition to the child's coenesthetic sensations. When the child is lifted and cradled in the mother's arms, pressed against her body and held securely during the act of nursing, it comes near to the blissful intrauterine state in which need tension never arose and the insecurity of our modern baby cot with its lack of support was unknown.

An excellent illustration of all that I have discussed above has been provided to me through the courtesy of a colleague from Habana, Dr. Carlos Acosta (1955). In the course of the analysis of an adult patient, Dr. Acosta noted a number of unusual dreams, hallucinatoryform visions and similar manifestations, of which I will quote a few.

Case O. V.:

O. V. is a twenty-one-year old white male. He came into treatment because of overt homosexuality. He is an extremely infantile individual, given to daydreaming which borders on the hallucinatory, with an I.Q. of 74. Both the testing psychologist and Dr. Acosta agree that the patient's I.Q. actually is higher and that the test situation is distorted through the patient's emotional difficulties. It was not possible to determine whether he is a case of arrested development or whether his symptomatology is the consequence of a regression; I would lean toward the former.

Four communications of the patient which bear on our discussion follow:

1. The patient visits his girl. Sitting next to her he falls asleep and on awakening he peeks into her decolleté and sees "the breast cloudy, with spots, like a glass from which milk was poured out, the glass remaining covered with a

film of milk, forming spots," which he compares to *"manchas en mujeres embara-zadas"* ("chloasmata in pregnant women").

2. Lying on the couch during treatment he hallucinates as follows: "There is a piece of white bread, shaped like a pear, with its point toward me, approaching me, coming closer and getting bigger. . . . Funny, now it has jumped suddenly to my thumb and is much smaller."

3. The patient reports on another day that the previous morning the chore of boiling the breakfast milk filled him with resentment because while the milk was on the fire, he was masturbating and indulging in fantasies, but worried that the milk would boil over. In his masturbatory fantasy he imagined that he was having intercourse with his girl and was sucking her breast. He associated the milk boiling over in the pot with that coming out of the girl's breast and with the sperm spurting out of his penis. In this fantasy part of the sperm was going into the vagina (and spurting out of the breasts), another part was splashing onto the floor.

4. When confronted with maternal-looking women, he gets a peculiar sensation when they look at him. He feels the inside of his mouth contracting (Analyst's note: like a contraction of the buccal and labial musculature), and he associates to this a "displeasure" in the stomach, like heat or emptiness. He had the same feeling in his mouth when he hallucinated the "clouded breast" vision of his fantasy. The contraction of his mouth muscles forces him to turn away and hide his face from such a maternal woman, because he does not want her to see him making faces. He remembers that he had this feeling as a very small child when mother carried him in her arms at her breast from one room to another; he also remembers the feeling of dizziness and nausea. This he has also at present when riding on a bus and "the air rushes into his mouth." The circumstances leading to his mouth sensations often also provoke similar sensations in the inside of the belly, which then contracts in the way the inside of the mouth contracted.

CONSIDERATIONS SUGGESTED BY THE CASE MATERIAL

In the various dreams and observations reported by Lewin and Isakower as well as by an ever-increasing number of analysts who in the meantime have written on the subject, a large number of the constituent elements of the picture we are concerned with can be found in one place or another. Some of these elements belong to dreams and normal states, others are found in pathological conditions. The case described by Dr. Acosta seems to bring together in one and the same individual all these elements. I feel, therefore, that it makes further examples repetitive because it is sufficiently representative of the large body of observations published on the subject.

Communications No. 1 and 2 describe phenomena which are strikingly similar to and in some particulars even more vivid than those reported by Isakower. That the patient brings together the breast-shaped object with his thumb, has particular significance for our further remarks. It impresses me as an example of the mode of operation of what, for want of a better term, we have to call the "psyche" in early infancy; this "psyche" causes different percepts with similar functions to be merged into one another; this merging is the result of a lack of differentiation. In the example quoted above thumb sucking and nursing have the same function, namely to release tension. The percepts are different, but the function is identical.

But Communication No. 4 suggests conclusions which are more far-reaching. Here sensations in the oral cavity, which refer to subliminal mnemic traces of the nursing situation, are brought into relation by the patient with sensations within the abdomen, on the one hand, envelopment in the mother's arms and body, on the other.[7]

In the case of Dr. Acosta's patient, the hand and simultaneously the equilibrium sensation (both in the "being carried" memory) as well as the intra-abdominal sensation are combined with the intraoral experience (French, 1929; Rycroft, 1953). It is this summative aspect of the nursing experience which has motivated me to speak of the inside of the mouth as the primal cavity. I believe that the data provided by the reports of Dr. Acosta's patient rather convincingly substantiate the opinion held by

[7] Two points are worth mentioning, although they do not belong into the framework of the present article. One is O. V.'s sensations of muscular contractions of his mouth region, which he associates with fantasies connected with the breast, with breast feeding and with seeing "maternal-looking women." He is so intensely conscious of these contractions that he has to avert his head for fear that "the woman may notice that he is making faces." This suggests that the *Schnauzkrampf* symptom in the schizophrenic may be connected with wishful fantasies of breast feeding and with the mnemic traces of the proprioceptive percept of mouth activity during nursing.

The other point is that, when the patient travels on a bus and "the air rushes into his mouth," he has a feeling of dizziness and nausea. He says that this feeling is like the feeling he had as a very small child when his mother carried him in her arms at her breast from one room to another. We may well add this finding to Freud's assumptions on the origin of flying in dreams (1900, pp. 271 f.; 393 f.) on one hand, on the other to his hypotheses on the production of sexual excitation (1905, p. 201). In the latter he specifically states that the stimulus of rhythmic mechanical agitation of the body operates in three different ways: on the sensory apparatus of the vestibular nerves, on the skin, and on the muscles and articular structures. He even mentions the impact of moving air on the genitals. He connects these childhood experiences with later developing train phobias. The contribution of Dr. Acosta's patient appears not only to confirm fully Freud's findings, but to add to them the information that the origin of the multiform traveling phobias may reach back to the nursing period of the infant in the first year of life.

Isakower, Lewin, and myself: intrauterine fantasies at a later age are based on a regressive imagery of early intraoral experience.

The patient's description bears out what I had postulated earlier: the oral cavity, in which the interoceptive and exteroceptive perceptive systems are united, forms the basis of a perceptive mode (we might call it "perception according to the cavity mode"), in which inside and outside is interchangeable and in which furthermore a variety of other sensations and perceptions find their focus.

It may be added here that this early intraoral experience consists of taking into oneself the breast while being enveloped by the mother's arms and breasts. The grownup conceives of this as two separate experiences. But for the child they are one experience, single and inseparable, without differences between the constituting parts, and each constituting part being able to stand for the whole of the experience. This is essentially the paradigma of Lewin's formulation: "to eat and to be eaten." It is a most vivid example of the mode of functioning of the primary process.

PERCEPTION OF ENVIRONMENT VERSUS PERCEPTION OF SOMATIC EXPERIENCE

There are certain aspects in the preceding discussion which are reminiscent of the brilliant, but in part erroneous, speculations of Silberer. Lewin has referred to them, and stressed how misleading many of his concepts were. In one of Silberer's articles, "Symbolik des Erwachens und Schwellensymbolik überhaupt" (1911), he states that symbolic imagery can express two things, content and the state or the functioning of the psyche. I believe that in my foregoing discussion it has become evident that his assumption has to be revised and that the infant's as well as Dr. Acosta's patient's experience can be separated into two perceptual aspects:

1. The aspect of perception mediated to us by our sensorium. This is the perception of the outside, the perception of things and events.

2. The second aspect is that of the perception of states and of functions; not, however, the states and functions of the psychic apparatus of which Silberer speaks, but rather the states and functions of the musculature, of joints, of position—in other words, an interoceptive perception. Dr. Acosta's patient describes a few of these perceptions of states and functions; I postulate their existence in the first period of nursing and probably, in a progressively decreasing measure, throughout the first year of life.

These two perceptive aspects, however, do not encompass the totality of the experience. We have already stressed several times that an instinctual gratification is connected with it. This implies the presence of affects and emotions of some kind, which provide the percept with its valency and with the quality of an experience. In the adult, affects may evoke visual imagery or, vice versa, visual imagery may evoke affects; but the two, affect and visual imagery, originate at two different stages in the infant's development. One may speculate whether the percept activates also the arousal function of the reticular system which, according to Linn (1953), is capable of mobilizing further affects.

LEVELS OF INTEGRATION AND PERCEPTUAL FUNCTION

We can now examine the degrees of regression attained in the dream screen described by Lewin and in the Isakower phenomenon. In dreaming, we relinquish the level of the verbal symbolic function and regress to the level of symbolic imagery (Freud, 1916, p. 143).

In the infant, the level of imagery is presumably reached after the third month; that of verbal symbolic function, approximately around eighteen months. According to our experimental observations, we may assume that somewhere from three to eighteen months the infant perceives mainly in images and operates mentally with the memory traces laid down by visual percepts. It is around eighteen months that verbal proficiency becomes sufficiently established, enabling the infant to begin to replace in his mental operations an increasing number of visual percepts by verbal symbols.

We believe that the infant passes in the course of his first two years through three stages, or, as we can call them also, through three levels of integration of increasing complexity.

1. The first level is that of the coenesthetic organization, when perception takes place in terms of totalities, because it is mediated mainly through the coenesthetic system on one hand, through interoceptive- and tango-receptors on the other.

2. The second level is that of diacritic perception, when distance receptors come into play, when visual images become available, but when the mnemic traces of these images are still impermanent, at least in the beginning. This is due to the fact that they are in the process of acquiring what Freud (1915a) calls in his article on the "Unconscious" in a specific context *"topisch gesonderte Niederschriften"* ("topographically separated records") (p. 108).

3. The acquisition of language marks the inception of the third level of integration. This presupposes an ego development, the development of the abstractive capacity, called by Kubie (1953) the symbolic function.

In waking life adults operate on the last of the three, on the level of symbolic function. In dreams they normally regress to the level of visual perception and imagery. This is the level at which Lewin's dream screen can become perceivable.

In his paper "The Forgetting of Dreams," Lewin (1953b) with the help of a reconstructive procedure arrives at formulations closely resembling mine. He deduces logically that if a regression occurs from the visual imagery level at which the dream functions, then there should be memory traces older than these pictures. Thus, as I do, he sees these memory traces "more like pure emotion," made up of deeper tactile, thermal and dimly protopathic qualities which are in their way "memory traces" of early dim consciousness of the breast or of the half-asleep state. And, if I read him correctly, he believes that it is to this level of integration that the subject regresses in the so-called blank dream.

It follows that the level of regression involved in the Isakower phenomenon harks back to an earlier period, that which precedes the reliable laying down of visual mnemic traces or at least to a period at which a significant number of visual mnemic traces has not yet been accumulated. I would be inclined to say that while the regression of the dream screen goes to the level of the mnemic traces laid down somewhere between the ages toward the end of the first half year and reaching to the end of the first year, in the Isakower phenomenon the regression reaches to the traces of experiences preceding this period. Obviously, these age ranges represent extremely wide approximations.

We may now examine the dream screen in the light of our assumptions. Following Freud, Lewin has pointed out that the dream itself already marks a disturbance of sleep. The function of the dream is to act as the guardian of sleep. The dream screen, which represents the breast, is derived from the infant's experience of going to sleep after nursing at the breast. This is exemplified by Dr. Acosta's patient who, when describing and reliving his hallucinatory experiences, frequently becomes drowsy and falls asleep on the couch. We might say that the dream screen described by Lewin is the achievement of a wish fulfillment, the gratification of a need, the symbolically used mnemic trace of satiated quiescence. The visual dream, on the other hand, is the symptom of the ego having become alerted to an extent sufficient to abolish the complete regression into dreamless sleep and to enforce a reversal of the regression to the level of visual perception, the level of three to eighteen months. The quality of satiated quiescence in the dream screen places the regression into the earlier part of this period.

It is not likely, however, that the dream screen is the visual image of the breast. It is much more probable that it is the result of a composite experience, which in the visual field represents the approaching face of the mother, but in the field of the other percepts involves the sensations within the oral cavity. This is perhaps also an explanation of the fact that in so many of the dream screen reports the dream screen appears dark, at other times colorless, amorphous. Lewin actually speaks of the dream screen being like a composite Galtonian photograph in certain dreams—only he conceived this as a blending of different images of the breast. I would rather call it a synesthesia of many different senses, the visual constituent of which is derived from the percept of the face.

What, then, is the relationship between the blank dream discussed by Lewin and the Isakower phenomenon? Perhaps it replaces in the sleeping state what the Isakower phenomenon is in the predormescent and pathological states. The level of regression in the two phenomena is comparable. Lewin considers the regression a topographical one in the blank dream. In the light of our findings on infant development we may add that it is also a genetic regression (in the terms of Freud, 1916, "a temporal or developmental regression," p. 143). It goes to a level which is earlier than the regression to the visual mnemic traces. It goes to the level at which mnemic traces were laid down in sensory modalities other than the visual ones.

This may provide the explanation why the blank dream is devoid of visual content. We know from Freud and from our daily experience with patients that the dream operates primarily with visual images. It operates much more infrequently on the higher level of verbal symbols; Lewin mentions this and Isakower (1954) in particular has commented on the phenomenon in his paper "Remembering Spoken Words." But the dream also has difficulties in representing emotional content as well as the mnemic traces which belong to the period in which they were not associated to imagery as yet. At that early period in life emotional content of a very primitive nature and the mnemic traces of bodily functions were associated to the traces of coenesthetic functioning. It is in good accordance with this that when reporting blank dreams, the subjects comment on the tone of affect which accompanies it, whether that be an affect of happiness or one of terror. And the coenesthetic mnemic association is confirmed by the fact that in some cases the blank dream is accompanied by orgasm—in the case of one of my patients orgasm could only be achieved in a blank dream.

We now may follow Isakower in his careful discussion of the processes which take place in the ego when a regression to the phenomenon observed by him occurs. He postulated two such consequences:

1. A disintegration of the various parts of the ego and its functions.
2. A dedifferentiation of the ego.

Isakower describes, within the many-faceted process of going to sleep, one specific consequence of the disintegration of the ego. This is the change which takes place through the withdrawal of cathexis from the outward-directed sensorium and a concomitant increase of the cathexis of the body ego. This formulation of the going-to-sleep process (in the adult) has an exact counterpart in our observations on the way in which the newborn functions. The newborn is incapable of perceiving the outer world. This has been shown in numerous findings of experimental psychologists as well as in our own. The sensorium is not yet functioning because, in terms of the dynamic viewpoint, the newborn has not yet cathected it.

The Stimulus Barrier and the Distribution of Libidinal Cathexis

This experimental finding enables us to understand Freud's concept of the stimulus barrier from the economic and the dynamic viewpoint, from that of the distribution of cathexis. The stimulus barrier is not to be understood as an obstacle in the path of the reception of stimulation originating in the environment. It is to be understood as consisting in the *uncathected condition of the sensorium.* In other words, the receiving stations are not energized as yet.

Conversely, the totality of the available cathexis of the newborn is directed toward his own body, a state of which we speak as the primary narcissistic stage. Isakower assumes an overcathexis of the body ego in the sleeping adult. Whether in the newborn one can speak of an *absolute* overcathexis of his own body, is questionable. There can be no question, however, about the disproportion between the infinitesimal amount of cathexis directed by the newborn toward the sensorium as against the enormous amount of cathexis allotted to his own body. We may speculate on this disparity in the distribution of cathexis. In a way, this condition is a continuation of the intrauterine situation. During the intrauterine period the mother has two roles: that of protecting the foetus from danger. In this role she carries out all the sensory and action functions needed for the purposes of adaptation to the conditions of living. Her second role could be described as that of assimilation because she also performs all the embryo's metabolic and catabolic functions. But after birth, these two roles are redistributed. The protective role against outside stimulation which the mother had during the period of gestation will be continued, for she still has the task of performing for the newborn the function of the sensorium as well as those of the action system. However, she can no longer perform the newborn's metabolic functions as she did during pregnancy. To survive, the organism of the newborn has to take over these functions and has to cathect the interoceptive system for the purposes of metabolic functions. Accordingly, toward the own body there will be no stimulus barrier. Therefore the responses of the newborn are a function of the messages transmitted by the interoceptive system; but as there is no localization within the interoceptive system's reception, these messages will be undifferentiated. They will operate in terms of the economic viewpoint, that is, of the pleasure principle. Such perceptions of himself as the newborn receives are of a total or global nature and cannot be assigned to specific systems; therefore the motor apparatus will respond to them by diffuse, undirected excitation and overflow.

In the adult's falling asleep as described by Isakower we have the withdrawal of cathexis from the sensorium and the increased cathexis of the body ego. We may add to this that the motor pattern of the sleeping adult also approximates that of the newborn in its undirected responses. The basic difference between the adult and the newborn lies in the fact that while the adult cathects a body ego, an organized structure of body representations in the psyche, there is no such thing in the newborn. The newborn has still to develop the body ego, and what we witness in the newborn is not a withdrawal of cathexis but a nonexistence of cathexis.[8]

CATHEXIS AND PERCEPTUAL EGO FUNCTIONS

The falling apart of the ego functions in the adult as described by Isakower might be spoken of metaphorically as a consequence of a weakening of the cohesive forces of the ego, which is a result of the process of falling asleep. In the newborn these cohesive forces have still to come into being and are only developed as a function of the constitution of the ego. It is an attractive hypothesis to assume that when the ego is weakened, be it by the process of falling asleep or by pathological processes, one of the first attributes of the ego, its cohesive force, will be diminished and the co-operation of the ego constituents ceases; or, in terms of present-

[8] It will be seen from this discussion that when I speak of the phase of nondifferentiation, I am referring to something much more inclusive and general than what Hartmann, Kris, and Loewenstein have described in "Comments on the Formation of Psychic Structure" (1946, p. 19). They refer specifically only to the absence of differentiation between the ego and the id, and the undifferentiated phase is the one in which both the id and the ego are gradually formed. My concept is much more closely allied to Hartmann's discussion of the same concept in "Ichpsychologie und Anpassungsproblem" (1939).

day communication theory, "intracommunication" becomes impossible (Cobliner, 1955).

The second consequence of the regression in the Isakower phenomenon is spoken of by him as a dedifferentiation of the ego. He believes that the dedifferentiation takes place somewhat later in the process of going to sleep than the dissociation of the ego components; therefore, when the body ego has arrived at this stage, when it is overcathected, it has reactivated an archaic developmental level. He stresses that on this archaic level perception is directed toward the processes of the subject's own body, toward the changes in intracorporal tensions, and not toward the external stimuli which may provoke them. He mentions that in the waking adult this mode of perception remains in function in one organ only, the vestibular organ. There it is the perception of intracorporal changes informing us (and frequently in a very disagreeable manner, indeed!) of changes taking place in our surroundings. We have nothing to add to these propositions of Isakower. By and large, they have been paralleled by our preceding discussion of the newborn's progressive development which corroborate his conclusions.

Freud (1915a, p. 111) stated that affects and emotions represent our awareness of discharge processes. The intracorporal sensations of which we have spoken actually are discharge processes. This may be the reason for their close connection with affects and in particular with anxiety.

Summary and Concluding Remarks

We may summarize by saying that adults, who operate on the level of the symbolic function, will regress normally to the level of visual perception and imagery in the dream; it is at this level that Lewin's dream screen becomes perceivable. When a disturbance of going to sleep occurs, as in febrile disease, or when a dissociation of the ego in waking states takes place, then a further regression to the level of the coenesthetic perception may occur in which the Isakower phenomenon becomes available.

The level of coenesthetic perception belongs to what I would call the experiential world of the primal cavity. It is the world of the deepest security which man ever experiences after birth, in which he rests encompassed and quiescent. It is to this world that man escapes when he feels threatened by pathological conditions in febrile states; also when in the waking state the ego becomes helpless through dissociation, as in toxic conditions. The method of escape has a double mechanism: the withdrawal of cathexis from the sensorium, on one hand, the hypercathexis of the body ego, on the other. The particular sector of the body ego representation which seems most highly cathected is the representation of the primal cavity. This distribution of cathexis makes the experience of the Isakower phenomenon possible.

From the point of view of therapy these considerations underscore the necessity of understanding the patient in terms of earliest orality, as has been stressed repeatedly by Lewin. When we deal with the adult, however, the approach to earliest orality is not a direct one, for the mnemic traces of earliest primal cavity experiences as such are not available to the patient and cannot be communicated to him by the therapist in terms of these experiences—the terms for them do not exist in language, they can only be paraphrased. Many, but certainly not all mnemic traces of the primal cavity experiences are attached in the course of development to memory traces in the nature of images, acquired and mediated by the visual and by the auditive senses. Later still, in the course of the elaboration of the symbolic function, word representations will be attached to these images. This is the linkage between the memory traces of object representations and the memory traces of word representations. The therapist, in his therapeutic endeavor, has to travel this road in the inverse direction, from the abstractive word to the concrete representation that evoked the original affect.

A better understanding of the intraoral experience and of its ramifications into experiences of hand and skin surface suggests nonanalytical therapies in the case of the deeply regressed psychoses. Up to now such therapies have scarcely yet been attempted.[9]

The world of the primal cavity is a strange one: indistinct, vague, pleasurable and unpleasurable at the same time, it bridges the chasm

[9] This communication was already in the hands of the editor when Louis Linn's paper "Some Developmental Aspects of the Body Image" (1955) was published.

His remarks parallel in many aspects the views expressed in my present paper. He reports on M. Bender's recent experiments in simultaneous sensory stimulation of adults. Bender's findings (1952) corroborate our direct observations on perceptual development and function in infants and their psychological concomitants.

Bender investigated two simultaneous stimulations of the *same* sensory modality. Our own propositions refer to simultaneous experience of stimulation in *different* sensory modalities. Linn's own work also deals with the fusion of two sensory modalities into a single perceptual event. We are referring to the patient who, when touched simultaneously on face and hand, reported this as "the hand of my face." The reader will note the similarity between Linn's observation and the conclusions drawn by me on the blending into a single event of the contact percept and the visual distance percept in earliest infancy (see pp. 222, 229). I am inclined to assume that the body ego originates from the sensations experienced in the oral cavity. The latter are vastly predominant in earliest infancy. This is in agreement with Linn's ingenious hypothesis on hand-mouth identity and with his explanation of the scotomization of the hand in adult perception.

between inside and outside, between passivity and action. The earliest sensory experiences of events taking place in the primal cavity are dealt with on the level of the primary process, yet they lead to the development of the secondary process.

In its nondifferentiation this world is the matrix of both introjection and projection, which therefore appear primarily normal phenomena, though we become really aware of their proliferation in pathological processes.

The perceptive modality of the primal cavity will also form the matrix for later developmental stages of perception in sensory organs with a very different function. The specific morphology of the particular organ will determine the mode of function—yet it will hark back to the inside-outside mode established by the intraoral experience, as for instance in the distinction between the "I" and the "non-I," the "self" and the "non-self."

We may say in conclusion that the mouth as the primal cavity is the bridge between inner reception and outer perception; it is the cradle of all external perception and its basic model; it is the place of transition for the development of intentional activity, for the emergence of volition from passivity.

When, however, the body relaxes diurnally in the passivity of sleep, the activity of the mind will retrace its way toward the primal process, and the primal cavity then becomes the cavernous home of the dreams.

BIBLIOGRAPHY

Acosta, C. (1955), Personal Communication.

Baerends, G. P. (1950), Specialization in Organs and Movements with a Releasing Function. *Sympos. Soc. Exper. Biol.*, IV.

Bender, M. B. (1952), *Disorders in Perception*. Springfield: C. C. Thomas.

Cobliner, W. G. (1955), Intra-communication and Attitude: A Methodological Note. *J. Psychol.*, XXXIX.

Drillien, M. (1948), Studies in Prematurity. Part 4: Development and Progress of the Prematurely Born Child in the Pre-School Period. *Arch. Dis. Childhood*, XXIII.

Federn, P. (1953), The Awakening of the Ego in Dreams. *Ego Psychology and the Psychoses*. New York: Basic Books.

Ferenczi, S. (1913), Stages in the Development of the Sense of Reality. *Sex in Psychoanalysis*. New York: Basic Books, 1950.

French, T. M. (1929), Psychogenic Material Related to the Function of the Semicircular Canals. *Int. J. Psa.*, X.

Freud, A. (1952), The Mutual Influences in the Development of Ego and Id. *This Annual*, VII.

Freud, S. (1900), The Interpretation of Dreams. *Standard Edition*, IV & V. London: Hogarth Press, 1953.

—— (1905), Three Essays on the Theory of Sexuality. *Standard Edition*, VII. London: Hogarth Press, 1953.

Freud, S. (1915a), The Unconscious. *Collected Papers,* IV. London: Hogarth Press, 1925.

—— (1915b), Instincts and Their Vicissitudes. *Collected Papers,* IV. London: Hogarth Press, 1925.

—— (1916), Metapsychological Supplement to the Theory of Dreams. *Collected Papers,* IV. London: Hogarth Press, 1925.

—— (1925), Negation. *Collected Papers,* V. London: Hogarth Press, 1950.

Fulton, J. P. (1938), *Physiology of the Nervous System.* New York: Oxford University Press.

Halverson, H. M. (1937), Studies of the Grasping Responses of Early Infancy, I, II, III. *J. Genet. Psychol.,* LI.

—— (1938), Infant Sucking and Tensional Behavior. *J. Genet. Psychol.,* LIII.

Hammett, F. S. (1922), Studies of the Thyroid Apparatus. *Endocrinology,* IV.

Hartmann, H. (1939), Ich-Psychologie und Anpassungsproblem. *Int. Ztschr. f. Psa.* XXIV.

—— Kris, E.; Loewenstein, R. M. (1946), Comments on the Formation of Psychic Structure. *This Annual,* II.

Hetzer, H. and Ripin, R. (1930), Frühestes Lernen des Säuglings in der Ernährungssituation. *Ztschr. f. Psychol.,* CXVIII.

Hoffer, W. (1949), Mouth, Hand and Ego Integration. *This Annual,* III/IV.

—— (1950), Oral Aggressiveness and Ego Development. *Int. J. Psa.,* XXXI.

Hooker, D. (1942), Fetal Reflexes and Instinctual Processes. *Psychosom. Med.,* IV.

—— (1943), Reflex Activities in the Human Fetus. In: *Child Behavior and Development,* ed. R. G. Barker, J. S. Kounin, H. F. Wright. New York: McGraw-Hill.

Isakower, O. (1938), A Contribution to the Pathopsychology of Phenomena Associated with Falling Asleep. *Int. J. Psa.,* XIX.

—— (1954), Spoken Words in Dreams. *Psa. Quart.,* XXIII.

Kaila, E. (1932), Die Reaktionen des Säuglings auf das menschliche Gesicht. *Ann. Univ. Aboensis,* XVII.

Kubie, L. S. (1953), The Distortion of the Symbolic Process in Neurosis and Psychosis. *J. Am. Psa. Assn.,* I.

Lewin, B. D. (1946), Sleep, the Mouth, and the Dream Screen. *Psa. Quart.,* XV.

—— (1948), Inferences from the Dream Screen. *Int. J. Psa.,* XXIX.

—— (1950), *The Psychoanalysis of Elation.* New York: Norton.

—— (1953a), Reconsideration of the Dream Screen. *Psa. Quart.,* XXII.

—— (1953b), The Forgetting of Dreams. In: *Drives, Affects, Behavior,* ed. R. M. Loewenstein. New York: International Universities Press.

Linn, L. (1953), Psychological Implications of the "Activating System." *Am. J. Psychiat.,* CX.

—— (1955), Some Developmental Aspects of the Body Image. *Int. J. Psa.,* XXXVI.

Lorand, S. and Asbot, J. (1952), Ueber die durch Reizung der Brustwarze angeregten reflektorischen Uteruskontraktionen. *Zentralbl. f. Gynäkol.,* LXXIV.

Lorenz, K. (1950), The Comparative Method in Studying Innate Behavior Patterns. *Sympos. Soc. Exper. Biol.,* IV.

Magoun, H. W. (1952), An Ascending Reticular Activating System in the Brain Stem. *A.M.A. Arch. Neurol. & Psychiat.,* LXVII.

Margolin, S. (1953), On the Psychological Origin and Function of Symbols. Paper read at the Meeting of the New York Psychoanalytic Society.

Minkowski, M. (1924/25), Zum gegenwärtigen Stand der Lehre von den Reflexen in entwicklungsgeschichtlicher und anatomisch-physiologischer Beziehung. *Schweiz. Arch. f. Neurol. und Psychiat.,* XV, XVI.

—— (1928), Neurobiologische Studien am menschlichen Foetus. In: *Abderhaldens Handbuch d. biol. Arbeitsmethoden,* V.

Montagu, M. F. A. (1950), Constitutional and Prenatal Factors in Infant and Child Health. *Problems of Infancy and Childhood.* New York: Josiah Macy Jr. Foundation.

—— (1953), The Sensory Influences of the Skin. *Texas Reports on Biol. & Med.,* XI.

Nunberg, H. (1931), The Synthetic Function of the Ego. *Int. J. Psa.,* XII.

Ostow, M. (1955), Behavior Correlates of Neural Function. *Am. Scientist,* XLIII.

Peiper, A. (1928), *Die Hirntätigkeit des Säuglings.* Berlin: Springer.

—— (1930), Sinnesreaktionen des Neugeborenen. *Ztschr. f. Psychol.,* CXIV.

Reyniers, J. A. (1946, 1949), Germ-Free Life Studies. *Lobund Reports,* Nos. 1 and 2.

Rubinow, O. and Frankl, L. (1934), Die erste Dingauffassung beim Säugling. *Ztschr. f. Psychol.,* CXXXIII.

Rycroft, C. (1951), A Contribution to the Study of the Dream Screen. *Int. J. Psa.,* XXXII.

—— (1953), Some Observations on a Case of Vertigo. *Int. J. Psa.,* XXXIV.

Scott, W. C. M. (1948), Some Embryological, Neurological, Psychiatric and Psychoanalytic Implications of the Body Scheme. *Int. J. Psa.,* XXIX.

Sherrington, C. (1947), *The Integrative Action of the Nervous System.* New Haven: Yale University Press.

Silberer, H. (1911), Symbolik des Erwachens und Schwellensymbolik überhaupt. *Jahrb. f. Psa. und psychopathol. Forschungen,* II.

Spitz, R. A. (with the assistance of K. M. Wolf) (1946), The Smiling Response. *Genet. Psychol. Mon.,* XXXIV.

—— (1947), *Birth and the First Fifteen Minutes of Life.* A motion picture. Studies of the Psychoanalytic Research Project on Problems of Infancy. New York: New York University Film Library.

—— (1948a), *The Smiling Response.* A motion picture. *Ibid.*

—— (1948b), *Genesis of Emotions.* A motion picture. *Ibid.*

—— (1949), *Grasping.* A motion picture. *Ibid.*

—— (1950a), Digital Extension Reflex. *Arch. Neurol. & Psychiat.,* LXIII.

—— (1950b), Experimental Design and Psychoanalytic Concepts. Paper read at the Symposium: Experimental Approach to Psychoanalytic Theory. 58th Annual Meeting, Amer. Psychol. Assn.

—— (1953), Aggression: Its Role in the Establishment of Object Relations. In: *Drives, Affects, Behavior,* ed. R. M. Loewenstein. New York: International Universities Press.

—— (1955), Genese des premieres relations objectales. *Rev. Franç. Psa.,* XX.

Tinbergen, N. (1950), The Hierarchical Organization of Nervous Mechanisms Underlying Instinctive Behavior. *Sympos. Soc. Exper. Biol.,* IV.

—— (1951), *The Study of Instincts.* London: Oxford University Press.

Volkelt, H. (1929), Neue Untersuchungen über die kindliche Auffassung und Wiedergabe von Formen. *Bericht über den 4. Kongress für Heilpädagogik.* Berlin: Springer.

Waelder, R. (1936), The Principle of Multiple Function. *Psa. Quart.,* V.

Windle, W. F. and Fitzgerald, J. E. (1937), Development of the Spinal Reflex Mechanism in Human Embryos. *J. Comp. Neurol.,* LXVII.

MOTOR PATTERNS AND GENITAL BEHAVIOR:

FETISHISM[1]

BELA MITTELMANN, M.D.[2]

STATEMENT OF THE PROBLEM

The following five aspects of skeletal motility may be distinguished during the early years of life: (1) "random" movements, i.e., not clearly purposive or expressive movements, which do not follow clear patterns; (2) affectomotor patterns, i.e., motor patterns accompanying emotional reactions such as joy, fear, and so forth; (3) well-organized, vigorous rhythmic patterns, e.g., rocking, bouncing; (4) skilled motor activities including control of posture, locomotion, and manipulation; and (5) motor phenomena that are indispensable elements in the function of another organ, of another striving (drive), e.g., sucking or biting as part of the oral activity.

In a previous presentation (Mittelmann, 1954), evidence was offered for (a) fusing some of these various elements to establish the concept of a motor urge (or drive), (b) a developmental scheme for the motor urge as a whole and for its various component elements, and (c) the concept of a period in development (starting with the second year of life) when motility is the dominant source of pleasure and form of mastery, expressed as a "motor level of ego and libido organization."

In this presentation, the accent will be on (a) affectomotor, (b) well-patterned rhythmic—often referred to as autoerotic (Spitz and Wolf, 1949; Kris, 1951; Levine, 1951)—motor phenomena, and (c) some of their implications for pathology. In these phenomena kinesthetic experiences and their effect on the body image are also significant. They further influence the development of "part and whole objects," in which process other sensory modalities, skilled manipulation and intellect also play a role. In particular, two aspects of pathology will be dealt with: (1) regressive motor phenomena in situations of strong affectivity, and (2) sensorimotor contributions to patterning and disturbances of the

[1] Presented at the Midwinter Meeting of the American Psychoanalytic Association, New York, December, 1953.

[2] From the Department of Psychiatry of the New York University College of Medicine, and the Psychiatric Division of Bellevue Hospital.

genital function. The case material to be presented is part of a study including some long-term observations, supplemented by moving pictures and drawings, of five normal infants followed up to three and a half years; five children and ten adults in psychoanalytic or prolonged therapy; and short-term studies of a large number of normal or sick infants, children, and adults.

The subsequent points will be developed in connection with scenes that have been filmed.

Motor Patterns Occurring During Emotional Excitement

Subject 1: A normal male infant with adequate physical and emotional care.

Scene 1: (13 weeks) The supine infant engages in random movements and the adult approaches with head nodding (Spitz and Wolf, 1946). The infant fixates the adult's face with his eyes, begins to smile. The random movements stop, then, within a few seconds, rhythmic, symmetrical movements of all four extremities, characterized by flexion and extension, appear.

Scene 2a: (31 weeks) In the supine position: the infant has discovered his feet and is holding them with legs extended, obviously preoccupied with his feet. In this psychological situation there is no smiling response to the otherwise very effective head nodding by the adult. After the infant releases his feet, he becomes responsive to the head nodding, but the motility pattern during the ensuing smile has changed from the earlier period. All four extremities are now held in extension. During crying the infant's posture is quite different: the upper extremities are in abduction and flexed at the elbow, the legs are somewhat abducted and flexed and bent at the knees. At times the right leg shows rhythmic flexion and extension at the knee.

Recurrently during the observation the infant is seen fingering his penis.

Scene 2b: After allowing a period for random movement, the experimenter restrains the infant's head by placing his hands with outstretched fingers on the sides of the infant's head; he also exerts moderate pressure on the infant's nose with his thumbs (Dennis, 1940). After a short period, the infant engages in two types of movement. The hands, in a semi-adaptive manner, move toward the hands of the experimenter. The rest of the body, particularly the torso, engages in vigorous jerky, rhythmic movements.

It may be mentioned here that, at a later period, when the infants are able to crawl or toddle, the usual reaction to the restraint of diapering is a vigorous flailing with all extremities and an attempt to turn into the prone position and to scurry away.

Scene 2c: The infant is of the same age, in a prone position. When the stimulus is presented, either in the form of a toy or the adult's face, one of two responses appears: the more frequent one, all four extremities go into extension resembling a swan dive; or the infant, leaning on one hand, slaps the surface on which he is lying with the other hand.

Scene 3a: (35 weeks) In the supine position, the motor pattern during the smiling response has again become rhythmic flexion and extension, mainly of the upper extremities, similar to the response of the earlier period except that the excursions are wider and more rapid.

Scene 3b: Prone position: When the father approaches with toys, the "swan dive" position occurs repeatedly, but the dominant pattern of the infant is slamming the ground on which he is lying.

Scene 3c: During pleasurable excitement the pattern in the upper extremities is particularly impressive when the infant is sitting: lively hand flapping occurs.

These films illustrate that (a) a characteristic motor pattern is observable in some infants during joyous excitement (smile), crying and restraint; (b) the patterning changes with the maturational process; and (c) in the process of developing new motor abilities the infant explores the lower part of his body, discovers his penis and his feet, and there is affective (libidinal) investment in the newly discovered parts of the body.

This infant is characterized by lively motility in general and also by particularly clear-cut affectomotor patterns. Both the regularity and individuality of affectomotor patterns should be stressed. Some rhythmic movement during smile can be observed in almost all infants if the stimulus is sustained long enough. But the pattern may not be clearly distinguishable from reactions to other affective stimuli, e.g., restriction and discomfort. In this infant, the pattern, right from the time of its first appearance, was specific. These differences in patterns between the various infants and the developmental changes seem to represent congenital differences,[3] although, as will be seen later, favored and accented by environmental effects. These statements apply also to the highly organized, vigorous rhythmic motor patterns. It should further be added that some affectomotor patterns, like the "swan dive," may occur with equal readiness during any kind of excitement, whereas the hand flapping occurs predominantly during joyous excitement, although it may also appear occasionally during reactions of distress, impatience or anger. The handflapping pattern gradually disappears as a rule after the second or third year of life.

Subject 2: A normal female infant receiving adequate physical and emotional care.

---

[3] Differences in "congenital activity types" have been postulated by Fries and Woolf (1953).

Scene 1: (17 weeks) Here again random movements of the supine infant are followed by joyous excitement (smile) in response to the mother's nodding face. In this infant, the movements of the lower extremities are much more prominent than those of the upper extremities. The movements are alternating rather than symmetrical.

This pattern remained the same up to nine months of age, and there was no period characterized by predominant extension. These differences between the two infants cannot be sufficiently accounted for by differences in environmental handling.

Scene 2a: (9 months) The infant crawls toward an object, picks it up in her hand, sits, flaps her hands while still holding the object and then mouths it. This infant shows the same hand flapping during joyous excitement as shown by Subject 1.

Scene 2b: While sitting on the mother's knees or astride the mother's thigh, the infant bounces.

Scene 2c: The mother is lying on the bed; the infant is on hands and knees beside her; the infant rocks. In this scene the infant at times is lying prone and in response to the smile and voice of the mother executes brief pelvic movements, some vertical, some sideways.

Subject 1 never showed the bouncing and rocking pattern. There was not sufficient difference in the handling of the two infants to account for this. The rocking occurred in the above scenes in close contact with the mother, thus representing clearly object-related movements. She displayed rocking on an autoerotic basis as well when she was alone in her crib mornings and evenings.

In contrast to the boy infant (Subject 1), up to this age the little girl was never observed fingering her genitals. While not universal, this difference seems to be the rule between male and female infants.

Subject 3: A normal female infant receiving adequate physical and emotional care.

Scene 1: (15 months) The adult stands next to her and puts his foot out; she evidences interest in his shoes and follows that by showing interest in her own shoes, and then looks up into the adult's face.

Here part of the infant's own body or clothing (feet and shoes) has been invested with interest which has been carried over to the object, thus there is interest in (libidinal investment of) the part object which plays a significant role in locomotion. The part object is then connected up with the whole object.

Subject 4: An essentially normal male infant with adequate physical and emotional care, with moderate social anxiety, who does not play readily with other children. He shows overattachment to parent or substitute.

Scene 1a: (13 months) After awakening, the infant, placed on the floor, crawls on hands and knees apparently for the purpose of satisfying his motor urge.

Scene 1b: He crawls around after a large ball—his favorite play activity. This illustrates the manipulative activity fusing with the motor urge.

Scene 1c: He is in the playpen with the ball outside the bars. First he cries, then he reaches for the ball through the bars but is unable to secure it. Then he turns away and rocks vigorously on hands and knees.

These scenes illustrate the occurrence of rocking as a clearly self-centered activity in a state of frustration, anxiety, and anger, also serving as an autoerotic substitute of more archaic character for motor play. This infant, like Subject 2, rocks in his crib mornings and evenings. The well-known rocking of infants in institutions is still more self-centered, with lack of variety of stimulation, limitation of motility, and substitute auto-erotic motor activity.

Another characteristic of this child has been mentioned in a previous article (Mittelmann, 1954): The ball is held outside of his reach by the mother; he struggles for a while to reach it, then cries and clutches his penis. Here a genital act replaces the motor activity in which the child was frustrated.

IMPLICATIONS FOR PATHOLOGY

Regressive Phenomena

The last infant described could be considered as presenting borderline pathology. While the rocking in the playpen was not clearly pathological, it did represent turning in on the self and a turning to self-centered activity in place of a manipulative and "creative" one. A case will now be presented of a child who was suffering from a psychoneurosis (neurotic traits and conduct disorder), in whom earlier forms of motility appeared in states of strong tension.

Subject 5: An eight-year-old girl manifesting anxiety (nightmares), fear of abandonment, and submissive behavior toward mates and aggressive behavior toward parents.

Scene 1: In the play session, she dramatizes a tea party in which she represents the mother, and the therapist represents the father. This is a fantasy attempt on her part to recreate the family unit. Her parents have been divorced for three years.

This scene illustrates that the motor behavior of the subsequent scenes represents special situations and is not of regular occurrence.

Scene 2: The child re-enacts a not infrequent scene with her mother to show the therapist "how I get into trouble." The mother is telephoning and the girl tosses herself around the bed (here represented by the couch) on which the mother is sitting, expressing her frustration and anger, and trying to force the mother's attention. In the midst of this tossing she gets up on her knees and flaps her hands in a manner similar to the hand flapping of one-year-olds.

Scene 3: The child is at the height of sexual curiosity and misquotes her father to the effect that the therapist will show her the male genital by exposing himself and asks, "Will you do it?" In the course of making this request she is bouncing up and down on the couch on her knees in a manner resembling the bouncing and rocking of one-year-olds. The bouncing-rocking behavior here is connected with sexual excitment and with anger over anticipated frustration.

It is to be noted that in both of these scenes the dominant mood of the patient is an unpleasant one, with genital excitement definitely present in the latter, possibly present in the former. One might call the appearance of hand flapping in this eight-year-old girl in situations of stress "cross regression," that is, a reappearance of more primitive forms of behavior which at an earlier age occur predominantly, although not exclusively, in the opposite mood. It is to be noted that this type of hand waving or flapping was not manifested by this girl in the course of normal joyous excitement. It is not present in the large majority of eight-year-olds, whereas it is very common in infants during the first and second years of life during joyous excitement and occasionally during annoyance, impatience or anger.

Motor Patterns Affecting Genital Symptom Formation

Subject 6: A five-and-a-half-year-old boy exhibiting fear of abandonment, submissive behavior, foot fetishism and prolonged masturbation. The history of the child and details of the symptoms will be given later.

Scene 1: The child is playing on the floor with fairly lively motility, making a fire truck collide with a cannon. On and off he stands up and, while talking, walks across the room or leaps. It is to be noted that affectomotor behavior here is manifested in increase of locomotor and manipulative activity.

Scene 2: The child is carrying a dish filled with water, with great care and excellent motor control, to the play table. He fills other dishes with the water, giving it to toy animals to drink. He then interrupts this activity to make drawings of skyscrapers. All of these activities consist of relatively controlled movements while he is stationary. He is well pleased with what he is doing. The activities are periodically interrupted by the following motor manifestation:

He gets up, may take a few steps, flaps his hands and jumps in the air several times.

This is a very clear joy reaction. It is highly characteristic of this child. He has manifested it, according to the parents' statement, since his motor development allowed such a performance. Before that, he would bounce, usually at the railing of his crib, so vigorously that, at the age of fifteen months he twice vaulted himself over the railing.

Scene 3: The boy's one-year-old sister is seen bouncing up and down in the crib holding on to the railing. The boy himself joins in the bouncing with great glee, standing outside the crib next to her. This illustrates how these congenitally based patterns receive reinforcement and are put to interpersonal use in relationship with the environment.

Scene 4: The boy bounces up and down a few times while standing on the couch and then lands prone without cushioning the fall with his hands. He repeats this series of movements a few times. The fantasy accompanying this behavior is the imitation of a clown. He does this maneuver on and off at home, and at times it is the preamble to his masturbation, to be described later. It manifests active and passive motor enjoyment, together with a sadomasochistic and genital component (uncushioned landing). The landing on his abdomen is preceded by the affectomotor pattern of the bouncing.

Scene 5: The boy moves his extremities and his head all at once in a vehement, rapid, alternating manner with a joyous smile, with deliberate uncontrol. At the end he throws himself on his back and swings his feet high up in the air. The scene has the character of both clowning and a motor ecstasy with exhibitionistic and later anal and genital components. This kind of behavior occurs rarely and almost entirely in the company of other children, who sometimes join in.

The main accent in these films was (1) on the great psychological importance of motility for this boy, along with a strong urge for activity, (2) on his affectomotor pattern during joyous excitement characterized by vigorous jumping up and down.

It has been mentioned that the boy's sister shows a similar affectomotor and motor autoerotic pattern. It may be added now, so did the mother up to the age of about eight years. The mother's father (the boy's maternal grandfather) had taken many films of family and playground scenes during the mother's childhood. In most of them she is seen jumping up and down at one point or another. Thus the congenital, hereditary aspect of the pattern is very probable. Apart from the scene of simultaneous jumping of brother and sister, it will be shown later that the environment (mother) has influenced the boy's genital motor behavior directly and indirectly through her handling of him.

Relation Between the Motor Patterns and the Boy's Symptomatology

At the start of treatment, the boy's symptoms were fear of noises; fear of being alone in a room even for a short time; submissive, whining behavior with mates; and, most relevant for our topic, excessive masturbation. He engaged in this for about four hours daily, two hours in the morning after waking and two hours at night before going to sleep. He executed vertical and sideways wiggling movements resembling adult intercourse while in a prone position, at the same time hugging and rocking a pillow with his upper extremities. Further, he had the fantasy during this activity of "fixing [i.e., healing] feet" with an instrument operated by a motor which he made revolve with his movements. His movements were so vigorous that the shaking of the bed could be heard all over the apartment.

It may be added that his drawings of the human figure in the figure-drawing test accented the legs predominantly, consisting of about two thirds lower extremities (see Figures I and II).

Figure I.—The child's drawing in response to the request, "Draw a person."

As regards the past history of his genital behavior, the following points are of special interest. Beginning with the age of about a year and a half, he used to fondle the feet of his mother or of his grandfather with affectionate excitement while they were lying in bed and would execute the movements described above against the legs of the adults (lying with his head at the feet of the adult). The mother discouraged this, but the grandfather allowed it. At two years of age, he was presented with a plastic doll, the surface of which resembled the texture of human skin. The doll became his most treasured possession and he called it "Brother Foot."

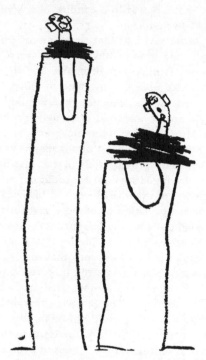

Figure II.—Spontaneous drawings by the child of "the giant and the giant's son."

Before detailing the mother's role in the child's history, it may be mentioned that she was a typical tom-boy as a child, engaging in lively motor activities. She usually sleeps in a prone position, and during intercourse strongly prefers to be on top, as a rule reaching several orgasms during each relation. She herself used to masturbate manually and reach orgasm in the supine position, since her childhood up to her marriage at the age of twenty-one. Because of this experience, she was forbearing with the boy's masturbatory behavior and never used stern repressive or punitive measures beyond saying to him impatiently, "That is enough, go to sleep." She usually put the babies to sleep in a prone position and patted them on the buttocks if they were cranky. For a period during the summer when conditions of sleep were changed, the boy's sister crankily wiggled her pelvis after being put to bed, in a manner similar to the boy's, apparently asking the mother to pat her buttocks. After returning to the city, this stopped and she does not masturbate.

The mother's handling of the boy in his infancy was somewhat inconsistent. They were living at the house of the mother's parents and the grandmother would insist that the infant be managed according to her ideas. The mother, having more "modern" notions, was in a conflict. She would yield to the grandmother, then, troubled, would change her mind, at the same time getting irritable and shouting at the child, at that time one or two years old. When the boy was nearing three, the grandmother became very critical of the boy's father because he was not earning enough money and the mother, after a great deal of excitement, prevailed upon her husband to move to a separate establishment. This, however, had the consequence that the boy could not caress the grandfather's feet any more. It was soon after moving that the boy's excessive masturbation started. Moving away from the grandparents' and the mother's irritability represented to the boy a threat of abandonment and a punitive attack including genital injury. The prolongation of the masturbation probably was brought about by the following factors: (a) He could not reach relief from tension (orgasm) because of the loss of the love object and his fears of abandonment and genital injury. (b) The masturbation acquired a restitutive quality; namely he was restoring his possession of his grandparents and proving through masturbation that his genitals were not injured ("fixing feet"). (c) The form of masturbation, because of his motor pattern, was such that the environment, particularly the mother, was always aware of it. As a result, partly through the mother's remarks, partly by implication, the environmental threat was always renewed. (d) The masturbation was accompanied by fantasies, revealed in the course of the boy's treatment, which in themselves could not be fulfilled and induced guilt.

In addition to the "foot fixing" fantasy, there were other fantasies: (1) He is behaving like a clown or is waiting for the clowns to appear. (Reference was made to this in the film scene in which he bounces high on the bed or on the couch in order to land prone with force, receiving a wallop.) This was an exhibitionistic, sadomasochistic and genital fantasy. (2) He is operating a machine which, on a long, whip-like thread, throws kisses at his father. (This fantasy will be discussed in a moment.) (3) Peter Pan, as in the Disney movie, flies through the air, attacking Captain Hook with a dagger. (4) A boy, the patient's classmate, who often shoves and punches him in school, is spanked by the teacher.

It should be noted that lively movement occurs in all of these fantasies. One of them, throwing kisses toward his father, has a homosexual connotation. The boy was more attached to his father because his father was more lenient than his mother, did not have a temper like the mother, and never expressed disapproval of the boy's masturbation. The boy frequently would wrestle with his father and then end up in the position of masturbation, lying across his father's thigh and often hugging a pillow without, however, moving. The boy was in the oedipal period, but dominated more by the negative than the positive type of the complex, although he was anything but passive.

The boy's genital orientation and symptomatology could be considered foot fetishism. Initially this was overt, later it was present in fantasy ("foot fixing"), and in the strong attachment he displayed to his doll, "Brother Foot." The observations previously mentioned suggest the following construction: Some attachment to his own feet and to the shoes and feet of adults occurs in a certain phase of development in most, if not all infants. In addition in this boy there was an unusually strong and persistent joyous affectomotor pattern, namely the vigorous jumping up and down. This undoubtedly goes with corresponding kinesthetic experiences in the feet and legs. Both of these factors further result in influencing the image of the body with an accent on the lower extremities, as shown in his usual drawings of the human figure. All of this would tend to lead to the foot fetishism which further shows the following mechanisms: his genital activity is based on the choice of a part object; he identifies then the whole object with the part object, and himself with the part object (the doll, "Brother Foot"); he also equates foot, penis, the object, and himself.

It should be added that in the course of a year and a half of treatment, along with the clearing up of the anxiety symptoms and the discussion and elucidation of masturbation fantasies, the duration of masturbation and its frequency dropped to three or four times per week, lasting about five minutes each time. The pattern, however, remained the same. The pattern fits the boy's congenitally determined needs and strivings much better than manual masturbation. I would still leave it an open question how much a possible role manual inhibition plays in the form of masturbation he exhibits. He himself always showed more guilt over the idea of his own form of masturbation. It seems that his manual impulses go into handling the object, namely, initially fondling the feet, later hugging and rocking the pillow.

The broader implications of the case, to be elaborated on later, are: (1) Motility plays a significant role in patterning of genital impulses and behavior. (2) Fetishism represents in part an intensification of a phenomenon occurring at an early phase of normal development, i.e., affective and libidinal investment of part of the body or an article of clothing when these are "discovered" in the course of the development of skilled functions.

AFFECTOMOTOR PATTERNS IN ADULTS

Subject 7: Hitler in a newsreel film.

Scene 1: He receives the news of the surrender of France. His reaction includes the following affectomotor features: He raises both arms with elbows bent and lowers them in a symmetrical movement resembling the hand flapping typical of one-year-olds. He lifts his right leg, knee high, in an exaggerated way and kicks out as he steps forward. Most people have interpreted this latter movement as a dance step, as if he were about to dance for joy. Actually it bears a closer resemblance to a single goose step, of the type, however, that was discontinued in the German army after the fall of the Kaiser, the "Parade March." The regular goose step carried in the hip joint with a stiff lower extremity. Thus it represents a self-magnifying regression in the adult period, but the resemblance is equally strong to the affectomotor kicking of the infant first shown at the age of thirteen weeks.

Scene 2: He is delivering one of his speeches at a mass meeting. At one point he starts a bilateral, symmetrical, rhythmic flexion and extension in the elbow and shoulder joints, with hands fisted. Simultaneously he exhibits a rhythmic movement of his rigid torso. These movements are sustained for about three minutes.

This primitive pattern is different from the gesturing of other statesmen observed in newsreels. The predominant mood of Hitler in this speech is one of rage, defiance, and vehement self-assertion. The movements of the upper extremities and of the torso resemble two of the types of movement seen in the first infant: (1) the rhythmic movement of the upper extremities during joy, (2) the rhythmic movement of the torso and the lower extremities when the head was held fixed and the nose was pinched. The latter component in Hitler's behavior could be considered primitive rage, rattling at the bars of a cage, and an attack on the enemy with the fists. The rhythmic, joyous component would represent what was referred to earlier as cross regression.

The primitive quality of these patterns is related to Hitler's psychopathology, and they regressively dominate his motility in these highly emotional scenes. However, the scenes indicate also the general rule that the infantile type of affectomotor patterns become integrated into the gestures of the adult.

Motility and Genital Behavior of the Adult

The patient to be discussed next has been presented in greater complexity in a previous article (Mittelmann, 1954). Here the relationship between motility, aggression and genital behavior will be elaborated.

Subject 8: A forty-year-old man entered psychoanalytic treatment because of severe anxiety states, attacks of asthma, and angioneurotic edema. In response to the request in projective testing that he "draw a person," he drew a nude woman in vigorous dance activity. This patient experienced his first consciously remembered genital excitement at the age of five when he was wrestling with a girl. As an adult he was attracted to two types of woman, one delicate and glamorous and the other muscular and athletic. His attraction to athletic women is usually impulsive; he asks them to resist him and wrestle with him during intercourse. He becomes more excited and has a quicker orgasm. His projective drawing actually combines the two types of women: the delicate type in the grace of form, the athletic quality in the vividness of the dancing. Motility plays an important role in his life in general. He usually displays lively gestures or body movements.

The patient's impulsive attraction to muscular women is difficult to classify. It can be considered as having a homosexual coloring and also as related to fetishism in that one quality of the object becomes dominant over the whole object (Freud, 1927). It became evident in the course of analysis that muscular women excited him mainly during periods of repressed resentment after some disappointment in his relationship with "feminine" women or occasionally after some occupational clashes with men. Thus the aggressive component was evident in this piece of behavior, as was already implied by the genital excitement during wrestling at the age of five and by his inclination to vigorous muscular activity to "work off tension." Further, this piece of sexual behavior turned out in the analysis to be connected with the family constellation in his childhood as dramatized by the following incident. His parents were separated. He lived with his mother, but his father came to visit intermittently. On one occasion when the patient was five, he remembers his father knocking his mother down with his fist and then twisting the arm of the patient's brother who tried to interfere. The patient himself felt "detached" during the scene and did not intervene. In his wrestling with muscular women the patient was identifying with the aggressor (father), also identifying the muscular woman both with his father and with himself, thus attacking his father and being attacked by him and at the same time sexualizing aggression in both directions.

The projective drawing by the patient, his history and his genital behavior illustrate what applies less dramatically to all adults, namely, that motility and aggression play a significant role in patterning adult genital behavior. To this may be added two further formulations: Infantile motor patterns, as displayed by the foot fetishist boy and two of the female infants described, becomes integrated into rhythmic muscular activity during intercourse and orgasm, although the larger part of the adult activity is probably learned. Further, in dancing, the motor urge, infantile motor patterns and genital impulses are fused with skilled activity for an aesthetic effect.

DEVELOPMENT OF THE IMAGE OF THE SELF AND OF THE OBJECT

Note on Fetishism

It has been stated earlier that the development of normal and pathological genital activity, including fetishism, is integrally connected with developmental processes of motor, sensory, and intellectual functions

(ego). The connection takes place via three intermingling steps: (a) In
the course of his exploratory activities the infant discovers, by oral, visual,
motor, kinesthetic, and tactile means, new organs in himself and corresponding organs in the persons in the outside world. (b) These organs
become invested with a great deal of interest and pleasure (libido). (c)
They are gradually recognized as parts of the total self and of the total
object. Thus the infant discovers his own hands first orally and, at about
the twelfth week, visually (Gesell and Amatruda, 1941). He gazes at his
hands held aloft with fascination for hours. Then he discovers the hands
of the adult. He may suck his own or the adult's thumb interchangeably.
Similarly, he discovers his own feet at about the twenty-fourth week, and,
more regularly than the female, the male infant discovers his genitals.
He may suck his toes, hold on to his feet or contact one foot with the
other for hours on end. Later, at about one year of age, he discovers his
shoes and the shoes and feet of the adult. These organs and articles of
clothing may best be called exploratory part objects, part selves or part-
object selves—the last implying that the infant takes part of himself as a
part object. They have a need-satisfying aspect (Hartmann, 1952), e.g.,
the hands satisfying oral needs, but the process also plays an integral role
in the development of the image of the self and in the differentiation
between the self and the outside world. The infant discovers that the
organs discussed are connected with the whole object, just as he has discovered that the same organs, his hands and his feet, are part of himself.
The whole object is connected closely with the face (head) as is noticeable in one of the films (in which the infant first looks at the adult's then
at her own shoes, and finally looks up at the adult's face).[4] These organs

4 It is useful to consider the ideas expressed here with related ideas of other
authors. Discussing the ego of the infant Freud (1915) says: "The objects presenting
themselves, in so far as they are sources of pleasure, are absorbed by the ego into
itself, 'introjected' (according to an expression coined by Ferenczi [1909]); while, on
the other hand, the ego thrusts forth upon the external world whatever within itself
gives rise to pain . . ." (p. 78).

Abraham (1924) assumes that early in the course of development of infants there
is a "stage of 'partial love with incorporation' [during which] the love-object is represented by one part of itself" (p. 497). He writes, "Another point to be noted in regard
to the part of the body that has been introjected is that the penis is regularly assimilated to the female breast, and that other parts of the body, such as the finger, the
foot, hair, faeces, and buttocks, can be made to stand for those two organs in a
secondary way. . . . This psychological process, by means of which the greater part
of the object is reduced to insignificance and excessive value is attached to the
remaining part, is seen to be the consequence of a regression of the libido to this
supposed stage of 'partial love'. . . . Those parts of the body on which the fetishist
tends to concentrate his inclinations are the same as those we meet with as the objects
of 'partial love'. . ." (pp. 490 f.).

Klein (1934) writes, "According to Edward Glover [1932], the ego, at first but play a role in part similar to the infant's favorite possessions or "intermediary objects" (Winnicott, 1953) as regards his emotional investment, his manner of handling them as part of himself as well as of the outside world, and in their partial consoling value in case of disappointment in the adult. The connection is illustrated by the observation that the boy with foot fetishism called his favorite doll "Brother Foot."

However, the author agrees with Winnicott that the average infant's attachment to his favorite possession should not be considered fetishism but only as containing an important component of that symptom. (For a contrary position see Friedjung, 1927; Wulff, 1946; E. Sterba, 1941.) The term "fetishism" had best be reserved for cases in which the reaction to the object includes genital excitement and manipulation. This may occur in some infants as part of the normal libidinal relation to exploratory part objects, perhaps facilitated by rhythmic affectomotor patterns. Subsequently additional motivational factors enter, namely, frustration, fear of abandonment, aggression, fear of genital injury, etc. These additional factors may then be responsible for the persistence of the activity or its recurrence in subsequent years. It has to be left an open question whether this sequence of events is the rule in fetishism. The case of foot fetishism in a child described in this paper is the only one of its kind

---

loosely organized, consists of a considerable number of ego-nuclei. In his view, in the first place an oral ego-nucleus and later an anal ego-nucleus predominates over the others. In this very early phase, . . . the ego's power of identifying itself with its objects is as yet small, partly because it is itself still unco-ordinated and partly because the introjected objects are still mainly partial objects. . . . As the ego becomes more fully organized, the internalized imagos will approximate more closely to reality and the ego will identify itself more fully with 'good' objects. . . . Hand in hand with this development goes a change of the highest importance; namely, from a partial object-relation to the relation to a complete object" (pp. 283 f.).

The ideas of Abraham are closely interwoven with his constructions about paranoia and manic-depressive psychosis, those of Klein with her concepts of the schizophrenic and depressive positions of the infant. Both center their construct around the oral function. In the author's presentation in the main text, perception, motility, intelligence—"autonomous factors in ego development," in Hartmann's (1939, 1952) language—are also taken into account and emphasis is placed on direct observation of the infant. (See also discussions of the development of the body image by Preyer, 1884; Bernfeld, 1925; and Greenacre, 1953.) The components mentioned exist in their own rights. Thus the twelve-week-old infant can carry his hand to his mouth—and does so a great deal—but he often "prefers" to *gaze* at it for long periods of time. The processes by which these components influence the development of the image of the self and its relation to the outside world seem at least in part to be different from introjection (incorporation) and projection processes usually attributed to the oral (or anal) component. Appropriate terms might be fusion, separation and equation, the last meaning the identifying of, or equating parts of the self with, parts of the outside world.

that the author has been able to find reported in the literature.[5] Many significant details would have been forgotten by the adult patient and because of the early years of their occurrence would not have been recovered by analysis. In the treatment of the child, of course, many of these details are obtained from the parents. The processes discussed in connection with exploratory part objects play a significant preparatory role not only in fetishism but also in other aspects of choice of love object ranging from the normal to the pathological. Preferences in choice based on color of hair, body form, shape of the nose or of the mouth are normal unless of impulsive, overbearing intensity. The choice of the patient who was periodically attracted to muscular women had pathological coloring. This type of behavior, in which the fetish dominates but is not completely separated from the whole object, may be called marginal fetishism. Another adult patient will be discussed briefly who presented hair fetishism as one of his symptoms.

Subject 9: The patient's mother was a feminist, disparaging toward men, including her husband. Women still wore their hair long, although sometimes only down to the shoulders, when the patient was a child. The mother let the patient wear a "page-boy" cut. At the age of four-and-a-half he asked his mother, in vain, either to let his hair grow or to cut it shorter, so that he would look completely like a girl or like a boy. A brother was born when the patient was five years old. It was a traumatic experience, accompanied by anxiety in the mother's absence during confinement, which increased considerably after her return. The mother favored the brother.

When the patient, a successful musician, came for treatment at the age of forty, mainly because of anxiety symptoms, he had close relationships with two women, one his wife, the other his mistress. The relationship with his wife was one of mutual dependence and had been free of sexual contact for about six years. While his wife was excessively submissive, his mistress behaved like a prima donna who had temper tantrums. It may be added that at no time in his life did he succeed in combining companionship and erotic relationship with a woman.

In addition to the sexual relation with his mistress, which was essentially adequate as regards potency, he engaged in masturbation which was almost never continued to the point of orgasm. If occasionally he did reach orgasm during masturbation, he had a severe anxiety state following it. The masturbation consisted of striking his penis with the palm of his hand after he got genitally excited by drawing abundant wavy long hair, reaching down as far as

---

[5] Lorand (1929) described the fondling and kissing of women's shoes along with increased sexual investigation in a four-year-old boy. He does not say whether the behavior was accompanied by genital excitement, and gives only a brief account of the boy's earlier years and relationship with his parents.

the ankles without covering the body, on the photographs of women which he had cut out of magazines.

On one occasion he bought a wig, with long hair, in a theatrical costume shop and, putting it on at home in front of the mirror, masturbated. In the succeeding days he spent all his free time in a similar manner. At the end of a week he had an unplanned emission and became panicky. This, combined with the alarm over his complete absorption in the wig, aroused his fear of insanity and he threw the wig into the river.

Two other comments should be made here in connection with the genital aspects of fetishism. It is a universal observation that fetishism is almost limited to males. It is usually assumed that this is due to the difference between the male and the female castration complex (Freud, 1927). Our observations add two additional factors. It seems that rhythmic motility in infancy is more apt to stimulate the penis because it projects more than the clitoris. These rhythmic movements occur, as in the boy observed, during the period when the first fetishistic activities may take place. Secondly, it seems that some fetishists have a strong genital urge which makes a relatively early appearance in their lives. This was the case with the boy and the two adults described in detail. The long hair fetishist remembered experiencing orgasm and something akin to ejaculation at the age of five. The early genital excitability with the concomitant tendency toward partial object choice is more common in male infants. According to Abraham (1924), some fetishists manifest decreased genital activity.

The phenomena of the exploratory part objects, which in a sense are the normal prototypes of one aspect of fetishism, occur at a period that precedes the differentiation between male and female and the castration complex. This does not contradict Freud's (1927) observation that in the adult the fetish represents the phallus of the mother, but it does imply that, in the earlier phase, the fetish represents an undifferentiated phallus, that is, as much of the father as of the mother. The boy discussed played as much with his mother's feet as with his grandfather's while executing the masturbatory movements with his body.

The three cases presented confirm the view of other authors as regards the roles played in fetishism by aggression or "sadism" (Gillespie, 1940; Glover, 1933; Payne, 1939; Romm, 1949) directed both toward the self and toward the object and by pregenital urges and needs. The aggressive motivation is dramatically illustrated by the ritual of some fetishists of tying themselves up with ropes (Kronengold and Sterba, 1936). The term "pregenital" is used by the various authors in three different senses: (1)

clearly meaning libidinal—oral, tactile, anal—urges (Bak, 1953; Gillespie, 1940, 1952; Payne, 1939); (2) relationships to the objects, referring particularly to disturbances in the mother-child relationship (Greenacre, 1953;[6] Payne, 1939; Bak, 1953); (3) disturbances in the function of the whole organism, e.g., during illness ocurring during the first and second year of life, leading to disturbances in the body image and resulting later in a revival of the fear of disintegration (Greenacre, 1953).

It has also been observed by other authors that patients may engage in the fetishistic activity following a current disappointment (Bak, 1953), just as the patient previously discussed was impelled toward muscular women during some tension with graceful women and with men in his occupation. The genetic and the current reactions mentioned can be integrated in a circular sequence of reactions that the patient manifests in relation to himself and to his environment. There are a variety of circular reactions that the fetishist may display. His genital excitement, arising partly from physiological sources, leads to fetishistic activity. The activity has to be fetishistic because of fear of rejection and of genital injury by the whole object. The orgasm leads to relief of the genital tension, but inasmuch as only part of the object is involved in the activity which also contains elements of aggression, it is followed by guilt, fear of abandonment and fear of retribution, including castration. These fears then incline the patient to evaluate various events in his life as meaning rejection, abandonment or retribution. Restitution against these factors would again take place in the form of genital activity and thus the renewal of genital excitement is facilitated. With this, the circular reaction is reinstated.

The circle described contains several other circles. Dependent needs are accented in the following sequence. The patient starts out with the feeling of abandonment and rejection by the whole object. He then engages in the fetishistic activity because genitality itself means uniting with the object again which, in the form of the fetish (Bak, 1953), he can completely control (Gillespie, 1952). This in part leads to a relief from the feeling of abandonment but with the realization that only the part object was obtained, the fear of abandonment is potentially reinstated and will again lead to the need for fetishistic activity. Aggression is accented in the following sequence: The patient starts out with aggression and hostility toward someone in the environment who would represent the whole object. This aggression becomes sexualized and is vented safely

6 Greenacre's article (1953) contains a thorough survey of the analytic literature on fetishism.

on the fetishistic object (Gillespie, 1952). This, however, leads to fear of retribution which in turn leads to defensive aggression and eventually to fetishistic activity.

These current circular reactions connect up with the infantile patterns in several ways: (a) The patient interprets current events in terms of infantile events, i.e., the fetishist may be afraid of abandonment because he previously destroyed the whole object via the fetish as well as because he interprets the situation in terms of fear of infantile abandonment, e.g., "My wife is rejecting me as my mother did." (b) Unconsciously the infantile and the current series of reactions reinforce each other. In other words, the patient feels that his interpretation of current events is justified in the light of infantile events and also feels that his unconscious interpretation of infantile events is justified in terms of current events, e.g., "My wife is rejecting me; this proves I was right in my feeling that my mother rejected me."

What has been described represents intrapsychic circular sequences. In reality, the reactions of the persons in the patient's environment who may display complementary neuroses (Mittelmann, 1944) have to be added to the links of these circular chains.

The hair fetishist's wife was even more dependent on him than he was on her. They rarely went out together or without each other, were sensitive to each other's moods and repressed all hostility toward one another. He escaped the all-engulfing and emasculating quality of the relationship and also expressed his hostility by having sex relations with his mistress instead of with his wife. The mistress, who was of the "Latin American" type, was imperious and had temper tantrums, and wore her hair, at his request, so that it reached to her shoulders. There was little intellectual companionship between them. He dealt with her tantrums with conscious amusement but then coped with his unconscious anxiety and hostility through the fetishistic masturbation. The latter also expressed his hostility toward his wife and during it he had control over the inanimate photograph. As dramatized by the incident with the wig in front of the mirror, the photograph with the long hair drawn in represented himself also on the basis of his infantile experiences so that in his masturbation he was narcissistically having relations with himself. The self-depreciation and guilt over the hostile and genital impulses and activities together with the exclusion of the whole object renewed his fear of abandonment by his wife as well as his fears of retribution and castration. The two women also related to two aspects of his mother, also represented by the photographs of long-haired women: his wife to the loving mother looking after all his needs, containing a great deal of infantile wishful fantasies, and his mistress to the domineering aspects.

Motor Activity and Fetishism

We may now complete our discussion of the relationship between motor activity and fetishism. For this purpose we have to discuss the infant and the adult separately. During the first ten months of life there is a great deal of maturation of skilled functions and spreading of emotional libidinal interest to new organs and activities. During the next year or two motility dominates the functions of mastery, integration, and pleasure, and it remains one of the dominant functions throughout childhood (Mittelmann, 1954). This has the following consequences: (a) The motor urge carries with it genital excitement and this genital excitement is apt to be of the variety that is the normal prototype of fetishism, i.e., it is directed toward a part object. (b) Other impulses, such as dependent needs, hostility, rivalry can easily be reacted to through an increase in motor activity. This motor activity then may further reinforce the transformation of any impulse into genital or other libidinal urges (Mittelmann, 1954). (c) Special reinforcement of the fetishistic trend can occur by a kinesthetic experience, namely, through rhythmic motor autoerotic activities. These rhythmic autoerotic activities may represent a self-centered, restitutive, consoling withdrawal from the frustration of the environment—an aspect which is common in fetishism. These statements apply to infants in general but with constitutional and experiential variations. The latter may facilitate the development of fetishism or other pathology. The "passive" motility of infants and children usually implies being cared for, held, fondled and moved rhythmically. For the purpose of this discussion, we add an active but dependent pattern, namely, clinging. In these experiences of the infant, anxiety, hostility, and libidinal impulses including genital excitement may play a role. The infant's behavior with favored possessions—transitional objects (Winnicott, 1953)—is both active and passive, e.g., going to sleep with the object, and includes the complexity of attitudes toward the parents. This too forms the normal prototype of fetishism.

In adults, the following motor variations occur, which may fuse with the infantile patterns. The same adult may exhibit several of the variations. (a) The general motor urge may manifest itself in organized sports or some other highly organized activity, and in that way the complex reactions to disappointment may be worked off. (b) In other adults, the reaction may lead mainly to general motor restlessness, and in that way undergo the same "transformation" into genital excitement and fetishism as described in children. (c) In other adults, the reaction described may go with passivity. Lying around or leaning back may be accompanied by distinct erotic sensations (Mittelmann, 1954), that is, muscle pleasure, and this then may be the link in the sequence toward the genital activity. (d) Action may be forbidden and inhibited in some constructive fields or in normal heterosexual activity, and the impulses remain in the realm of fantasy. The general tension then leads finally to the fetishistic activity.

SUMMARY

1. The following four aspects of motility were discussed as being of special psychological interest in infants and children: (a) affectomotor patterns; (b) well-organized, vigorous rhythmic patterns, usually referred to as autoerotic; (c) skilled motor activities; and (d) motor phenomena that are indispensable elements in the function of other organs.

2. These various functions may be fused in the concept of a motor drive which follows a developmental scheme both as a whole and as regards its component parts, the second year of life, with some extension, being the motor phase of ego and libido development (i.e., motility being the dominant source of pleasure and mastery). This paper deals mainly with the affectomotor and the vigorous rhythmic phenomena and their pathological implications.

3. In the course of exploratory activities resulting from sensory, motor, and intellectual development (ego), the infant "discovers" and becomes preoccupied with parts of the body and articles of clothing (e.g., hands, feet, and shoes). This preoccupation has libidinal qualities. The infant eventually realizes that these organs and articles of clothing belong to the "whole self" and the "whole object."

4. Bilateral rhythmic motor phenomena occur in infancy during joyous excitement—showing both general characteristics and individual variations. In some infants the joy patterns specifically differ from motor patterns of crankiness mixed with rage and anxiety and restraint, whereas in others differences are slight or inconsistent. The patterns change in the course of development. These patterns seem to be largely congenitally determined. The same applies to vigorous rhythmic (autoerotic) motor phenomena, but the frequency of their occurrence, their intensity, and their predominant psychological structure depend to a greater extent on environmental influences. These patterns too show individual variations.

5. Affectomotor patterns and vigorous rhythmic motor phenomena may have pathological implications in two ways: (a) They may appear regressively in older children or adults during intense excitement. (b) They may contribute to the patterning of symptoms in disturbances of the genital function in general and, fused with exploratory part objects, to fetishism in particular.

6. In a child manifesting anxiety and foot fetishism, the normal libidinal investment of feet was intensified by the kinesthetic experiences that accompanied his affectomotor joy reaction, namely, vigorous jumping up and down. The latter affected the image of the body also. These factors, combined with disturbed relations with the environment, contributed to the symptom of foot fetishism and prolonged masturbation.

7. The infantile affectomotor and the vigorous rhythmic patterns are incorporated into the adult gestures and the motor behavior during intercourse and orgasm.

8. Fetishistic activity frequently follows current disappointments. The infantile patterns are fused with and are reinforced by a circular sequence of reactions containing dependent needs, hostility, guilt, fear of abandonment, fear of genital injury, and the defensive and restitutive use of the fetish as a reliable, controlled, and defenseless part object. The use of the latter potentially reinstates the attitudes and impulses with which the patient tried to cope.

9. During the period of exploratory part objects and later when skeletal motility dominates the functions of mastery, of integration, and of pleasure—then dependency needs, hostility and anxiety are readily carried over into active or passive motility and may in turn lead to genital excitement with part object choice.

The same connections may exist in adults with motor restlessness, passive muscle erotism, and significant areas of motor inhibition.

BIBLIOGRAPHY

Abraham, K. (1910), Remarks on the Psycho-Analysis of a Case of Foot and Corset Fetishism. *Selected Papers on Psycho-Analysis*. London: Hogarth Press, 1927.
—— (1913), A Constitutional Basis of Locomotor Anxiety. *Ibid.*
—— (1924), A Short Study of the Development of the Libido, Viewed in the Light of Mental Disorders. *Ibid.*
Bak, R. C. (1953), Fetishism. *J. Am. Psa. Assn.*, I.
Bernfeld, S. (1925), *Psychology of the Infant*. London: Kegan Paul, 1929.
Dennis, W. (1940), Infant Reaction to Restraint: An Evaluation of Watson's Theory. *Trans. N. Y. Acad. Sci.*, II.
Ferenczi, S. (1909), Introjection and Transference. *Sex in Psychoanalysis*. New York: Robert Brunner, 1950.
Freud, S. (1905), Three Contributions to the Theory of Sex. In: *The Basic Writings of Sigmund Freud*. New York: Modern Library, 1938.
—— (1915), Instincts and Their Vicissitudes. *Collected Papers, IV*. London: Hogarth Press, 1925.
—— (1927), Fetishism. *Collected Papers, V*.
Friedjung, J. K. (1927), Wäsche-Fetischismus bei einem Einjährigen. *Ztschr. f. psa. Päd.*, II.
Fries, M. E. and Woolf, P. J. (1953), Some Hypotheses of the Role of the Congenital Activity Type in Personality Development. *This Annual*, VIII.

Gesell, A., and Amatruda, C. S. (1941), *Developmental Diagnosis*. New York: Paul B. Hoeber, 2nd ed., 1947.

Gillespie, W. H. (1940), A Contribution to the Study of Fetishism. *Int. J. Psa.*, XXI.

—— (1952), Notes on the Analysis of Sexual Perversions. *Int. J. Psa.*, XXXIII.

Glover, E. (1932), A Psycho-Analytical Approach to the Classification of Mental Disorders. *J. Ment. Sci.*, LXXVIII.

—— (1933), The Relation of Perversion Formation to the Development of the Reality Sense. *Int. J. Psa.*, XIV.

Gostynski, E. (1951), A Clinical Contribution to the Analysis of Gestures. *Int. J. Psa.*, XXXII.

Greenacre, P. (1953), Certain Relationships between Fetishism and Faulty Development of Body Image. *This Annual*, VIII.

Hartmann, H. (1939), Ego Psychology and the Problem of Adaptation. In: *Organization and Pathology of Thought*, ed. D. Rapaport. New York: Columbia University Press, 1951.

—— (1952), The Mutual Influences in the Development of Ego and Id. *This Annual*, VII.

Horney, K. (1937), *The Neurotic Personality of Our Time*. New York: Norton.

Klein, M. (1932), *The Psycho-Analysis of Children*. London: Hogarth Press, 2nd ed., 1937.

—— (1934), A Contribution to the Psychogenesis of Manic-Depressive States. *Contributions to Psycho-Analysis*. London: Hogarth Press, 1948.

Kris, E. (1951), Some Comments and Observations on Early Autoerotic Activities. *This Annual*, VI.

Kronengold, E., and Sterba, R. (1936), Two Cases of Fetishism. *Psa. Quart.*, V.

Levine, M. I. (1951), Pediatric Observations on Masturbation in Children. *This Annual*, VI.

Loewenstein, R. M. (1954), Some Remarks on Defenses, Autonomous Ego and Psycho-Analytic Technique. *Int. J. Psa.*, XXXV.

Lorand, S. (1929), Fetishism in Statu Nascendi. In: *Clinical Studies in Psychoanalysis*. New York: International Universities Press, 1950.

Mahler, M. S.; Luke, J.; Daltroff, W. (1945), Tic Syndrome in Children. *Am. J. Orthopsychiat.*, XV.

Mittelmann, B. (1944), Complementary Neurotic Reactions in Intimate Relationships. *Psa. Quart.*, XIII.

—— (1954), Motility in Infants, Children, and Adults: Patterning and Psychodynamics. *This Annual*, IX.

Payne, S. M. (1939), Some Observations on the Ego Development of the Fetishist. *Int. J. Psa.*, XX.

Preyer, W. (1884), *The Mind of the Child*. New York: D. Appleton & Co., 1914.

Romm, M. (1949), Some Dynamics of Fetishism. *Psa. Quart.*, XVIII.

Sadger, I. (1912), Haut-, Schleimhaut-, und Muskelerotik. *Jahrb. f. psa. & psychopath. Forsch.*, III.

Spitz, R. A. and Wolf, K. M. (1946), The Smiling Response: A Contribution to the Ontogenesis of Social Relations. *Genet. Psychol. Mon.*, XXXIV.

—— —— (1949), Autoerotism. Some Empirical Findings and Hypotheses on Three of Its Manifestations in the First Year of Life. *This Annual*, III/IV.

Sterba, E. (1941), An Important Factor in Eating Disturbances of Childhood. *Psa. Quart.*, X.

Washburn, R. W. (1929), A Study of the Smiling and Laughing of Infants in the First Year of Life. *Genet. Psychol. Mon.*, VI.

Winnicott, D. W. (1953), Transitional Objects and Transitional Phenomena. *Int. J. Psa.*, XXXIV.

Wulff, M. (1946), Fetishism and Object Choice in Early Childhood. *Psa. Quart.*, XV.

SOME CONSIDERATIONS IN THE INTRODUCTION TO THERAPY IN PUBERTY

SELMA FRAIBERG (Detroit)

The analytic method encounters special problems in work with the child in puberty. In a real sense we can say that the aims of puberty and the aims of analysis are hostile to each other. At a time when the ego must strengthen its defenses against the powerful resurgent drives, analysis must disturb the defensive structure in order to do its work. The precarious balance of the pubertal ego makes exceptional demands upon the analytic method. If the method succeeds in undermining the pathological defenses, it may, in some instances, precipitously release the dammed-up impulses to wreak new havoc upon the character of the child and upon the environment. If the method is perceived as a threat to the defensive structure, the ego may further strengthen the defenses, bring forth new defenses and elaborated symptoms, and marshall its resistances against the intruder, the analyst. The therapist, therefore, must walk a tight-rope in his work with the pubertal child.

As we pursue the problem further we see other contradictions of aim. Puberty is the age of secrecy. It closes the door upon the prying adult; it suspects the well-intentioned overtures of the parents, the invitations to confide. It hoards its secrets and, at times, sees the world of adults in grand conspiracy to spy upon them and ferret them out. The classical analytic technique requires the surrender of secrets. The spectre of the analyst as Spy who haunts the dreams of patients in analysis can be a tangible flesh and blood enemy to certain children in puberty. Where the enmity between parents and child is very strong, the analyst is certain to be suspect. Isn't he "hired by" the parents "to find out things"?

The pubertal child fears analysis for other and darker reasons. He is aware, as his parents are, that powerful forces are disrupting his psychic equilibrium. He experiences strange, overwhelming impulses, new sensations. He is frightened by the cyclic swings of affect which buffet him between the poles of depression and elation. He does not know this new self; his body seems to be inhabited by a stranger. But even his body has become a stranger to him! He observes its changes with mingled wonder and alarm, for with all its new excitements this oldest, most intimate and substantial fact of existence and personal identity has changed its landmarks. The stranger inside is the tenant of a house which does not seem to be his own. The sense of identity is assaulted from all sides. The pubertal child seems constantly preoccupied with the question, "Who am I?" and, as if to remind himself, he fills his school-books, his notebooks and scraps of paper with his name and address in various fancy scripts and styles of lettering. And all of these things, the alienation of parts of the psychic structure, the altered body image, the disturbance of the reality sense, the masturbatory conflicts, give rise in puberty to terrible speculations regarding sanity. So he is afraid of analysis for these other reasons. "I'm not nuts!" he says. "I won't go to a nut doctor!"

The dilemma of the therapist lies not only in the technical problems which arise in the treatment of pubertal neuroses, but in the fact that puberty may bring forth the most severe symptoms, depressions, phobias, compulsive disorders, character disturbances and delinquencies in their most virulent form—symptoms which demand our immediate assistance and which cannot wait for a more propitious time in life for their treatment.

If we decide, in view of all these handicaps, that a pubertal child must have treatment, we are faced with our first and most difficult problem, that of overcoming the resistances to treatment which are commonly presented by the child of this age. While this is the problem which I have set out to study in this paper, it becomes immediately apparent that in order to do justice to this subject we would have to investigate every aspect of the condition of puberty. My intentions in this study are very limited in scope. They are to review some of my own cases of girls in early puberty in order to examine the early reactions to treatment and the technical problems posed by these reactions.

II

Almost all writers recognize the adolescent's negative reactions to beginning treatment, and the powerful initial resistances, as factors which require special handling in the early hours of treatment. The possibility of an "introductory" phase in adolescent analysis is proposed by Spiegel (1951), who also suggests that some of Aichhorn's techniques for establishing contact with dissocial adolescents may find applicability here. Zachry (1945) gives special attention to the unfavorable position of the adolescent at the beginning of treatment. He might seek help himself except that to do so "is the result not of his own feelings in the matter but of the urging of his parents from whom he is seeking to free himself." Under such circumstances, Zachry stresses the importance of showing the patient that the therapist is not the authority from which he seeks independence, but someone who stands with the patient. This view is similar to Aichhorn's (1925), who, in speaking of the neurotic child with symptoms of delinquency, shows how the therapist must act toward the child "in such a way as to prevent a repetition with the worker of the situation with the parents which led to the conflict." In the case of the child who is in open conflict with society, Aichhorn found it necessary completely to take the child's part in order to win the child's confidence and bring him into a positive transference. In a case report of a twelve-year-old bed wetter, Anny Angel Katan (1935) describes the initial difficulties in the analysis due to the child's belief that the analyst was in league with the mother. Until the child's suspicions could be dispelled the analysis could make no progress. Deutsch (1944), speaking of the prepubertal girl, remarks on the special difficulties encountered by women therapists with this age group. The hostility toward motherly persons makes it necessary, Deutsch believes, for the therapist to adopt a role which is similar to that of a girl friend. Ella Sharpe (1950), supporting the view of Melanie Klein, believed it necessary to dissolve the initial resistances of the adolescent through early direct interpretation of symbolic actions.

Anny Katan (1951) examines a problem of resistance to the analytic process in the pubertal child in her work on the mechanism of "removal" and the pubertal defenses against incestuous strivings. The critical task of puberty is that of object removal, the displacement of the incestuous desires onto new objects. The term "removal" is employed by Anny Katan to differentiate this mechanism from displacement, and to give specificity to a process which has a single aim and direction (in contrast to displacement). The direction is forward moving and away from the incestuous objects, and the mechanism is exclusively concerned with the incestuous desires. The implications for analysis of the pubertal child are of the greatest importance. In an illustrative case, Anny Katan shows how a satisfactorily progressing analysis of a fourteen-year-old girl was abruptly terminated by the girl herself when she fell in love with a boy. There were no indications from the analytic material that this termination was a hostile act. The analyst saw this termination as a normal and necessary step. The girl's falling in love was seen as a successful object removal. Analysis would inevitably have disturbed this process in examining the repetitious nature of the new love and bringing forth once more the incest anxiety which impelled the removal. "In puberty," Anny Katan (1951) says, "... one is confronted with the entire force of the developmental thrust counteracting the analysis."

The negativism of puberty (which can become a formidable resistance to treatment at times) has been illuminated by Anna Freud (1952) in her "Studies in Passivity." The negativism which is investigated in these studies is a specific type, a primitive mode of defense. It is encountered in male homosexuals of the passive type, in certain borderline cases as an extreme defense against object relations, and as a characteristic of two developmental phases, the second year and puberty. Analysis reveals a common danger which is warded off by this defense. The danger is surrender, of complete submission to the love object—not alone a sexual danger, a danger of castration—but a danger of merging with the object, hence of losing the self and personal identity and of returning to an archaic oneness with the object. Here, love of the object would mean complete surrender to the object, loss of the self in the object, and the defense of negativism is employed against the object and against the danger of loss of personality. Such persons as these described by Anna Freud, are afraid "to be like" someone else, since "to be like" is "to be one with" the object (my paraphrasing).

In adolescence, Anna Freud shows how the two aspects of this process, negativism and emotional surrender, can exist side by side and are seen in the manifestations of passionate devotion to objects and, alternately, extreme negativism to the same object. In a brief case illustration Anna Freud also shows how an extreme form of negativism in a child patient dissolved in adolescence to reveal the most passionate longing to surrender in a love relationship, as seen in her abandoned love for a man.

It is significant that our greatest progress in understanding puberty has come out of the developments in psychoanalytic ego psychology. In Anna Freud's study of negativism and emotional surrender, as in earlier studies of "defense motivated by fear of the strength of the instincts" in *The Ego and the Mechanisms of Defense* (1936), the study of puberty is incidental to a larger study of defense, but in each work puberty is illuminated by the study of defense at the same time that it serves the study of defense.

We understand that under conditions of severe stress, and puberty is one such condition, the ego behaves as if it were in danger of extinction and falls back upon primitive defenses which originated in the earliest struggle to preserve and maintain the boundaries of the emerging self from the danger of the backward step, of fusion with the object world. In any discussion of the therapy of puberty these defensive processes must be counted among the chief resistances.

For these reasons, and many others, there is disagreement among analysts regarding the treatability of adolescents. The relative weakness of the adolescent ego is regarded as a contraindication for treatment by Gitelson (1948). Zachry (1945), on the other hand, writes positively and optimistically about the possibilities of psychotherapy in adolescence. She regards the adolescent's introspective tendencies and his conscious recognition of conflict as specific advantages in treatment. Spiegel (1951), in his survey of the analytic literature on adolescence, notes the tendency among analytic writers to dwell upon the unfavorable aspects of analytic treatment in adolescence while comparatively little attention has been paid to the possibilities of "adapting psychoanalysis to the adolescent's particular situation."

III

I have limited my own study here to cases of girls in prepuberty and early puberty. I should begin by explaining this selection.

It was my original intention to survey all my cases of adolescent girls within the age range, roughly, eleven to eighteen. I had expected, of course, to find important differences in the treatment of the very young adolescent and the older adolescent, but a preliminary review of the cases in this wide age range revealed such large differences that I could not justify the study of eleven to eighteen as a single group. I was struck by the fact that when we speak of "the special problems in the treatment of the adolescent," we are often not speaking of the wide range of adolescence but the phases of prepuberty and early puberty which precede the shift in object choice.

We know that the decisive point in adolescent development is the abandonment of the incestuous aim and the replacement of the infantile objects. While we recognize that this is a gradual process, the achievement of "object removal" distinguishes the later phase of development from the earlier and permits us to speak of two major phases of adolescence.[1] This achievement is reflected in ego changes, for the perilous

[1] Our present nomenclature gives no descriptive categories for these two major phases of adolescence. Helene Deutsch's categories "early puberty" and "later puberty" take cognizance of the shift in object choice which sets off one phase from the other,

balance between ego and drives which characterized the earlier phase has shifted and thrown the scales on the ego side. When this decisive step has been accomplished, however badly or contaminated by the incestuous motives, the ego has triumphed. A neurosis may persist with a change of personnel and scene, but the relative positions of ego and drives have changed and the implications for therapy have altered accordingly.

Now when I grouped my cases independent of age and only in reference to the phase of development as told by object choice, I achieved a much clearer picture. The "characteristic" problems of treatment which we speak of in connection with adolescence were actually characteristic of only the first phase, corresponding roughly to the age of biological puberty. Problems involving the early resistances to treatment and the establishment of a positive transference, technical considerations in interpretation, depth of analysis permitted, dangers of acting out, actually faded in importance when applied to the second phase, that which we sometimes speak of as "later adolescence." It almost seemed as if there were less differences between the analytic method employed for the "older adolescent" and the classical procedure for adults, than between the analytic methods employed for these two groups of adolescents with their separate developmental achievements. The "older adolescents" often strongly desired treatment for themselves; they understood its necessity, willingly accepted its conditions and showed readiness and aptness for the analytic process. Most important of all, this second stage of adolescence, marked by the successful removal of object choice, fulfilled the conditions for the development of a transference neurosis which altogether changed the character of the treatment from that employed with the pubertal child.

For these reasons I decided to limit my study to those girls who properly belonged to the earlier phase of development, the period which precedes object removal and which is still under the influence of "the biological onslaught of puberty," to use the phrase of Helene Deutsch (1944).

---

but her scheme presents certain problems when, for example, she employs the term "adolescence" for the period which follows puberty and which is characterized by maturation and consolidation of trends set up in puberty. Current usage argues against standardization of the term "adolescence" in this special sense. More frequently now it is being used to designate the whole period of development commencing with the onset of puberty and ending with sexual maturation. There is evident need for a workable nomenclature which brings the phases of adolescence into the framework of the libido theory and for standardizing the terms "adolescence" and "puberty" which are used ambiguously and even interchangeably in our literature.

IV

The problems of initiating therapy, of overcoming the initial resist-
tances, are always in the foreground of discussions of treatment of the
child in puberty. We find that if we are able to engage the child in a
positive transference, many factors in the situation of puberty and the
strong currents of puberty will come to the aid of therapy and work
toward a favorable outcome.

1. *Initial Reactions to Treatment*

From the beginning some children of this age show the strongest
reactions to the idea of treatment even before the first meeting with the
therapist. In only two of my cases did I have reason to believe that the
parents themselves might have given a punitive tinge to the idea of
treatment in preparation of the child for seeing me. Further, these
negative reactions seemed to have little to do with the type of disturbance
manifest in each case. We can understand that a delinquent girl or a
youngster with conduct disorders can show strong resistance to the idea
of treatment, but among other cases in the series studied were severe
neuroses and symptoms of a type which critically handicapped the child
and which we should expect might provide strong incentives to the child
to come into treatment.

Some of these initial reactions seem worth while cataloguing:

Jeannie, who was eleven, was referred for treatment of a severe compulsion
neurosis. There was a hand-washing compulsion, ideas of contamination through
breathing, ritual prayers and hypochondriacal fears of cancer. Now, also, there
was a reluctance to go to school.

She refused to come into my office to see me and pleaded with her mother
not to seek help for her. In view of the severity of the disturbance I visited her
first in her home in order, I hoped, to dissipate some of her exaggerated
fantasies of me.

Upon seeing me the first time she burst into tears and cried out hysterically,
"I'm not crazy! I'm not crazy!" then ran wildly out of the room.

With the greatest difficulty, in three visits to her home, I was able to
reassure her and help her gain some degree of confidence in me.

Patty was eleven. She was a deeply unhappy child, without friends or special
interests, and was failing in school in spite of better than average intelligence.
She was biting and sarcastic to her parents, complained bitterly that she was
a girl. She was untidy and flaunted her unkempt and unwashed appearance.
Only girls, "sissies" washed and cared about how they looked.

Yet her loneliness and misery was evident to everyone. A sympathetic teacher found her sobbing behind a book one day, and took steps with Patty's parents to get her into treatment.

Patty's reaction to the idea of treatment was forthrightly hostile. "I don't need to go to see anybody. There's nothing wrong with me." And in her first visit to me she was hostile and uncommunicative, except that every now and then, she said, "I don't need to come here. There's nothing wrong with me."

Martha, aged twelve, referred for a serious conduct disorder and compulsive stealing, burst into tears at the entrance to my office on her first visit. "Mama, I'm not a psycho! Am I?"

Margery, aged twelve, was referred to me by her school. She was a stormy, defiant child who was so disruptive in the classroom and openly abusive of her teachers and parents that she could not be influenced by anyone in her environment. Yet, she spent hours in her room brooding and crying hopelessly. There was nothing wrong, she insisted, and she was not unhappy.

She protested with tears and tantrums when her parents proposed that she come to see me. Finally she capitulated and said craftily to her parents, "All right. I'll go to see her. But I won't talk to her. She won't get me to talk!"

At the time the child comes to us many fantasies about therapy and the therapist have already taken shape. Sometimes we are able to obtain these fantasies in early hours of treatment and make use of them in dissipating the child's fear of the treatment. But more often we may not get the content behind these initial reactions until a later stage in treatment.

At the beginning of her treatment, Judy, then twelve years old, would sit in complete silence with me. She suffered with a severe phobia which began as a school phobia and had extended itself to all areas outside of the home. Her apathy and withdrawal, her inability to communicate, had caused a psychiatrist to diagnose her as a schizophrenic the year before she came to see me, but this diagnosis was withdrawn after a period of observation.

Months after I had gained her confidence and our therapeutic work had progressed favorably, I asked her the question which I had asked at the beginning without getting an answer. "What did you think I was going to be like when you first came to see me? What did you think I would do?" She said, "I thought I was going crazy. I thought I had a brain tumor and that when you found out about it I would have to go to the hospital and have an operation."

I do not think that this fantasy was much influenced by the actual experience of a psychiatric interview, for it can be seen again and again, how such fantasies about treatment exist independent of experience in puberty.

Susan, fifteen, was a stutterer, a shy, lonely child who longed to be like other children. She was not unwilling to come to see me at first, but in the early interviews with me she found herself unable to talk and would sit wretchedly in a chair in evident agony. Once, in an early hour, she asked shyly if I didn't have to take notes, and in discussion of this I learned that she had expected me to behave like the movie psychiatrist who is equipped with a clip-board and fountain pen. But I learned nothing more about her fantasies about treatment at the time.

Then one day during a silence which was difficult for her, I asked her to tell me her thoughts. And then she blurted out, "I was thinking of a movie I saw." I asked her to tell me about it. "It was a mystery. There was a psychiatrist who was really a crook posing as a psychiatrist and he took notes to blackmail the patients."

The protests of these patients were, as we should expect, the first clues to the neurotic picture. But usually it was only later in treatment that the significance of these reactions became clear. It does not surprise us that in the case of Jeannie, the analysis of the hand-washing compulsion revealed her defenses against masturbatory activity, and that her hysterical protest, "I'm not crazy!" was the confession of her fear that her masturbation had made her crazy. Her fear of treatment was the fear that her secret would be discovered, a fear of the "examination." The reiterated protests of Patty, "There's nothing wrong with me!" testified to the deep fears that something *was* wrong with her, and I learned in the later treatment that she believed that she could become pregnant through her masturbation. Again the resistance against treatment was based on her fear that her secret would be discovered. Judy's fear that she was going crazy and that I would discover that she had a brain tumor for which she would have an operation, stemmed in similar fashion from the belief that she had damaged herself in sexual activity and from fantasies of impregnation through sexual activity with a sister. Susan's paralyzed silences in the beginning of her treatment had a direct relationship to her symptom, for her stuttering represented, among other things, the fear that she might blurt out forbidden words and thoughts. Her thoughts of the psychiatrist who blackmailed his patients with their own words stemmed partially from her own fear that she would betray (hence "be betrayed by") her own words. The behavior of Margery to the suggestion of treatment was seen to resemble that of a person accused of a criminal act who fears that if he speaks he will give evidence to the court, hence her absolute refusal to talk to the therapist. "I'll go but I won't talk to her. She won't get me to talk."

The occurrence of these reactions at the outset of treatment, even in many cases prior to the first meeting with the therapist, suggests that the therapeutic situation is ideally suited for the transference of certain elements of the pubertal neuroses. The fear of the pubertal girl that her secrets will be discovered finds rich possibilities for amplification in the girl's view of therapy and her view of the parents' motives in bringing her into treatment. The fear of "being found out" even reaches beyond the therapeutic hour. There is the fear that "others will find out" about their treatment. "What shall I tell the other kids when they want to know where I go so many afternoons? ... If anyone of my friends found out I'd die." When asked: "Why?" she replied: "Because they'd think I'm nuts and had to go to a nut doctor." We find them making excuses to their friends regarding their absence from some after-school activities— most commonly, "I have to go to the dentist." We find that this fear of "others knowing" is a greater factor in puberty than at any other age. Our younger patients usually show such a casual disregard for "others knowing" that they may present embarrassing problems to their parents who do not wish the fact to be broadcast. Again in later adolescence there seems to be much less secrecy about treatment.

The factor of "being made to come" by the parents will also require skillful technical maneuvering on the part of the therapist. In the analysis of younger children the problem is quite different. Although the small child does not initiate the treatment and comes to his first hours chiefly because of his parents' wish, he is still dependent upon his parents and their influence will be sufficient usually to overcome any objections of his own at the beginning of treatment. But the child in puberty may actively resist the treatment *if only* because his parents wish it (Zachry, 1945). If we are not successful in divorcing our treatment from the pubertal tug-of-war with the parents, we may find that treatment can become a new battleground, ideally suited in some ways, for the continuation of the struggle.

In the case of very strong hostility between patient and parents, resistance to treatment may satisfy revenge fantasies against the parents.

Leslie, eleven, amused herself during unproductive hours of therapy with exhilarating fantasies, during which she calculated how much money her parents were throwing out on her treatment. (Her mother had once told her the fee when she asked.)

I have also suspected, at times, that "being made to come" satisfied certain masochistic tendencies which are so open and exposed in the early stages of puberty. It would have the significance of "being forced into intimacy with a woman," an idea which is both compelling and alarming to the pubertal girl during the period of her struggle to free herself from the incestuous tie to mother. I saw this most clearly in the case of a twelve-year-old girl who actually had entered treatment voluntarily; had requested treatment herself without any "pushing" from her mother.

In spite of the fact that Eleanor had come to treatment through her own expressed wish, and on the basis of her deep unhappiness, her depressions and her withdrawal from normal interests of her age, the first signs of resistance appeared in this striking way: In the fourth hour of her treatment she announced that she had no problems, that she saw no reason for coming here, and only came here because her mother made her! I knew that no pressure had been put on Eleanor to come into treatment or continue treatment. I reminded her that nobody had "made her come" here and that I would not wish this to be the reason she came for treatment. (My attitude, I felt, was a very neutral one. The implication was, of course, that no one would make her come here against her own wishes.)

She reacted with evident disappointment, but characteristically did not discuss this further with me. Later, in an outburst to her mother she said, "Selma was mean to me. She said if I didn't want to come in I didn't have to."

She arrived the next hour with intentions (she told her mother) to end her treatment. But as soon as she came in she relaxed, then said, "It's funny. I came today to tell you I didn't want to come any more but when I'm here I don't feel that way." When I encouraged her to discuss her feelings earlier of ending treatment she said, "I felt I *had* to come here and I didn't like it." I asked, "Did you feel that I was making you come here, too?" "Yes, that's what I thought. But I know you weren't really. That's what I can't figure out."

From the content of later hours I could understand the nature of this first resistance. For this hour ushered in a period of strong positive attachment to me, during which she tried to emulate me in many small ways, compared me, my house, my way of living with her mother, her house and her family's way of life to the latter's disadvantage, of course. She wanted to become a therapist one day and, as if to make a beginning, promptly had her hair restyled like mine.

It seemed to me, then, that the thought "I am being made to come here" alluded to the "compelling" nature of the emerging positive transference. It was this which the child felt must be resisted and was seen by her as a force emanating from the outside; I was "making her come"; mother was "making her come." We observe that my neutral attitude toward her continuation in treatment was interpreted by her as rejection. I was "mean" to her.

Here, we see how without any external pressure on the young patient to enter treatment or continue the treatment, she behaves like so many of our other youngsters for whom the beginning of treatment is actually the outcome of the parental initiative.

2. Technical Considerations at the Beginning of Treatment

If an adult patient enters treatment with fantasies of a dangerous and powerful Spy-Psychiatrist who will wrest his innermost secrets from him, we will certainly hear about this spectre or see him in the patient's dreams, for the patient is bound to the analytic rule. The young child patient, if he has such fantasies, will bring them forth in Spy games, or robber games, or often in interminable guessing games in which he tests the therapist's ability to "read minds," for the small patient easily translates his fantasies into games and makes them accessible to us. But the pubertal patient can neither be bound to an analytic rule, nor will he act out his fantasies in play. We feel as if we are left without familiar access to the patient's inner life. I am reminded of a time when I spoke such thoughts out loud to Eleanor during an hour which was particularly difficult for her. She was evidently upset that hour and several times fell into paralyzed silence during which she could think of "nothing." Finally I said, "At your age it's so hard. The little ones who come here can play and they tell me their thoughts while they play. And grownups, you know, agree to a rule where they tell everything that comes into their minds . . ." Eleanor stopped me right there with a horrified look on her face. "Do you mean," she said, "they tell *everything* that comes into their minds? *Everything!* Why that would be terrible! That wouldn't be . . . that wouldn't be *polite!*"

It seems to me this story nicely capsules the pubertal dilemma in treatment. We understand from Eleanor's reaction that she was struggling with such "impolite" thoughts about the therapist, but a therapy which should insist upon the telling of such thoughts stands for corruption to an ego which has concentrated its forces to resist corruption. This fear of "having to tell" can be dealt with even in puberty at later stages of treatment, but during the initial phase of treatment anything like an "analytic rule" would be countered with the greatest resistance by patients of this age.

How, then, can we deal with the initial resistances to treatment which have such critical importance for the future of the treatment? If the child brings transference fantasies to the treatment which are withheld from analysis, there is seemingly no means for the dissolution of the negative transference.

I have been impressed in work with some girls of this age with the fact that at the beginning of treatment, almost any interpretation, no matter how little, how superficial, constitutes a threat to the patient. Behind the transference fantasy of the sinister psychiatrist, the mad hypnotist, the "nut-doctor," is the image of the omnipotent parent, all-seeing, all-knowing. A display of the analyst's insights into the workings of the mind, however "correct" the interpretation may be, will only convince these youngsters that they are in the hands of the powerful superbeing of their fantasies. So we find, in the early stages of treatment, that we can best win the confidence of the pubertal girl by negating the transference image of the omnipotent psychologist if we cannot analyze it, and we can do this through being quite simply human, open, unmysterious, and not too clever. We may put aside, at first, our professional interest in dreams and fantasies for the more urgent worldly sorrows of youth—the traitorous girl friend who spreads lies about our patient, the math teacher who likes to humiliate students, the blue-taffeta dress or the lime velveteen for the school dance Saturday night. We are interested in whatever the patient brings to us and we demonstrate from the beginning our sympathy, our special understanding of youth, and our ability to be helpful, very practically, on all manner of problems, small ones as well as big ones.

The transference fantasy of the omnipotent psychologist provided most valuable clues to me in the handling of the initial resistances to treatment in puberty. For when we consider this fantasy in another light, the danger of the therapist to the pubertal child is also the danger of *loss of autonomy,* of submission to a powerful being. In this connection, too, Anna Freud's "Negativism and Emotional Surrender" immediately comes to mind.

It is characteristic of the pubertal struggle that the ego, torn between two masters, should regard its loss of autonomy as the most terrible danger of all. In the transference fantasies of the omnipotent psychologist, the mad scientist, the mind reader, we see how the fear of being overpowered, of submitting, is a powerful determinant. Similarly the fear of "going crazy," while certainly connected with sexual ideas, is also a fear of loss of autonomy.

It appears then that if our therapy is to appeal to the pubertal child, the introduction to treatment must be managed in such a way that the threatened ego is given some measure of control in this new and strange situation, assurance that it will be an active, not a passive partner in this treatment. We will not only dispense with the analytic rule, we may find it advisable to reverse the analytic rule, as Aichhorn did with his delinquents, "You don't need to tell me anything you don't wish to," to which one can safely add, "Though when you know me better you may *want* to tell me some things so that I can help you better." And since we understand the significance of the pubertal fear of the strength of the drives we will in no way reveal, at the beginning, our special interest in the instinctual sources of his conflict. We ally ourselves from the beginning with those forces within the ego which seek harmony and equilibrium, and we hold out to the ego the promise that our treatment will restore its autonomy.

The case illustrations which follow permit a more detailed analysis of some of these special problems of technique in the beginning of treatment in puberty.

The introduction to treatment begins, of course, before the introduction to the therapist. The manner in which the first consultation is presented by the parents to the child will greatly influence the initial reactions to the therapist, even, as I mentioned earlier, when the parents have not given a punitive tinge to the idea of "help."

I have found it very useful to give the child the initiative whenever possible, and this can actually be done in many instances. In noncritical situations where an immediate consultation with the child is not necessary, there is a great advantage in a "preparatory period" at home.

Nancy, fourteen, suffered with depressions which were of sufficient concern to her parents and me so that therapy seemed indicated, but the general picture of the child was not so alarming that immediate consultation was necessary.

When the suggestion of therapy was first made by her parents, Nancy reacted unfavorably. She was sure she could help herself, she protested, and she didn't need to go to an outsider. She couldn't talk about "personal things" with a stranger anyway. At my suggestion her parents did not press their offer but proposed that Nancy wait a while and think things over. For weeks Nancy tried valiantly to help herself, then the depressions returned. Her parents, following further advice from me, talked with her again, told her that even when parents loved their kids very much they could not help with such problems, and Nancy herself had tried so hard, yet could not help herself either. They asked Nancy if she would like to reconsider the possibility of "outside help" and this time Nancy asked questions about this "help" which were well answered by her parents. A few days later Nancy made her own decision to come to see me.

This was a good beginning for the therapy that followed. Had the parents been insistent at the beginning, we would certainly have encountered a negative youngster in the early hours of treatment, and much labor would have been expended on the achievement of a favorable attitude toward treatment which was better accomplished through waiting and permitting the child herself to come to terms with the first step in obtaining help.

I think there is an important indication in Nancy's initial protest and her wish to "help" herself. To seek help meant for Nancy (and for other youngsters, too) to admit a failure in control, a loss of autonomy, a dreaded admission in puberty. We know that the adult patient, too, finds it painful to acknowledge his own failure in dealing with his problems at the time that he comes to terms with his need for treatment, but the child in puberty is often terrified by his failure to find his own solutions to his problems. The pubertal fear "I am no longer master of myself" is realized in the admission, "I need someone to help me."

In more critical situations a "waiting period" during which the child can come to terms with the idea of treatment may not be desirable at all. In many such instances we are confronted with the need for an immediate consultation with a youngster who is strongly opposed to the parents' suggestion. Yet here, too, if we can bring the patient to the therapist with a more favorable attitude, if we can turn this disadvantageous situation into one which is advantageous from the point of view of the child, we stand a much better chance for a favorable outcome.

Diane, who was twelve, had displayed the most determined resistance to the idea of coming to see me. Her parents had consulted me following a rash of stealing episodes at home and in the community. Diane had long been a problem to her family. She was negativistic and obstinate, was passionately envious of boys, told "tall tales," and was having serious difficulties in school in spite of good average learning ability.

"I don't need to go. I'm not crazy!" she insisted when her parents introduced the idea of treatment. Although her parents had tried in every way to get across to her that I would be understanding and kind, she was suspicious of their motives and, of course, displayed the same obstinacy to this proposal as to most other proposals her parents made these days. She was reassured again and again that coming to a therapist did not mean one was crazy, but all this had no effect on Diane.

Of course I did not want Diane to feel she was being forced to come to me. I suggested to the parents that they tell Diane frankly that they had come to see me and that I felt I could not understand the situation without Diane's point of view, in fact that it would be most unfair to Diane if we had only her parents' view and not her own. I also suggested that the parents explain to Diane that it was quite possible that mother and daddy had not understood the problems of Diane, even though they had tried, and that Diane could tell the therapist everything she wanted to help her understand Diane's point of view. If she felt mother and daddy had made mistakes she could tell these things to the therapist, too. (With this last suggestion I was very careful, of course, to help the parents understand my reasons for saying this, and to assure them of my own uncritical attitude.)

This approach was successful. Diane came to see me willingly; she talked freely with me, and I was able to interpret treatment to her and to get her own consent to continue work with me.

The suggestions which were employed by the parents were based on the assumption that Diane would resist a visit to me if only because her parents had suggested it, and that she felt treatment itself was to be an "accusation" against her for her thefts and her other "crimes." The advantages, so far as Diane could tell, were all on the parents' side in this therapy business. When the parents surrendered part of their advantage to Diane (she could state *her* grievances, too), her own situation was changed from that of "being made to come," being passive, to the active role, choosing to come to state her own case.

In the case of twelve-year-old Martha (stealing, conduct disorder) the initial reaction to her parents' suggestion was also hostile and defiant. She, too, was afraid she was "a psycho."

Martha was very uncertain of her adoptive parents' love for her and feared that she might be sent away for being "bad." Here, I suggested to the parents that they tell Martha that because they loved her they could not bear to see her so unhappy and had consulted me to see how they could help her to become a happier girl.

Martha was really very much touched by this explanation. She agreed to come to see me, although still worried that she might, after all, be "a psycho," and tearfully asking for reassurance as she came to my office.

In this case treatment which is first perceived by the child as a punishment, a banishment by the parents, is reinterpreted so that it can be seen as an act of love on the part of concerned parents.

In recent years, through giving more attention to the manner in which the child is introduced to treatment by his parents, I have been impressed to see how my work in initiating treatment has been lightened. As I review cases from the earlier period of my practice I observe how I tended to give "general" kinds of advice to parents in introducing the subject of therapy to the patient and did not concern myself sufficiently with details. I assumed, somehow, that the parents would manage to induce the patient to come to the first consultation and I would employ my own skills to bring about a positive transference. In the case of the negative adolescent, I burdened the early hours of treatment with the problems of undoing certain resistances which need never have arisen had I paid sufficient attention to the preparation at home. Granted that only the therapist should assume the task of *interpreting* treatment to the patient, only the parent can introduce the suggestion of treatment, and I am sure through my later experience as a therapist that even the most well-meaning parents can err in this without careful advice from the therapist. It is my practice now to counsel parents almost step-by-step in this process. The suggestions for introducing treatment are specific in terms of my knowledge of each child as far as it can be acquired through the parent consultation. If the adolescent patient does not react favorably to the parents' suggestions, the parents do not press or coax but are asked to discuss the child's reactions with me once more so that we can handle this in terms of the child's feelings. In this way we avoid the situation (some examples of which are provided earlier in this paper) in which a sullen and determinedly hostile youngster meets the therapist for the first time.

There still remains the very important work of the therapist in making treatment significant to the anxious and still uncommitted young patient. The question has been raised by Spiegel (1951) as to whether an "introductory phase" of analysis might have value in the treatment of adolescents in the same way that it has proved useful in the analysis of young children and delinquents. In her introduction to the last edition of *The Psychoanalytical Treatment of Children,* Anna Freud modified her earlier statements regarding the need for an introductory phase. Progress in psychoanalytic ego psychology and the study of defense mechanisms has made it possible for the child analyst to analyze the first resistances of the child patient and in this way to shorten the introductory phase or render it unnecessary. In general these remarks seem to apply as well to the treatment of the adolescent patient.

Our understanding of the nature of the pubertal conflict provides us with the means for dealing with the early resistance. What the child in puberty fears is loss of control, surrender to the demands of the drives. What he fears in therapy is the further disturbance of his precarious equilibrium. What he longs for most of all is the restoration of harmony. If our treatment is to have meaning for him, if we can hold out to him a concrete goal, we need to help him see therapy as a means of re-establishing his equilibrium, of helping him become master of himself.

Nancy had recognized her need for help and had entered treatment willingly following the period, earlier described, in which she tried heroically to help herself. Now her depressions at home had alternated with violent outbursts against her mother, but early in her treatment, when she tried to tell me about these outbursts, all the circumstances fled from her mind and she could neither recall the events nor the strong emotions which had accompanied them.

She became afraid that coming to see me would make her worse. She begged me to arrange for her to go away to school. She considered giving up her treatment (then barely started). She was filled with self-loathing because she could not control herself. And she began eating enormous quantities of food which caused her now to castigate herself because she could not control her appetite. "Now that I come here I can't hate myself the way I used to and now I can't stop eating!" she wept. All interpretation was directed toward her fear of losing control and I assured her that therapy would help her achieve control. I showed her how her attempts to control through self-punishment had not worked, but that with help she would learn to control herself without being cruel to herself.

In one of these early, critical hours when she expressed her shame at letting me see her anger and her fear that she was getting worse I made a promise to her in the form of an interpretation. I told her that the more she was able to talk about her feelings here, the less she would lose control outside and that I could promise her that if she were able to do this she would actually gain more and more control over her feelings.

Nancy was really very much impressed with this statement. This made it possible for her to offer her co-operation in a very painful period in therapy, to begin at last to express feelings and to tell me for the first time about her obsessional symptoms.

This is, of course, a type of interpretation which we are accustomed to employ in order to penetrate a resistance which is produced by fear of the strength of the drives. I only wish to make special mention of the value of such interpretations in therapeutic work in puberty.

A variation of this interpretation served an important purpose in the very first hour of Diane's treatment.

When Diane tried to speak of her thefts in this first hour, she turned pink with shame and could scarcely find the words to tell me. I remarked sympathetically on her feelings of shame. Diane: "I feel very badly about it. Most of all because I've hurt mother so. I *really* don't want to do it. I wish I could stop it. But I can't!" I told her I thought I understood, that she was telling me that she really didn't want to steal but at times she felt she had to and couldn't stop herself. Was that right? Diane: "That's right. Oh, and I really don't want to be bad. I want to be good so people will like me. And sometimes I can see money and it won't bother me. And sometimes—well it's just like eating." (Gesturing toward her round belly.) "I'll see it and I'll have to have it."

Now I said, "It must be very frightening to have a wish to do something which you know is not good and yet not be able to control it." Diane was very much moved by this. "That's just it!" she said, and seemed close to tears. . . . "I'm so glad I'm coming here. You know all about that, don't you?"

On this basis I interpreted treatment to Diane. I explained how it was as if another part of her makes her do these things against her better judgment. If Diane wanted me to, I would be able to help her so that she would gain control over that other part of her. A look of relief came over her face and then another thought seemed to cross it. "But some things which have good beginnings have bad endings," she said with worry. I asked if she were afraid that I might not be able to help her. She quickly denied this. Then I told her something of how I would help her and why it would take time. I explained that there were reasons behind her problem which neither of us understood now. But as we talked together we would be able to understand what made her do these things against her will and then she would be able to control them.

On this basis Diane herself agreed to regular appointments with me. This proved to be a good beginning for therapy which was successfully concluded. Diane, throughout her treatment, accepted her own responsibility and her own need for help.

Here, then, we appeal to the child's anxiety in being at the mercy of uncontrollable urges. The promise of treatment is directed toward the part of the ego which strives for restoration of control over these urges.

When we encounter a well-established neurosis in puberty, we frequently find that the neurotic equilibrium will be preferred by the young patient to any possibility of relief which we can offer him. We can understand this very well for these symptoms which have been motivated by dread of the strength of the drives are regarded as indispensable by the patient. (They may, in fact, be indispensable, and we know how carefully we must judge the clinical picture in treating such patients analytically.) The ego which has achieved control in this way through pathological defense cannot easily be bribed through our therapeutic promise.

By the time Judy, then twelve, entered treatment her phobia embraced almost every area of functioning. It had started as a school phobia and she had not been in school for over a year. She rarely left her house, could not answer the door or the telephone. She had abandoned all friendships and even her relationships with her family were perfunctory and empty. The only thing in the world that she loved was her dog. The only traces of anxiety which remained were, of course, in connection with "going out" and "having dizzy spells" (which were chiefly connected with going out). Her fear in connection with the "dizzy spells" was that "people would see me and think something was wrong with me."

She came to her hours without fuss and without the slightest manifest resistance—but she was unable to talk! At best when she had reduced me to banal questions or leading remarks I would get from her a low "yes" or "no" or "maybe." Once I was rewarded with the longest speech she ever made to me. "But if I get rid of my dizziness, then I will have to go back to school." I promised her that I would never force her to go back to school and placed the emphasis in treatment on relieving her dreaded "dizziness.' I think she believed me and trusted me, and yet she was unable in the hours that followed to talk to me.

It was a transference symptom which provided the first opportunity to make treatment meaningful to her. One day I observed a symptom which had never been reported to me by the parents. It was a leg-tic. The right leg moved jerkily up and down, pantomiming a motion of stamping the leg on the floor. I waited that hour to see if I could obtain any clues through behavior. None appeared. When the tic appeared again the following hour I called Judy's attention to it. She reacted with acute embarrassment. I said sympathetically, "Can you stop that if you want to?" She made a desperate effort, but the tic persisted. Then I told her that sometimes when we are unable to talk, our bodies do the "talking" for us. It was as if her leg were stamping the floor as someone might do when angry. Was she afraid to feel angry about something or toward someone. Perhaps me? Now to my surprise Judy burst into a tirade—not against me—but her sister Janie. It was an outburst that lasted several minutes. How she hated Janie. How Janie used to beat up Judy and threaten her. How Janie would get Judy into trouble, then blackmail her with threats of telling the parents. She went on and on in a voice full of impotent rage, cataloguing the grievances against her sister. (These were objectively correct statements.)

During the angry tirade the tic had ceased. I chose a moment after the outburst to draw Judy's attention to her leg. I showed her how, when she was able to talk about the feelings of anger and fear the leg had stopped its "jerking." She was surprised, even incredulous, and then broke into a smile of recognition.

Now in some respects I feel that this technique was disputable. It was successful (this marked the beginning of a true therapeutic attitude) but risky. With more experience in the treatment of puberty I would not be so sure of myself and would not so confidently undermine a defense before I ascertained the capacity of the ego to deal with smaller quantities of affect.

I can justify this technique, however, on the basis that it rendered inoperable the resistance of silence which completely blocked my efforts.

It demonstrated to Judy that one can "talk" through a symptom. It also demonstrated that putting feelings into words could dissolve a symptom which she had demonstrably been unable to control. I, then, had the means to help her bring the disagreeable symptoms under control. It goes without saying that this technique worked only because this was an alien and embarrassing symptom. The phobias were not, of course. Above all this hour opened up the possibilities of exploring the negative transference which led us by way of the tyrannical sister whom she must placate to an infantile dog phobia, the prototype of the present neurosis. Her muteness in those early hours was the muteness of terror as well as repressed rage. One must not show any emotion to the dangerous animal or he will jump on you and bite you. Be nice to him. Make friends with him. And so she had! The only thing she loved when she first came to me was her dog. But I was a new dog, the strange dog.

Initially my therapeutic usefulness to Judy had to be based entirely on those symptoms which she herself found disagreeable. These were the conversion symptoms, the symptoms that "showed." Gradually as she lost her fear of me I acquired a role which became my greatest asset therapeutically. I became the watchdog, in effect, the one who protected her from dangers, from her father's rages (which I could "tame"), her sister's tyranny, and even (for a while) from going to school. Only when I had become the indispensable watchdog could I begin to approach the school phobia and encourage her to face the greatest danger of all.

In the following case we see how a short "preparatory" period was essential to reduce the anxiety of a child who was terrified at the prospect of treatment.

Earlier I mentioned Janet, the eleven-year-old with hand-washing compulsions and obsessional rituals. Her parents could not even induce her to come to the first interview with me and it was necessary to visit her at her home during the first hours. We recall how in the first hour she screamed hysterically upon seeing me, "I'm not crazy! I'm not crazy!" and fled from me in panic before I could speak to her.

Clearly there was nothing to do under these circumstances but to attempt to gain her confidence in me through whatever means seemed best. With her mother's help we induced her to come back and stay with me long enough so that I could offer some reassurance to her. While she sobbed, "I'm not crazy!" I managed to quiet her and to assure her that I knew very well that she was not crazy. I told her that she did not need to tell me anything about herself or her problems until she felt like it, in fact I would prefer that she tell me other things about herself, the kinds of things she liked to do, the subjects she liked in school, such things as that. She eagerly accepted this opportunity and asked if I would like to see her weaving and some of her metal work. She then brought me samples of her handwork which I wholeheartedly admired, and we talked enthusiastically about crafts methods.

In the next hour, still at her home, we continued to talk of her interests in crafts, school subjects, basketball, movies and books. She talked a great deal as if almost fearful that if she did not talk fast I might still change my tactics and begin to ask "psychiatric" questions. But more important, I could see how she wished to impress me with her normality and her good intelligence, to show me she was not "crazy."

In the third hour we continued our exhaustive survey of her interests.

In the fourth hour (now at my office) our patient announced that she was cured. "I'm feeling much better now. I think all my problems are solved." I told her I was surprised but glad to hear of this, and, if this were so I certainly could not take any credit for it, since we had not talked about her problems at all. I asked her with professional interest, how she had achieved this.

"Well, I'm all better now," she said bravely, but then couldn't go on because her voice shook so and she added, "Except my hands." And now she told me in an outpouring how she must wash her hands over and over because if she touches anything she might get sick, she might get cancer. She told me of her ritual prayers at night which keep her awake for hours and how she must sometimes hold her breath because if she breathes on someone, "they might get sick and die."

I am sure that in this case only such an introductory period could have brought the child into treatment. In such instances interpretations related to the child's fear of the therapist will only increase the anxiety and bring forth stronger denials and suspicion of the therapist. We understand that Janet needed to demonstrate to the therapist how well she was before she could admit she was ill. She had to show the other side of her "handwork," the good things she could do with her hands before she could speak of the bad things she did with her hands. And the introductory period probably succeeded in correcting the transference fantasy of the omnipotent therapist and an "examination" which would show that she was "crazy," that she had damaged herself.

V

In many ways the introduction to treatment and the early hours of therapy appear to be crucial. In my own experience a case is more likely to be lost in the early stages of treatment, that is in the initiation to treatment, than any other time. If we can overcome these initial resistances and establish a therapeutic attitude we find many factors in the pubertal situation which go to work for us. I do not need to mention all those factors in puberty which do *not* work for us, the rigidity of defense, the fear of the homosexual transference, the acting out, etc. But the morbid aspects of the clinical picture in puberty are counterbalanced by the tremendous forward thrust of the drives. It is also, then, a time of hope and of promise and while the clinical picture in puberty can at times be alarming and can resemble in every aspect certain morbid disturbances of later life, the impetus toward growth, fulfillment, toward the future can work for puberty toward a favorable outcome. So it happens that a depression in puberty and a depression in the climacteric will present the same clinical features, but puberty is "not yet fulfilled" and the climacteric is "unfulfilled," and the therapeutic difficulties are by no means as great with the young patient as with the older one.

BIBLIOGRAPHY

Aichhorn, A. (1925), *Wayward Youth*. New York: Viking Press, 1948.

Deutsch, H. (1944), *The Psychology of Women*. New York: Grune & Stratton.

Freud, A. (1936), *The Ego and the Mechanisms of Defense*. New York: International Universities Press, 1946.

—— (1946), *The Psycho-Analytical Treatment of Children*. London: Imago.

—— (1952), Studies in Passivity. Address before the Western Reserve Medical School, October 25, 1952.

Gitelson, M. (1948), Character Synthesis: The Psychotherapeutic Problem in Adolescence. *Am. J. Orthopsychiat.*, XVIII.

Katan, A. A. (1935), From the Analysis of a Bed Wetter. *Psa. Quart.*, IV.

—— (1951), The Role of "Displacement" in Agoraphobia. *Int. J. Psa.*, XXXII.

Mahler, M. S. (1945), Child Analysis. In: *Modern Trends in Child Psychiatry*, ed. N. D. C. Lewis and B. L. Pacella. New York: International Universities Press.

Sharpe, E. (1950), Contribution to Symposium on Child Analysis. In: *Collected Papers on Psycho-Analysis*. London: Hogarth Press.

Spiegel, L. A. (1951), A Psychoanalytic Theory of Adolescence. *This Annual*, VI.

Zachry, C. B. (1939), Contributions of Psychoanalysis to the Education of the Adolescent. *Psa. Quart.*, VIII.

—— (1945) A New Tool in Psychotherapy with Adolescents. In: *Modern Trends in Child Psychiatry*, ed. N. D. C. Lewis and B. L. Pacella. New York: International Universities Press.

CLINICAL PRESENTATIONS

"SAY YOU'RE SORRY"[1]

LAWRENCE S. KUBIE, M.D.[2] and
HYMAN A. ISRAEL[3] (New York)

Occasionally, fortune presents to us an unexpected opportunity to teach basic dynamic facts in a form as transparent and clear as a precise laboratory experiment. Such an opportunity occurred a few years ago during a clinical conference at the New York Neurological Institute. These weekly conferences are attended by the house staff, clinical psychologists, psychiatric social workers, nurses, medical students and a scattering of visitors. The leader of the conference never knows what clinical problem will confront him until he arrives for the session.

The Conference

On this particular morning a crib stood outside of the conference room. In it sat a gaunt child of five with pale, parchment skin and deep circles around her dark eyes. She sat erect, motionless and mute in the middle of the crib, touching nothing, saying nothing, merely turning her head silently to follow the doctors as they filed by on their way into the conference room. The leader of the conference stopped by the crib, leaned down to smile and slowly put his hand out toward her. The child neither drew away nor moved toward him, but looked at him unsmiling and without a sound. He checked his tentative overture and went on into the conference room, where the house officer told the following story:

The child was the younger of two children. The older was a boy of twelve. About the relationship between the two, little was known except that the boy had teased the little girl. The child was a bright youngster who had learned to speak at an early age. Suddenly, a few weeks prior to her admission to the hospital, which had been a few days before the

[1] As read before the meeting of the American Psychoanalytic Association, December, 1954.

[2] Clinical Professor of Psychiatry, Yale University School of Medicine; Faculty, New York Psychoanalytic Institute.

[3] Director, Inter-Agency Guidance Center.

conference, something had changed. First the child had refused to answer to her name, insisting either that her name was that of a little girl who lived down the street, or of a boy. Presently she stopped talking almost completely, and practically stopped eating. Then she refused to remain in her bed, or to use any bed covers, or the pink pajamas and robe of which she had previously been particularly fond. She would wrap herself in a dirty blanket, rolling herself up in it with her face to the wall in the corner of the bedroom, where soon she began to wet and soil as she lay mute and unresponsive. Nothing had succeeded in arresting the progress of these regressive symptoms.

After a few weeks the child had been brought to the Neurological Institute with the idea that this was either an acute, rapidly progressive schizophrenic process, or else the result of some unusual type of encephalopathy or of an intracranial neoplasm. All neurological, X-ray, EEG and other laboratory examinations had proved negative. During the period of intensive neurological examinations, she had been negativistic and destructive, and her rare speech consisted chiefly of explosive fragments of profanity and obscenity. Her partial mutism was interspersed with a few recurrent phrases such as, "Don't let her call me honey!" (apparently referring to her mother).

Without waiting for further anamnestic data, it was decided to show the patient briefly to the group; and the nurse was asked to roll the crib into the conference room.

As before the child sat unmoving in the middle of the crib, looking silently at the examiner, and making no response when he put an arm around her shoulder, or asked her name, or where she came from, or whether anything troubled her, or whether he could do anything for her, or whether she minded being there. Each such advance was met by the same blank, staring silence. The examiner drew away, and stood by the bed for some minutes smiling silently at the child. Slowly the child began to hum a rhythmically repeated sound. This was so insistent that the examiner turned to the nurse and asked, "Has she ever done this before?" The nurse answered, "Yes, I think so." The examiner then asked, "Has there been any time when you could make out anything that sounded as though she were trying to say any words?" The nurse answered that on one occasion, as she had stood in the doorway of the child's room out of the child's direct range of vision, she had thought that in this same sing-song rhythm the child might be saying, "SAY YOU'RE SORRY." At hearing the nurse use these words the child turned slowly and looked at her searchingly, then turned back to the examiner silently.

This gave the examiner his cue, and he leaned toward the child, took her hand, and said to her seriously and solemnly, "I am sorry, I am very, very sorry." The child looked back at him in silence, then turned to the house officer who stood at the shoulder of the conference leader and said to him as clearly as the words could be spoken: "Say You're Sorry." The house officer answered: "I am sorry too." Then the child turned toward the other doctors who sat in the front row of the conference room, and said to each in turn, "Say You're Sorry." Each of the young doctors rose to the occasion by answering earnestly, "Oh, I am Sorry Too. I am Very Sorry."

Then the child turned back to the examiner, looked at him a few moments and asked, "What's your name?" He answered, "My name is Larry." The child then turned to the doctor at his side and asked, "What's your name?" He answered, "My name is Joe." Then the child turned to each doctor in turn and then to a number of the nurses, social workers and clinical psychologists and asked the names of each; and each replied. Then for the first time the child turned back to the examiner with an obvious show of relief; and when the examiner asked her, "And now what's your name?" the child smiled, and gave her own name correctly.

At this the examiner again ventured to put an arm around her shoulder. This time the child leaned against him. He then asked her, "Would you like a piece of candy?" And when she said, "Yes," eagerly, there was a rush on the part of the house officers to fetch some from the vendor on the floor below. Nothing more was said to the child on this occasion; and the child was rolled out, sucking on a candy.

One week later the child was again shown in conference. This time she came running into the room, climbed up on the examiner's knee, and talked to him freely.

Further History

In the meantime, the following additional facts about the child's life had been ascertained. The mother had not wanted this child. How much attention, thought and feeling she had given to the older brother is uncertain. He was said to have been docile and submissive with his mother; and there is a possibility that he had taken out his frustrations on the patient. The father had been gentle and loving, but the struggle to make his way forced him to work early and late, so that he had little time for his children. The child's closest emotional attachment was to a general houseworker, who lived in and who took care of the household and of the children. There is some uncertainty as to where the child slept at different stages of her life. In her parents' bedroom at eighteen months she had gone through a period of sleeplessness which kept her father awake. Later she and the housekeeper shared a bedroom. Then came a day when the father's financial state began to improve. This made it possible for him to move to a larger home, so that the child could have her own bedroom. Thereupon the child became restless in her sleep, wakening frequently and showing increasing anxiety. Soon after this move, the general houseworker had to leave, presumably because of illness. This precipitated the child into storms of panic and night terrors, with screaming attacks and intensified unruliness, none of which could the mother handle.

The crisis followed an occasion when the father had come home more tired than ordinarily, and in a sudden explosion of anger had spanked the child. It was this which seemed to precipitate the onset of the acute illness.

Shortly after her admission to the Neurological Institute, the child had shown a slight improvement; but no significant changes had occurred until the conference described above and the subsequent week.

Subsequent Developments During Therapy

The first collateral effect of the dramatic improvement that followed the clinical conference had been to convince the hitherto reluctant parents that the child needed psychiatric treatment. Through the social service department psychotherapy was scheduled with one of us (H. I.), who has now seen the child regularly ever since. From the first, efforts were made to induce the mother to accept similar treatment herself and to co-operate with the child's therapist; but throughout the first year she was unable to force herself to keep regular appointments, preferring telephone calls and occasional visits. Nevertheless some progress was made with the mother, as well as great progress with the child. The treatment uncovered much additional anamnestic data.

Additional History

The mother was a person of strong personal interests, which she pursued intensively. Yet when she was alone and also when she brought the child for therapy, she frequently lapsed into sleep.

The patient had been a premature child, born close to the onset of her mother's menopause, and admittedly unwanted. From the first she had been unusually active, bright, and vigorous, in contrast to the older brother who was placid and perhaps more like the mother. Indeed this contrast was so marked that from an early age the patient had ruled the family. Although her older brother sometimes was aggressive, the patient seems to have provoked much of this aggressiveness. Indeed the child would use many tricks to disrupt the family activities and to focus on herself the attention she could not otherwise enjoy. She would dawdle or she would rush. She would order the adults around, and frequently succeeded in commanding their obedience, particularly that of the housekeeper. There is a story that once when she had ordered the housekeeper to sit down on the sidewalk, the woman had obeyed.

The father was feelingful but not forceful. He was closer to the children than the mother, but had little energy or time to give them. He worked hard; and at home he wanted peace at all costs.

The child's first manifest neurotic symptom had been precocious, certainly in its nature and perhaps in age of onset. It is difficult to evaluate this part of the child's history because the mother's guilt over earlier neglect may lead her to project onto the child some of her own concealed phobic maneuvers, and also to excuse herself by predating the manifestations of illness to infancy, as though to prove thereby that the child was ill "from the start" and before the mother's behavior could have exerted a deleterious influence. For whatever it may be worth, then, the mother's story is that at some time between the ages of one and two the child had developed what seemed to be a phobia of having anyone touch the baby carriage. For instance, if anyone touched the carriage in the elevator, she would cry until her mother went back upstairs and started out with her anew. (Specifically one wonders here whether this was the baby's phobia or the mother's.) However that may be, during her illness a comparable phobia developed in the child, focused on her beds, both at home and in the hospital.

It is interesting also that in the subsequent course of her treatment the child played out another version of the original phobia on her doll. Thus she placed her doll precisely in the center of the room, just as she herself had sat in the middle of her crib before the conference. She then identified with her mother by placing some of her own baby clothes in the doll's lap. Thereupon she could hardly bring herself to enter or to leave the room, and went through many avoidance rituals and phobic maneuvers so as to avoid even looking at the doll. Characteristically the mother was unable to deal with this problem effectively, until the therapist had instructed her precisely in what she should do.

The child's initial reaction to therapy was excellent; but she then went successively through a long series of reactivated earlier phobias about contacts and smells, with related compulsive avoidance rituals.

One example is particularly illustrative. She cuddled with the therapist, sat on his lap, then retreated from that position to strike and kick at him. Then came the following interchange:

Patient: "Do you ever think of duty?"

Therapist: "What do children think of duty?"

Patient: "They like to put it in their mouths."

Therapist: "They cannot tell what is duty and what isn't, and, therefore, they smell it."

Patient: "But you like me, don't you?"

Therapist: "Oh yes."

This precipitated a discussion over what belongs to whom.

Another illuminating episode illustrates the child's need for symbolic reassurances. When her mother said to someone: "I like your hat," the patient would plague her with repeated questions, "Did you say you like *her* hat or *mine?*" until the mother would say that she liked the patient's hat.

The patient allowed the therapist to call her by her real name only after she had first gone through a long period of concern about sexual anatomy, making vaginas and penises out of clay. Finally came the day when she said, "Girls are prettier than boys"; and when the therapist had agreed with this, she finally accepted her own name for good.

Her sexual games continued to take interesting forms. She had accepted her own name and abandoned a boy's name; but she would turn her pocket into an imitation of the fly of a boy's trousers. She made a family of valentines, printing the names of each member of her own family on the backs. She still insisted that she had feelings which other children did not have; and when she referred to her stay in the hospital it was as though she spoke not of herself but of some other child who had been in the hospital.

In the course of the first year of therapy, the child developed an intense and complex relationship to the therapist, variously expressed by compulsive, hilarious laughter, by expressions of affection, and not infrequently by calling the therapist "Daddy." As this developed, signs of improvement became clear. Although she continued to be demanding and intrusive in her relationship to adults, her tolerance for frustration increased. She became able to attend a kindergarten, and could even accept a substitute teacher without running away as previously. Her mother could leave her to go shopping or even to make an out-of-town visit. The youngster could sometimes play with other children, and in general was able to accept more give and take in all relationships.

The ritual about the doll in the center of the room gradually became less exacting and rigid. She could turn her head toward the doll, which she had not previously been able to do; and eventually she permitted the mother to remove the doll from the room altogether.

Other symptoms persisted. Sometimes she still had to remain in her bed when she felt guilty; as for instance when she had stolen a fountain pen from her brother, or an object from the therapist's playroom. On the bus and in public she sometimes made loud and embarrassing personal remarks. At times she had a compulsion to touch fur coats; but into these symbolic acts she developed a great deal of preconscious and conscious insight.

The conflict between her attachment to her father and to the therapist was marked. On one occasion her father, while taking care of her, could not avoid causing her some pain. After this the patient turned on the therapist in anger and said, "See what you made me do." On another occasion when she heard that her father had visited the therapist to seek advice, the patient cried and ran out of the therapist's office and sent her mother in instead. When she returned she spoke of her fear that the therapist would tell her father that she had once said that she wished that the therapist was her father.

Finally, the great danger of self-injury through an artificial and compulsive "fearlessness" has been replaced by a more realistic caution. Occasionally when furious at a mistake which she had made, she still would say, "It's all your fault," and then would quickly add, "Say You're Sorry."

Further Progress in the Second Year of Therapy

As the patient's progress continues, she has become less provocative and less ritualistic. Occasionally she makes repetitive statements, to which she demands ritualized responses in precise words and even with precise intonations which she defines. Though in the past she had stubbornly refused to show or accept signs of affection at home, she occasionally seeks her mother's lap and permits her mother to comfort her.

Recently during a play session with dolls, she created a "poison statue" around which she wove the story that it had poisoned all the members of her family, until finally an imaginary "good uncle"—a policeman— came along and destroyed the poison statue and brought all the members of the family back to life.

The therapist is now seeing the mother regularly, in spite of her continuing resistances. In order to do this he has had to make her into a co-therapist. In this role she is quite observant and objective, while keeping everything at arms' length emotionally. Slowly she is beginning to focus on some of her own problems. The mother often says of the patient that she "is trying very hard," in words which are reminiscent of the patient's needs for ritualistic responses; and to this the therapist must answer, "Yes, and you are, too."

The brother, at thirteen and a half, is consistently firm as he accepts her attacks, and he is always rewarded by his parents for his forbearance in dealing with her. Of the family he alone had always insisted on calling the patient by her own name, whereas the others yielded to her demands to call her by the name first of another little girl and then by the name of a boy.

Current Status

Both the patient and her mother are now being seen regularly once a week. As the child improves there are periods when the mother becomes restive about the regimen. Nevertheless she continues to co-operate. The child also becomes resentful at times, or at least puts up a front of sham objections to coming. This may be linked to a lessening of her identification of the therapist with her father.

Many signs of improvement are interwoven with evidence that the process of illness persists. It is possible to observe a gradual shift in the distribution of control between conscious, preconscious and unconscious forces. At times it is hard to decide whether there is a lessening of some of the conflict-laden drives, or an increase in repression; but the general increase in flexibility makes it likely that the conflicts themselves are actually lessening. For instance, most of the earlier bizarre behavior has disappeared. She no longer takes down her panties to urinate in the waste-paper basket. She shows a normal reticence and modesty about herself and toward her companions. The bed wetting never occurs on the nights when she is going to school, although it reappears occasionally on the evening before a week end. Her play with other youngsters is freer. She still oscillates in her sexual roles, but in forms which are more or less standard for her age; and she does it with a twinkle and with full awareness of what she is doing. Thus she says that she wants to be a little girl, but that she also likes to be a cowboy; and when she wears blue jeans, she slicks her hair back and plays the cowboy role freely.

The contamination fears are lessening, but still are manifested around her doll. She can allow her friends to play with the doll; but there are sudden regressive flare-ups, as when she said that her father must not touch the doll with his "dirty hands." Subsequently she could join in the family laughter about this, which would formerly have been quite impossible for her to do. Again when she is playing with her doll she sometimes insists on wearing fresh clothes, because no other children can have touched them.

Thus the process oscillates back and forth between obsessional rituals and freedom. Occasionally she will revert to some rigid sequence; and when this happens she cannot allow this sequence to be interrupted, without insisting on going back to the beginning to start all over again, even returning to the very spot in the room from which she had started.

In the above description of this patient's progress in therapy, we have tried to avoid overoptimism about both the progress and the current status. Several problems remain. The child is still subject at times to sudden overwhelming moods and anxieties, leaving her troubled and temporarily inaccessible. We wait to see how well she will be able to rise to the challenge of the first grade in public school. Certainly the end of the story is not yet at hand; and it is impossible to predict the ultimate outcome. Nevertheless this record first of the powerful psychological forces which swept the child into malignant regressive illness, then of how she turned toward health during the initial conference, and finally of the steady advances under treatment have important technical and theoretical significance, in addition to its dramatic values.

Two recent episodes provide moving evidence of the change which is taking place. Thus she watched a little boy climb a tree, and could say that the little boy was a better climber than she is. Then she could add, "But I'm good in art."

And when one considers the significance of the ritualistic phrase *"Say You're Sorry,"* it is equally significant that now when she is gently but firmly reproved she can say, *"I'm Sorry."*

THEORETICAL DISCUSSION

This brief clinical story does not pretend to tap deep layers of analytical data or insights. It is presented because of its moving quality, because it demonstrates that during these early years an ominously disintegrative process can remain remarkably labile and reversible, and because it is a challenging manifestation of certain facts about technique which more frequently are encountered in hypnotic procedures and hypnotic research.

Milton Erickson, in his communications with dual personalities (whether by word of mouth, by drawings, or by writing) (1938), and in experiments involving the translation of automatic writing or doodling (1940); and Farber and Fisher (1943) in their brilliant experiments with the translation of hypnotic dreams, have shown that in its use of verbal symbols the unconscious is as precise and restricted and literal as a child. It is a direct consequence of this that when it aims to be exact, every word of an interpretation must be chosen with a precision that is formidably exacting, if the interpretation is to fit precisely into the dimensions of the unconscious expectation and of the unconscious need. It is as though each unconscious constellation was a lock which can be unlocked by only one key, which consists in turn of a unique and precise constellation of words. When the words fit precisely, their effect is instantaneous and almost magical. One sees this frequently in hypnosis. In analysis one encounters it only occasionally, in the sudden and always exciting response to the rare "just exactly right" interpretation. This case history demonstrated this principle with the precision almost of a laboratory experiment. The principle has significance for all techniques of psychotherapy, for the validation of psychoanalytic interpretations in general, and for the elucidation of various baffling problems of insight; i.e., both its acquisition and its therapeutic leverage.

We do not mean to imply that the psychotherapeutic process *always* depends upon fitting the precise word to a precise need or conflict. A great deal of nonverbal communication may also be potent. The scientific questions which confront us here are both searching and important; i.e., what are these situations in which effective interpretative communication can be nonverbal? What are the situations in which effective interpretation can be approximate and general? What are the situations in which effective communication depends upon the unique and precise word? An ultimate answer to these questions is essential for our understanding of the psychotherapeutic process, whether in children or adults.

There are other important implications in this brief clinical story: implications for the concurrent and simultaneous interweaving of conscious and unconscious processes both in the evolution of this illness and in its resolution. More specifically there are implications with respect to the distortion of symbolic functions as these evolved in this child, starting at the moment of origin of her first overt phobic reactions to being touched or to having any of her possessions touched. Her subsequent neurosis became an obligatory, idiosyncratic sign language, in which carriages, dolls, clothing, her own body, her eyes, the bodies (or more specifically the hands and eyes) of others, body products and their smells, all constituted a wordless symbolic language by which the child linked her inner "I" world to her outer "Non-I" world (Kubie, 1953). Obviously during the acutely regressed phase of her illness, the link between the two was severed; to be suddenly re-established during the initial teaching seminar, and clarified gradually and more completely during the process of treatment.

Here again we have what was almost an experimental demonstration of the appearance and disappearance of a psychotic state in childhood out of a neglected pre-existing neurosis. The fact that this malignant process was caught in time to be reversible was the happy outcome of a moment of exceptional clinical good fortune, not only for the child, but perhaps ultimately for psychiatric and psychoanalytic science in general.

BIBLIOGRAPHY

Erickson, M. H. and Kubie, L. S. (1938), The Use of Automatic Drawing in the Interpretation and Relief of a State of Acute Obsessional Depression. *Psa. Quart.*, VII.
—— (1940), The Translation of the Cryptic Automatic Writing of One Hypnotic Subject by Another in a Trance. *Psa. Quart.*, IX.
Farber, L. H. and Fisher, C. (1943), An Experimental Approach to Dream Psychology through the Use of Hypnosis. *Psa. Quart.*, XII.
Kubie, L. S. (1953), The Distortion of the Symbolic Process in Neurosis and Psychosis. *J. Am. Psa. Assn.*, I.

THE STUDY OF A PROBLEM OF AGGRESSION

DAVID CROCKER, M.D. (Cleveland)[1]

INTRODUCTION

In this paper I will attempt to present some of the factors in the development of a thirteen-year-old boy, leading to such severe asocial outbreaks of aggression as to necessitate separation from his home and community, and admittance to a residential treatment center. Although his intelligence was superior, he had fallen far behind his potential schoolgrade, because of his inability to read and work intellectually, and because of his intolerable, aggressive acting out. Although there was considerable question whether his acting out could be managed, even in a residential center, and especially during certain phases of psychoanalytic treatment, the intense anxiety and neurotic suffering of this boy made it seem possible that analysis could succeed in enlisting his ego gradually in the work of recovery. The difficulties of the analysis (until the acting out was brought under control) served, in part, to mobilize the interest of the analyst around the meaning of reality in an analysis—for both the patient and the analyst.[2] Some of the contributions at the symposium, led by Anna Freud in Philadelphia, in May 1954, emphasized the importance of technical deviations that may help to shift the balance of forces so that the work of analysis can proceed. While in this paper the development and manifestations of aggression are the subject of study, they are inextricably tied up with the disturbance of reality testing and the gradual improvement in reality testing with the progress of the analysis. Inasmuch as aggression is connected with the disturbance in this boy's contact with reality and, eventually, with forces leading to a mastery of reality, that aspect of it will be dealt with. Other data having to do

[1] From the Department of Psychiatry, School of Medicine, Western Reserve University, Cleveland, Ohio.
[2] I owe a great deal to Dr. Anny Katan for her support in this regard.

with the development of a sense of reality, and the mastery of reality will be the subject of another paper.

Summary of the Problem

Since Freud's original conception of aggression as an ego instinct, there have been many observations tending to support the thesis that aggression is mobilized mainly as the result of the frustration of libidinal drives. However, there has been a steady change, both in Freud's ideas, and in other contributors', which tends to view aggressive drives as inherent in the biological nature of mankind, and as subject to some of the same modifications and eventual use in the service of ego functions as libidinal energy (Hartmann, Kris, Loewenstein, 1949). Recently work has been published which tends to support the view that aggressive drives can be observed at work from early childhood, and that their fate is subject to some of the manifold and variable modifications that affect libidinal drives (Anna Freud, 1949). This paper will attempt to trace some of the ways in which aggressive drives become deflected from the main course of the development of the ego, to show how these deflections developed in the personality of my patient, and how the analysis uncovered successively in different layers, aggressive and libidinal drives which (when brought to consciousness and worked through under guidance of the reality ego) served to effect the utilization of aggression in a form more integrated with outer reality and with the patient's own ego, seeking mastery.

Family History

S. was the second of four children. He had an older sister (two and a half years older) who was subject to aggressive outbreaks since very early childhood, characterized by severe temper tantrums, soiling and withholding, stubborn behavior, and a constant, intense fear that she might be abandoned by her mother. During her latency she was sent away for psychiatric treatment in a residential setting. After treatment she returned home improved but continuing to exhibit rebellious and acting-out behavior, mainly in attempts to control. She remained very exhibitionistic and competitive with S., and precipitated many fights with him, especially over suspicions of his sexual activities. (She suspected that she visited prostitutes with his boy friends when he went out for rides with them in a car.)

S.'s father, in his middle forties, was a very weak, impulsive, insecure man who fought his anxiety by compulsive work habits. He tried to dominate every situation by any means which he thought would gain him control, and he had outreached himself in his automobile business, in financing operations and in his social life to the point where the whole structure of his life was threatened. He continued to bluff, cheat, threaten, plead, seduce in order to maintain his status quo, and had succeeded so far in maintaining an outward appearance of a successful self-made man, although his reputation with his local social agency and credit institutions was poor. After a terribly insecure childhood with many changes, and having started early in life to develop an automobile business, he continued to build his life around this and the security of a home. He was so threatened by the fear of military service and separation from his business in the last war that he worked nights in a vital factory to be declared essential, and had no energies left to help his wife or take responsibilities toward his two oldest children at this time. Because of great anxieties then he sought psychiatric help, which did give supportive direction to the education of the two younger boys, and to the need for placement and treatment of the two older children. It also increased the intellectual psychoanalytic armamentarium of the parents, and accentuated in some areas an acting out on the part of both parents that made the placement of S. outside the home imperative. This behavior could be characterized by excessive bribing and seduction, followed by excitement and lack of controls in S., then resulting anger in the parents, leading to harsh controls, physical beatings and rejection by isolation. Maturer ego patterns could only be established in periods of relative quiet when supportive, outside controls steadied the situation or when internal anxiety subsided.

S.'s mother was a tired, intelligent forty-year-old woman whose seductiveness was used by her, like so many other defenses, to control the situation when she became anxious that she could not cope with reality. She could not handle the responsibilities of caring for her children, and, particularly in the case of the two oldest, left them often in the care of a maid while gaining solace for her helplessness and loneliness in the social activities of high society. She entered treatment at the time of her daughter's treatment and placement outside the home, but she was not able to use it.

At first the anxiety about S. made co-operation with the parents feasible (though difficult) in maintaining environmental controls, but later when S. began to improve I was able to establish a more positive relationship which the parents' need to control (when they became anxious at home) threatened continuously. The mother tried to seduce me, to control me and regard me as her miracle worker—just as she did her own psychiatrist, her husband and S. It was by using this narcissistic attitude that I was able at times to bring accession to demands for more realistic and mature responsibilities on the part of both parents. If those measures failed, I reminded them that S.'s problems were not solved, and that I was anxious to know how *they* would meet the situation should treatment be stopped or invalidated by their attitude. That is, I mobilized anxiety in them by emphasizing that S. was their responsibility, and offering my help if they would co-operate.

History of the Illness

S. was not planned for and during the mother's pregnancy she made several unsuccessful attempts to abort. She was already having trouble bringing up her first child (temper tantrums), and she stated that S. arrived two weeks early because of a sudden fright. S. was never breast-fed, and his mother felt depressed by the responsibility of caring for him, feeling helpless to know what to do, and delegating responsibility to servants. There was a good deal of sporadic concern about feeding which the mother tried to control at intervals by taking over and demanding that everything be done her way and on a rigid schedule. On the other hand, S. was still on the bottle at times until he was three. At the age of one and a half it was noticed that he began to exhibit marked restlessness, frequent bouts of crying which came with the least provocation. His mother told me: "He had an awful life. I neglected him and I know he suffered from not getting enough. He seemed dissatisfied all the time." At the age of three he had a tonsillectomy which was advised because of frequent colds. Colds were associated with fever, irrational behavior, and one seizure which he had had at eight months with a high fever. One gets the impression that S.'s parents were in a constant state of anxiety about things getting out of control which led to alternating periods of desperate measures and giving up. When he was about two he sucked his thumb a good deal and attempts were made by varnishing his finger, spanking and removal of satisfactions to stop him. It resulted in alternating periods of quiet, depressed behavior, and occasional temper tantrums, during which he was destructive of property. At four he had mumps, and at five was subjected to a thorough medical check-up because of the complaint of headaches and stomach aches for which no organic cause could be found. Generally S.'s behavior until he went to school was depressed, passive, restricted, and he was interested, curious about mechanical things but destructive when anxious. He did not start to act out severely until he was six (in first grade) when his reading difficulty began to be apparent, as well as anxieties about performing individually and in the group. At this time his mother was beginning to get psychiatric treatment, and she began to accentuate a previous tendency to be seductive, encouraging him to express his anger freely in every way—even encouraging him to hit her. She felt that her understanding in treatment was giving her the insight that it is better for children to express their impulses, to see their parents naked, and to know all. (It is interesting that S.'s educational disturbance was related to inhibitions in *seeing* and *succeeding* and very great anxiety in these areas, which underlay the acting-out behavior.) S. stayed in the public school through second grade, but his behavior was intolerable a great deal of the time. He did as he pleased, defying all rules and authority, and he became a leader in delinquent acts, inciting other children to destructive behavior. The parents' main method of disciplining him was to spank him with many resultant fights in which he would taunt them until they got out of control. Failing all else, they would isolate him in a locked room with the result that he became more anxious and more destructive, breaking everything in the room. When anxious he always had a chip on his shoulder, was teasing and provocative—and, as his anxiety (and anger) mounted, he would try to throw everything into hopeless disorder. He would throw clothes into the burning fire in the fireplace. Despite this pattern he had a passion for fairness and loyalty, especially in dealing with boys that he liked, and he always insisted that he be kissed, and tucked in at night. He made many demands, especially for food and candy—but when his demands were met he was often anxious and scornful.

At the age of seven (about the time that his sister was sent away for psychiatric treatment), he ran into a car and broke his right arm. At this time he suffered from nightmares whose content was repeatedly that his sister was killed in accidents. (These dreams recurred in the early stages of analysis when his fear of things getting out of control and insanity was so great, and in these dreams his parents died as well as his sister.) They were also related to his own guilt and separation anxiety.

When S. was ten he discovered a right inguinal hernia and right chordee and insisted on an immediate operation, although it was considered elective. He thought he had done something to himself by doing too much in sport activities.

From the age of eight to eleven S. had to be removed from public school to a special private school because of his completely unmanageable acting out in public school, and because he had fallen seriously behind in his academic work. It was noted that he could perform at his age level in mathematics, but in all other subjects dependent on reading and writing S. was three to four years behind his age level. He was very withdrawn, depressed and inhibited socially on admission to this school, saying very little and being very sensitive about recognition. He began to express himself in sports first, and enjoy himself there. (He has always remarked that this was one area where his father had helped him and done things constructively with him, spent time with him individually.) At times he was a leader, a model of fairness and standing out for controls, at others (when excited or hurt or let down by someone or when he felt not trusted or without support) he would break down completely and try to control everyone around him by being sadistic and destructive. He would try every conceivable attitude—sullenness, stubbornness, running away, uncontrollable rages, teasing to try the patience of those in charge. When he could not succeed he became desperate and terribly anxious—broke into sobs and depression. This was dealt with fairly successfully—at times by his teachers—but their firmness and interest was not sufficient. Because of the inability of his parents to handle him at home his anxiety remained at such a high level that he could not gain ground academically, although he showed that he was of superior intelligence in many ways. His parents both indulged him in different ways—his mother by seducing and encouraging him to express himself and his father by spoiling him with presents, bribes—then leaving him to his own devices. When S.'s anxiety mounted he would become unmanageable and destructive—then rigid and harsh controls would be necessary, leading eventually to continual rejections by both parents. They sided with him against his teachers, then withheld from him that they were planning a new change, then would suddenly take him out of school or have him see a psychologist without the school's knowledge. Despite all this it was recognized at school that S. had fine qualities, and that he was constantly being disappointed by not being able to reach impossible standards he had set for himself. He stole from a dime-store and from his parents—but it was apparent that his delinquency was related to an internal conflict. If he gave his word he would keep it—but if he thought he couldn't he wouldn't promise.

Finally, one year before he entered psychoanalysis he was sent to a psychologist for treatment. The school was not informed and S. was told he was going for treatment of his reading problem. This dishonesty on the part of the parents was typical of the problem that S. and his school had to put up with, and which eventually discouraged them in efforts to gain his trust.

S.'s behavior problem continued unabated and his treatment was another instance of a program impulsively intiated by the parents which led to a rejection and abandonment. S.'s anxiety was mobilized by his mother's acting out. She would encourage him to slap her on the face and body, saying, "I know you hate me and this might make you feel better." The impulsive attitude of his parents was also related to their own guilt and anxiety. The report of his treatment shows how he became fearful that he was hopeless, that he would be seduced and eventually rejected—and this is what he succeeded in making of his treatment. He was aided and abetted by his therapist, who encouraged the expression of his aggression and increased S.'s anxiety, instead of trying to interpret his ego anxieties and to work *with* his ego. S.'s acting out made termination of the treatment inevitable since his anxiety pushed him to further acting out and attempts to control the terrifying treatment situation.

Because he was making no significant academic or behavioral progress at school (except in mathematics he was behind four to five grades in almost every subject), and because he was acting out in a dangerously aggressive way at home (stealing from his parents and outside his home, threatening with knives to hurt his siblings, destroying hundreds of dollars worth of property, and hurting himself psychically by provoking punishment, physically by pulling his hair out), the recommendation was made that S. be removed to a residential treatment center (a) for relief from the uncontrolled situation at home, and (b) for treatment of his internal conflict.

PLACEMENT IN RESIDENTIAL CENTER

S. was sent away, like his sister, to a residential treatment center. He was prepared by his parents with their usual seductiveness and dishonesty, like a child that is seduced into hospital for a tonsillectomy by a dishonest ruse and then abandoned. He was told that he was going to an expensive, high-class boarding school and that he was going there because of his school difficulties. (His parents had become desperate and terrified of him because they could not control him and he thought he was going to a place for crazy children, that he was being abandoned.) He was assigned to a woman caseworker who had considerable warmth and understanding of children. S. did not show his aggression so directly to women usually, but displaced it to acting out, by running away, by not coming, by trying to control the situation (asking for things, then not accepting them). In the institutional school with men teachers, in his cottage with the cottage father or with older boys, S. was teasing and attempting to get them to lose control, and he became extremely destructive of property during the nine months before he started analysis with me.

The first day of his placement, he became acutely anxious that he was in an institution for criminals or crazy children. He was suddenly exposed to a great deal of sexual talk and acting out, he saw one boy packed off to the detention home, and another attempt to stab a boy with a knife. He tried to run away, and called his family many times on the phone. Because of aggressive outbreaks with stealing, breaking of windows, furniture, linen and clothes, he had to be isolated at times in the infirmary. His cottage parents became afraid of him because his provocative behavior, when he was anxious, turned the cottage into pandemonium, and got the parents upset. He was constantly playing everyone off against each other, and his parents against the institution, running up large telephone bills. At times he was an enjoyable member of the group, especially in sports where he excelled. He set high standards, especially in his demands for fairness and cleanliness, and actually was considered too neat and feminine. In this connection he became attached to several delinquent boys who were stronger than he, and he not only used them as protectors, but became involved with them in homosexual play, and excitement in the shower rooms and bedrooms. (S. showed some overt feminine traits at this time and was called "Mrs." by some of the boys.) One or two of these boys were plainly headed for criminal careers, and S. joined them in off-campus stealing, gambling and fights, destruction of property. At night they were involved in forays to show that they were above the law (like Raskolnikov), breaking into the record files, the store, and offices of the workers and administration. They were also asking for controls which could not be offered at that time. In many ways S. was headed for serious difficulties, including overt homosexuality and delinquency that might easily have led to juvenile court action and more punitive disposal.

In school (he had to be placed in the institutional school because of his severe academic difficulties, and his truancy, aggressive acting out) he could accomplish little in most academic areas because he was so far behind, but in mathematics where he could be relatively sure he was right, and protect himself against being in need of help, he worked at a seventh grade level. He would blow up in anxiety if he was praised, try to destroy his work, and to ward off any excitement that success might bring him.

So long as he was unchallenged leader in sports or with younger boys he was fair and was not aggressive or sadistic. In everything he did he was compulsive but fought off success if it involved him in demanding relationships, situations where he would be involved and subject to the danger of relationships controlling him.

In group activities or in his cottage he would submit to the rule of a strong protector, or to a gang leader, and he reacted favorably to grownups who did not get too involved with him or who became afraid of him. He could only work with the protection of someone staying with him constantly, and he used his passive attachment to a tough, strong boy to allay his anxiety. When this attachment weakened at times (because of this older boy's delinquent behavior and trips to the detention home) or when the relationship made too many demands on him and excited him too much, S. became very destructive—provoking his cottage parents, spending many dollars on phone calls to his parents, breaking and stealing furniture and other personal property, making impossible demands on his worker and in general trying to control his whole environment. At these times he had to be isolated in the infirmary, and he often welcomed rigid controls then. Even when running away from his limited interviews with his worker, he showed a tendency to want help from her behind his defense of "do not touch me." It was not possible for anyone to interpret his anxiety to him successfully because of his acting out at any time he was approached in interviews.

He would not accept the institutional rules about money, clothes, going off campus and in many areas—and his keenness in detecting unreasonable and unfair arbitrariness was diabolical.

S. showed signs of great concern about his condition at times, and occasionally showed depression and self-punitive attitudes, indicating severe guilt and suffering which made it seem that he was basically neurotic and might be treated. Although his conflict with his environment was great, he seemed to have an internalized neurotic conflict with tremendous anxiety about controlling his inner excitement. If his acting out could be controlled externally and by interpretation of his anxiety, it was felt that this boy might be reached through psychoanalysis.

Course of the Analysis

When I heard about the attitude of the parents and their illness (their apparent difficulty in co-operating in a treatment program), when I thought of the limitations in an institution to setting firm limits for adolescents, when I heard of the tremendous amount of property damage inflicted by S., and of the great academic difficulties he was in, when I thought of the repeated traumas at home, school and attempts at treatment with eventual abandonment of S. in each case, I felt quite doubtful about the possibilities of psychoanalytic treatment. If something about him had not appealed to me from the beginning I am doubtful if I would have had the courage to tackle this problem.

I became aware from observations of him, from reports of him generally that he had an above average intelligence and areas of potentially strong ego activity, a strong sense of reality which only succumbed to an impoverishment of functioning under the stress of great neurotic anxiety. If I could mobilize his healthy ego in the process of recovery, it seemed a possibility to help him. Unless I could convince him gradually that I would be his ally and become indispensable to him, I did not feel that my relationship with him would be strong enough to stand the trials of penetrating his defenses. We began the analysis with a deceptive quiet, eyeing each other warily.

Up to the time of the start of his analysis, S. was seen for eight months by a woman caseworker. He developed a considerable attachment for her, showing his dependence in many reality needs. She was encouraged to interpret some of his anxieties to him—for instance his fear of success—but these attempts only resulted in increased anxiety on the part of the worker because S. ran away or became aggressive (though never toward her personally). At the time of preparation for his analysis S.'s attachment to her was minimized, and his failure to show up for interviews, his negative attitude was assumed to show a lack of relationship. Consequently it was felt that S. would react favorably to a transfer to an analyst, and when this seemed to be the case, his worker assumed wrongly that feelings of rejection and hostility were not involved. Recognition of this problem proved to be one of the ways in which I could align myself with the patient's ego, and deflect some of the tremendous anxiety and hostility about myself. In addition I was aware from the first that a failure to recognize the reality situation, and an eagerness to embark on any but reality interpretations touching on the internal conflict would land me in enemy territory.

S. came to see me in an office in the institution which was relatively isolated at the end of a hall where the caseworkers had their offices. It had two closets, one sky light, two windows. It had a wicker couch with pillows and mattress, a desk, a telephone, and three or four chairs. There were some children's drawings and paper illustrations on the walls. The office next to mine was that of his former caseworker, and loud sounds could be heard from her office but never discrete words. From the first, however, a steady stream of interfering and noisy children stormed the hallway, and controlled the interviews going on by standing just outside the doors, often actively interfering. One of the first reality measures I insisted on (with S.'s full knowledge) was the introduction of a hall door which prevented any but *bona fide* visitors to have access to the hallway.

When he came to see me on the first day of the analysis S. was well aware of problems for which he needed help. He had begun to speak of them increasingly to his cottage mother. He always mentioned that he came to the institution for his reading problem first—and then furtively brought out others, such as inability to control his stealing and destructiveness, his worry about his body and physical health. He had begun to mention openly that no one liked him, that he would end up in the Detention Home. His defiant breaking of up to fifty odd windows at one time was followed by calm acceptance of restrictions, and by intense efforts to please and to be favored. He could not stay in school quietly for long without provoking his teachers and truanting. As soon as anxiety returned he had to provoke his whole environment into an uproar. He managed to keep everyone in a constant anxiety and despair, approaching his own.

In marked contrast to this provocative, and destructive behavior was his compulsive neatness, his need to ingratiate, and his passivity. I saw predominantly this side of him the first day he came, but his anxiety forced out his aggressive and threatening attitude from the beginning. Although he was polite and quiet at first, he soon showed a surly resentment and said, "I'm not going to tell you anything," waiting to see what I would do. I told him that I would see him five times a week because I knew he had troubles that were causing him pain, and kept getting him in difficulties with his surroundings, and that it would take a long time for me to get to know those troubles with him through what he could show me. I said that anything he could tell me about himself would increase my knowledge of him and therefore my ability to help him. He agreed that he did have troubles with learning in school and getting out of control but showed me right off that he was interested in seeing whether he could trust me in practical reality areas—for instance, whether I was interested in seeing him get an opportunity to go home on vacations. His distrust of me became focused immediately on his betrayals and desertions by all those who had dealt with his problems before he came to me, and in order to combat his anxiety he became aggressive, controlling, threatening, bribing and at first did not want to hear any interpretations around his fear that I would not like him or be there solely to help him. He wanted proof of my interest in concrete evidence that I would help him to gratify some of his reality needs, but if I did this (and I had to anticipate his threats, to surprise him) he then grew anxious and doubly suspicious that I was all-powerful. If he could (on the contrary) threaten and control me, he became more aggressive from anxiety about my weakness—or ran away. He tested me thoroughly in the first few months of the analysis on both counts, (1) to see if I would use my power unscrupulously to gain control of him, and (2) to see if I was weak and could be controlled by him. After telling me that it would take him two to three years to get to trust me, and laying down *his* rules for the analysis, he showed that he could be reached by reason and fairness at times, that he was miserably unhappy (he cried over what he felt was a severe rejection by his caseworker) and that he wanted help (he came *every day* to see me).

I tried to show him in every threat to control me and every need to make me all-powerful how fearful he was that both fears (that I would be weak or powerful) were essentially related to his fear that I would not like him—would desert him, or would take advantage of him. I used his feeling of rejection by his worker and the administration and previous teachers and therapists to show him how he was anticipating it from me—and I emphasized that my function was an entirely different one from those who had previously worked with him, (1) that I saw his need to work confidentially and closely with *me on his side* to help him regain his health; (2) that the work of coming to know his problems would be a gradual process, and that I would depend on his help. In this regard I had an opportunity to show him that I would neither decide for or against his going home on vacation, nor would I remain inactive if I could learn with him what he wanted. On the other hand, I could not promise him that the director would do as I suggested as I did not run the institution—but I would go to bat for him when I knew what he wanted. (I had at one point made the mistake of saying that S. ought to stay for his analysis during the short vacation—but had a chance to admit that this was unrealistic—and this admission that I was human, along with the recognition of other mistakes, brought me closer to him.)

He began to test me to see if he could get me to be active by leaving early, by threatening that he would tell me nothing, by telling me that he was sure I wouldn't be able to help him, by trying to catch me off guard in some way that would show me to be representing some other interest than his own (his parents, the administration, a psychiatrist trying to see if he is crazy, someone trying to control him, someone who would desert him when I found out his secrets). He wondered if his analysis would take six months (either I would be superman or give up)—or six years (it would take that long for him to trust me or his problem was hopeless). In addition to interpreting his fears around his reality experiences to show him that I understood he had real basis to mistrust me from past experience, I reacted to his need to get definite answers by saying that it might be two years—or more—I didn't know—that it would depend to some extent on our working to understand his thoughts and fears together—and that would be best accomplished in one way, *by talking about them.* Whenever he would act out, or demand an answer, or tell me of the possibility of some impulsive motor outlet for his aggression or a sexual impulse—I would urge him as calmly and firmly as possible, appealing to him to work at the analysis with me, "Let's talk about it." (S. later told me that what helped him the most in the analysis and formed the core of his understanding of analysis was my reminder, "Let's talk about it." In a way I think that it served, as the couch does, but without the anxiety attending the passivity of lying down, to focus the synthetic or evaluating side of the boy's ego on the essential process of analysis—to let the flow of associations come and to regard a motor expression of the conflict as a hindrance to the work of recovery.)

But my attempt to secure myself as a source of encouragement for this side of his ego was a precarious and intuitive business. It involved the recognition of the dangerous forces threatening him, partly through identification (how human his impulses were), but also the recognition of how painful it is to have those forces out of control and causing trouble because they were not acceptable to him or his environment. I tried to make myself indispensable to him in supporting any attempt to master reality, and in recognizing how his illness interfered with this process. My aim was to show him that I recognized this need for mastery and would go out of my way to strengthen his reality gratification both outside the analysis and within it, but that we needed to work together to see what often prevented this and threatened the whole therapeutic process. Once when I came to his school for an open house, some of the administrative staff were teasing S. by suggesting that he tutor one of the other students, a girl, in mathematics. Knowing that he wondered where I stood with him, I showed him by whispering in his ear, "Tell them you will if they pay you for it." As often as possible opportunities like this were used to consolidated his awareness that I was with *him*.

At first difficulties showed up in S.'s attempts to control me in a series of aggressive maneuvers that he employed with considerable skill. He had learned through long experience that the best defense is a good offense—at least to bewilder people and keep them from hurting him. Although the first layer that had to be reached was his alternate fear of desertion and fear of being taken advantage of, I was only partially successful in showing him gradually that he was identified with the aggressor and was taking this role because of his great anxiety about me being the one to hurt him.

This was a crucial and difficult time for me because S.'s acting out frequently aroused my own anxieties, and made me act out too. There were times when I felt that my own resourcefulness and stability would not be sufficient to get S. to focus on the therapeutic process of evaluating what was going on. It takes a certain kind of ability on the analyst's part to maintain a quiet, firm attitude of evaluation of the situation when the necessity to defend oneself emotionally and physically is a prominent part of the picture. I did not always succeed in maintaining my own equilibrium, and I made many mistakes, especially when I became too anxious myself. For instance, to decrease his fear of me professionally, I told him he could call me by my first name. This was felt by him to be an attempt to placate him, a weakness, to which he reacted aggressively and contemptuously, "You dope."

At first S. attempted to control me by seeing how far I would go in interfering for him about vacations, and in many realistic situations which were difficulties for him. I tried to get him to work at these problems with me, so that when I did interfere for him, the decision had been reached by him. This brought out his anxiety that no one liked him, that they felt he did everything wrong, that he could not control himself. He began to try to control the number of hours he would come a week, or how long he would stay in the interviews, or get me to tell what time it was. This led to alternating periods of anxiety, depression and concern if I could ever find out what his trouble was, and when his anxiety about his secret thoughts became too great, he tried in a multitude of ways to make me anxious, and to control me. He would ask me if I would help him in some realistic way, and when I showed him that I could, he would show me that whatever I did, it was no good. He tried to trip me up, to make a fool of me, to threaten me, to ask me specific questions about myself, or the time, and when I would not answer anything but one or two questions that seemed important reality fears (what was my position in the institution? did anyone else use the office?) S. would push further in a kind of third degree, trying to undermine me by asking, "Why do you answer some and not others?" or by adopting police methods, "Why don't you answer me? You know God-damned well what kind of a car you've got—answer me 'Yes' or 'No.'" Often he would leave early, "I guess I'm not going to get anywhere with that stupid son-of-a-bitch, no use sticking around here. Good-bye, stupid." Often, if I would try to interpret to him his fear of me and how he seemed to be treating me the way he might be afraid of being treated—like a bad, stupid person with secrets, like a criminal—he would intensify his attack, copy me or upbraid me that I had been of absolutely no practical use to him thus far.

About a week after his analysis started he announced that the authorities had told him that he could go home for vacation. I looked surprised and asked how he felt about it. His answer was characteristic of his dilemma, "You're the first person who seems to be able to do anything for me—I suppose you think you're pretty damn good—well don't get too confident—if you make any mistakes that's the end." I pointed out how much he tried to put everything on me—that is, how much he must fear I would blame him and desert him, be disappointed in him.

At about this time his nickname had changed from "Mrs." to "King" and with me he struggled against his increasing awareness of his anxiety about going home and about the analysis by becoming increasingly provocative and aggressive. His behavior in school became unbearable, and it became apparent that he was very concerned about his going home for the vacation, as well as about the analysis. Although he almost always came on time for his hour, he gradually became more provocative with me—pulling things out of desk drawers, calling out on the telephone, throwing pillows out of the window, sitting in my seat, and trying to control everything that was said during the interview. Whenever he made any direct attack on me physically or my clothes, I stopped him. He tried to steal my handkerchief, or my cigarette lighter by subtle and bold feints and sleight-of-hand. His aim was to show he could make me powerless and get me out of control, and I said that if he wanted to stop the analysis because he was so afraid, he could do it so much more easily in a less arduous way. I said I did not think he wanted to stop it really because he came every day, but that he was afraid I would control him or leave him—as he had forced everyone else to do. He had shown unmistakable signs that he was anxious about leaving me and going home, as well as anxiety that things would get out of control in the analysis, and I told him that he did not have to go, and that he did not have to come to see me but that I felt we should try to find out what he was so afraid of so that he could make up his mind what he wanted to do.

The day after I showed him that he would not be forced to do anything, but that his anxiety was at the bottom of his behavior, he came determined to provoke me and to get *me* to take some action. He attacked from the beginning, verbally trying to put me on the defensive by saying that the trouble in the analysis was all my fault, that I thought

I knew too much, I didn't trust him, I was just like all the rest. "You know everything—you—great big scientist, supposed to know how to help people. If you're so God-damned good why is this place in such a mess, why aren't you helping me. All you are is a jerk." As he proceeded to demolish the furniture, kick through the doors of the closets, and approach trying to hurt me and get me involved, I told him I thought he was desperately trying to get me to kick him out and stop the analysis so that he could say, (1) I did it, and (2) that I was the one who got upset. I repeated (what I had said) that he wouldn't behave this way unless he were terribly anxious about something in his thoughts—that he had to prove he could get me to give up—just as he felt hopeless and frightened about himself. He made a concentrated physical attack on me with chairs, books, pillows and broken pieces of furniture, yelling, "You can't stop me—I can lick you with one hand." He became so provocative physically that I was afraid that if I did not stop him he would hurt me, and I could not let him—so at the first opportunity I grabbed him and held him firmly saying, "I just want to show you that I can stop you, S.—that's all." He fought furiously and demoniacally and said I wanted to hurt him. I said I thought that was why he wanted to hurt me—because he was so afraid in his thoughts that he would get me angry like everyone else. Then he cried for awhile, and said, "I'll promise to stop." (I said I would trust him if he promised.) When I let him up he said, "I never promise anything I can't keep—so sometimes I won't promise." There was a silence and then he said, "Can I go now—you won't let me go—will you?" I said I thought he couldn't trust me because he didn't trust himself. After he got outside the door, he kicked through the door and said, "When I came outside, the promise was over—are you sorry for what you did?"

When his provocative behavior continued the next day I told him that I had not stopped him the day before because I thought it would help him but because I wanted to show him that I could stop him if I wanted to. I told him that he could easily stop the analysis in a much easier way, and that of course I couldn't help him if he was determined to stop it. Because he came back every day I couldn't believe this, and I was here to work with him on his troubles. To do that we would have to discuss things together, and only by learning his troubles from him could we find a way together to talk out his problems. I assured him that acting his problems out would not help at all, but that if I gradually came to know him with his help we might both, by talking, work together to help him with that side of him that he feared so. I said this all sitting on a chair backed up in a corner where he could not enjoy attacking me—and I paid as little attention to the destruction going on about me as was realistic—and put the emphasis on the evaluation of what was going on. After I remained quiet and not interfering in any way physically, he suddenly sat down on a chair near the door and started to cry. A vista of his inner misery broke through.

He then said he was angry with his teacher because he hit him and would I help to stop the teacher from hitting him. I agreed with him that hitting and physical fights would not solve problems—and that although I could help to stop the teacher from hitting, I thought it might help even more to see what S. had done to provoke the teacher to hit him, just as he had tried to provoke me. This led S. to remember his terrible troubles in school when he was hated by all his teachers, and was abandoned by them. He said despairingly, "They would never give me another chance." I took this opportunity to say that he must be afraid I wouldn't be on his side in trying to understand and help the side of him he felt to be so bad. He must be afraid that instead of talking with him and working on it with him, he would seduce me to fight and get excited, and then give up, as the others had done. S. cried and said then that he was afraid to go home, where he had lost control and struck out in blind despair and anger when his parents' inconsistent attitudes had left him not knowing where to turn. As an example he told me that his mother had told him seducingly how much she realized he loved his radio set, and then had thrown it away when he had left home to go to camp. Another example was that his father had told S. he would never pay for anything he broke again and then showered him with presents all the time. These two examples were intimately related to his unconscious anxieties, and to his aggressive outbreaks from the time he was a young child. At this time he told me he was very sorry over what had happened and from this point on he fought a dramatic and tempestuous struggle within himself over his growing attachment to and dependence on me.

In the two weeks before returning home for vacation, a month after the analysis began, he was torn between a desire to stay with me and fear of it, and the same ambivalence about returning home. He tried to get everyone either to force him to go home or to keep him at the institution. He asked what the laws were regarding the punishment of sixteen-year-old murderers and began to show great anxiety about staying more than a few minutes with me in his treatment hour. If he saw me on the campus, he would call out loudly, "Hah-ya Sam, hah-ya Joe," and at times he would try to get me to discuss his anxieties about coming so often outside of my office. He tried to get me involved with the personnel at the institution by stealing my hat and getting them anxious about it—but eventually his anxiety and my nonpunitive waiting made him bring it back. Then he would start to test me all over again, mostly in my office because I gradually perfected my technique of not letting him get at me outside that office, and I knew his dependence and anxiety would bring him there. Once he grabbed my wrist to look at my watch and see the time, and I pointed out his anxiety to him, saying I thought he couldn't trust me because of his thoughts. He became the scornful tough guy—"You wouldn't frighten anyone—you—a doctor—ha—Sam!" I said, "You sure have to bring me down a peg, S. and try to keep me under your thumb so you won't feel how scared you are." This led him to ask if the director had spoken to me about what went on in my office: "Wait till my parents know!" he threatened. I said, "Why don't *you* tell me how frightened you are of me?" At this S. said, "There—you see—you're making me do it," and he started on another destructive assault on the office furniture, this time overturning the desks, and breaking the drawers, turning the room into a shambles. I tried to sit quietly in the corner, slowly shaking my head and said barely audibly— "I've never seen anything like this before," and later, "It certainly would make some people think you were crazy." S. whirled around when I said that and shouted, "I heard you say I'm crazy." I shook my head and let my gaze wander over the debris. I told him I didn't think he was crazy at all, but I thought he was showing me how afraid he was that he was. I emphasized what a great difference there was between two concepts. "You said I'm crazy" became his war cry, and in a new burst of aggression he kicked out the door panels again, saying that he was not returning to see me anymore but would see his worker. The next day he was back, surprised to see that the room had been fixed, and that there were only two pieces of furniture in it—the chair I was sitting on and a wicker sofa. Failing to control me by all previous means, he asked if I played checkers, and I said I did. When he asked if we could play, I said that we could as long as I thought it would be a help in his analysis, and I found another way to intrigue S. in the work of the analysis, not lying on the couch, but sitting across a desk from me and gradually getting to his anxieties through the way he approached me and through getting him to participate with me in looking at himself. He began to reach out to me in tenuous ways to ask my help—would I help him to get his teeth straightened, would I see that he got a referral to a good eye doctor to clear up any part of an old injury might play in his difficulty in reading

and his headaches, did I think he was too small, what was his I.Q.?
I tried to tell him what I honestly knew or could find out about all these
matters and then directed his attention to his own fears about himself.
I even predicted that he would find the doctors to whom I sent him no
good, like his need to prove me no good. Shortly thereafter (though he
had been well prepared for the effects of homatropine) S. came to my
office in great anxiety and asked to be allowed to stay there till I came.
When I did, he was lying on the sofa, apparently asleep. He gradually
became more alert and spoke of his anxiety that he was going blind, and
that I had sent him to a lousy doctor who had assured him that his eyes
were perfectly normal, but had maimed him.

Beginning with this hour (a few days before he went on vacation)
S. responded to acute anxiety by resorting to his old attempts to control
me, or by lying down and either pretending to go to sleep or by going
to sleep. But before he went home (his own decision) he began to use
his stays on the sofa to listen to my interpretations of his fears at home
and with me, and my reassurance that if things did not go well he could
return and that I would see him regularly.

Although he attacked me for giving him for his birthday a book on
the history of football with anecdotes that interested him, he was obviously pleased. He was angry because he said I gave him a book when I
knew he couldn't read well. I supported other educational ventures—
that he be encouraged to read anything he liked and within a short
while after his return from vacation, he began to show an increasing
effort to help himself both educationally and in the work of his analysis.
On each occasion that he would bring me symbolic material, dreams, or
other seductions to interpret unconscious material I would refrain and
try to point out his anxieties about his previous treatment and things
he might have been told at home (he had frequently referred to his
parents being in treatment).

During the next three months S.'s behavior in his treatment hour,
alternating from *controlling* and *attacking* to *withdrawing and sleeping*,
gradually changed to more and more of S., the Detective. He paid acute
and painfully scrutinizing attention to my weaknesses, especially in
checkers, but sometimes he reported observations that his detective work
uncovered about himself. In addition to his concern about his body size,
his eyes, his tendency to nose bleeds, weakness, he began to mention a
concern about the lack of ability to control his thoughts. He brought
the anxiety in connection with my repeated explanation that to be crazy
and to fear that one is crazy are two very different things. When he
told me of his fear that he could not control his radio, that he was afraid

that he had to think certain things and had to go back to be sure he had closed doors, etc., I was able to show him that what he was afraid of was that he could not control his inner thoughts and feelings—and that I thought it was some other problem, not his ability to turn his radio off, that he couldn't control. For three months S. tried to put me on the defensive in every way—by telling me I was crazy, that I was afraid of him, that I was hopeless and he would leave me, that he would steal things of mine, and that he could beat me at chess any time he wanted to. He got an immense pleasure out of beating me, just as he got a great pleasure when he could show that people in his environment were afraid, made mistakes, had secret problems. He became the grand inquisitor of the institution, and became concerned about my need for psychiatric treatment. I found that I could use all these things to advantage by showing him how anxious and angry he got when I beat him, and how much he enjoyed being my master, or being the psychiatrist. There were periods of silence too when he was obviously anxious about his thoughts, or when instead of being aggressive he would try to change the subject or to lie down and ignore me.

Gradually he began to show me more openly how afraid he was that I would find out that he was crazy, defective, that I would make snappy, symbolic interpretations like those which had been made to him before, that I would seduce him and find out his secret thoughts, that he would get so excited that he would break things, or more and more, parts of his own body. He was continually hurting himself. Each step nearer to his secret thoughts was accompanied by warning bursts of aggression and an attempt to control me. This defense alternated with going to lie down on the sofa where he sometimes feigned sleep, but seemed to go to sleep at times, only to wake up with a jerk or get up suddenly from the couch with "It's no good lying down there—it's too hot in here—I get restless—this isn't helping." He was obviously excited and frightened. He began to show me how he was continually hurting his hands, and getting punished—and mentioned one of the reasons for his provocative behavior and uncontrollable fights with his cottage parents. He didn't like the way they looked at him, they seemed to see things in him, their eyes look frightened and accusing, they pried into his secrets so he became more provocative and this led to further physical attempts to control him which he fought with fiendish cleverness. I was able to show him that he feared that his secrets would excite and frighten them, that when he saw this he got frightened, had to attack and get the others to lose control. Finally he became so excited and frightened by the sexual talk and play in his cottage that he asked a counselor to whom he was attached if he thought S. could be a sex maniac. The counselor was encouraged to be supportive of his talking about fears so common to boys of his age—but also to tell him if he wanted special help with his fears to take them up with me. Shortly after that S. asked me: "Just what would you like to know most." I asked him to tell me what bothered him most of all—the worst problem. He then told me how he was afraid there was something wrong with his mind, he was too small, he kept hurting himself, his nose kept getting infected, that he was afraid I would drive him crazy—"Look at my hands." I told him that I thought we both knew what he was worried about now—that we both knew how common it is for boys of his age to be worried about these things, afraid they might go crazy—and that it all came from masturbation and loss of sexual control, as well as the punishment for it. I told him how afraid he must have been that I would find out these secrets, and say it's hopeless. He was silent—and eventually said, "How do you know you're right?" But he returned the next day to say "Maybe you're right" and to commence gradually to show me how concerned he was that his sexual thoughts and masturbation had hurt him. "Does smoking stunt your growth?" "Am I small for my age?" led to my repeated interpretations around masturbation anxieties which S. would listen to quietly while I reviewed all he had told me about things getting out of control and injuring him. At first he would answer noncommittally, "Maybe you're right," but continued to bring more and more material around his acting-out anxieties. He began to tell me about how the lack of controls in the institution tempted him and other boys, and then how they went out at night and raided the offices, store and records, took keys, picked locks and felt such an excitement about being above the law. They couldn't get caught. I showed him how this must represent another problem which he had been so afraid would be found out—his secret thoughts, and that he had to deny the danger on the one hand, and that he could be caught and be punished on the other. He began to tell me more and more about earlier fears about his size when he was four, about his sister being crazy and his anxiety when he was seven leading to his breaking his right arm, and then to his discovery of his right inguinal hernia when he was eleven, and his fear that he had injured himself forever. He remembered that his penis had bent to the right and that he had vague fears that that and the hernia came from the same thing, his masturbation.

S.'s aggression toward me became greatly reduced at this time, and he began to want me to help him and protect him—fearing openly that no one liked him, and showing his depression about the restrictions his illness placed on his mastery of reality. He started to go to public school where the principal let him go at his own speed, allowing him to come part time and to take only subjects he wanted to. His work in school was supplemented by tutoring outside school. He had nearly four years of academic work to make up in every subject but math and his reading was four to five years behind his age level. Although his energies (and aggression) became more available for reality mastery, such a considerable amount of aggressive acting out remained in the treatment situation that I was not able to transfer him to my private office until ten months after the analysis began.

S. began to go to public school about four months after the beginning of his analysis, and during the ensuing four months, his analysis was mainly concerned about the relationship of his anxiety and his aggression to his masturbation fantasies and their relationship to the transference (as manifested in his verbalizations and his acting out both within and outside the analytic hour). In general the material he brought was concerned with the fear that he would be seduced and his excitement would get out of bounds, or that he would not be enabled to develop a mastery of himself and his environment because of arbitrarily imposed controls—imposed by outside forces that would interfere with and frustrate his inner needs before he could come to grips with them himself. Aggression, therefore, was released to control (and destroy) the environment whenever inner or outer mastery was threatened.

I would like to give some examples:

(1) Soon after he began to go to public school, S. began to be greatly concerned that a policeman, who supervised the bus-stop areas near his school, was out to get him, and was a persecuting figure. He became very anxious that he would be detected (that his weakness would be found out), but also that the policeman would take advantage of him and attack him. His aggression became more and more provocative with the aim of getting the policeman to get out of control and to lose his position, but it also put him closer and closer to being attacked and hurt. He became terrified that his aggression would only succeed in getting him in the detention home where he would be deserted and subject to punitive measures (as he had in childhood).

(2) He felt the analysis as a very seductive and dangerous situation where I would lure his secrets out of him and then trap him. His fear was that I would abandon him and treat him as though he were crazy (like his parents). He was afraid that I would read things into his mind, seduce him with interpretations, and invite him like his mother to lose control. Then when he got an erection or intense passive excitement about having a vagina, he would lose his mastery of himself and be abandoned.

(3) In his cotttage he was in a constant terror that the sexual talk and behavior of the other boys would excite him so greatly that he would get out of control by masturbating or being involved in passive homosexual activities, mainly fellatio. This led him to make counterattempts to get the others out of control. It forced constant punitive action and at times his isolation in the infirmary.

(4) The thought of lying down on the couch was felt by him to be an expression of my wish to take something away from him, to castrate him, but it also intensified his passive homosexual fears. This led to his attempts to steal from me, to castrate me, to excite me and leave me hopeless, and then to stimulate anxiety in me that he would desert me, get me in trouble, find out my sexual problems and be my analyst.

In all these situations, despite his attempts to seduce and control me neurotically, he showed increasingly his need for me to be a protective figure and to stick with him patiently in his effort to come to grips with a mastery of reality himself. Despite all the difficulties of his life related to the inconsistent and neurotic attitudes of his parents, he had a great appreciation of their assets. His libidinal attachment to them had roots in real strengths of theirs which he exaggerated and idealized. He began to do the same with me, and it was the analysis of this passivity which eventually freed his aggression from its defensive and regressive outlets, and made it available for a more mature ego mastery.

At first he showed this in his great concern that he was castrated, and his need to have his father protect him. His father knew better than all the doctors, and so did I. Gradually it became possible to show him that he wanted my penis, to have me attack him, to give him a baby, enemas, to do it for him. His utilization of interpretations, although at first met by waves of aggression and negativism, were particularly dramatic on this passive basis. His success in life would be because of his father's wealth, my fame as an analyst; he would use his father's penis; he would get well because of my interpretations; he would only succeed in school if his tutor went over his lessons with him. As he felt he could never make up himself for what he had lost in the fundamentals of school work, he also was telling me that he felt he could never make up for the loss of standards and consistent training, steady love from his parents, that his penis was no good.

Behind this passivity lay the great anxiety that he had been injured, that he was defective, unloved, and at the same time afraid to venture, not only failure, but also success. To be left alone and helpless, to be abandoned was not only a guilty anticipation but a fear connected with losing control, and to succeed brought the same fear. Whenever his feminine excitement or his masculine excitement threatened to get out of control, S. felt strong castration anxiety which brought forth volleys of indiscriminate aggression. He did not want to do too well, nor too poorly, and he became a genius at just getting by. About five months after his analysis began, I unwisely told his parents that I thought S. might get well. They told him, and he gave me ample evidence that he could wreck the analysis if he wanted to. His acting out during the treatment hour became nearly unbearable. He feared I would see his intense excitement about succeeding, and he feared that I would get very excited and seduce him into succeeding too. He thought I had a detecting machine in a closet in the eaves, and when he looked in there and found none he threw loose plaster at me for days, and brought knives to attack me. He did not ever come close to really trying to hurt me with the knives, but used them to threaten and to test me. When I told him that the analysis could not continue with knives, he never brought them again. The fear to see and detect some secret or to be seen and detected led, however, to the memory of being discovered by his father (through an intercom system) in the act of seeing his sister un-dressed (when he was four or five). This led to many recollections of seeing his mother undressed, and how seductive and provocative she was. At this time he began to bring many of his masturbation anxieties in connection with similar fantasies, and began to show an exhibitionistic and pseudo-heterosexual interest in some of the girls in the institution who had a tendency to promiscuity. He became preoccupied with the word vagina, and the need to look and feel what was there but he did not have an erection when with such a girl. Instead he showed a renewed outburst of identification with helpless castrated people, and spoke again of his fears with the policeman who patrolled the bus stop near school. In some way he provoked the policeman's attention so that the latter called him into the police car, and talked dirty, insulted him, said he never had any use for the institutional children. S. did not help matters by telling the policeman, "You wouldn't have as much Kotex as a flea." Although I emphasized how provocative he was in this situation, and in many others, relating it to his behavior with me, I was only able to interpret the passivity in it gradually—how he would be attacked and made helpless in the analysis too. His fear of going to sleep, becoming weak, stunted, he related not only to overindulging and hurting his penis through activity, but it came out more and more clearly that his anxiety about lying down on a couch (as he knew adult patients did) was ter-rifying to him because he became passively excited, expecting me to attack him like the policeman. Shortly after this he told me of recurrent dreams that his sister, brothers, father and mother had died violently, and his associations led to his fears that through his masturbation fantasies and masturbation he had hurt his penis, and gotten his hernia, that an emission weakens you permanently—and "what happens if you have nose bleeds that won't stop?" He began to want to go home, was afraid he would never get away from me, and, after superficial interpretations of his fears around being passive, he started to talk about his fears of active and passive fellatio. Just as I had been cautious about insisting that S. lie down on the sofa, interpreting mainly from the side of his fear to lie down (ego anxiety about his unconscious wish), I attempted to interpret mainly on the defensive side his fear of my attack. When he continued to have aggressive outbreaks during the hour, or to steal things out of my car, I interpreted his fear that I would attack and steal from him, make him helpless. He tried once to grab at my genitals and I could show him his fear that I would attack him, as well as wanting to arouse me. As far as I could stop him when he attacked me or my car, I did, and continued to show him how afraid he must be to talk about his thoughts. I hid my car, and took every possible opportunity to rob his acting out of any gratification, to show him how it hurt him realistically and impeded the analysis.

A visit of his parents brought out his anxieties around exposure to the primal scene, and to going home for a vacation. He told me how his parents had him sleep with them in their hotel room, though in a separate cot. His main fears were that he would get into uncontrollable rages with his mother because of her seductiveness, and would be envious of his sibling, and would become a slave to his father's wishes. His father was continually threatening, bribing and seducing S. with presents which he lost or broke. He pictured his father as a strong, self-made man who was a big-time operator, owned considerable real estate, nice cars, etc. He feared he could only succeed by getting something passively from his father, and yet he was terrified because it meant "You can never have an adequate penis of your own." If he got a new watch without having to be accountable for losing or damaging the old, it meant that he could never do anything about the damage sustained through masturbation.

At this time S.'s aggression continued to come out in attempts to control and to be the psychiatrist—asking if I was afraid of him, if I had some secret, "Why don't you answer?" Several times I mimicked him, pounding the table, and once I said, "Dr. M., you don't frighten me but I'll sure scare you." He could laugh with me at this point, and then he told me spontaneously that he had noticed one thing, "When I think about sex and get excited, then I get angry; but now I don't want you to end the hour." As vacation came nearer he spoke of wanting to leave early, and he came to see that his aggression was partly to ward off his passive wishes, and partly to beat me to leaving. He went home expecting to stay four days, afraid he would not be wanted, and would be exposed to excitements he could not master. But he had a good time, and both he and his parents expressed very warm feelings about the successful vacation.

From that time on S.'s aggressive acting out in the hour was typically adolescent behavior, and in a relatively short time he was coming to my private office and lying down on the couch. A good many of his fears of having an erection and exciting me, or of having a passive excitement and exciting me to attack him sexually came out while he was moving on and off the couch in an experimental way. When he had tested me and himself enough to be sure he would not bring about a sexual acting out between us—but could more safely bring his fantasies and apply the analytic work to areas where his ego activities were restricted socially, athletically and in his school work, he stayed on the couch.

After his return from summer vacation S. began to try to get me to tell him what he had to do in school, during the hour, and fought taking the responsibility for giving his associations, for working at his problems, but by now his wish to take part actively in the resolution of his neurotic problems had become so strong that he was readier to face the anxiety of giving up, not only his aggressive acting out, but, to some extent, his passive dependence on me, as a protector. He began to engage much more actively in social life at school where he attended classes all day, as well as in athletics, and in his studies. He was anxious about the change to my private office in that he would be alone with me, but he felt it as a promotion (in accord with his own increased confidence in himself). He began to work through some of his anxieties that he had hurt himself through masturbation, and could not take an active role in learning to master football, and mathematics within his real potentialities. He showed in many ways his fears to make mistakes and learn by them, and to lie down on the couch, to expose himself to the passivity of having his thoughts come freely, to expose his secrets. He began to show how afraid he was to be admired, to be successful because of the danger that he would be valued for his success and not for himself. He feared being seduced and used in the analysis both for my selfish sexual and professional gain, and this led to the emergence of his memories of many experiences with his parents where he felt that he had been the victim of their exhibitionism, and their need to have him gratify their sexual needs as well as to be their scapegoat. He brought out wishes to have big things like his father's and eventually began to realize that he wanted his father's penis (and in the analysis, mine). That is, he valued me for my penis. On the other hand, he feared the weakness that this narcissistic need was associated with. He feared to see that I had human weaknesses and that behind his narcissistic idealization of me lay the poverty of inner strengths that he felt in his parents and himself. He associated this with his passive, homosexual attitude. He began to be much more active in doing his school work, in taking an active part in his tutoring, in football, in his analysis; as he did, his anxieties about his sexualization of his activities became more prominent. He was afraid that he would be endangered by competing with other boys in two ways, (1) as a rival, and (2) by exciting their attack homosexually. He was afraid that his tutor would resent his growing activity, and also that he would provoke him to take advantage of his helplessness. He was afraid that the other boys and coach would be jealous of his ability to play football, and try to take it away from him. In this regard he became aware of his jealousy of me when he saw how he coveted my car, my pencil, my job, my personal attributes, and actually tried in moments of acting out to grab my penis. He also wanted to deny his homosexual wishes to get something from me, to get me to be active, to mobilize my aggression and interest by being feminine. It was this attitude that he could be passive and feminine that corresponded to his acceptance of lying down on the couch and his enjoyment of my power as his analyst. (In his mind he was also competing with his parents who had been in treatment, and doing them one better.)

His bisexual conflict came out clearly in one football game where his team lost 28-0. One of the key players on his team was missing, and S. felt that it represented the danger of a one-man team. No one person should become too important. I might let him down, and he might let me down. He related this to his penis which might be hurt by masturbation. He felt he had been weak at certain key moments that might have saved the game—because he had masturbated the day before. The excitement of the analysis might hurt him and reveal his weakness in the same way through punishment for his aggression and the emergence of his femininity. He feared I would take over 28-0, and he feared to be outstanding in victory himself. He wondered whether I would be like his coach—get excited when he did well, or interfere because of my own needs (like his parents) or get disgusted because of my personal interest in the outcome of the analysis and yank him. It was a fear that I would be like S. too, and then it would be the blind leading the blind. It led to his fantasy that he would destroy me through his passive homosexual attachment to me, steal my penis and wreck it. He had passive fantasies dating back to his earliest memories of being read to and receiving a magic gift to protect himself, and prevent the helplessness that his masturbation excitement had brought on him, either that he could not control erections and aggressive behavior toward me, or fantasies of having a vagina and being raped on the couch. And yet, despite his continual need to get magic presents, I showed him how great his fear was that his father's presents meant "You are hopeless, you need magic." It was only gradually that the analysis came to belong to S. and to be something he could work at for himself. His attitude toward his penis was the same. His anger continually broke out whenever I attacked defenses which protected him from looking at his helplessness, his wish to avoid responsibility. On the other hand, he showed me how much he valued and feared me as his analyst. He told me that the difference between a psychiatrist and a psychoanalyst was that the first did not stay with you but the latter did, so that gradually you could have free speech when you finally got to trust him ("When you die, Doc?"). He told me a story of a man who told *all* but got hung because his lawyers forgot the divine right of kings. This led him to ask who Freud was—then to questions what my powers were? Did I have secrets about being a father and starting a baby, or a mother growing one, both secret wishes. In his anxiety about his fantasies (which I related to the primal scene) he became very aggressive and became the analyst. He had fantasies what I did with a pretty woman patient, and did I prefer her to him. He wanted to know if there were any good women psychiatrists so he could talk "just between us girls." More and more he brought his fantasies that masturbation had made him feminine, no one respected him, how would he ever be anything but a hopeless criminal. Could I save him? Will he ever stop breaking pencils, chewing gum? As he got closer to his innermost problems, he showed his concern about secrecy in the analysis, and would I run from or be alarmed about his secret. He tried to show me how he provoked others to get out of control and struggled not to drink, drive fast in cars, be under homosexual sway of other boys. (I supported him in not acting out but talking about it in the analysis. Instead of trying to ingratiate delinquents passively, I reminded him how talking about problems had increased his mastery of himself.) This led to his fear that I would see his sexual secrets which would lay him open to the danger I would think him crazy, or take advantage of his passive fantasies.

When his parents came to visit again, he became very excited, afraid he would steal, was preoccupied with committing the perfect crime, could he stop chewing gum, would he be able to show he could succeed at school. He was afraid he would have to sleep in his parents' hotel room again, and brought out fantasies of wanting what his father had. I told him I thought he must have seen something exciting that made him wish to steal his father's penis. (S. was worried and I told him I thought he was old enough to have his own room, and supported him in his attempt to educate his parents.) He brought out his fear to be impotent with girls when dancing, to have his car stall, to make mistakes, to lose control, to fail if he were president of his class. In all was his fear to be castrated because of his bisexual primal scene fantasies. After this followed a remarkable anxiety in which he could not decide whether to be *active* or *passive*, to *succeed* or *fail* in which his associations led to the perfect crime again. He had seen a movie where a crime is committed (murder) which cannot be detected or proven, although the criminal was suspected and put in jail. When he is acquitted, he confesses, but "he can't be tried again or circumcised." S. had meant to say circumstanced—but it led him to the thought of wanting his mother, and wanting to have a foreskin. He wanted me to protect and cover him like a woman when he got his football letter at assembly, but he did not want me exposed, like his penis. Then he thought of the secret on the battleship at the atom blast in Pacific—KILROY WAS HERE. He stole a pencil on my desk and held it up when he got to the door to show me—ran out defying me.

After this S. made rapid strides in school despite the fact that he said that I was standing in his way. "Do you think I like being your slave all the time? I know what I want now." He was afraid I would interfere too much in his life, and when he read to me about Ben Franklin, the self-made man, and Teddy Roosevelt who changed from an asthmatic weakling to the man with the big stick, he was waiting for me to interfere when he flubbed. Then he would break out in a frenzy of anger, and if I let him struggle or praised his improvement, he also became very angry. Soon after this he went home for a vacation, anxious that he would see his mother naked, or find his father alternately in a rage (castrating) or helpless and weak. In reality he had a good time, partly by avoiding acting out with his parents. On his return from home, he began to take a position of leadership, and criticize the delinquency in his cottage, suggesting more realistic standards and controls, and elimination of the most disturbed delinquents. His aggression became directed to reality and ego-mastering activities in a sudden spurt, but he was afraid of succeeding too much lest (1) I would be jealous, and (2) I would get too excited. These fantasies were correlated with fears (1) that he would have to face rivalry with other boys if he showed too much interest in girls at school (who openly showed their wish he would be more aggressive), and (2) that girls were helpless and passive. He became very excited and upset over his social worker's pregnancy because he felt attracted to and identified with her. Increasingly he showed me his fears of succeeding in the analysis, with his school work, in studying on his own. He became very aggressive verbally and in action over his fear that if he lost his symptoms I would say he was ready to leave, and he would be left at the mercy of fantasies not yet mastered, of uncontrolled masturbation. He continued to show marked aggression whenever he felt I would interfere (because his thoughts were dangerous) or that I would abandon him while his inner conflicts were still unsolved. He became more and more critical of my deviations from the analytic rules (if I helped him with his reading or would not think he needed more analysis after his symptoms cleared up). It was during the next six months (twelve to eighteen months after his analysis began), that his interest in the work of the analysis became a constant struggle for increasing ego mastery and a fusion of aggressive and erotic energy as this became more and more available for reality testing and gratification. Here are some examples of this:

(1) He stole a doughnut in the cafeteria at school and was caught by the assistant principal. When the potential seriousness of this was pointed out to S., he reacted with real concern about himself. "How could I take a chance with something that means so much to me?" was his question, and he looked anxiously at his own inner lack of responsibility and concern for others. He offered to help stop all petty thievery in the dining room, and began quite courageously to take a position of leadership in this regard.

(2) One day in recess he was wrestling playfully with another boy in the hallway while waiting for a short walk to the bus in the cold. An overprim, unpopular teacher wrongly accused S. of other actions that day which he had not been involved in, and S. told him too honestly that he was wrong and criticized him for being impulsive—which he had been. When S. was sent to see the principal, the latter was very understanding and agreed with him that the teacher was annoying and difficult. Then he said, "But S., you could have done better, though you have improved a great deal. It's not what you say that's out of line, it's how you say it." S. was impressed that this was right and wanted to figure out how he could handle the teacher better the next time. "Help him to stop what scares him" was his thought.

He began to realize that he had many fears about being helpless in the analysis, about having me see something first, look over him as he lay on the couch, see him have an erection (how I influenced him), or see his passives wishes. He gave many examples of being identified with his mother and girls, passive boys, and of inviting attack by his helplessness. He wanted to steal or get a present from me, and though he feared a woman's helplessness, he felt that a woman can hurt and castrate a man too. His fear of woman was partly based on his feeling that they would seduce him if he was aggressive, that their passivity frightened him, and that he felt their envy and their castrating potentialities would then be unleashed. And so he brought out his feeling that it was safer to be a woman in ways and get his father's riches that way. He also brought up many fantasies that he was imperfect when he was born, too small, too much trouble, that he was not loved, that he would never get a real chance to grow without interference or abandonment. He had fantasies much like those of Tristram Shandy that his whole life had been affected by circumstances at the time of his conception, something had gone wrong, and he connected this with fears that a fight would break out in the analysis, that he would come to no good end in the analysis, that I would not give him the love to enable him to continue. He began to be able to speak about his love for me, for what he felt to be my humanity and interest in him, and how fearful he had been to show his need to give and take affection. He used more of his aggression in working at the analysis, in trying to work at school, and to take more and more responsibility in his cottage. He wanted to show me what he knew about chess, to speak about the analysis as a piece of work which fascinated him. He wanted to become a scientist, an analyst, and he worked on a project of building a box which was a periscope in reverse. It was to look in from outside into his secret life, it was to look into his parents' bedroom, it was to divine the secrets of my life and how I came to have such an enviable and gratifying life work. And when he became anxious that I was getting too near his secrets for comfort, he wanted to attack me in chess and take my queen, or he viewed analysis as a sadistic weapon of the analyst, and he attacked me in every area where he could see any weakness. "Don't you ever clean under your chairs? Been seeing any analysts lately? Why do you help me sometimes and not others? Mighty poor technique, Dr. Crocker!" He would talk to keep me from saying anything.

One year and six months after his analysis began, S. had caught up in every subject except English, and his greatest difficulty remained in reading. He related his fear of success to the fear of becoming excited and injuring himself through masturbation, and he became obsessed again with the thought of having a hole, a vagina, and being raped. Success would lead him to lose his mastery of himself, he would be punished, and it seemed as though his femininity emerged behind this. He went through a period of passive idealization of me and his father. He brought out his interest in his mother's erotic interest in her analyst. Despite his great gains in school and in his social life, in his increasing independence with his family, he remained attached to me passively and could not succeed without me, and feared very much the ending of the analysis (which I tentatively set for six months ahead).

An increasing amount of material began to emerge around S.'s fear of dirt, and his increasing compulsiveness, secrecy and interest in acquiring money and power. He was afraid of an excitement that would lead him to explosions of dirty anal talk, and of being jumped on by his cottage parents and losing control over his clothes, money. He began to say that his cottage mother had no control over him, and to show outbursts of his old aggression over her attempts to control him.

At this same time S.'s father had begun to have great anxieties about his son's increasing independence and leadership in his home, and also about his own finances. Although he was having business reverses, he refused to sacrifice any of his extensive property to pay his bill at the institution. The extent to which he cheated in buying railroad tickets for S., and his dishonest accumulation of money at the expense of others, made more understandable some of the lacunae in S.'s superego. S. revealed many fantasies at this time, related to memories of his father getting repeated enemas from his mother, about his own similar wishes in the analysis. And at the same time he brought out a tremendous aggression against his mother, and blamed his father's weakness on her. He described his uncontrollable fury that she would encourage him to buy his own clothes, and then control the purchase of every piece of clothing, that she would give him money, and then tell him what to do with it. I drew his attention to his expression, "It's a lot of crap." In his fear that I would abandon him before he had attained a mastery over his productions, or that I would have to control him rigidly, and interfere with his freedom to use his new-found energies, I was able to show him that he was having the same conflict in the analysis. He went back to memories of how as a child he had been alternately seduced and rigidly controlled so that he had not been able to develop a mastery of himself. He remembered having to wait so long once that he soiled his underwear when he became frightened by a fight his parents had. He was humiliated by his loss of control. On the other hand, he remembered having a temper tantrum and throwing things around in a hopeless mess, when his mother in her anxiety tried to come into the bathroom when he was having a BM to see how he was doing. His father's ultimatum that he was stopping S.'s analysis hit him the same way. It brought out the deepest sadness and misery within him over the feeling of abandonment, a panic that things would get out of control, and a rage that he felt might lead him to wreck the institution, his home, and kill his father. All the fierce resentment over having his gradually emerging mastery interfered with seethed in him. Despite this S. was able to take a strong stand with his father, and at the same time to understand his father's illness and reach out to him (because of his own experience). Fortunately, I was able to mobilize the father's energies enough (as I described earlier in this paper), so that the analysis continued as I had planned.

After a relatively happy summer vacation, during which he worked on his reading, consolidated his social life at home, and tested his new-found independence at home, S.'s analysis bogged down for two months in the fall while his father threatened to stop the analysis, and fought with the institution about money. The log jam was broken by firm reminders to S.'s father that the reading problem and other difficulties needed further work, and that S. needed time to separate from me.

The final layer which emerged in S.'s analysis came largely out of the analysis of some of the reasons for his reading problem, and his symptoms of alternately swearing off gum and cigarettes and chewing two or three packs of gum during the hour, smoking furiously after he left. He was afraid I would let his reading problem, his gum chewing and his smoking go untended—and that as the end of the analysis grew closer he would lose his power to do anything about them. He was also afraid that I would help and control him too much, and prevent him from gaining a mastery in that way too. He was afraid to look at the words and to take them in—just as he was afraid to listen to me many times, and he gradually became aware that he had impulses to suck my penis, which he had to ward off. These were associated with memories of the excitement of taking showers with his father, and seeing his penis. His inability to read the word "success" at all brought out its connection with this conflict. It also had active aggressive meanings for him. Finally it was related to fantasies around sucking his thumb, nursing and fears that it couldn't be controlled—as well as to memories of rigid interference with his sucking his thumb, drinking out of a bottle, and the freedom to learn how to feed himself, and eat what he liked. His oral aggression came out in explosive bursts, and was related to his feeling that he could not have the freedom to choose what he read or ate or take what he wanted from the analysis. He was afraid he had to do what I wanted.

I was interested in the last two months of S.'s analysis (after the anlysis of this oral material) to see the emergence of his activity, and the many ways in which he showed an increasingly aggressive but creative responsibility for himself and his milieu. He took a very active leadership in his cottage; he had a tendency to attack the director of the institution but in a much more reasonable and realistic way (that is, to fight for constructive changes). He became quite popular at school, and was very touched when his classmates gave him a party when he left. He caught up in all his subjects and enjoyed athletics because he had learned to profit by mistakes, and not to be so afraid of success.

Throughout the last six months of his analysis, he became more and more attached to a girl in his class, and able to show his jealousy of other boys and compete for her. In his associations he found how much this girl resembled his mother and in the transference—me. Two main themes stood out in the last few weeks. S. became increasingly concerned about his positive feelings toward me and that they might get out of control, and lead him to act crazy, to have an explosion. He felt I was not doing anything to stop this, and that his girl friend was exciting him too much. On the other hand, he expressed increasing sadness and anger that the analysis was stopping, as well as relief. He told me that he was going to move his bedroom away from being next to his parents' bedroom at home, and that he was afraid he would not find someone as important to him as his girl friend at home. The analysis of his fear of girls brought out very strongly his fear and guilt that he would hurt them, and be a victim of their counterattack. In another way he felt that they would excite him too much and then humiliate him by leaving him. He developed considerable anxiety in the analysis that he might shout, that we might get in a fight and that he would hurt me by succeeding in many ways. He was especially afraid that he might say "mother fucker" to his science teacher—a man, and he said it frequently to other boys. He pointed out to me how sensitive they were about this. Shortly after this S. developed acute anxieties (connected with a doctor's prophecy, reported in the papers, that the end of the world was at hand) that his end was at hand. He was afraid that I would throw him out of the analysis if he mentioned fantasies about my having intercourse with my wife. He was not only afraid of his rivalrous feelings in this regard, but was afraid that my anger would be particularly great if he proved superior to me in any area. He thought of Disney's movie of the elk and the fights of the males. "Boy when they're through, they're through." He tried out his new-found strength on me, and after a long, searching criticism of me, he said, "Well I guess you can take it." But it was necessary to show him his passive defense against his aggression in many areas before he could finally tell me of his fears to take his mother away from his father (by taking showers with her, by having her come to witness his success at school and in his analysis). He connected this with the memory of getting an erection once when his mother exposed herself to him in the bathroom, and asked him to look at her. He turned away, but saw her in the mirror. This led to an aggressive outbreak of destruction (yelling and throwing things at her), after which he was isolated and beaten by his father. After this he told me that his parents were going away for a vacation soon with all the children. S. told me there were four bedrooms where they were going, one for his parents, one for his two brothers, one for the maid, and one for him and his sister. When he had told me this he became very anxious, and, for the last time, acted out his aggression in my office. He accused me of ending the analysis and sending him away too soon, threw some papers off my desk and threatened to telephone the police. When I said, "What are you so frightened of you can't talk about?" he screamed at me, "What else can I do—there's no other room for me to sleep in than with P. What's so bad about that?" I said I thought he could do something about it, but that he was afraid, because of his previous excitement with P. and his mother that he couldn't, that no one would stop him, least of all his father—so he had to provoke someone to stop him. S. got back on the couch and related then how frightened he had been when P. had gone away for treatment, that their incestuous behavior had made her crazy, and he connected this with his feelings about circumcision—that he had lost his foreskin for the same reason. "Why do I feel like standing up and shouting—I almost said shitting?" I said it made me think he might have seen his parents having intercourse, and felt terribly excited, cried out. Shortly after this the father of a boy at the institution died just as the boy was about to return home for good. S. was terribly understanding of this boy and spoke to him with deep sympathy. It was genuine and was related to his coming loss of me. That it was related to his own feelings of anxiety over his aggression toward his father was revealed in S.'s remark about the worst part of it, "He'll probably think he did it." Whereas he would get angry and hurt or leave his girl three months earlier whenever he got too excited, he was successful later in getting moved to her classroom and in having the courage to show her that he liked her and would miss her.

In connection with his increasing ability to stand up to the director or to do his own work, S. told me of his increasing disillusionment with his father, and his realization that I was human. He reviewed jokingly and warmly some of the mistakes I had made as his analyst—"remember the time you told me to call you David"—"remember the time you told Mrs. W. she was wrong—you sure got sucked in that time." "You told my parents you could cure me. How did you know?" He told me he had decided to become a lawyer—"I don't want to be a scientist any more— I enjoy arguing and winning, like I used to beat you in chess, too much." These attitudes were related to the ability to see his own penis as valuable, and see how he had idealized his father and me.

The analysis ended with the recognition that he was ready to go home, and that he still had many problems, one of which was his depression at being left by me. He related it mainly to fantasies of being left out and secret thoughts that I loved someone else better. They were related to the primal scene. I told him that I hoped he would get in touch with me if he wanted to see me for any reason. This was in answer to his question, could he come to see me once in a while after he saw how things were going? One of his practical worries was about his reading. While he was up to the ninth grade in all other school work, and well able to compete in public school, he did need continued remedial work in reading which was still at seventh to eighth grade level. I also had considerable doubts about the effects of his parents' difficulties on his further progress—even though I had evidence that his analysis had strengthened him a good deal.

Summary

Uncontrolled aggression was at first mainly an expression of the ego's loss of mastery of libidinal conflicts, and was used defensively in an infantile, destructive and controlling way. As the libidinal conflicts gradually came more under the control of the ego, and the conflicts around masturbation and the primal scene were analyzed, the aggression could be fused more with libidinally realistic activities, and contribute to the ego mastery of reality. The crucial trauma seems to have taken place around the uncontrolled, and seductive stimulations which took place in all phases of libidinal development, which led to a breakdown of ego mastery, and the release of aggression in temper tantra and other destructive ways, some of them self-destructive. Another source of the outbreaks of aggression was the interference with ego mastery in all phases of libidinal development, characterized by times of rigid control of oral, anal and genital behavior (Buxbaum, 1947). The resultant frustration of libidinal gratification through overstimulation and rigid control brought the release of aggression in an uncontrolled way. It was also used defensively to control the dangerous environment, but not realistically. Hence the severe conflict with reality. Important sources of uncontrolled aggression were connected with difficulty in the mastery of oral and anal libido, and the analysis of earlier material connected with these then led to a more complete emergence of the oedipal material. This led to the uncovery and working through of fantasies around the primal scene in which loss of control and castration and violence played a prominent part. The aggressive acting out was thus a direct representation of the primal scene excitement as well as a defense against his homosexual excitement. In his fantasy of injury at conception lay the excitement which he felt he could not master, which had injured him psychically and emotionally.[3] This may have represented the origin of his aggression, a reaction to the helpless excitement of witnessing the primal scene. As energy involved in his conflict became available to the ego for reality mastery in his social relationships, athletically and his school work, S. took a more and more responsible and masterful position, and was able to use his aggression for healthy narcissism and to deepen his object relationships. He was able to succeed in many areas, as well as to learn from failure. Whether he became strong enough to deal with the illness of his parents remains to be seen. I should think it would depend on the strength of the fusion of aggression and libido in developing and maintaining stable reality satisfactions and ego functions and the extent to which the unconscious conflict has come under the sway of the ego, guided by his own superego.

BIBLIOGRAPHY

Buxbaum, E. (1947), Activity and Aggression in Children. *Am. J. Orthopsychiat.,* XVII.

Freud, A. (1949), Aggression in Relation to Emotional Development: Normal and Pathological. *This Annual,* III/IV.

—— (1954), Problems of Technique in Adult Analysis. *Bull. Philadelphia Assoc. Psa.,* IV.

Hartmann, H.; Kris, E.; Loewenstein, R. M. (1949), Notes on the Theory of Aggression. *This Annual,* III/IV.

[3] I wish to acknowledge the suggestion of this idea and further ramifications of it to Dr. Maurits Katan, who elaborated it when I first presented this paper.

THE INITIAL PHASE OF CONCOMITANT TREATMENT OF TWINS

ELINOR W. DEMAREST, M.D. and
MURIEL CHAVES WINESTINE, M.S. (New York)[1]

The concomitant treatment of preschool age fraternal twins is presented in its initial phase because it provided an unusual opportunity to understand further the implications of separation of twins from each other as revealed during the therapeutic process. The initial phase of therapy,[2] a period of three months, encapsulated two main problems: how the introduction of therapy upset the formerly established equilibrium between the twins, and how each differed in her ability to utilize treatment. This initial phase shed some further light upon the problem of individuation[3] and the development of object relationship in twins, an area of focus in the growing psychoanalytic interest in twins. The treatment of these twins within the Council Child Development Center[4] provided a unique opportunity to observe their behavior prior to and following the introduction of therapy.

Prior to the influence of psychoanalytic theory, studies on twins traditionally focused upon the problem of heredity versus environment. It became apparent that material obtained during the adult analysis of

---

[1] This case was seen in joint supervision by Augusta Alpert, Ph.D. The authors wish to express their deep appreciation for her supervisory help and for her criticism of this paper.

[2] Upon the termination of treatment, the authors intend to report more fully on the treatment process and ensuing development of the twins.

[3] The term individuation is used to denote the degree of separation of the child from the mother and, in this case, from the other twin.

[4] The Council Child Development Center is an agency devoted to the treatment of emotionally disturbed children and their parents. The Center program consists of a therapeutic nursery for children of two and a half to five and a half years; of a clinical department for the treatment of selected children from the nursery who are seen three times a week in a setting physically separated from the nursery; and of an outpatient department for the purposes of intake, diagnostic study, and referral service. The twins were assigned to different therapists. Susan is being treated by Dr. Demarest and Ann by Mrs. Winestine.

a single twin promised to contribute to our greater understanding of sibling relationships (Karpman, 1953; Orr, 1941). Burlingham (1952), while not basing her observations and conclusions on data obtained in an analytic situation, reported painstaking observations of identical twins by persons who were in close living arrangements with the children. Indeed, hers is now the definitive, conceptual work in the area of twin relationships and delineates the phases which take place as the twinship unravels. Although the problems of fraternal twins do not exactly parallel those characteristic of identical twins, a common denominator does exist—a sibling relationship in siblings who happen to be born at the same time. "It would seem that feelings of being identical are established even in fraternal twins if only because they are living in the same stage of development and in close proximity and constantly see their own emotions played out in front of them" (Burlingham, 1952). Her material was collected in the Hampstead Nurseries, a residential home for children in England during World War II. While she richly describes how the twins jockey for the attention of mother substitutes, their prolonged separation from the real parents prevented an adequate evaluation of how the real mother consciously and unconsciously experienced and influenced each twin. When twins reside within their own home, there is bound to be one twin at one time who is preferred by the mother and the other twin may substitute other persons in the family constellation (including her twin), in an attempt to compensate for the loss of the mother to the chosen twin.

The study of this pair of twins impressed the authors with the complications that "twinship" adds to the development of object relationship. A twin not only has the problem of individuating himself from the mother but also from the other twin. This need to individuate himself from the mother and from the other twin will occur at the same stage of development and so presents each twin with a dual task. It could be hypothesized that the twin can make one individuation while not making the other, or rather that this is a quantitative process in which one individuation will be more complete than the other.

Historical Background

Problems of Twinship: The twins, Susan and Ann, now five years of age, were enrolled in the nursery at the Council Child Development Center at the age of three years seven months because of difficulties which the mother attributed to their "twinness." It seemed clearly established that while feelings of sadness and happiness oscillated between them, a dominant-submissive pattern was rigidly established, to a degree greater than is typical of twin relationships as reported by Burlingham (1952). Susan was the dominant and controlling of the pair, while Ann was the submissive and compliant. Ann imitated and followed Susan's lead, so that mutual play acquired a character imposed by Susan.

Inbreeding in the Marriage: A brief account of the complicated inbreeding of this family will serve as an additional framework in which to see the twins. Mr. and Mrs. A. are first cousins whose respective mothers were sisters and who had also married first cousins, two brothers. Mrs. A.'s mother died when she was fourteen years of age, at which time she and three older siblings moved into the home of Mr. A.'s family. She continued there as a regular member of that household until the time of her marriage to Mr. A. It is known from studies of primitive peoples, that the arrival of twins, while sometimes a good omen, has been considered to be the work of the devil and a portent of ill luck. While speculation upon this matter would go beyond the scope of this paper, it seems likely that in this marriage the production of twins intensified the anxiety in the mother and provided an additional basis for having markedly polarized her ambivalence toward an accepted and a rejected twin.

Developmental History: The parents had planned a second pregnancy to provide companionship for the first sibling, Harry, who is three years and three months older than the twins. The mother reacted to the news that she was going to bear twins with depression and dejection. The father responded with exaggerated humor and denial of the responsibility of rearing twins. The twins were full-term infants, Susan being born first and uneventfully. Ann followed three minutes later in a breach presentation with the aid of low forceps. Care was administered alternately to each infant by the mother and a succession of maids. The mother felt she sacrificed emotional care for the exigencies of routine. The twins were bottle fed according to a schedule that was established for both children by Susan's rhythm. Ann was often awakened in order to be fed at the same time as Susan. Ann frequently vomited after such feedings. Susan seemed to have a greater sucking need, making sucking motions and noises between meals. Ann evidenced a need for more sleep than Susan and was disturbed by the latter's cooing. Susan needed a blanket at bedtime while Ann became fussy, requesting the mother's presence. Frequent attempts were made to restrain Susan when she wished to be active and Ann required quiet.

Susan's developmental curve preceded Ann's by approximately two months. Ann showed marked awareness of Susan's advanced achievements and strove to emulate her. Bowel training was introduced simultaneously for both children and proved to be an arduous and traumatic experience for them both. It was characterized by their resistance and withholding, which was handled by inconsistent and punitive behavior from the mother and maid. Ann, it was thought, was the more fearful in this area, hiding her movements, whereas Susan told the mother and insisted that only the mother could change her. Ann also seemed more fearful regarding dogs, new situations, and social groups. Susan had more physical illnesses than Ann, developing a "bronchial asthmatic" condition about the age of three. At the age of four years and eight months, Susan was hospitalized upon the mother's insistence, for the removal of a benign neck cyst, following a removal of a breast cyst in the mother.

Mother-Twin Relationship: The mother complained of her inability to gain full satisfaction from either child and, during their infancy, yearned to be with one child at a time. Nevertheless, a strong preference for Susan over Ann was early established because Susan was the first-born and more wanted child. She felt Susan bore a stronger family resemblance than Ann who, although prettier, seemed like an "outsider." Indeed, it was from outsiders that Ann gained more attention, and the mother used this fact further to rationalize her tendency to favor Susan. The mother also expressed preference for the more dynamic and active personality of Susan in contrast to Ann whom she thought the less interesting and more phlegmatic. The mother attempted to help others differentiate the two girls and attempted to follow the latest advice regarding the rearing of twins, for example, dressing them differently. Nevertheless, the above-described factors determining her preference and her own ego deficiency mitigated her capacity to individuate herself from each twin. Thus she fostered problems of individuation and object relatedness in them. She consistently permitted Susan to thwart Ann's early attempts to seek contact with the mother: Susan shouted Ann down when the latter attempted to talk with the mother; Susan could not sleep unless the mother left Ann's bedside and the room, until Ann finally stopped all her requests for the mother's presence; Susan attacked the mother when Ann attempted to seek solace from her at times when Susan had sat on Ann or had forcibly taken something from Ann, until finally Ann also stopped these overtures. The mother worked part time for a short period when the girls were two and a half years of age. Susan then began to have temper tantrums and could only be calmed by the mother picking her up and removing her to another room where they would be alone together. The mother felt that each twin had a negative effect upon the other, thus creating a more difficult task for her: Ann would have been less difficult to rear without the stimulating effect of Susan; Susan displayed fears only by "contagion" and exposure to Ann. The mother expressed unmitigated hatred of Ann whom she perceived as being cold, mechanical, and remote. Ann did not communicate her needs, and the mother felt incapable of understanding or meeting them. Although Susan was the more troublesome, the mother felt that she could empathize with and help Susan and that there was a mutual satisfaction derived from their closeness. The mother, who has been receiving psychiatric treatment since the twins were approximately three years old, responded to the twins' treatment by overidentifying with and unconsciously reinforcing Susan's resistance to treatment. At the same time she sensed the readiness with which she handed Ann over to her therapist.

Father-Twin Relationship: The father employed denial as a major defense against his anxiety concerning the marriage and sought little close contact with the twins. He preferred the company of Harry to either girl. Since Ann often chose to be with Harry, she was indirectly in contact with the father whom she tended to perceive as a big brother, a bigger Harry. During his absences from the home, Susan dictated long letters to him which were written by the mother. Susan responded to him more affectionately upon his return than Ann who showed more interest in his gift than in his person.

Twin-Twin Relationship: The dominant-submissive relationship between Susan and Ann has been described above. As depicted by Burlingham (1952), a gang pattern of behavior developed between the ages of three and four years. They became wild, noisy, and destructive of the furniture in their bedroom, which they shared. Susan instigated this behavior and Ann invariably followed her lead. Their speech was a gibberish, well understood by each other and addressed to each other. Only gradually did it improve so that others could also understand it. Susan was remarkably more verbal than Ann, having long talks with the mother. Susan shouted down Ann when the latter attempted to talk with the mother. Susan did not appear particularly upset during a separation from Ann, while Ann showed anxiety when Susan went away from her and considerably more joy upon their reunion. Ann revealed greater manual dexterity and ability to concentrate upon tasks, frequently finishing such tasks for Susan. The mother summed up their relationship by saying: "Ann serves as Susan's hands, but Susan is like a drug for Ann and Ann cannot do without Susan."

Sibling-Twin Relationship: From an early age, Harry played more with Ann than with Susan because Ann yielded completely to his domination whereas he and Susan clashed. He provided Ann with the only relationship unmonopolized by Susan, since Susan tended also to gain the attention of household help. Susan offered no objection to the relationship between Ann and Harry because at these times she enjoyed the uncontested possession of the mother. The latter subtly sanctioned the couple of Harry and Ann during which time she was free to be alone with Susan. Harry had a sexually stimulating effect upon Ann as well as upon Susan when she occasionally joined them in "roughhousing." He expressed appreciation of Ann's talents and manual dexterity, and she frequently designated her productions as presents for Harry. While this relationship with Harry is overdetermined, it seems clear that he represents for Ann a model of singleness in contrast to her twinness.

NURSERY EXPERIENCE

On the basis of the intake study and prolonged observation of the twins in a weekly group, it was decided to separate the twins and to place them in different nursery groups. This constituted their first significant separation from each other. From the initial evaluation it was felt that Ann's greater manual dexterity would enable her to use the older group, while Susan's possessive need for an adult could better be met by the teachers of the younger group.

Both girls are thin, brown-haired and brown-eyed with a marked pallor and deep circles under their eyes. They both present a generally bedraggled appearance and often are shabbily dressed. Ann remains the prettier of the two.

Initially Ann demanded the mother's presence in school more so than did Susan, who consistent with past behavior displayed greater ease in initially adapting to a new situation. After Ann's demands diminished, Susan increased her demands for the mother. She also established a clinging, demanding relationship with her teacher, verbalizing "Only me, just me." It seemed unlikely that she would have been able to remain in school without the mother's constant presence had not this teacher been available to her. She missed many school days because of illness. Susan's clinging utterly immobilzed this teacher, making it impossible for her to comfort Susan. Ann also developed a pattern of clinging to adults, but the tone and intent seemed clearly different from that of Susan. Ann entwined the adult's arms about herself in exactly the position she desired, thus directing and mobilizing the adult toward granting her satisfaction, while Susan imprisoned the adult's arms and legs so they could not move. Ann's hands rather than her language seemed to be her means of communication. Susan was determined to monopolize the attention of her favored teacher much as she did the mother's attention at home: she pretended helplessness to obtain the teacher or verbally demanded this attention; and if her demands were not gratified, she physically attacked the teacher and had to be removed from the room and comforted alone by the teacher. If she was unable to possess this teacher, she would sullenly withdraw and often at these times masturbate. In contrast, Ann failed to show any preference for a single teacher, and the distribution of her "affection" rendered a quantitative rather than qualitative coloring to her relationship. Ann, too, had temper tantrums during which her needs remained uncommunicated but, unlike Susan, Ann recovered very quickly and appeared oblivious of what had occurred a moment previously. This contributed to a picture of considerable emotional lability in Ann. She demanded attention with dressing and other routines, but frequently she reversed or counteracted her own orders, thus making it impossible for a teacher to satisfy her.

Susan was able to become occupied with another child more readily than Ann who made a peripheral adustment to her group and passively observed the other children. Ann never formed a relationship with another child which paralleled the pattern of that with Susan, but she was able to accept the friendship of a little girl whose outstanding social maturity aided Ann in becoming a more integral part of the group. When this "good sister" child left the group, Ann relapsed into her former peripheral position. Susan tended more to duplicate in her play some of the qualities that characterized her play with Ann at home. She sought out another little girl who was very excitable and with whom she could play mother-child games. Although there was some interchangeability of roles in this play, Susan usually triumphed in her wish to be the mother. If she did not, she would accept play in which both girls were big sisters. Susan encouraged this girl into mischievous, disruptive behavior in which Susan sometimes was the observer with vicarious enjoyment and at other times the partner.

Initially Ann requested many visits with Susan during which time her face lit up and she would imitate Susan's activities. Immediately prior to therapy, Ann's therapist observed one of these visits which took place in Susan's group. Susan shoved, directed and pulled Ann with an insistence which resembled fierceness. Susan seemed to enjoy the visit more so than did Ann, who seemed very sad and lifeless. Ann looked at the other children as though she might have preferred to be part of their group, but had to submit to her sister's monopoliza tion. An evaluation of the twins after their first year of nursery experience suggested that little change had occurred in their basic relationship with adults and other children and that sufficient psychological separation from each other had not occurred.

During the second year of nursery, each girl was advanced to an older group, thereby giving Susan Ann's former room and teachers. Susan's initial response was a spurt in development; she began to paint, increased her group participation, and accepted help with less clinging and attacking of the teacher. Ann's initial response was characterized by increased sadness, cessation of painting, and aimless wandering about the room. In school as at home, Ann expressed a wish for a private place free of other children and sought such a place during her rest period.

Following the introduction of therapy, Susan insisted upon more visits with Ann, as insurance against the loss of her twin, and wanted to be more frequently in the latter's group. Accompanying this was her wish to be included in Ann's therapy appointments where they would share Ann's therapist, thus repeating the pattern of one adult and two twins, with Susan undoubtedly striving to monopolize the therapist. Ann responded to this by insisting upon visits being held in Susan's group, implying that she did not want Susan in her group with her teachers. During these later visits, she appeared more independent of Susan and even threatened not to visit unless Susan permitted her to do as she pleased.

TREATMENT OF SUSAN

Individual therapy was recommended for Susan because of her need for sole possession of an adult, of her inability to use this or any other adult in an educational setting, of her inability to join or use group activities, and of her inability to use materials. In Susan there appeared to be a drive disturbance. When she was not involved in the loving-attacking relationship with her teacher or the bossing-provocative relationship with her friend, she was the picture of an angry pathetic child, kicking the dirt with her foot or sitting alone at the edge of the group doing nothing.

Her initial recognition of the therapist in the nursery was one of ordering the therapist to help her, to dress her, and to get things for her. This was followed by a week's absence from school due to her illness. Upon her return, she recognized the therapist and in the nursery room moved from her teacher to the therapist. She started with her entire body in the teacher's lap. Then she gradually straddled the teacher's and the therapist's laps, finally moving entirely into the therapist's lap. She could then, with the teacher's expressed approval, participate in an activity with the therapist, during which time she questioned the therapist as to her name, her function and her clothing. She asked whether the therapist saw Ann and then added her knowledge that Ann had appointments, stating, "I bet you didn't know I knew so much." On her way to the therapy room she stopped in Ann's nursery room to make sure that Ann saw her therapist.

During the initial hour she differentiated the therapist from the mother by stating, "Ladies don't play. My mother doesn't play. You do." She interchanged the roles of baby and mother with the therapist and succeeded in taking the therapist through all the activities that she did with the mother. The hour was ended by clinging to the therapist and leaving only when her teacher came for her. In the next hours Susan attempted to identify with the therapist by herself becoming a doctor, under the name of the mother's dentist. In this play she treated the therapist, then a doll which was first the therapist's baby and then Susan's. In this play she was much concerned about whether things as candy pills, thermometers, and the doll's eyes were "real." She had difficulty in differentiating her own needs from the therapist's, the parts of her own body from the same parts of the therapist's body, and animate things from inanimate things. She identified the family dolls as mother, daddy, boy, and, after difficulty, decided the girl doll was a "white bride." In enumerating her own family she called them "my mommy, my daddy, my big brother, and Annie—she's my sister."

At first Susan would start each hour by showing the "grown-up things" she could do, what big steps she could take, etc. This followed her showing the therapist the room she had been in during the first year of nursery school, stating, "That is the room for babies." This pattern then changed to one in which she would request to be carried to the therapy room, but she would never allow this request to be fulfilled. This change was associated with her increasing baby play during the therapy hour. She would start to feed the baby as the mother, then as the big sister, and finally to feed herself as the baby with the therapist as the mother. As she moved closer to the therapist in this manner, she could begin to express her fears of thunder, bears, wolves, and finally to state that the baby had no mother, that there were too many babies and the mother was too busy. She could then throw out the baby doll she had previously insisted upon taking into the cradle with her.

Each session was ended by Susan carefully arranging the room for next time, stating that things should not be moved, and turning out the light. If things were moved she would demand to know who moved them, where new things came from, and finally whether the therapist saw other children. She showed anger that she was not the therapist's only patient and that others used the same therapy room. (At this time she did not know that Ann used the same therapy room—an unfortunate necessity.) Her anger was associated with requests for bandaides which she put first on the therapist and then on herself. This often was followed by sharing out of candy, in which she gave the therapist and herself the same number and the same colors. Gradually she would take more for herself, selecting her favorite color red for herself and leaving only the brown ones which she did not like for the therapist.

She often stated that she was fooling the therapist and that she would not answer questions for fear that if she did answer "the big bad robber would shoot her." Then she demanded that the therapist not talk, look, or listen unless she were allowed to by Susan. In this way she attempted to immobilize the therapist and transfer upon her the submissive, puppet-like role of Ann. If her demand was not recognized she would shoot the therapist "all dead." It was only during the last session before Christmas vacation that, through denying that Ann had appointments, she could express her wish to be the only twin to have appointments. The impending separation from the therapist produced a flood of bandaides which she placed first upon the therapist and then upon herself in lesser number, stating her wish to throw the therapist out of the window and that the bandaides were needed for cuts obtained by so much "falling down." Thus she expressed her fear of the violence of her own aggression and showed her expectation of retaliation. This was associated with a fantasy of a boy she knew who died because he was angry. She could accept reassurance that appointments would be resumed but insisted that the therapist wear the bandaides until after the vacation. She parted from the therapist after showing her newly acquired skill of tying a bow knot.

During this first month and a half of treatment, Susan's clinging to her teacher decreased. She appeared happier and freer in her play. Her behavior resembled the initial spurt she had shown upon returning to school.

It was originally planned that each girl would get a letter from her therapist during the vacation, but due to unforeseen circumstances Ann was called on the phone by her therapist. Susan's therapist was notified of this too late to call that day and called the following morning. Susan could not take the phone but Ann did, stating that she was Susan and that she did not like the therapist and did not want any more appointments. The mother interrupted at this point to tell the therapist that it was Ann on the phone not Susan, but Susan had already left the room, stating that she would not come to any more appointments. The therapist attempted to rescue the situation by telling the mother to tell Susan that the therapist knew it had been Ann on the phone and that she, Susan, would have appointments with the therapist after vacation. (The mother was also undergoing a period of separation from her therapist which she experienced as a rejection.)

During the vacation, the mother reported, Ann became more assertive with Susan and Susan could not cope with Ann, could not fight back, and would be reduced to tears by Ann's taking her things.

On the first contact with the therapist following the vacation Susan attacked her and then clung to her, not allowing her to talk. The second hour Susan consented to come to the therapy room only if the teacher would come too. She told of Ann seeing her own therapist and of Ann's having told her the name of the child in Ann's group whom Susan's therapist also treated. She stated that she was wearing Ann's overalls, which she was, and claimed that it had been she, Susan, on the phone during Christmas, refusing to listen to the therapist's statement that she knew otherwise—that she was not confused by Ann or Ann's overalls. Susan insisted upon leaving with the teacher. The third hour Susan refused to come to the therapy room and demanded the presence of both the teacher and the therapist, stating, "I had two alone"—two people to herself.

For the next four weeks Susan was torn by her ambivalent feelings toward the therapist. She refused to come to the therapy room saying that she wanted a room of her own, not Ann's, but was unable to accept a different room. When the therapist spent the appointment hours with Susan in the nursery room, Susan attacked the therapist verbally and physically, demanding that the therapist leave the room and declaring that she would only come with the therapist if she could hit the therapist first. She provoked her twin substitute into also attacking the therapist. This attack she would either gleefully watch or join as a participant. When the therapist did not leave and did not allow Susan or her twin substitute to attack her, Susan clung to her teacher or sat pathetically outside the group, unable to accept verbal or physical contact with the therapist. Any offer of contact by the therapist provoked a renewal of the attack. At the end of one such hour, Susan told her teacher: "I tried not to have an appointment, but Dr. Demarest wouldn't let me." In the nursery her clinging increased and was focused upon one teacher. It assumed a new intensity which made it impossible for this teacher to manage it. When the second teacher separated Susan and removed her from her teacher, Susan became calm almost immediately. Susan subtly attempted to manipulate other people to resolve for her her ambivalence toward the therapist. For example, knowing the therapist was waiting for her downstairs, she started down the stairs saying, "I wonder where I am going—the nursery is upstairs." The teacher responded, "Yes, it is," and Susan turned and went upstairs. Later that day she accused the teacher of "forgetting to remind her" of her appointment. She also stated that she could not go to appointments because Ann would pull her hair and the mother would then punish Ann.

Susan's attack of the therapist was accompanied by letters to the therapist in which she declared her love for the therapist, for the appointments, and for the new therapy room, which she had never seen. These letters were written by the mother at Susan's request and dictation—another attempt at resolution of her ambivalence by projecting the conflict onto a third person. These letters increased the mother's fear of losing Susan and resulted in expression of the mother's hostility toward the therapist, as misaddressing the letters, questioning the feasibility of Susan's treatment. The mother brought the doll, which the therapist had given Susan for Christmas, to an appointment with the therapist, stating that Susan had forgotten it and she, the mother, would have to return it to Susan.

Throughout this period of treatment the outstanding feature was Susan's inability to accept or gain satisfaction from any situation which did not mirror her relationship with the mother or with Ann, or which threatened to disturb the equilibrium of these relationships. She was desperately "acting out" her struggle to accept and to fit the therapist into her life, i.e., to cathect the therapist, without causing a loss of any other cathected object. As better stated by Susan, "What do you expect me to be—an octopus?"

Because of the lack of individuation between Susan and her mother, Susan had experienced no sense of deprivation in the relationship. Therefore, the therapist could offer her no satisfaction as a mother substitute which did not constitute a threat to this relationship and, as such, had to be rejected. Ann's growing strength, gained through her acceptance and utilization of her therapist, allowed her further to individuate herself from Susan, and she no longer had to submit as much to Susan's manipulation. This deprived Susan of her "puppet," creating for Susan a need which the therapist could fulfill. At the time of the writing of this paper, Susan has returned to the therapy room, the attacks and letters to the therapist have ceased. Susan directs, commands, and demands in her hours. She also includes the therapist as a partner in a game in which she peeks, spies and attempts to fool Ann.

TREATMENT OF ANN

Individual therapy was instituted for Ann because she revealed ego deficiencies which could not be helped solely through the nursery experience; she experienced little feeling of self-completion without Susan; her object relationships with adults were faulty; her activities did not appear self-motivated; and she showed a lack of aggression, verbalization, and fantasy play. Marked sadness, bordering on depression, also suggested disturbances in her affective responses.

When the therapist, after becoming acquainted with her in the nursery, suggested the idea of private appointments just for Ann, she planted a kiss on the therapist's cheek and proceeded to enumerate that she had a "sister, Susan; brother, Harry; father, William—and a mother, Mrs. A." It became clear how remoteness characterized for Ann, as well as for the mother, the nature of their relationship. She displayed little means of coping with Susan other than through submission or avoidance. A statement, "I am tired," soon emerged, accompanied by physical activity—jumping on the stairs, walking rather than using the elevator. "I am tired" usually occurred when going to and from the therapy sessions—an expression of her dissatisfied state prior to sessions and upon their ending. The discrepancy between her statement and her activity was reflected back to her to enable her to identify the "I am tired" as an emotional rather than a physical state.

The depressed quality of this child appeared more strikingly after therapy began. She limited the therapist's role to providing her with materials and to getting things out of her way. The therapist was stripped of any personal contact and was much like the earlier drawings of ladies without arms which Ann had made in the nursery. She demanded things in great quantity but was unable to refuse her sister's demand for candy, when in the therapists' presence she met Susan on the staircase. Finally she played that she was the mother and had five sets of twins and only one milk bottle. She demonstrated the frenzied, tired behavior of the mother. The suggestion was made that she was both the "tired" mother and also the deprived babies, and she agreed that she would like to have just one baby. She then played for hours with one baby and ten bottles. This play was repetitive, monotonous, and abortive in nature, with the ten bottles usually ending up in her own mouth. (It had been reported that at home she seldom played with dolls and never endowed them with any tenderness.) It was this wish to be the only baby with a boundless supply of oral gratification that set the early goal for therapy.

It was the therapist's impression that Ann's reversing and counteracting her demands was her statement of the adult's, i.e., the mother's, inability to satisfy her. It also suggested an introjected Susan who made it impossible for her to know or to obtain what she herself wanted. Her manipulation of the adult's arms to obtain affection further stated a condemnation of the adults—they themselves would not know how to show her love. In spite of her expenditure of energy in her relationships with adults, she derived little gratification.

Her lack of individuation appeared to have been the blocking agent in her actually assuming the role of baby and assigning the role of mother to the therapist. Once she heard another child playing baby in a neighboring therapy room. She listened with intent and envious interest. Upon the therapist's invitation to do likewise, she sadly stated, "I cannot play baby because there is no other child here for me to watch." Also, attempting to model a baby in clay, she said to the therapist, "I want this to have your smiling mouth," but upon completion she had added "crying eyes" —her own. These sessions were otherwise characterized by a remarkable lack of verbalization and aggression.

Following a canceled therapy session she asked to be alone—without Susan—with her mother at home for the first time in her life. Amazed, the mother granted this wish only to be confronted and baffled by Ann's crying, frustration, and inability to state what she wanted. It seemed clear that she was attempting to share the aloneness with the mother which she had missed with the therapist because of the canceled session, but was unable to experience this with the mother.

During sessions, defecating and urinating were accompanied by eating food. When asked what would happen were she not to do this, she said, "I would not grow." The wish to have the therapist present and watching during this procedure was not interpreted nor understood as seductive. Rather it had the quality of a younger child who was willingly producing for the approving, giving, noninterfering adult.

Ann admitted that Susan told her of her wish to come to Ann's therapy session. Ann said, "I pretended that I did not hear her." It was suggested that she feared that Susan's wanting something of hers meant that she could take it away from her. She seemed surprised but did not react ver-

bally to the further suggestion that she might say to Susan, "It is mine—
I won't give it to you."

During Christmas vacation and separation from the therapist, Ann
cherished a gift from the therapist in contrast to disappointment and in-
difference which otherwise characterized her reaction to Christmas. It was
during this vacation that her aggression in the form of extreme possessive-
ness emerged toward Susan. She impersonated Susan on the telephone
when the latter's therapist called—after a call from her own therapist—
saying, "This is Susan, I do not like you, and I do not want to have any
more appointments with you." When Ann resumed sessions after vacation,
she extended her relationship with the therapist so as to include her in
games (dominoes) and there was mild verbal assertiveness, "I want it right
away—I want everything closer to me." When her wish to take away from
Susan was explored, she denied this—"I never said that"—and it was
suggested that her feelings said it for her.

At home she became more assertive with Susan. She was overheard
saying to Susan, "Why are you so bossy? Why do you always have to boss
me? Why do you always have to play the mother when we play?" Finally
she began to grab things back from Susan, hit her back, and redoubled
her efforts to be with Harry. Susan seemed utterly disarmed by the new
Ann. Ann made a puppet in the nursery, confided to the therapist that its
name was "Susan" and it remained in the therapy room, hanging limp
and inactive. It was as though she had become less of a puppet with
Susan, and envisaged a reversal of roles. She was delighted during games
when the therapist would follow her lead, such as tracing her markings
through a maze.

Ann soon indicated her wish to have her session precede that of another little girl in her nursery group whom she knew had been in treatment for a long time with the therapist. At no time did she express any
direct aggression toward this child, and only gradually developed a more
altruistic[5] attitude toward her. Upon the therapist's arrival in the nursery
she would hasten over to the other girl to tell her it was her "appointment
time," as though saying: I have my appointment after yours but it's not
spoiled by yours coming first—mine is as good. It is significant that with
Susan she never appeared to have graduated from the submissive and
jealous role to one of altruism.

The first real aggression aimed at the therapist followed another canceled session. Ann brought a present—a crayoned design—for the thera-

[5] The term altruism is being used here as a phase of development in twinship in
which the twins are able to seek equality with each other as a resolution of their
rivalry. It does not imply the mechanism of defense as described by Anna Freud (1936).

pist that had initially been intended for Harry. She called it a "surprise" and agreed with the therapist that it was a nicer "surprise" than she herself had received, the canceled session. With a little encouragement from the therapist she shifted to a urethral form of aggression, spilled water at the therapist and tricked her into sitting on a wet chair. Following acceptance of this aggression, she permitted the therapist to provide her with direct gratification. She climbed into a baby carriage and directed the therapist to push her. She directed the activity, as though she still could not believe that the therapist would know how nor want to please her. After several such sessions she gazed at the mirror on the wall and was delighted when the therapist bent down so that Ann could see the image of herself being pushed in the carriage by the therapist. This image of togetherness, of mother and child, had been so lacking, whereas the mirroring of her sibling had been so omnipresent.

Finally she verbalized with contentment, "I am the baby and you are the mother," and gave the therapist some of her favorite possessions to hold as she pushed Ann in the carriage. She then darkened the room and played that she was the baby going to sleep. She again reverted to directing the therapist as to how to make her comfortable, but was assured that the therapist really did know. After making her comfortable, she sent the therapist away. When asked whether she did not wish the therapist to remain at her bedside, she responded, "But mothers always have to work." When assured that this was not the case with the therapist, she said, "Then come closer," and reached out to hold her hand. These sessions were characterized by a marked diminution of her requests for sugar lumps during the sessions, and she verbalized, "Now I only have to have the sugar when the appointment is over." She had finally been able to express and receive what she really needed during the session, and the sugar tided her over to the next session in lieu of "I am tired."

Her behavior in the nursery somewhat reflected an increased aggression and assertiveness with other children. She stopped entwining the teacher's arms about herself and she stopped thwarting her own wishes. But she frequently wandered about the room, still appearing as though she did not know what to do.

DISCUSSION

The initial phase of therapy made it apparent that there had been insufficient individuation in each twin from the mother and from each other. The effect of this on each twin's personality contributes to an understanding of the marked difference in their approach to and utilization of therapy.

Susan's lack of individuation from the mother made it impossible for her to accept another adult, i.e., the therapist, in a way other than the unindividuated mother-Susan relationship, and she could not successfully transfer the mother role onto the therapist. So long as the transference focused on this unindividuated relationship it could not be utilized because it was too threatening to both Susan and the mother. When she was faced with the Christmas separation from the therapist, this attempt to project the mother role onto the therapist was terminated. The assertiveness which Ann showed as exemplified in the phone conversation, confronted Susan with the loss of Ann as a puppet and produced for Susan a new problem which therapy could better satisfy. She then transferred the puppet role onto the therapist. In one way Susan used Ann in the mother's absence, as another child might use a doll, to reverse her passive role with the mother into an active role (Anna Freud, 1936). In another way, Susan used Ann as a puppet to immobilize Ann as a rival who might threaten her relationship with the mother. This was aided and abetted by the mother's preference for Susan out of her own conscious and unconscious reasons, Susan's accelerated developmental curve, and Ann's acceptance of the puppet role imposed upon her by Susan.

Ann's initial attempt to gain the real mother in a relationship free of Susan's presence was thwarted by Susan's constant interference and the mother's preference for Susan. She gradually submitted to a domineering Susan and reflected an insufficient individuation from Susan. It would seem likely that Ann experienced the mother indirectly through Susan. We do not know what role substitute figures other than Susan actually played in Ann's development. It seems probable that Harry provided a refuge from Susan and also offered Ann a model of an individual in contrast to her own twinship.

Ann's drive toward finding a private place for herself without the presence of Susan or any other child provided her with an initial impetus to accept therapy. Her faulty object relationship with a mother figure made it difficult initially for her to cathect the therapist as an object, and as with the mother, she cathected things rather than the person. She forced the therapist into a limited role, transferring the remoteness characteristic of her relationship with her mother. She responded with increased depression as she re-experienced the original deprivations, but her perceptive functioning was well enough developed to recognize the potential which was available within the therapeutic situation. Still, she was unable to attempt a mother-child relationship on her own, the image of mother having always been accompanied by another child. After violently ejecting Susan, through the telephone incident, she was able to expel her from the domineering role. It is unlikely that she ever completely relinquished the image of the real mother as object because of the relative rapidity with which this was achieved. The lack of cathexis of the real mother minimized the conflict in her wish to then adopt the therapist as object and paved the way to a positive transference.

Although Ann has achieved greater individuation from Susan, her ego deficiencies continue to be markedly apparent through deficient differentiation and integration in her functioning, while Susan's drive disturbance is apparent through her lack of fusion of the libidinal and aggressive drives.

BIBLIOGRAPHY

Burlingham, D. (1952), *Twins.* New York: International Universities Press.
Freud, A. (1936), *The Ego and the Mechanisms of Defense.* New York: International Universities Press, 1946.
Hartmann, H.; Kris, E.; Loewenstein, R. M. (1946), Comments on the Formation of Psychic Structure. *This Annual*, II.
Karpman, B. (1953), Psychodynamics in Fraternal Twinship Reactions. *Psa. Rev.*, XL.
Orr, D. (1941), Psychoanalytic Study of a Fraternal Twin. *Psa. Quart.*, X.

EMOTIONAL IMPACT OF NEARNESS AND SEPARATION FOR THE ASTHMATIC CHILD AND HIS MOTHER[1]

LUCIE JESSNER, M.D., JOHN LAMONT, M.D., ROBERT
LONG, M.D., NANCY ROLLINS, M.D., BABETTE
WHIPPLE, Ph.D., and NORMAN PRENTICE, M.A.

(Boston)[2]

The point of departure for this study is an observation, striking both in our own cases and in the literature; namely, that often when an asthmatic child goes to the hospital or away to camp, the asthma dramatically improves, and equally dramatically recurs when he comes home (Abramson, 1952; Hallowitz, 1954; Rogerson, Hardcastle, and Dugid, 1935; Unger and Unger, 1952). Although some authors interpret this as a result of isolation from allergens (Unger and Unger, 1952), others believe it to be a result of the child's separation from the emotional climate at home (Abramson, 1952; Hallowitz, 1954; Rogerson, Hardcastle, and Dugid, 1935), and, as such, evidence of the importance of emotional factors in some cases of asthma. In their studies on psychogenic factors in asthma, French and Alexander (1941) have stressed the central role of fear of estrangement from the mother in producing the asthma attack. These authors and subsequent writers (Gerard, 1946; Saul and Lyons, 1955) have discussed the strong dependent and orally regressive needs in asthmatic patients. Similarly the asthmatic children we observed were intensely dependent on their mothers.

What appears to be a paradox—namely that the child threatened with alienation from mother may react with an asthma attack, yet be free from asthma when separated from her—points to the need for scrutiny of the meaning of separation.

[1] This investigation was supported in part by a research grant (#MH-66 and supplements) from the National Institute of Mental Health, U. S. Public Health Service, and in part by the Harvard Medical School.

[2] From the Child Psychiatry Unit, Massachusetts General Hospital, Boston, Mass.

Our observations are drawn from a group of 65 asthmatic children and their mothers, seen by the Child Psychiatry and Pediatric staffs of the Massachusetts General Hospital since 1947. Of the total number serving as a background for this investigation, 28 cases have been studied by the authors as a group. We selected 14 boys and 14 girls in the age range between 5 and 16.

This observation, of improvement in the child's asthma on hospitalization and recurrence on return home, is conspicuous in our cases, especially in a few who had as many as twenty or thirty hospitalizations. The asthma would subside within a short time after admission, and medication which had failed at home would bring relief. At times the mother of the child would remark on this with chagrin, wondering if the doctors were using a new drug.

Yet it was evident from a review of our cases that mere physical separation did not necessarily lead to relief from asthma. The following case may serve to introduce some of the complex factors involved.

Deborah, a girl of ten years, eight months, was referred because of chronic asthma and anorexia. Asthma began at two and a half, with attacks increasing in frequency and severity, leading to numerous hospitalizations with temporary benefit. Since four years of age Deborah had eaten poorly and lost weight.

Her mother was a thin harsh woman at her wits' end with the patient, feeling unable to understand and cope with her. The father seemed strict, but with an unusual understanding of the patient. He felt she resembled him. Several times, illness in the patient had preceded or followed an illness of his. The father was unusually eager to participate in casework, nearly excluding the mother.

Both parents describe the patient as isolated, well-behaved, undemanding, and a "diplomat." The parents first emphasized how well she and her brother, Harold, got on, but later stated that the patient seemed to get extremely annoyed with him, though she tried to keep her temper. As well behaved as she ordinarily is, she gets wild at night when she has asthma, screaming for her parents.

The patient was weaned suddenly at six weeks because mother's milk was considered "bad." Thus there was an early estrangement between mother and child, with feelings of frustration on both sides. The mother withdrew with hurt feelings and Deborah sucked excessively. To make matters worse, Deborah had eczema and boils from four months to two years. Whatever skin contact and comfort existed was restricted to the application of medicine. The sight of eczema and the repulsive smell of ointments made the mother disgusted with the baby and resulted in greater estrangement. After a number of colds, asthma was diagnosed when Deborah was two and a half. Shortly thereafter the mother became pregnant with Harold, born when the patient was three and a half. Deborah was annoyed because no one told her to expect a baby. During this time her father took care of her, dressing and feeding her, putting her to bed, giving her suppositories and injections during asthma attacks at night. She became the father's favorite; he felt he understood her because he, like her, had been imaginative and apprehensive. Following the birth of Harold, the patient would wake up screaming, would grab her tongue with her fingers, yelling she would swallow it and die. It was our impression that the patient was frightened by oral impregnation fantasies concerning her father. At this time the patient began to eat poorly. She seemed tender and affectionate to her brother, never showing jealousy, until she was seen by a psychiatrist at another hospital. Although first inhibited, she eventually brought out many aggressive fantasies against Harold and irritation at the whole family. Harold, she said, would stay by her bed and laugh at her when she got asthma. She wished she had a good fork—she would put it into his head and mash him to pieces as though he were a potato. (Would she eat him after she got him mashed up?) "No, I would throw him into the garbage can and get rid of him for good." The day she brought this out she had a severe attack. Then she ate better and had less frequent attacks. At this point the parents and Deborah broke off the contact.

On admission to the Massachusetts General Hospital medical findings were severe asthma, emphysema, pigeon-breast, state of depletion. Skin tests were positive to a number of allergens. Deborah was a pathetic-looking, pale, thin girl with beautiful eyes and an appealing, resigned expression, mixed of sadness and serenity. She looked like a poster for Hungry and Abandoned Children.

She was friendly and talkative, saying she had not been in school since Christmas. "I didn't get my asthma in school. I got it at home." It comes mostly at night, then she calls for her father "because my mother, you know, works all day." The asthma may also occur when she plays with her brother Harold. In several remarks about her siblings she left out the baby. Reminded of his existence, she replied that she gets mad at him and added, "I know what I am going to be, a nurse for children. I might get married too." In every interview the patient indicated that she likes to overcome her rage by being good and helpful to persons who annoy her. Reaction formation seemed the most outstanding of her defense mechanisms.

While at another hospital, she was homesick every night. "I don't know anything about that place. I forgot all about it." This recurred whenever a particularly painful experience was brought up. Suppression was another frequent defense. She mentioned "when I don't feel so good, my mother reads to me or talks to me and that helps. Sometimes my mother says I am talking too much." At this point she scratched her head and bit her upper lip. She started to cry. "I know I am thin but I don't think about it at all. Sometimes I eat an awful lot. I might eat and eat all day long. It all depends on how I feel." The patient here looked at the therapist with suspicion and tears. "Everybody says I don't eat. My mama doesn't say anything about it." There was a bitter resigned tone in her voice when she indicated that her mother did not care.

These main topics, and her special way of dealing with them, were brought out in the course of her interviews:

(1) She says her mother neglects her and she feels uneasy with her father. She showed the therapist a very conventional empty letter from her mother. "She didn't write much. I forgot what else she said," was the patient's characteristic comment. She expressed similar disappointment with other females, e.g., her grandmother and her therapist. When asked whether the therapist could keep poems she had written for her, she exclaimed "Oh, to show everyone how I can't spell!"

(2) Her jealousy of her brother also played a prominent role in her feelings. Once in a play interview she was quite intrigued with two dolls and mentioned that she once smashed the head of a plastic doll at home. "I wouldn't do that now. It was not only an accident." She added that this particular doll looked quite like a real baby. (Your baby brother?) "He is like a doll but not like a doll." (One can't smash his head?) Patient chuckled, saying no, that wouldn't do.

(3) Her aversion to food seemed on the conscious level an expression of reproach and defiance. Once she said, "I didn't eat hardly anything for breakfast. I won't eat today. They woke me up out of a dead sleep with breakfast." Her parents had visited her the day before and she had gotten angry with them, then displaced the anger onto the nurse who woke her up.

Her greatest food aversion was hamburger, which she called chopped raw meat. She says here she will eat only what is good. She loves blood. One day she had her finger pricked for blood samples every hour. She sucked the blood with delight and showed it with pride, commenting that she enjoys it when she has cut her finger. When her brother cuts himself, however, she doesn't like to see it, adding, "Some people would." When asked whether she doesn't also, she said that sometimes she likes to see someone else hurt, but she feels badly for having such a thought.

One night she had been wheezing, which started before she went to bed. She commented spontaneously: "I know why. Gloria [another asthma patient] and I did so much laughing and giggling about a new game, 'What went into the soup?'" (What?) "Oranges and pears, my father's belt, a finger and [giggles] blood from my finger, a nice soup, don't you think?" At this moment her luncheon was brought in. She gulped the milk down, pushed her fork into the mashed potatoes with vigor, making sure that she didn't get much on the fork. When asked what went into the mashed potatoes, she laughed, "Just potatoes, nothing else." Thus eating seemed so strongly related to unconscious cannibalistic and castrating tendencies that the defense against them necessitated refraining from eating.

(4) Concerning her asthma, Deborah emphasized the coincidence of her attacks and returning to her home. Often there is a question of eating combined with the breathing difficulty. In one interview she said, "I had a wee bit of asthma. I had it after my mother was here. I know what I ate the day before, cheese and something else." (Does that have anything to do with your asthma?) "No, usually if I don't feel good and get a pain in my stomach, then I don't

get asthma. Sometimes when I have a bit of asthma and I get mad, it may get worse."

At another visit, the patient was angry, and her mother, accepting the social worker's suggestion, told the patient it was all right to be angry. At this, Deborah looked slyly, replying it was all very well for mother to say this, but she knew mother didn't love her when she was angry.

During hospitalization there was a definite change in her attitude. She first appeared as a most unhappy child, who participated in activities of other children only when she was made to do so, following each order most obediently. She became increasingly more relaxed, childlike, whimsical and joking. Her weight increased and there were few asthma attacks. She made a real friend of another asthmatic girl, younger but more enterprising than the patient. They had together a teddy bear whom they called "The New Patient." Deborah was his doctor; her friend was the head nurse. She told the following story: "Once there was a teddy bear and he came to the hospital to get well. We took good care of him and he is getting well. We gave him medicine. He gained two pounds. He is always better in the hospital than at home. He doesn't feel good so he doesn't want to eat."

When the possibility of her leaving the hospital was raised, she looked distressed and said, "I guess I'll stay a little longer."

The teddy bear a few weeks later was replaced by a doll. Again Deborah was the doctor and her girl friend the nurse. She said, "The baby won't eat at home and coughs, nobody knows why. I guess it will do all right here." After a few weeks she announced that the baby was almost cured, and that she herself would like to go home soon to attend a wedding. Deborah also hoped her friend and she could leave together. She was discharged a few days later, was very willing to return for further interviews.

On her first return visit she was talkative but evasive. The day after the wedding, which she had been so eager to attend, was her birthday and then she started to wheeze. She reported she had been well for the first four days. Mother said that only the first night was peaceful. After that she would call for her parents several times and ask for her spray. The parents couldn't sleep because of the patient's screaming.

One week later Deborah came to the outpatient department, crying, wheezing and moaning. The mother came into the psychiatrist's office while Deborah sat with her father, screaming, "Give me a needle, or I'll die; give me a needle or I'll kill myself; give it or I'll never come to see you again." She gave the impression of a two-year-old in a temper tantrum, a marked contrast with her usual sweet obedient self. After several weeks the patient again appeared waif-like and had to be readmitted to the hospital. Here she was free of asthma except for one night, which she connected with a visit from her mother. She remarked that when she returns from any place, she'll have asthma as soon as she arrives home.

Deborah was then sent to a ranch for convalescent children. Although her asthma was better she complained bitterly, asking the psychiatrist over and over, "Why is it worse at home?" She seemed depressed and homesick. The housemother spent a great deal of time with the patient, telling her to be "relaxed and expressive." After a few weeks Deborah became gay, talkative, and easy, remarking with a coy smile that her wheezing doesn't go on to become asthma.

In a follow-up interview with the mother seven years later, the patient was reported still to have asthma, although not so severe, and her ambition was to be a nurse who would care for children while still in their own homes.

Anorexia and asthma seemed interwoven and overdetermined by the wish to be fed and protected by the mother, the oedipal fear of the father, the fight against oral impregnation and oral devouring wishes. She tried to please her mother by being sweet and obedient. She expressed disappointment by hunger strikes and rage by asthma attacks. Both conditions improved in the hospital which provided the patient with accepting mother figures (nurses and psychiatrist) and allowed a passive anaclitic form of existence. Psychotherapy with parents and patient improved their interrelationship to a certain degree, but not sufficiently to outweigh disappointments and frustrations incident to her return home. A permanent improvement in symptoms and in personality development was achieved at the convalescent home, where a mother substitute gave her constant attention and "forced" her to eat and get well.

In this case, where hospitalization and subsequent placement led to improvement of asthma, a number of factors play a role: gratifications obtained through mother figures, release from the tensions arising from the frustrated longings for her mother, a positive transference and identification with the psychiatrist, expression of her cannibalistic impulses, and opportunity to verbalize and play out her true feelings and still be accepted.

When we reviewed instances of less definite separation, such as going to school or the mother's leaving for a short time, we found that they often were followed by an asthmatic attack. For example, a six-year-old boy had his initial asthma attack on his first day of school; at the time, his mother was home in bed, nearly at term in her second pregnancy, and a new nurse had been hired to take care of the boy. These subtle forms of separation brought on the threat of losing mother's love, which, as French and Alexander (1941) pointed out, is so crucial for the asthmatic patient. Thus situations like the arrival of a sibling, emotional withdrawal of the mother through nursing or illness, awareness on the child's part of feelings which are unacceptable to his mother, such as forbidden aggressive or sexual impulses, contained the threat of estrangement from mother and brought on an increase of asthmatic symptoms. These might bring on an attack of asthma, even if the mother is not immediately present.

The following case illustrates the conflict of separation and closeness between mother and child, and its effect on the child's asthma.

David M., a ten-year-old boy, had been in psychotherapy for the past eighteen months because of asthma. He is the second of four boys. In the family history of allergy, mother's oldest sister, Mary, had eczema, and Mary's son, Gerald, had asthma. Once, when eighteen months old, David stuffed his mouth full of peanuts. His mother fearfully grabbed those remaining in his hand. David screamed, choked, turned blue, and gasped for breath. The next day he was hospitalized for the first of a series of respiratory disturbances diagnosed as croup. Asthma was diagnosed about one year later. Attacks continued, worse during the winter, mostly at night, and were particularly severe at two and a half and five, when his two younger brothers were born. An asthmatic attack at age nine following an argument with a woman counselor at camp convinced David's mother that emotional factors were important, and she sought psychiatric help.

Special circumstances surrounded the onset of David's asthma. Mary, the mother's older sister, was ill in Washington with cancer of the breast. The mother visited her frequently until Mary's death when David was five. The mother recalled her own irritability and resentment of her children who prevented her from being with Mary all the time. She felt tired, said she hated the children and always seemed to be pregnant. Mrs. M. had always felt closest to Mary whom she admired for her intellectual interests. Mary was like a mother to Mrs. M. and told her the facts of life. Long after Mary's death, Mrs. M. constantly dreamt of her and felt as if she would meet Mary every time she went to Washington. "I guess I never buried Mary," said Mrs. M.

Mrs. M. could not talk with her own mother, and saw her as a drudge who strictly adhered to her religion. Mrs. M.'s mother had abandoned an infant in Europe when she came to this country. Mrs. M. recalls with anxiety scenes between her parents, relating them to her own discomfort when she sees her children fight. Her parents were divorced when she was ten. In her teens she rebelled against her mother's old-world ways and religion, and entered nurse's training.

At twenty-five Mrs. M. married an executive, a college graduate. She describes him as a perfectionist who demands a high standard of performance from the boys. In their marriage mother and father avoid arguments, with but occasional outbursts from either parent toward the children. The father's work often keeps him away from home, which Mrs. M. resents, as she feels the added weight of the family responsibility.

The mother has special feelings about David. While the three other boys remind her of her husband and his family, temperamentally David is like herself. She compares him also with Mary's son, Gerald, who, like David, developed asthma at eighteen months.

She feels that David demands more than she can give. On the other hand, she overprotects him since "he is ill and cannot do as much as the other boys." She was terrified during his attacks, fearing he would not catch his breath and might die. Yet she resents his illness. She wishes she were not burdened with the children, yet wonders if it is abnormal that David wants to spend the night away from home with a friend. She describes him as having many friends and outside interests, and asked if this is normal.

In interviews, David readily expresses in play and fantasy the conflicts arising from his relationship to his mother. Early in treatment his mother planned a trip to New York but feared David would have an asthmatic attack. He did. It occurred the night before she left. In the next interview, while his mother was away, he wondered if he and his female therapist would use the same room they had used before. He looked out the window and reassured himself that the State House dome was still in the same place, saying, "Anything can happen in this world. . . . The earth might be bombed by people from Mars. But if there is life on Mars it must be different from life here because there is no oxygen on Mars." David showed indirectly that he felt abandoned in an unpredictable world. Later in the same interview he played out a fantasy of two fathers fighting over a mother (who was blackmailed for $10,000). Both fathers were killed. The little boy hit mother in the face and she fell dead with the others. The boy himself almost fell to his death but was rescued and carried away by a Palomino. He expressed in this the fantasy of his mother's meeting another man. Three months later, Mrs. M. planned another trip to New York. There was a difference between the two departures. The first time she wanted to get away. David sensed this and felt she was going to see someone more important to her in New York. The second time she was able to let him discuss his feelings because she felt less guilty, and David had no asthma.

Concerns of losing his mother were expressed in the transference situation. David brought the therapist a miniature suitcase and said that she too might be doing some traveling. Later when the therapist was thinking about seeing David less frequently he "bought" the whole hospital, including his doctor, for $60,000,000. When the interviews were reduced he baked cakes and fed the therapist, showing that he needed no one to cook for him. In reversing roles he showed his concern about not getting enough and a denial of his dependence.

Many fantasies dealt with the wish to be in an enclosed place symbolizing the mother. David spoke of the fun he had exploring the dungeons of an old castle, and in interviews he delighted in exploring the subterranean parts of the hospital. His Thematic Apperception Test stories are filled with treasure hunts and adventures into mine shafts.

While there is the wish to be in an enclosed place it brings on the fear of suffocation. David said children might accidentally be locked in ice boxes and suffocate. The good air is replaced by bad air which people breathe out. He proved that a candle needs oxygen to burn, and that the flame goes out when he puts a jar over it. In one fantasy bad children were put into cages by their parents. They escaped through a trap door into a passageway, which led to a secret room. Here was a magic fireplace in which they could take trips to faraway places like Africa. The parents knew nothing about the secret room; although they stumbled into it a couple of times, they thought they were dreaming.

Closeness to the mother and dangers associated with this are expressed vividly by David. He said that coral is formed by the young attaching to the mother after her death. But soon the young coral also dies. To be separate from mother is equally dangerous. While David was coloring a picture of a man being shot out of a cannon, he said, "I wouldn't want to be shot out. I'd rather stay inside; it's safe."

Often David fantasied prisoners getting shot by guards as they escaped from the roof at the Charlestown Jail nearby. When a notorious jail break actually occurred, he was anxiously preoccupied with the dangerous escaped criminal and his whereabouts. David finally had him recaptured and killed in the electric chair. Aggressive (and sexual) impulses lead to confinement, escape from which is fraught with danger.

David shows intense rivalry with his brothers. In play, David forced a toy bottle down each doll's throat, saying, "Drink this." The doll fell over and died, complaining its throat hurt. This was repeated until all the dolls were dead. Then he said vehemently, "This boy does not care at all that he is left alone. Now he can have all the toys in the world to play with." The other dolls suddenly came to life and there was a long bitter fight. One doll, held responsible for the mass killing, was finally defeated and killed. Many other fantasies express this concern of being the only one left.

During therapy, Mrs. M. became warmer toward David as her attitude toward her own mother was worked through and became more positive. One way she showed this was by accepting some of her mother's religion and traditions.

Concurrently, David's asthma has become much less frequent. Formerly he had attacks in the winter. During the first year of treatment he had one winter attack and has been free of asthma for one year. As David improved, his mother tended to transfer her close attachment to her youngest son. David, who seldom talked about his asthma, once said he felt his youngest brother was most likely to get it. As treatment continued, the fantasies became less rich and numerous. David was more able to express his feelings directly in real situations.

This case illustrates many of the features which we felt characterized our group of asthmatic children and their mothers. We saw how the ambivalence over closeness and separateness reflected itself in the concerns of both David and his mother. We saw how both mother and child tended to preserve the unique quality of their attachment by inhibiting impulses which tended to endanger it. Further, we saw how the source of the mother's need to keep David close derived from an early dependent relationship with a mother surrogate. Lastly we were able to glimpse the complex interaction between allergic propensities, respiratory illness, and the special emotional climate that surrounds the asthmatic symptoms.

CHILD'S NEED TO BE CLOSE TO MOTHER

The need for closeness to the mother is striking in our cases. Rogerson, Hardcastle, and Dugid (1935) found that asthmatic children had unusual difficulty in leaving their mothers for play sessions. Some of our cases showed this, but it may as often be expressed in other ways. The child may insist on being dressed or cared for in ways inconsistent with his age. Many asthmatic children want only the mother to take care of them, particularly during an attack. They may insist on sleeping with the mother (or the father), so that in these families ordinary sleeping arrangements are constantly disrupted.

The conflict between the wish to remain forever close to mother, and the wish to grow up (as well as anxieties over being enveloped and extinguished) are expressed clearly by Jean, a seventeen-year-old girl, who has been known to our clinic since she was eight years old. Her asthma began at two, shortly after the birth of her sister, and became severe at six, after her father's death and the birth of her youngest sister a few months prior to father's death. Her mother had a grief reaction after father's death, requiring hospitalization. Jean grew up feeling that babies, sickness and death were linked. She said that as a little girl, she thought babies came from the sky and the parents reached up and caught one. When people die, they are reborn into the same family, as babies coming down from the sky. In this way life goes on and on.

Her mother felt Jean was different from the other children. She was overprotective and treated her (in Jean's words) "as if she always had one foot in the grave." The mother at the same time used Jean as a companion to unburden herself of her own problems, thus neglecting Jean's dependent needs. Jean's need and fear to be close to her mother was expressed symbolically in a dream at nine years. She was in a house being washed out to sea, but felt comfortable because the whole family was together inside. She had a terrifying dream of circles coming toward her from the darkness and feared what would happen when they got to her. She told of her fear of the darkness all around her, and of lifetime fears of water and wind which are stronger than she. For Jean, darkness meant both mother's womb and sexual temptation.

Jean recalled the first day of school when she was six years old. "It was raining and the mothers brought the children, left them with the teacher, and waited outside. When the mothers left, the children began to cry." Shortly after this, her asthma became severe, and for the next three years she did not return to school.

At seventeen, Jean had a prolonged asthma attack. This began when the mother was upset because her sister, with whom she had always been close, decided to move away. The mother reacted by yelling, nagging, and taking her troubles to the children. Jean's asthma kept her home with mother. "There was always something missing with mother," she said. She wept and complained she never got from her mother what she should have. Since mother was unable to tell her the facts of life, which Jean resented, this knowledge came from the therapist. Jean then asked what happened when there are twins—do they fight to get out? Are babies born in pieces? She enviously criticized her sister, who was ahead of her in school, although a year and a half younger than Jean. The sister is out with her friends all the time, fights with mother, does exactly as she pleases and is "too independent." Jean's longing to receive from mother and be close to her prevented her even as an adolescent from turning to out-siders for guidance and help.

Jean's need for closeness to mother, her anxiety over separation, her fears of school, water, darkness, etc., are reminiscent of phobic states in children. We have observed phobic trends in other cases.

Frequently the children symbolize their need for mother in terms of houses or caves, but the protecting shelter is often seen as dangerous. Intrauterine fantasies have been observed by others, especially empha-sized by French and Alexander (1941) and Saul and Lyons (1955).

Like David, eight-year-old Danny enjoyed wandering through the cellars and tunnels of the hospital. One day, while exploring a deserted cellar with his therapist, he stepped on a wire which injured his foot. He shrieked, cried, was afraid he would be operated on, and thought something would be cut off. "Something always happens here," he said through his tears. "From now on we will stay in the playroom." Later, he squeezed between two shelves and in panic said he couldn't get out; what was he to do? Danny's wish for and fear of the enclosed place are linked with his suffocation fantasies and ideas about asthma. He had a cowboy caught in quicksand, submerged, and suffocated. "Suffocation is the worst kind of death there is," said Danny, "I know I feel suffocated when I have asthma." The cowboy came back and fell in the quicksand again but was rescued. Finally, because he didn't listen to what people told him, he went back, fell in and died. "Like not listening to what mother tells me. She says not to stay out in the cold because this brings on asthma." His mother reported that Danny refused to go to camp because he might get sucked into quicksand. A little later, Danny told of going with mother in water up to his neck. He was frightened at first but got used to it. On another occasion, he was blowing bubbles into water and associated this to being smothered by asthma. The therapist introduced the idea of unborn babies in water. Danny thought they must have gills so they could breathe without difficulty. Fish have gills to get the air out of water. He and his sister have water gun fights. As he told this, he impulsively stuck his head under water. He was attracted to the water and at the same time feared it. He asked about breathing under water and wondered if it hurt as if still feeling one can literally breathe under water. He was fond of water play and often had dolls diving, swimming, sinking, drowning, and fighting under water. A woman took a boy into the water to drown him because he had hit another boy with glass. Then Danny changed his story so the boy killed the mother.

Felix Deutsch (1947, 1955) has pointed out the importance of water fantasies in patients with respiratory illness, and their significance as symbolic of purification and rebirth, and return to the mother. Mickey, a five-year-old boy, made a picture and explained, "Someone is under water with a tube that he uses for breathing. There's no one around to talk to him. He just lies there underneath the water."

Rickie, a five-year-old boy, was seen once a week for over a year, and a few times in follow-ups. From the first, three themes dominated his play and his fantasies—water, separation, and sickness. Water was the major vehicle of play during the early sessions: he splashed, spilled, filled and emptied, and refilled every container he could find. He said to the therapist, "You and I will be floating by the time we are through." (I like floating.)

The meaning of water to him was richly overdetermined. It was good milk, to drink. He pushed the toy animals into water, the cow in the toilet, the chicken in the sink, saying that they wanted to drink. Later, he named one of the dolls Lollipop, and through her played out his fantasies over many weeks. Lollipop was three years old; like himself, she had a seven-year-old brother named Jimmy. Although he usually referred to Lollipop as "she," her sex was vague. When asked whether she was a boy or girl, he said, "Both." Rickie said, giving Lollipop a bottle, "Here, Lollipop dear, drink it, it is sterilized milk, no germs, no sickness." On another occasion he said he had drunk three gallons of water the day before and Jimmy had drunk ten. He wanted to drink more than Jimmy. "Jeepers, I love it. Isn't it beautiful, this cool water. I want to drink more than Jimmy because it is beautiful." Water, as milk, was not only beautiful, cool, germ-free and safe, but healing. Once he played being angry, and said, "I am in a rage. I am mad as the dickens. I drink water to calm my rage." Hence water becomes medicine. In the third hour, he filled all the bottles with water, saying they were filled with medicine. He said he took medicine for his cough; so did Jimmy; and grandmother took a lot.

Water is not only to drink, but also to bathe in. First the animals were put into the water; then Lollipop was put over and over into the bathinette. "Lollipop needs a long bath; she gets so awfully dirty. She always promises me not to get dirty." Rickie identified with his mother, in bathing as in feeding. "I am her mommy. I don't do anything to her, I don't spank her. Jimmy, her brother, is always clean: I never spank him." Once, when the therapist asked after Lollipop's and Jimmy's health, he said, "They are healthy. I go crazy when they are sick. I give them a bath before bed. Jimmy is the dirtiest one." In one play session, the water was both milk and bath: "Jimmy will have a milk bath because he gets dirty. Sometimes he is the cleanest, but now he is dirty. Besides he was fresh."

There is an undertone here that the bath is punishment, and in fact the children often don't like it. Rickie says, "The water is cold, and Lollipop would like to get out: his dad is pushing his face in the water." Again, "She doesn't like it," and he throws Lollipop across the room. Or he pulls Lollipop out of the bathinette, saying, "He is dripping; I can't stand that," and throws her away. "How do I dry this drenched thing?" and throws her down. The mother, enacted by Rickie, doesn't like the wet baby and so throws it away. (Rickie was enuretic.) Not only does the mother reject the wet child, but the water is here seen as cold and uncomfortable. Once he described a visit to the beach, said he and Jimmy had been jumping into the water. "It was cold. Mother didn't go in the water. She was afraid it would bite her. It was biting me plenty."

The themes of being thrown away for being bad came up over and over. Just as Lollipop was thrown away because she was drenched or didn't like her bath, animals were thrown away because their legs were broken off: they were no good any more; Lollipop is thrown to the floor when she drips, with the shout, "Pee, Lollipop, pee." Rickie, mixing paints till he had a brown semi-solid mixture, said, "Beautiful, isn't it?" Then he seized a doll and threw it across the room. One is thrown away for being wet, damaged, or dirty. Sometimes he would throw the animals around and throw himself on the floor at the same time, shifting from playing to acting.

Bad means being wet, dirty, disobedient, and leads to illness. When the bathinette leaked, Rickie tried to tape the hole, abruptly turned on Lollipop, saying, "Dirty child. There is no way of fixing this bathinette. I tried it twice. Lollipop has got a cough; I have to bandage it." He said another time that he had a bunny at home. The bunny was sick with asthma: he got the asthma from playing in mud puddles. After he had missed two appointments because of asthma and a sore throat, he explained to the therapist that he had gotten a sore throat from mudballs; he had only smelled them but had gotten a sore throat. When his mother was ill, he said she got sick from drinking from a dirty pot.

Once, when his mother was angry at him, he said to the therapist: "I was too wild," then ran and yelled, returned to bang and throw the elephant, saying, "I will fix this elephant. I will put it into water. How do you like it, Mr. Elephant? Time for you to get sick." He took him out, and put him in a blanket. "I bundle him up so he will not catch cold. He needed a bath. He got dirty in the mud puddle." Then he explained to his mother at the end of the hour, "The elephant had a bath. He got dirty because I was throwing him around." The sequence is: he was thrown away, he got dirty, he gets a bath, he gets sick. The asthma serves to bring the discarded (and bad) child back to his mother. He has to get sick because he was bad and because he left mother.

The therapist asked on one occasion if Lollipop and Jimmy had been sick. Rickie answered by saying, "They get so dirty when they are in bed that I have to beat them." He immediately went on to say that Lollipop liked to go to parties and wear evening dresses, while Jimmy liked baseball. The asthma is punishment for being dirty and enuretic, as well as a return to mother, but is tantamount to castration. While playing with a broken doll, he wanted to dismember it and fix it. As he did so, he said, "The baby is spoiled. Mommy is sick; she has pneumonia since yesterday. She went for shots. She likes to give shots too. She gives them to me. I like them." He cuts off the doll's fingers and toes, saying, "It looks like a monkey with a long tail. I cut off his long tail." Getting the needle from mother is equated with being passive, castrated. Then he embarked on a repetitive game of putting a clip on the hose from the bathinette and taking it off again so that the water ran out. After summer vacation, one of his first questions was whether the bathinette still leaked.

Over the course of the first year, the theme of sickness was woven into conflicts proceeding from oral to anal to phallic levels. One got sick from drinking dirty water, but could keep well by drinking germ-free milk. Later, one got sick from playing in mud puddles or smelling mudballs, and had to be bathed; but the bath is cold, too; he said to the elephant as he put it in the bath, "Time for you to get sick." The same sequence follows with wetting and enuresis. Gradually his play shifted to problems of castration, having babies, and oedipal wishes. He became more assertive, and dealt more actively with the threat of separation. The horses had a "running away habit"; he played a repeated game of running and shouting, "Block my way."

Only gradually, and never altogether, was the feminine identification given up. Lollipop had been both boy and girl, preferred evening dresses and parties to baseball. Rickie played a mother's role to Lollipop; he said, "I am the mother; grandmother is waiting outside." In time, Lollipop was replaced by the elephant and the horses. When he played with the rifle, he alternated between putting a rifle in water and hiding it in a blue box (blue is his mother's favorite color).

Fire may also be used in fantasies concerning mother. Leonard, at six, drew a picture of a woman with red hair and named her for his mother. He dreamt of "mugging" with an old witch who chased him, tied him, put him in a cracker box and set fire to him. He added that when he was young, he wanted to hug his mother that way.

Sometimes the children expressed the mother-child union as a physical bond. Peter drew a large, blushing rose with a green stem and attached a bud saying it looked like a radish. He added thorns to the stem and said, "Rose is my mother's first name; I guess that's what made me think of it." We assumed Peter was the bud, still growing on its mother.

Jacky said there are two kinds of eggs, those that stay under the brooding hen and those in the stores that are eaten. Chickens which don't hatch eggs are also eaten. Jacky seemed to be saying it is only safe when mother and child are together; one without the other may be eaten.

Jim symbolized the bond by connecting the mouth of one doll to the mouth of another doll with a piece of wire saying the goodness would go from one to the other.

The Thematic Apperception Test stories also reflected the children's central preoccupation with a strong mother-child bond and their anxieties over being enveloped and smothered. Jackie, who was seven, told this story for the first Thematic Apperception Test card: A boy had a violin which kept getting broken. He would get it fixed and play it again. "It got bigger and bigger until it got so big that he climbed into it and then he was in Mother Goose Land."

On another TAT card depicting an operation, a boy was bitten by a poisonous spider while he was walking in a cave. They had to cut open his stomach to get the poison out.

The fearful consequences of wishing to be separate from mother are described in another story. A boy wants to go to the carnival, but his mother won't let him because she is sick and she thought he was too little. The boy goes away with the carnival man while mother gets sicker and phones an ambulance. The boy thinks: "Oh, it's just a joke. My mother is just doing it to make me come back." But he saw mother was really coming out on a stretcher and he went with her to the hospital where she died. The boy went to his grandmother who said, "I'll never let you do to me what you did to your mother." The boy was made to stay in his room for two weeks and after that was restricted to the yard.

These fantasies were the asthmatic child's wish. The wish is for shelter and protection, for the intrauterine position, where all needs—even breathing—are automatically met. But the claustrum is as much frightening as desired, as much reflecting helplessness, frustration, and death, as gratification and safety (Lewin, 1952).

MOTHER'S NEED TO BE CLOSE TO CHILD

The child's need and the mother's need for closeness complement each other. One mother complained about her five-year-old son's infantile traits, but unconsciously she preferred him as a baby. Mother had to be present while he urinated. When she left to answer the telephone, he would stop and wait until she returned. If he had to urinate while sitting for a bowel movement, mother had to hold his penis. After he moved his bowels, he would lie across mother's knee while she wiped him. Refusal to help, led to temper tantrums. He once threatened: "You will die if you don't come and help me." He also insisted mother be present while he dressed. He sucked on a diaper at night which he called his "yum yum." He was interested in cooking and would have a tantrum if his mother baked a cake without him. Mickey told his doctor that his mother used to teach music but now she has to stay home and take care of him, emphasizing she had to be with him when he "catches bronchitis." Mother was unaware of her wish to keep him infantile and dependent on her, but showed it indirectly when she frequently questioned the need to continue treatment and when she resented the suggestion that Mickey wipe himself.

Another mother showed her involvement with her child in a different way. For two weeks after the birth of a boy, who later developed asthma, she felt there was another baby inside her. Many of the mothers experienced their pregnancies as pleasant and had difficulty in parting with the child at birth. (Labor was induced artificially; mother would be unable to bear down, etc.) It was as if they were saying the perfect relationship is between a mother and her unborn child within. What Helene Deutsch (1944) described as the experience of pregnancy for the motherly woman—the fulfillment of mankind's eternal yearning for identity between the ego and the non-ego—is for this mother not relinquished when the child is born.

The need to keep the child close often led the mothers unconsciously to foster the child's asthma. As the asthma begins to improve in therapy, the child usually becomes more openly aggressive. At this point the mother's anxiety increases, and she often questions the need to continue therapy. Such was the case with David M., where the asthma served as a safeguard against aggression which mother could not tolerate. As Mrs. M. said, "It's better to have asthma than to fight in a foxhole."

Jane's mother was happy that she herself had asthma when she was young. Otherwise, she might have run around, gone to parties, gotten into trouble, and she would never have met her present husband in church. She had the same fears of sexuality for Jane and felt Jane was protected by her asthma. Jane, six years old, disclosed in therapy how she shared mother's fears. She clung to her mother and did not dare show her fondness for her male therapist in her mother's presence. Alone with her doctor, she became quite seductive. She told how babies grow in Mummy's tummy and how the doctor gives the mother a sleeping pill, cuts mother open and takes the baby out. Then she told her doctor, "When we get married, we'll take sleeping pills right off and have a baby."

This special closeness of mother to her child leads to an inability to see the child as a separate individual. The child becomes identified with a figure from mother's past incompatible with the reality of the child in the present. Jane's mother was anxiously overprotective. She was afraid to let Jane out of sight to play with other children, and she was overly concerned during the patient's asthma attacks. Jane, to mother, was herself in the past, the little girl with asthma. As a child, the mother had resented her own mother's solicitude and preference for her younger sister. Her own mother never allowed her to go to parties. She had felt that attention was showered on her only because she was sick. Similarly, the mother now prefers Jane's younger sister and finds the latter a much easier child to raise, but hovers anxiously over Jane. In the course of therapy, the mother was able to allow Jane more freedom, and asthma attacks became less frequent. At this point, the mother's concerns shifted from Jane to the younger sister who developed transitory asthmatic symptoms.

The mothers are close to the asthmatic child in many ways yet reject him in other ways. They usually do not have the same conflicts in relation to their other children. Some mothers on the surface reject their asthmatic children and appear to fit into the concept of rejection, suggested by Miller and Baruch (1948), which, we feel, describes one aspect of a complex relationship. The paradox of the mother clinging to her child and pushing him brusquely away toward premature independence can be understood in terms of the mother's unconscious need and her defense against it.

SOURCE OF MOTHER'S NEED TO BE CLOSE TO CHILD

The source of the mother's special bond with the asthmatic child became apparent in the light of the mother's experiences in her past life. With Jane, described above, the mother repeated the unresolved hostile dependent relationship she had with her own mother.

In many cases we found that the mothers had an anaclitic and obligatory relationship with another person, often a sister. Mrs. M. maintained her close attachment to her sister Mary long after Mary died. Another mother had a twin sister on whom she leaned. The twins went to music school together, jointly taught music, and became pregnant at the same time. When Mickey was born the mother's twin was in a distant city having her baby also. The mother felt very much alone and said she had no one to turn to. She had trouble with Mickey from the very beginning. He was a feeding problem and developed eczema at six months. Later the mother became so attached to her aunt that she was afraid to move away and establish her own home with her husband. She found herself unable to function as a separate individual when her twin moved away. She kept Mickey tied to her like a baby long after this ceased to be appropriate.

Harry's mother had a twin brother with whom she shared everything from childhood on. As an adolescent, she never went on a date unless her twin came too. When she was twenty-four, this brother suddenly married, moved away, and she has not seen him since. She felt very lonely, and longed for a woman friend to confide in. Harry is the oldest of three children. He is undersized for his age, shy, sensitive, clinging to his mother and unable to hold his own with his peers. His mother asserted that she treated all the children exactly alike, "as if they were triplets," making no allowance for age differences. She is afraid to treat Harry according to his age and at the same time resents his inability to defend himself in fights. The mother's need for a close relationship first with her twin brother and later with her son seems related to earlier experiences with her own mother, a nervous person with little to give.

The twin theme has proven to be one striking way in which the unconscious symbiotic need is expressed both by the mothers and by the children. One mother had always been very attached to her older sister, "We were often taken for twins," she said. She very much wanted twins and indeed had as first-born twin girls, one of whom died at birth, leaving the mother grief-stricken. Three years later, a boy was born who subsequently developed asthma. Unconsciously the mother identified her son with the dead twin. In later years his birthday was celebrated on the birthday of his older sister. He was small for his age, shy, and afraid to fight. He told his therapist that the milkman thought he and his younger brother were twins. Twin fantasies were another derivative of the symbiotic need shared by mother and child. In some cases the mother did not develop a close tie to another person, but remained ambivalently dependent on her own mother. Susan's mother complained that she had to grow up after her marriage. The youngest child in a family of six, she had assumed she would always be "the baby in the family." She had always shared a bed with one of her sisters and had never slept alone in her life. She did not want the responsibility of children, and became pregnant only because her husband's family insisted on it. Her own mother spent six months of each year in California. While she was away, Susan's mother would write voluminous letters to her and save all her sewing for the grandmother to do on her return. A few months before therapy began, the grandmother died of a carcinoma of the womb. Susan's mother experienced numerous abdominal pains during her mother's illness and after her death. She quickly formed a relationship to the social worker and became strongly dependent on her. At first she described her mother in positive terms, but gradually after the course of several years became able to verbalize her resentments. She felt that her mother had neglected her to care for mother's feeble-minded older sister. Susan's mother said, almost tearfully, that it was hard to let your children be independent and grow up, but it is much better for them if you can do that. As she became more adult herself, striking changes occurred in her relationship to Susan. She saw Susan as an individual and felt warmer toward her, although they continued to irritate one another. At present the patient is no longer a source of anxious worry to her mother, and she has been asthma free for the past two years. In several cases like Susan's, where a mother identifies the asthmatic child with a sibling, the significance lies not so much in the identification itself as in the revival of the mother's conflict with her own mother.

DIFFERENCE BETWEEN BOYS AND GIRLS

The central conflict is essentially the same for boys and girls. They experience intense longings to be close to mother and at the same time feel threatened by such closeness and need to escape from it. However, on the surface, the mothers of girls expressed more negative feelings, while the positive aspects more often colored the relationships between boys and their mothers.

Doris Q. was referred to the clinic for behavior problems as well as for asthma. Though Doris and her mother were very irritating to each other, Doris was unwilling to separate from her mother for interviews. Mrs. Q. asserted that the patient was always very good when she was out with her father, but difficult to handle when she was with her mother. On the surface Mrs. Q. is very rejecting of Doris. When she was an infant the mother had an impulse to stuff her down the toilet. At the beginning of therapy the mother identified Doris with a series of devalued figures: a feeble-minded cousin, a retarded maternal aunt, and her father.

In therapy Doris acted out her aggression toward her mother with three female therapists who saw her at successive periods. She depreciated them, swore at them, tried to hurt them, and get them dirty, whereas she was friendly and coquettish with two male therapists.

With the girls, the mothers were more outspokenly resentful of the asthma attacks and would accuse the child of doing it on purpose to get her own way. One mother refused to give her girl "asthma pills" during the attack. Another said, "I could have murdered her," because the child kept the neighbors awake.

However, a tender intimate mother-daughter relationship was found in two cases where the mother also had asthma. In these cases there was an intuitive understanding of each other's needs and feelings, often at a nonverbal level (Unger and Unger, 1952).

The girls respond with aggressive feelings toward mother figures, expressed quite directly on the projective tests. One of the patients told a story to TAT card #12F about a girl who "wished that her mother would die for she was so mean to her. Her wish came true and she lived happily ever after with her brother."

In contrast, the relationship between the mother and the asthmatic boy appears more affectionate. The mothers were frequently seductive and encouraged the expression of oedipal wishes but tolerated aggression poorly. On the projective tests the boys told far fewer directly negative stories about the mothers. Their hostile feelings toward the mother figure could only be expressed symbolically, as e.g. in a story about a poisonous spider or witch.

The relationship between the father and the asthmatic child has not been studied intensively. Projective tests, occasional contacts with fathers, and information brought by the mothers have led to the impression that the father's relationship with the son does little to enhance his masculine identification. In the case of David M., the mother subtly interfered with David's relationship with his father by taking up all of father's time when he was home. In many cases, the father's relationship with his daughter, however, was unusually warm and understanding. Deborah's father considered her a special child and in many ways like himself. In one case, the father slept with his four-year-old adopted daughter, and in many ways assumed a motherly role. He brought the girl to the hospital and he, instead of the mother, had regular interviews with a social worker. Seductive behavior on the part of the fathers toward their daughter endangered the relationship between mother and daughter. Some mothers were outspokenly jealous of their daughters. We feel the central conflict of the asthmatic child and his mother, involving a mutual need for closeness and mutual fear of estrangement, was intensified by the girl's oedipal wishes.

Marked passivity needs are shown by the boys in their TAT stories, in which the hero was asleep, lacking in ambition, and afraid of mother's criticism. This was true even when the boy on the surface appeared to be active and masculine. Passive needs in the girls were also prominent but more frequently were masked by reaction formations.

DISCUSSION

The development of asthma in the child appears to be the result of a number of influences reinforcing each other:

(1) *Allergic constitution.* An allergic predisposition is an essential factor. It is possible that allergic children are generally more sensitive. Certainly in many of the cases there is a history of hypersensitivity, irritability, excessive crying, and feeding difficulties from the very beginning. As a result, the mother-child relationship is altered. The child makes special demands which are less easy for the mother to satisfy. She may feel rejected or particularly needed. Infantile eczema and other allergic symptoms are often forerunners of asthma. Because of eczema, physical handling of the child becomes less satisfying to both mother and infant. For the child, the inevitable frustrations in feeding and handling are intensified, leading to greater fixation at this infantile level. For the mother, the child may be less satisfying, may mobilize guilt and a feeling of inadequacy; or he may provide gratification, through his difficulties proving how much he needs her.

(2) *Early respiratory infection.* The early occurrence of respiratory illness may, as suggested by Felix Deutsch (1951), link respiratory

symptoms to critical conflicts and predispose further to the development of asthma. Such illnesses heighten the mother's concerns with disease, suffocation and death. In addition, the respiratory tract may have undergone pathophysiological changes. Often the onset of asthma is closely associated with respiratory infections, or with other breathing difficulties, and only later emerges as a distinct clinical picture.

(3) *Ordinal position.* Cobb and McDermott (1939) made the observation that the asthmatic is frequently the oldest child. Our series confirms this. Two of our cases were only children and seventeen of twenty-eight were the oldest child. In this position he may encounter greater anxiety and uncertainty on the mother's part than do his siblings.

(4) *Special emotional conflicts of the mother.* The asthmatic child assumes a special place in his mother's feelings. She unconsciously regards the child as a part of herself, without which she feels incomplete. These feelings derive from her own past and are not ego-syntonic. Often she has turned away from or been disappointed in her own mother, and her struggle between individuality and dependence on another person continues. Consciously, she may feel free of her mother, may devaluate her, or may still feel bound. But the unconscious need for the mother persists. Several of the mothers transferred this infantile attachment to another person, e.g., an older sister. This person then became the good mother without whom they could not exist. With the child they repeat the symbiotic relationship with the mother figure. The still active conflict between dependence and independence, between closeness and distance, is transferred to him. They hold on to him and push him away at the same time. The child responds in kind. He feels the wish for closeness and protection, and at the same time the drive toward independence and growth. As one asthmatic girl said, "Don't come too close but don't go away." He feels enveloped and choked by his mother's need to keep him so close. This is often expressed symbolically in his fantasies in the image of a claustrum or womb, which is both an inviting shelter and a dangerous trap. For both mother and child, the asthma itself may become a vehicle for the expression of feelings of protection and rejection, surrender and rebellion. This conflict is intensified when the child is with his mother and lessened when he is away from her. These profound regressive and oral wishes are akin to those expressed by psychotics, but the asthmatic has usually erected more adequate defenses against them. Often the defensive system resembles that found in phobic children. While the personality is immature in the sense of

failure to establish independence, in other ways the ego continues to develop.

Those features which were striking in many, but not all, of the cases, such as passivity in the boys, or closeness to father in the girls, appear to be secondary to the more crucial issue of closeness and separation between mother and child. While such a conflict is to some extent universal, with the asthmatic child it seems to be of outstanding intensity and central significance. Mere physical separation brings only temporary relief. The aim of psychotherapy is to achieve a genuine differentiation between mother and child so that both can tolerate being together as well as apart and are free to establish true object love.

BIBLIOGRAPHY

Abramson, H. A. (1952), Psychodynamic Pharmacology of the Treatment of Asthma. *J.A.M.A.*, CL.

Cobb, S. and McDermott, (1939), A Psychiatric Survey of Fifty Cases of Bronchial Asthma. *Psychosom. Med.*, I.

Coolidge, J. (1954), The Asthmatic Bond—A Special Mother-Child Relationship. Read at the Annual Meeting of the American Orthopsychiatric Association, New York, March, 1954.

Deutsch, F. (1947), Artistic Expression and Neurotic Illness: The Respiratory Neurosis of Charles Kingsley. Read at Smith College, July 27, 1947.

—— (1951), Thus Speaks the Body: Some Psychosomatic Aspects of the Respiratory Disorder, Asthma. *Acta Med. Orient.*, X.

—— and Murphy, W. F. (1955), *The Clinical Interview*, Vol. I. New York: International Universities Press.

Deutsch, H. (1944), *The Psychology of Women*. New York: Grune & Stratton.

French, T. M. and Alexander, F. (1941), Psychogenic Factors in Bronchial Asthma. *Psychosom. Med. Mon.*, IV

Gerard, M. N. (1946), Bronchial Asthma in Children. *Nerv. Child*, IV.

Hallowitz, D. (1954), Residential Treatment of Chronic Asthmatic Children. *Am. J. Orthopsychiat.*, XXIV.

Lewin, B. D. (1952), Phobic Symptoms and Dream Interpretation. *Psa. Quart.*, XXI.

Miller, H. and Baruch, D. W. (1948), Psychosomatic Studies of Children with Allergic Manifestations. *Psychosom. Med.*, X.

Rogerson, C. H.; Hardcastle, D. H.; Dugid, K. (1935), A Psychological Approach to the Problem of Asthma and the Asthma-Eczema-Prurigo Syndrome. *Guy's Hosp. Rep.*, LXXXV.

Saul, L. J. and Lyons, J. W. (1955), Motivation and Respiratory Disorders. In: *Recent Developments in Psychosomatic Medicine*, ed. E. D. Wittkower and R. A. Cleghorn. New York: Lippincott.

Sperling, M. (1949), The Role of the Mother in Psychosomatic Disorders in Children. *Psychosom. Med.*, XI.

Unger, L. and Unger, D. H. (1952), Treatment of Bronchial Asthma. *J.A.M.A.*, CL.

A SHORT COMMUNICATION ON A TRAUMATIC EPISODE IN A CHILD OF TWO YEARS AND SEVEN MONTHS

ELIZABETH GERO-HEYMANN (New York)

This brief communication concerns a little girl. The material that I am presenting was gained during the analysis of her mother, who had two children. The eldest, a boy, was seven and the little girl, whose case I am presenting, was at that time two years and seven months old.

In the last stage of her analysis, Mrs. M. came to her session and immediately told me that the previous day Lily had had a traumatic experience.

Lily had been riding in the car with the baby sitter, holding her doll on her lap. She had twisted the doll's head, and the head had suddenly popped off into the air. When the mother came home about an hour after this had happened, she found the child white and motionless. Only after a long time did she relax enough to cry, but could not be consoled.

At night Lily made all sorts of magic gestures when she took her other dolls to bed. She spat on them and murmured some words, which the mother could not quite understand. For several weeks Lily had difficulties in falling asleep.

Lily was completely accepted by her mother. The mother nursed her for six months. The weaning was smooth. The analysis was interrupted when Lily was born and during the first fifteen months the mother did not leave her at all. The toilet training was smooth, too. The most disturbing factor in Lily's life was her four-year-old older brother, who often handled her roughly, snatched things away from her and teased her a great deal. Lily admired him, but she was also very afraid of him. Before the doll incident happened, Lily had tried to urinate standing up like her brother. She had often seen her brother's genitals and had shown her envy very openly.

Lily's father was always kind to her, but his interest in the child was still rather limited at the time of the accident. He was more interested in the older boy. When Robert was little, the father had at times been rather critical of his wife's handling of the boy. His wife could not take his criticism and had at times felt deep anger toward her husband as well as to her son.

The mother's attitude toward Lily was entirely different. This time her husband did not interfere. One could say, Lily was her very own child. So Lily received a great deal of love and warmth from her mother, but she must have sensed some lack of interest in her father. The only person Lily felt sure of was her mother.

When the mother had to leave Lily in order to come to her sessions, Lily resented it very much. She used to look very sad when the mother left. As the family lived in a suburb, it meant that the mother had to be away for at least three hours.

A day or two after the doll incident, Lily burst out crying, when she looked at a picture on the wall that showed her mother holding a baby in her arms. It is a picture of the mother holding the elder child Robert, when he was a baby. The mother took the picture away to spare Lily the frightening experience. On the picture the mother is bending down and there is an obvious wrinkle showing on her neck. The mother understood that Lily was afraid that the mother's head would come off. Lily asked for the picture, saying: "I am two years old, I won't be scared."

During this period Lily complained that her vagina hurt and she tried again and again to urinate like her brother. The mother could not move her head without causing anxiety to Lily, and Lily did not dare to touch her mother's head.

The mother tried to help Lily in all sorts of ways. She bought clay, she made dolls of clay, dolls of rags to re-enact the story. Nothing helped. At last the mother had the idea of singing the whole story to Lily, who seemed to like this and always asked for all the details.

At this time the mother read a story to Lily in which a farmer, Mr. Mac-Gregor, chased a rabbit with a sieve. On one page one sees Mr. MacGregor's hand holding the sieve, just his hand, no arm. Lily was afraid to look at this picture, and the mother explained that there was not enough room to include the whole figure. Lily's brother drew an arm for her. Lily demanded that her mother include Mr. MacGregor in the new song.

When I heard about the singing I made two suggestions: The first was to sing that at the time when the doll's head had come off, Lily had been very angry with Mummy because Mummy was not at home. To this Lily remarked at first with great emphasis:

"I was not angry."

The mother said, "I think you were, Lily, but Mummy was not angry."

"Why not?" asked Lily.

"Because I love you," the mother answered.

After the mother had for the first time included in the song that Lily had been angry, and Lily had emphatically denied it, Lily said at the end of the song with a sigh of relief: "I like these songs."

The second suggestion I made with regard to the song was the following: When Lily had twisted the doll's head and the head had come off, Lily was afraid that Mummy's head could come off but Mummy was quite all right.

I would now like to give you the whole song in its final form.

There's a picture hanging on the wall
Of Mummy holding Robert,
And there's a big wrinkle in her neck
Because she's holding her head back.
And Lily was walking up the stairs
And she saw the picture,
And she got terribly scared
Because Lily had a dolly that
The factory didn't make so good
And Lily was in Mrs. Miller's car,
And she turned the dolly's head
And the dolly's head popped off
And fell in her lap.
And the foam rubber came out—
And Lily was very, very scared
And she was very, very mad at Mummy,
Because Mummy wasn't there.
She had gone to school and shopping.
But Mummy isn't mad at Lily
Oh no!
And Mummy is quite all right
Oh yes!
And children get mad at their Mummies
When they have to go shopping or to school,
But Mummies don't get mad at their children for this.
And Daddy fixed dolly's head
So now it's good again
And he made the dolly squeak again
And now it's all right.

There's a picture of Farmer MacGregor
In the Peter Rabbit book,
And it shows the hands of Farmer MacGregor holding a sieve.
And Lily got scared because she thought they were broken.
But Mummy said, "No, Lily, it's only a picture and there
Wasn't room to draw the rest of Farmer MacGregor."
And Robert said, "Don't be scared, Lily,
If you want, I'll draw some more of the hands for you."
And he did.

The mother and Lily sang this song for about two weeks, when Lily wanted
to look at the picture again. The mother said: "Alright. Let us see whether
Lily is still afraid of the picture." Lily looked at the picture and said: "I hate
this Mummy, she does not like me."

This was the turning point. The next morning the mother saw Lily looking at the picture and she heard her saying: "This is the old Mummy, I am going to my nice new Mummy."

Some days later Lily said with contempt in her voice: "I am not afraid of this picture any more."

After Lily had felt all right for some time, she and her brother played a game one evening, in which they rolled off the bed holding each other. Robert said in jest: "Lily, you nearly broke my neck." Lily got white, and it took her mother some time to calm her down and to explain that she had not hurt her brother.

Some time later, when she felt quite all right, Lily said to her mother one day: "Mummy, let us talk." Her mother agreed.

Lily said: "All girls have ginas."

"Yes," said the mother.

Lily: "All boys have penises."

Mother: "Yes."

Lily ended the talk, saying: "But most people have penises."

After Lily had overcome her fear, she had a short period of trying very hard to be tough, obviously imitating her brother. When she was about two years and ten months old, she showed signs of being more pleased with being a girl. She wanted to show her "breasties" to her mother, and she discussed with her mother how it would be to nurse babies.

This is the condensed story of Lily's traumatic experience and of her cure. Phyllis Greenacre (1953) has pointed out that penis envy and castration anxiety often occur between two and a half and three years. Lily certainly did not leave us in any doubt as far as her envy and her fear were concerned. Her brother's aggressive teasing must have contributed a great deal to stimulate Lily's envy as well as her anxiety.

The doll accident happened at a time when Lily was preoccupied with the lack of the penis, with her strong envy of her brother, and with her aggressive feelings toward her mother, whom she needed so badly at the same time. The fact that the accident happened while Lily's aggressive fantasies were so strong explains why the experience was so traumatic.

What was it that caused the resolution of the child's trauma? Her penis envy and her castration anxiety were not interpreted to Lily. The two interpretations that had the therapeutic effect were:

(1) Lily wanted to hurt Mummy, but Mummy is quite all right.

(2) Lily was mad at Mummy, but Mummy was not mad at Lily.

Lily's mother was an unusually warm and accepting mother to Lily, but she occasionally had rather explosive outbursts of temper toward

Lily's brother. These probably added to Lily's fear. The main reason for Lily's neurotic spell, however, was the fear of her own aggression. Lily was afraid of her own destructive fantasies toward her mother who had deprived her of a penis, and toward her brother who had the desired penis. She was afraid to have the magic power to destroy mother and brother. At the same time she was afraid of retaliation. She had projected her own aggressive feelings onto her mother. The mother's patient and repeated interpretations, as well as her acceptance of Lily's anger, helped Lily in two ways. She became less afraid of her own magic power to destroy, and she modified the image she had of her mother. The "nice new Mummy" was less aggressive and more accepting of Lily. What is more, Lily had the experience that she could hate and still be loved. Thus a positive relationship with the "nice new Mummy" laid the foundation for a healthy superego development.[1]

BIBLIOGRAPHY

Freud, A. (1949), Notes on Aggression. *The Yearbook of Psychoanalysis,* VI. New York: International Universities Press, 1951.

—— (1953), The Bearing of the Psychoanalytic Theory of Instinctual Drives on Certain Aspects of Human Behavior. In: D*rives, Affects, Behavior,* ed. R. M. Loewenstein. New York: International Universities Press.

Freud, S. (1926), *The Problem of Anxiety.* New York: Norton, 1936.

Greenacre, P. (1953), Penis Awe and Its Relation to Penis Envy. In: *Drives, Affects, Behavior,* ed. R. M. Loewenstein. New York: International Universities Press.

[1] By now more than a year has passed since Lily's traumatic experience. Her mother finished her treatment nine months ago. I asked her how Lily had developed during that time. She told me that Lily, who is now three years and nine months old, is a well-developed child. She enjoys going to a nursery school where she participates in all activities. She is very fond of a little girl friend in her school. Lily also occupies herself well at home. She gave up all attempts to urinate like her brother and stopped complaining about her vagina.

She competes with her brother, but she also enjoys helping her mother in her household chores. On the whole she presents a picture of a healthy child without undue difficulties.

MAD LAUGHTER IN A SIX-YEAR-OLD BOY[1]

MARTHA WOLFENSTEIN, Ph.D. (New York)

Tommy was the most unfortunate child I have known, and the one who laughed the most. At a time in his life when he was acutely threatened with being abandoned by his mother he began to laugh incessantly. His laughter could be produced at will, like that of an accomplished actor. It had an exaggerated, crazy sound which filled the hearer with uneasiness; no one laughed with him. Tommy's laughter was an attempt to deny and ward off unbearable anxiety. It was also a means of attack, a provocation, and an expression of impulses which could not find other outlet. It was associated with a reduction of verbal articulateness, with the shouting of isolated incomprehensible words and phrases, and also with unco-ordinated motor activity as he threw himself on the floor and rolled about. In this it expressed a regressive tendency, the reverse of the normal development of a child entering the latency period, in which there is an increased capacity to use speech in isolation from emotionally expressive movement.

I

When Tommy was five, his mother brought him to the child guidance clinic because he was unable to stay in nursery school; he could not be separated from her. She reported that his behavior was unruly and uncontrollable; she was unable to take him anywhere. The two of them lived in almost complete isolation, incessantly together. Tommy's father had deserted his mother when Tommy was three months old. The mother's own parents had died shortly before this, and she became understandably deeply depressed. She was especially vulnerable to

---

[1] I wish to express my appreciation to the Jewish Board of Guardians of New York City for permission to use the material of this case. I treated Tommy in the Child Guidance Institute of the Jewish Board of Guardians over a period of about a year and a half. During the first six months I saw him once a week and also saw his mother weekly. When contact was resumed after the summer holiday about two months later, the mother was seen by a social worker. During the following ten months I saw Tommy twice a week. (Throughout, there were many interruptions due to his frequent illnesses.) At the end of this time Tommy was placed in the Henry Ittleson Center for Child Research. I am grateful to the staff of the Ittleson Center for putting their observations of Tommy at my disposal.

the extremity of desertion which she suffered at this time. From childhood she had been intensely clinging toward her mother, often embracing her and begging her never to die. She had felt that she could not go on living without her mother. Thus, fears of abandonment, undoubtedly motivated by her own ambivalence, had haunted her life, and now, just after Tommy's birth, her worst fears had been realized.

As I would reconstruct the situation in Tommy's infancy, the little boy was confronted by a mother withdrawn in depression, and he discovered then that he could rouse her to life, to excitement, and to contact with him by naughty, provocative behavior. At the time I knew him Tommy showed an almost incessant impulse to do whatever was not permitted, and I would suppose that the need to rouse his mother from depression into excitement was one source of this behavior. That he also had wished to console her with his love is suggested by an episode from the time when he was in nursery school (shortly after beginning treatment). There was only one child in his class with whom he had any contact, a sad, withdrawn, little boy, who sat apart and did not join in the play of the other children. Tommy repeatedly approached this child and embraced him. This may have been a repetition of his behavior toward his depressed mother.

From the time that her husband left her, Tommy's mother continually debated whether she should not place Tommy in a foster home. She said that she had once approached a foster home agency, when Tommy was not yet a year old, but that no arrangements could be concluded because her husband would not give permission for the child to be placed. While she thought constantly of getting rid of Tommy, she also clung to him desperately. He was, as she said, all she had, her whole life. When he had been little she had often smothered him with kisses. She still slept in the same bed with him. The mother's impulse to get rid of Tommy in part expressed an identification with the aggressor; she had been the victim of abandonment, she in turn would be the one who abandons.

Tommy not only overheard his mother discuss with neighbors the possibility of placing him, he also was repeatedly threatened with this when he misbehaved. I think this was a second major motive for his provocative naughtiness. He could not bear to have this threat hanging over him with its terrible uncertainty. He had to test over and over again whether the threat would be carried out. If he was bad and the mother still did not throw him out, then for the moment he was reassured. But the threat was really not removed, and the test always had to be repeated. He gave a demonstration of the same thing in the office with me. After he had known me for some time and had become attached to me, he asked me whether bad children could come to my office. I assured him that he could always come and asked if he thought he was bad. He said no, but then proceeded to shout, seized a box of candy and asked if he could empty it on the floor, and, when I said no, dumped it all out. He seemed to be checking on whether I meant what I had said, that I would not throw him out even if he was bad. There was also in this a wish to control fatality; if it had to come, then it would be because he made it happen; he would not be a passive victim. In this sense, he sometimes asked me to say to him in an angry voice that I was going to throw him out.

Tommy's mother was particularly anxious to have him go to school because she wanted to be able to go to work. She was living on a small allowance from a public welfare agency and on payments from Tommy's father, where, however, the father was giving only part of what was due. When Tommy was about three and a half, the mother had made the first attempt to put him in nursery school. This separation had been especially difficult for Tommy because it followed closely on a traumatic separation experience when he had been in a hospital overnight for a tonsillectomy. At nursery school he had not been able to let his mother leave the room for the first three months, and after this, when she had left him and gone to work, he had been so frequently ill, with colds and ear infections, that the doctor had advised her to withdraw him from school. Now, with Tommy approaching his fifth birthday, the mother was very anxious to renew the attempt to get him to school. She had tried unsuccessfully to enter him in a public school kindergarten; he had refused to stay there without her, and the teacher and principal would not allow her to stay in school with him. The mother's view of this was that Tommy is thrown out everywhere; nobody wants him.

Shortly after Tommy started coming to the child guidance clinic, it was arranged for him to be readmitted to his former nursery school. The mother was allowed to stay at school with him until he should be able to remain without her. At school Tommy was afraid of the other children and said that they hit him. Toward the teachers he was very aggressive. He frequently told them: "Get out of here!" He was again turning passivity into activity, identifying with the aggressor, saying to others what he felt his mother was saying to him. He also anticipated, as his mother did too, that he would be thrown out of school, and he was telling the teachers to get out before they had a chance to say this to him. To the considerable alarm of the teachers, since he showed little awareness of the real damage he might do, Tommy attacked them with hammers and saws. At home, Tommy's mother frequently lost control and hit him and pulled his hair. He probably expected similar punitive violence from the teachers, and hastened to attack first, to ward off his fear of being attacked. But he also had some positive attachment to his teacher, which he used in an attempt to demonstrate to his mother that he could do without her. When it was time to leave school in the afternoon he would sometimes tell his mother that he was going home with the teacher rather than with her.

When the attempt was made to have Tommy remain in school while the mother returned home, he began running out of the school building into the street in an effort to get back to his mother. I learned that at this time the mother had renewed or intensified her threats to send Tommy away. (This seemed in part related to my having told the mother that I would soon be going on my vacation. Whenever she felt abandoned she was impelled to abandon Tommy.)

The school director felt that Tommy's running out of the school into a busy and dangerous thoroughfare involved a risk for which she could not assume responsibility. If he did not stop, they would not be able to keep him at school. At this point I suggested that the mother should again remain in the building while Tommy was at school. After I left on my vacation, however, the attempt was renewed to have Tommy stay in school without his mother. He again ran out into the street, and was expelled from school. I think that his repeated running out was not only an effort to get back to mother, but was also motivated by the need to test whether the threat that he would be thrown out of school would be carried through.

During the time that Tommy was in school he showed some effort in his play to master his separation difficulties. He played with me over and over a game which we called "the good-by game." This game also reflected another separation experience which had occurred in the office. In order to be able to talk with his mother alone, I had (shortly after he first came to the office) introduced him to a secretary, whom he called "Miss Betty," with whom he went off to play while his mother talked with me. Subsequently he had also become able to stay in the office alone with me while his mother remained in the waiting room outside.

The "good-by game" was played in this way. Tommy seated himself in my revolving chair, instructed me to turn the chair so that he turned away from me, and to say, "Good-by, good-by." As the chair turned full circle round and he was again facing me, I would say "Hello," to which he would reply, "Good-by!" turn away again, and laugh. This laughter was more appropriate than the crazy laughter which he produced later; it was related to a joke he was playing on his partner in the game and was meaningful in this context. The laughter represented an attempt to master the anxiety of separation and was substituted for the tears he had shed when his mother left him at school. The game was based on Tommy's favored mechanism of identification with the aggressor; he became the one who went away, and the other person had to suffer being abandoned. After we had played this game for some time, I said that I did not like him to go away and leave me, that I was going to cry. This alarmed Tommy and he jumped down from his chair and wanted to stop the game. He needed to deny the sadness that was involved in separation by making it a laughing matter. A little later, however, he incorporated the idea of my crying into the game, regularly instructed me to cry when he said good-by, and reassured me that he would have Miss Betty stay with me.

In the fall following Tommy's dismissal from nursery school, and before I saw him again, his mother attempted to enroll him in a public school first grade. On his one day in school he continually barked like a dog. He had recently been frightened of dogs, and in the nursery school he had been afraid of the other children. In barking like a dog, he was again trying to frighten others as a defense against his own fear of them. He was not accepted in the first grade, and an attempt by the mother to enter him in public school kindergarten was equally unsuccessful, as the principal refused to admit a child who cried for his mother and whose mother would have to stay at school. The mother then gave up hope of being able to get Tommy into school. I believe that from this time on her long-term, though until now wavering, resolve to place Tommy in a foster home or institution became fixed. It was then that Tommy's mad laughter began. His psychotic tendencies, whether because of their inherent impetus, or because of his intensified emotional danger, or both, now became increasingly manifest.[2]

II

The first time I heard Tommy's crazy laughter it was set off by a word that he shouted over and over, the word "odor." This pattern of inducing laughter in himself by a cue word persisted over a period of several months, the words used for this purpose varying from time to time. He felt no need to make the cause of his mirth intelligible, and it was often not possible to extract from him the context from which his cue word was derived. In the case of the word "odor," however, I was able to learn from him the immediate situation from which he took it. He told me that as he had been going out through the hall of his apartment house with his mother, she had exclaimed: "What an odor!" in a disgusted tone of voice which he reproduced very convincingly. The source of the odor was a garbage can in the hall. I would make a guess that the little boy thought at first that he was the source of the odor that so roused his mother's disgust, and experienced great relief when he discovered it was the garbage can. His laughter was in part a celebration of triumph at having escaped the danger of being repudiated by his mother for making an odor.

In Tommy's mind, one of the reasons why his mother wanted to get rid of him was because of the disgust which his excretory processes aroused in her. According to the mother's account, which was doubtlessly incomplete, Tommy was a "very clean baby," who from the time she started to train him, at one and a half, was very co-operative and dry even at night from the age of two and a half on. However, no baby is clean to begin with, and admittedly Tommy had not been clean for the first year and a half. In calling him a clean baby the mother was denying his initial dirtiness and her own disgust about it. Tommy, with his intense ambivalence toward his mother, had strong impulses to continue to be dirty, which he greatly feared would alienate her. He gave an indication of her reactions to his messing up the house when he would mess up my office and then tell me to scold his pig, his favorite toy which he often brought with him. I should tell the pig he was very bad for making a mess and that it was a lot of trouble to clean it up.

There was also a memory from his first nursery school experience, which he

<hr>

[2] A neurological examination of Tommy when he was six and a half did not reveal any organic pathology. Two attempts to give Tommy a psychological examination at about the same time were unsuccessful. Examination by a staff psychiatrist of the Jewish Board of Guardians confirmed the diagnosis of schizophrenia.

had told me about repeatedly when he first came to see me. There had been a teacher (whose name was very similar to his mother's) whom he said he had liked, but about whom he recalled that he had thrown paint all over her dress, and "Was she mad!" Though this may have been quite literally true, it probably also cloaked more important memories about his mother's reactions to his dirtying impulses. In my office he often made rolls of clay which he called snakes, which he would alternately throw in the wastebasket and on my dress, expressing his conflicting tendencies to defecate in the right place (complying with mother's wishes) or in the wrong place (angrily soiling her).

The day when Tommy first started shouting "odor" during his visit with me was the same one on which he asked me whether bad children could come to my office and tested whether I would throw him out by dumping things on the floor. He also combined his laughter and his shouts of "odor" with the good-by game, calling out, as he turned away from me in the revolving chair: "Good-by, good-by! Odor! Odor!" and laughing loudly. When I responded with, "Good-by, you odor," he accepted this as very funny.

For some weeks Tommy continued to shout "odor" repeatedly and to follow this with his prolonged, wild laughter. This was among other things a provocative and aggressive act against his mother, who found this behavior unbearable. During this time Tommy acted out soiling activities in the office, breaking up cigarettes which he found in my drawer, spitting into the tobacco, throwing it on the floor, saying, "It's duty on the floor," and then picking it up and throwing it on my dress. This was followed by the production of a new key word, which he shouted over and over, and which set off fits of laughter: "Dr. Feigel!" When I tried to find out what was so funny about Dr. Feigel, Tommy told me: "Dr. Feigel put tobacco on the floor." He wanted me to telephone Dr. Feigel and scold him; I should tell him not to do that any more. I learned from the mother that Dr. Feigel, while he had not recently treated Tommy, had during this period administered a penicillin shot to her, an operation which Tommy had witnessed. What Tommy took to be the sexually attacking behavior of the doctor toward the mother, he translated into the dirtying of the room. In this way he repeated the aggressive activity of the doctor and also attempted to ward off the threat of this dangerous father figure by his laughter.

Tommy's laughter seemed not only to be associated with thoughts and symbolic representations of excretion, but to be itself equated with an excretory act. While his mother was talking with a social worker in another office during Tommy's hour with me, he said he wanted to go into the office where his mother was and "giggle all over the floor." While this may have referred to his throwing himself on the floor, as he sometmes did in his fits of laughter, it also seemed analogous to his throwing the tobacco ("duty") on the floor. He treated his laughter like excretion when he frequently announced that he was going to do it: "I'm going to giggle, I'm going to giggle now," like a well-trained child letting mother know when he has to defecate or urinate. When he stopped laughing, he often instructed me to ask him: "Aren't you laughing any more?" at which he would produce renewed outbursts of laughter. It seemed as though this might represent a teasing game which he had played with his mother, when she would ask him after a prolonged session on the toilet whether he was finished and he would produce more feces which he had been holding back.

The extraordinary way in which Tommy controlled his laughter, announcing when he was going to laugh, and producing it at will, may also have been related to a feeling of panic at the increasing loss of control involved in his psychosis. In making himself the master of laughter, he may have been demonstrating his control over loss of control: if I lose control it is because I choose to. That his laughter expressed uncontrollable excitement is evidenced by the fact that, according to his mother's report, he also laughed in his sleep. A wish to control others by his laughter was expressed when he once instructed me not to move while he laughed. He had asked me to cut out some pictures for him, but then demanded that I interrupt this as long as he would laugh. More often he would summon others into action by his laughter, as when he would announce his arrival in the waiting room by loud and continuous laughter in order to call me from my office, or when he would provoke his mother into hitting him by throwing himself down in a laughing fit on the street.

For Tommy, laughter, excretion, and also genital excitement were all equivalent. In one episode he performed what for him was a sexual act in terms of excretion, but then again substituted laughter for it. Tommy had not seen his father for a long time. Until he was about four, his father had taken him out occasionally, but then had stopped. That Tommy feared his father is suggested by the fact that at night he was afraid that a bear or a lion would come into the bed which he shared with his mother. The image of the father as cruel was kept vivid by his mother's frequent and tearful complaints about how the father made her suffer, particularly by not paying what was due for Tommy's support. Finally she appealed to the Domestic Relations Court to call her husband to account. Tommy went to court with his mother. To his excited imagination the prospect of the confrontation between the suffering mother and the cruel father seemed to have the impact of a primal scene. As it turned out the father did not appear in court, sending the excuse that he had broken his leg. This news added to the disturbing effect of the occasion.

When Tommy came to my office after returning from court, he pulled down the blind and in the darkened room told me that we must talk very softly because there was a bear under the desk who would come out if he heard us. He whispered the word "fuck," and said, "Oh, there's that terrible word again." He then said he would make "pee-pee" in the office, and before I could stop him took out his penis and urinated on me. Then he ran out to get some water to clean up, spilled a good deal on the floor, said it was the Pinocchio doll that had spilled it, and told me to scold Pinocchio. The anticipated confrontation of his parents had roused his erotic and hostile impulses, and the reported injury of his father had filled him with triumph and alarm. In displaying his penis and urinating on me, he was performing what for him was a sexual act, and at the same time assuring himself of the intactness of his organ by the response which he wished to evoke from me. In his characteristic way he was also testing by provocative behavior whether feared punishment would overtake him, whether the bear under the desk or I would attack him for his erotic activity. The castration theme was further manifested in his leaving in the office at the end of this hour his toy pig, from which he was usually inseparable and without which he could not go to sleep at night. He came back some time afterwards, looking quite dazed, to reclaim his pig.

The sexual excitement which on this occasion was expressed in urination was at other times manifested in laughter. Tommy received a great deal of sexual stimulation from his mother, in sleeping with her, in watching her dress and undress. In the following hour he confided to me: "I giggle when I see my Mommy's brassiere." He also told me that he laughed in order to wake his mother up in the morning. Thus his laughter not only expressed his own excitement but served to rouse his mother from withdrawn immobility, to get her excited too. He complained to me that his mother objected to his giggling in bed and hit him for it. He then proposed that he would come to live with me; he would sleep in my bed, and I should let him giggle as much as he liked.

The key words which set off Tommy's giggling frequently seemed to be associated with his father. For a time he shouted, "Uncle Pete!" and followed this with shrieks of laughter. Uncle Pete was a brother of his father's who had formerly sometimes taken Tommy on outings. Another favorite name, used similarly as a cue for laughter, was "Robert." All I could learn of Robert was that he was an older boy who lived in Tommy's apartment house, that he was "stinking," and that he had a father. However, once when Tommy's thoughts seemed to be related to his father, and I told him this, he exclaimed: "I won't talk about him! Robert! Robert!" From this it seems evident that Robert was one of the substitutes for Tommy's father. The laughter about these male figures (Dr. Feigel also being one of them) probably aimed at warding off and denying Tommy's fear of his father. Thus his oedipal feelings, both of sexual excitement in relation to his mother and fear of punishment from his father, were expressed in his laughter.

Tommy's laughter was both an equivalent of release of impulses (hostile, excretory, and genital) and a defense against anxiety. The central and overpowering anxiety in his life, as I have indicated, was the well-justified fear of being abandoned by his mother. With his reduced powers of articulateness, his tendency to compress a whole drama into a single word, he summed up this anxiety with the word "tired," which he began to repeat endlessly, followed by laughter. This word symbolized the mutually tormenting struggle in which Tommy and his mother were entangled. First his mother had said he made her tired. This was an expression of her finding him unbearable, which of course alarmed him greatly. Bringing into play his favorite defense, Tommy in turn began to say that he was tired—tired of the toys his mother had bought for him, which he would refuse to play with after a short time, tired of the paper cutouts which she made for him, which he would throw away. He was treating the toys and the cutouts the way his mother treated him. The mother then would become very cross, complaining and angry at his losing interest in his playthings. In a rage she would throw a toy which he had rejected across the room and break it, or refuse to buy him a new toy which he wanted, anticipating that he would very soon get tired of it. Tommy said to me: "Tired, tired, he always gets tired of it." And he told me: "My mother said it and now I have to say it."

Tommy enacted with me many times the drama of ambivalence which pervaded his relation with his mother, the ever-present danger that one would be overwhelmed with the impulse to get rid of a loved object. He wanted me to make endless paper cutouts for him (particularly of buses, to replace the toy bus which his mother had broken in anger). As I was drawing a bus and cutting it out, he would say repeatedly: "I like it, I'm going to keep it, I'm not going to get tired of it, I'm not going to tear it up, I'm not going to throw it away." But sooner or later he would feel that he did not like it, he wanted to tear it or throw it away; he would crumple it up and consign it to the wastebasket. This was partly also a test of whether I would, like his mother, get impatient with his destruction of my gifts, or whether I would keep providing him with more. He expressed similar ambivalent feelings toward his favorite toy, the rubber pig which he frequently brought to the office with him. He would hold the pig to his cheek, and murmur, "Piggy," in the most affectionate tone. He would ask me, "Aren't you glad Piggy is here?" But then he would invent tales of Piggy's misdemeanors (Piggy made a mess, or Piggy went for a ride on the bus alone when he had been told there was no money for a bus ride), and I would be instructed to scold Piggy severely. Or he would become angry with Piggy, throw him in the wastebasket, say he did not want Piggy, that he would leave him in the office and not take him home. When I would say how bad Piggy must feel, he would take Piggy out of the wastebasket and fondle him again.

Tommy could not tolerate having the sadness which his laughter aimed at denying brought into the open. When he had been shouting "odor" endlessly and laughing all the time, I had told him that I thought he could not stop, that I felt sorry for him, and I said, "Poor Tommy." He had been greatly distressed by this, had told his mother that I had said, "Poor Tommy," and that she must tell me never to say that again. At another time, when he was forcing out repeated bursts of laughter, I told him that he really did not seem very happy when he laughed like that. He immediately became sober and frightened, and wanted to run out of the room.

At a time when definite plans were finally under way for placing Tommy in an institution, his laughter gave way almost entirely to another emotional expression, one of indignation. The object of his indignation was a pregnant woman who lived in the same apartment building and with whom his mother was friendly. Tommy expressed the most intense rage about this woman, Helen, calling her a "bum," a "bitch," and a "fuck." He would say in desperate tones that he just couldn't stand it any more having her around, and would seize the telephone, demand to speak to the police, and tell the police to come and take that Helen away, put her in jail, kill her. He told me repeatedly that he hated Helen like poison, that he called her names and slammed the door on her when she tried to come to visit his mother. He repeated alleged conversations with Helen in which he told her "Drop dead," and she said, "Go to hell yourself." In this rage against Helen, whom he could not stand, and wanted the police to take away, we may suppose that he was expressing what he sensed as his mother's feelings and intentions toward himself; his mother could not stand him any more and was about to send him away. Apparently at this time he felt that it was on account of his genital strivings that he was being thrown out, and these became projected on the pregnant woman, whose sexual activity was patent from her condition, and whom he violently berated as a bitch, a bum, and a fuck.

When Tommy was six and a half he was placed in a small residential center for treatment of disturbed children. I should like to mention some observations reported by those who worked with him there. He continued for some time his laughing fits, the most frequent cue for which remained words and acts expressive of soiling and dirtying. He would, for instance, shout "Doody, doody!" (duty = feces) over and over, and follow this with prolonged laughing. He continued to announce that he was going to giggle. He did a lot of spilling of chocolate milk (which he called "doody" and at first refused to drink, laughing as soon as it appeared at table), and also juices and water, again often announcing that he was going to spill them on the floor, and following the act with laughter.

It would seem that in this spilling and messing Tommy was repeating voluntarily earlier wetting and soiling from the time when he still lacked control of these functions, and was probably greatly alarmed by his mother's reactions, fearing that she would repudiate him for these acts. His deliberate repetition would then be an attempt to master these painful experiences and to deny the original involuntary character of the acts which made him feel so helpless. In a similar way one can often see a young child who has had a painful tumble immediately afterwards throwing himself down in simulated falls and making a great joke of it. Tommy emphasized the controlled quality of his spilling and messing with his announcements beforehand. He was also probably testing in his characteristic fashion whether this messing and wetting would draw down the feared punishment, feeling for the moment reassured if it did not.

In a game which Tommy was observed to play repeatedly with a little girl, the two children pretended they were married and had a baby. They would alternately assure each other that they would not tease the baby, and then go off on long trips leaving the baby behind. Tommy also pretended that his little playmate was his second wife, and would speak of his first wife in very condemnatory terms: she was very dirty, made cocky in her pants, and so on. We can see here again how strongly Tommy felt that his mother's abandonment of him was because of his dirtiness. (Incidentally, in the time I knew Tommy he neither soiled nor wet, and according to the mother he had been completely trained since the age of two and a half, though she related that he had once wet himself at school in the first period of his attending nursery school, and had been very much ashamed.) In playing that his first wife had been dirty and had soiled her pants, Tommy was again identifying with the aggressor: he was the one who abandoned his mother, and he projected his dirtiness onto her.

I saw Tommy again, at the center, shortly before his eighth birthday. Though he had not seen me for a year and a half, he immediately recognized me with a wide-eyed hurt expression, and then greeted me with his current repetitive phrase: "I'm gong to make fahtzy doody." He wanted to know if I remembered how he used to laugh when he arrived in the waiting room to let me know he was there, and announced several times that he was going to giggle, but did not do so. He also said: "Pee-pee on the floor." As I remarked that he had once made "pee-pee" on the floor in my office, he said without much conviction that he would make "pee-pee" on the floor now, but did not do it. He said there was "fahtzy doody" on the floor at the other end of the hall, told me one of the other boys was dirty, made a grimace and covered his eyes.

III

Tommy's laughter illustrates the variety of functions which this mode of expression can serve. It was a substitute for tears in an effort to reverse painful emotions, and served as a defense against anxiety. At the same time it provided a release for aggressive and sexual impulses and particularly functioned as an equivalent of excretory acts.

The intimate relation between laughter and tears is well known (cf. Byron: "If I laugh at any mortal thing 'tis that I may not weep," etc.). Darwin (1904) pointed out the antithetical relation between laughing and crying, in respect to respiratory pattern, applying his hypothesis that many emotional expressions reveal their meaning through such inverse relations. Ernst Kris (1939) has remarked on the indeterminate expression of the infant who may be about to laugh or cry, as well as the situation of older persons under extreme emotional stress who do not know whether they feel like crying or laughing. In Tommy's case, not only did he laugh where he had formerly cried, as in the "good-by game," or where he might currently feel impelled to cry (e.g., in connection with the word "tired"), but he also used laughter as an infant uses crying to summon an absent person whom he needs. Thus Tommy laughed to waken his mother in the

morning and to summon me from my office when he arrived in the waiting room.

The reversal of affect in the substitution of laughter for crying is
closely related to the use of laughter as a defense against anxiety. Kris
(1939) has cited a case of compulsive laughter in a young man patient and
indicated a series of reassuring meanings which it had: you are not dangerous; I am powerful and triumphant; I am harmless, just a laughing
fool. Brody (1950) has observed how laughter may be substituted for a
wide variety of distressing emotions. According to Grotjahn (1945), in
the rare instances where laughter occurs in dreams, it serves a similar
function of warding off painful feelings. In my study of children's
humor (1954), I have tried to show how pervasive the motive of defense
against anxiety is in the joking of children.

Freud (1905) demonstrated how jokes release aggressive and sexual
impulses. The act of laughter itself has a similar significance. In young
children laughter is often an expression of sexual excitement. Fenichel
(1945) has also remarked how outbursts of laughter, particularly at
inappropriate times, may express a feeling of triumph in the fulfillment
of destructive wishes. Tommy's laughter not only provided an outlet for
his sexual and aggressive impulses, it also served to excite his mother
and make her angry. Thus he induced her to participate in his excitement and to intensify it by hitting him.

Perhaps the central and unifying theme among the many motives
which overdetermined Tommy's laughter was its being equated with an
excretory act.[3] Excretory activity seemed to be laden with particularly
intense erotic feeling for Tommy. At the same time it was most dangerous: it was that for which his mother wanted to get rid of him. By
repeating excretory acts constantly in the substitute form of laughter he
actively precipitated the danger situation and tested whether his mother
would really get rid of him. But the laughter as an excretory act was
in itself a way of getting rid: getting rid of the incessant strain of inner
tension, and symbolically perhaps getting rid of the introjected mother.
We know how continuously Tommy used the mechanism of turning
passivity into activity. If his laughter had the significance of getting rid
of the mother who to his overwhelming alarm wanted to get rid of him,
this would be another instance of the same mechanism.

While there were special circumstances in Tommy's case which
strongly determined the use of laughter as an excretory act, I would
wonder whether this significance may not be a component in all laughter,

---

[3] In a similar way Phyllis Greenacre (1945) has shown how crying may be used as an
equivalent of urination.

what is common being only more intensely highlighted in the exceptional instance. Laughter would then be a slightly later addition to the processes by which the infant rids himself of bodily distress: urinating, defecating, and crying. Laughter, along with these other manifestations, would have the significance of relieving the body of bad things inside it (bad impulses and painful inhibitions in the case of the laughter released by wit [Freud, 1905]). The loss of control in laughter may have a particular value because it is the only excretory act in respect to which loss of control remains publicly permissible.

Tommy's wild laughter in which he would sometimes roll on the floor represents the opposite of what we see in the normal development of children entering latency. Normally at this time there is a reduction of the expressive use of the whole body and an increase in capacity for verbal expression in isolation from motor activity (Kris, 1939). In my observations of children's joking (1954), I found a marked shift in this respect in normal children from the age of five to the age of six. Children of five and under, when asked to tell something funny, would usually begin to teeter and topple, to jump up and down, or they might roll over backwards after saying something they considered absurd. For them saying something funny and acting funny remained inseparable. Starting at six one could see a striking change: the children acquired a repertoire of verbal jokes which they could relate without any large muscle activity. This isolation of the verbal joke from motor manifestations was one of several isolations which characterize latency period joking: isolation of manifest from latent content, isolation of the joke from the surrounding context. (In keeping with the latter, latency period children did not say, as older children so often did, that to tell jokes they would have to be in the mood.)

As I have tried to show elsewhere (1954), the requirement for brevity in wit is initiated in latency. I am tempted to say that Tommy's one-word cues for laughter represented an unsuccessful counterpart to the process of condensation which characterizes typical latency period jokes. Apart from his shouting isolated words, such as "odor," to set off his fits of laughter, he spoke in complete sentences. As with condensed joke forms, Tommy's one-word cues stood for a wealth of meaning which he wished to conceal from himself. However, it would probably be more correct to say that he employed a form of joke common on the four-year level (where verbal joking may be, though it is not always, extremely unelaborated), where a shout of "Doody!" passes for a good dirty joke.

Tommy's lonely laughter and incomprehensible one-word "jokes" contrast in a number of other ways with the development of joking in normal children of his age. The favored jokes of normal latency period children represent a working over of emotional problems of preceding phases of development whose urgency has become reduced. Tommy's laughter aimed at release from the immediate and continuing pressure of acute emotional difficulties. Where the normal latency period child takes up conventional modes (learned jokes and joke forms) to obtain social sanction for the motives he expresses, Tommy's jokes remained exclusively personal. The normal child of this age is able to combine the wish for concealment with the wish to be understood, the result being an intelligible manifest content cloaking a suppressed or repressed latent meaning. For Tommy the requirement of making himself understood did not operate. The normal latency period child is able to postpone immediate physical gratification, to substitute verbal for motor expression, and wants to elicit an admiring response for his skill. Tommy could not postpone the immediate physical gratification which he obtained from his fits of laughter and aimed at getting an equally physical reaction, the blows of his mother which his repeated "jokes" and incessant laughter provoked. Normally the aggressive provocation of the joke becomes moderated by the gratification which it offers to the hearer. In Tommy's case there was no such moderation; his hilarity offered nothing to the hearer but provocation.

While Tommy's peculiar way of joking and laughing represents a failure in development, there remains something impressive in the phenomenon of a desperate and helpless child struggling to laugh off the tragedy of his life.

BIBLIOGRAPHY

Brody, M. W. (1950), The Meaning of Laughter. *Psa. Quart.*, XIX.
Darwin, C. (1904), *The Expression of the Emotions in Man and Animals.* London: Murray.
Fenichel, O. (1945), *The Psychoanalytic Theory of Neurosis.* New York: Norton.
Freud, S. (1905), Wit and Its Relation to the Unconscious. *The Basic Writings of Sigmund Freud.* New York: Random House, 1938.
Greenacre, P. (1945), Urination and Weeping. In: *Trauma, Growth and Personality.* New York: Norton, 1952.
Grotjahn, M. (1945), Laughter in Dreams. *Psa. Quart.*, XIV.
Kris, E. (1939), Laughter as an Expressive Process. In: *Psychoanalytic Explorations in Art.* New York: International Universities Press, 1952.
Wolfenstein, M. (1954), *Children's Humor.* Glencoe, Ill.: Free Press.

CONTENTS OF PREVIOUS VOLUMES

VOLUME I

VOLUME II

VOLUME III/IV

VOLUME V

VOLUME VI

VOLUME VII

VOLUME VIII

VOLUME IX

WESTMAR COLLEGE LIBRARY